ALSO BY CARL P. RUSSELL

Guns on the Early Frontiers

FIREARMS, TRAPS, & TOOLS
OF THE
MOUNTAIN
MEN

FIREARMS, TRAPS, & TOOLS
OF THE
MOUNTAIN MEN

Carl P. Russell

SKYHORSE PUBLISHING

Skyhorse Publishing books may be purchased in bulk at special discounts for sales promotion, corporate gifts, fund-raising, or educational purposes. Special editions can also be created to specifications. For details, contact the Special Sales Department, Skyhorse Publishing, 307 West 36th Street, 11th Floor, New York, NY 10018 or info@skyhorsepublishing.com.

Skyhorse® and Skyhorse Publishing® are registered trademarks of Skyhorse Publishing, Inc.®, a Delaware corporation.

Visit our website at www.skyhorsepublishing.com.

15 14 13 12 11

Library of Congress Cataloging-in-Publication Data is available on file.

ISBN: 978-1-60239-969-3

Printed in the United States of America

To Betty

whose contributions were most important
and never-failing

FIREARMS, TRAPS, & TOOLS
OF THE
MOUNTAIN
MEN

A NOTE ABOUT THE ILLUSTRATIONS

All the drawings by Glen Dines have been prepared especially for this book.

Those drawings not otherwise credited are by the author.

See index for references to specific illustrations.

PREFACE

SEVERAL MOST EXCELLENT WORKS PUBLISHED IN RECENT
years have done much to improve the popular image of the
historic beaver hunter. They accurately detail the magnitude of
trader-trapper accomplishments in shaping our national life and in
making our country one nation, they remind us that enduring *good*
reputations were made in the Western fur fields, and they prove
rather conclusively the authenticity of heroism among trappers in
the wilderness. Regarding the mountain men: "Their very names
now sound like the blast of trumpets and the tuck of drums."

The role of the mountain man in our westward expansion was a
brief one; his era began with the Lewis and Clark Expedition,
1803–6, and ended rather abruptly with the beginnings of westward emigration in the early 1840's. There was no repeat performance. As a type, the mountain man was distinct, yet one cannot say
that either his possessions or his methods were unique. Everything
that he brought into the West and much of his *modus operandi*
were inherited from his predecessors in the Indian trade. Almost
everything that transpired on the Yellowstone or on the Green
rivers during the early decades of the nineteenth century was
largely an adaptation of trapper-trader procedures on the Cumber-
land, on the upper Ohio, or on the Maumee during the 1700's.

Probably the most distinctive characteristics of the Western
beaver business relate to the horse Indians who inhabited the
Western realm, and to the vast, seemingly limitless wilderness in

which the drama was enacted. In almost every part of his range, the mountain man was constantly subject to Indian raids. Deprived of horses, he was doomed or, at best, reduced to an ineffective existence, often given to dodging enemies while he sought the most direct route to safe haven and more horses. Even the direct route usually involved long, painful travel, and the trapper on foot sometimes elected to recover his own animals or steal others. In any case, he resorted to Indian stealth and strategy. The Rocky Mountain cliché "Wal, now, I took ya fer an Injun" was not altogether inept; the successful beaver trapper tended to think like an Indian, look like an Indian, and behave like one, too. Generally his paraphernalia did not differ greatly from that of the Indian; in the mountain man's time the plains and mountain tribes had obtained and adopted as their own much of the white man's equipment. Especially did they take unto themselves the ironwork of the trader-trapper.

The present book pertains to this ironwork. Since the ironmongery of the Plains and the Rockies was derived from its earlier counterparts in Canada, Iroquoia, and the Old Northwest, attention is given to the progenitors. Perhaps the most striking eduction herein is the persistence of seventeenth-century matériel in the nineteenth-century scene so far removed from the St. Lawrence and the Hudson.

Appropriately, I think, the core of this story is the three-dimensional object itself. Some two hundred collections of historic fur-trade artifacts were drawn upon in making the selection presented. With few exceptions the individual specimens were examined, and measured sketches or photographs were made by me. In some instances photographs were supplied by museum curators, and in all cases museum officials or owners of private collections were cooperative in giving written permission to publicize these specific items among their holdings. Sixty of the plates of finished drawings here reproduced were made by National Park Service artists at the Jefferson National Expansion Memorial, St. Louis, in accordance with specifications provided by me. Most of these plates are the work of William Macy; some the work of James Mulcahy. The drawings are used here by the kind permission of the Superintendent and the Chief of Museums, National Park Service. Thirty-two drawings by Glen Dines were created especially for this work.

The illustrations, of course, are vital to the interpretation as presented, and I acknowledge, gratefully, the important contribution of the artists to this work.

Numerous librarians, historians, historian-archeologists, museum curators (including the nationwide staff of the National Park Service), private collectors, manufacturers of tools, and officials of historical societies and related organizations have collaborated in assembling my materials and in the interpretation of findings. The work has been in progress for thirty-five years and has extended over much of the United States and into Canada. My indebtedness in this connection is great, and to some degree I express my thanks more specifically in the acknowledgments section. So far as possible, the footnotes and the bibliography also identify some unusual documentary sources that I drew upon.

Alfred A. Knopf over a long period of years has encouraged me in the pursuit of my goal, and his very constructive advice has been important to the completion of the work. I have been fortunate in getting the guidance of an "old beaver hunter," Angus Cameron, editor at Knopf, who has been direct, discerning, and entirely helpful and understanding in meeting the problems broached by my presentations. Also at Knopf are Mrs. Ellen Fertig and Mrs. Judith Pomerantz who collaborated in shaping the final format. Mrs. Pomerantz, copy editor, did yeoman service in combing out inconsistencies and in readying the manuscript for the printer. Finally, I acknowledge a very big debt owed to my wife, Betty Westphal Russell, for consistent help given through almost a lifetime as she stood up under the peculiar assaults related to a museum conscience. She has given patient encouragement and expert secretarial support, which have been all-important to the consummation of my studies and writing.

CARL P. RUSSELL

August 1966
Orinda, California

ACKNOWLEDGMENTS

W ORK ON THIS BOOK WAS INITIATED IN 1930–4 WHEN IT devolved upon the writer to organize the story of the mountain man for museum purposes in Yellowstone National Park. Since that time, Western fur-trade studies have been one of the author's major interests, both in official work and in purely personal endeavors. In the early years of the studies, a few venerable pioneers of the Plains and the Rockies were still available for interviews. These old-timers cannot be classified as mountain men, but they had associated with mountain men in the time of the long shadows of mountain-man life. From the lips of these witnesses came some interesting testimony, and from their places of last retreat came a few fur-trade "relics" with known histories. Particularly, a debt of gratitude is owed to J. P. V. ("Trapper") Evans, Captain H. Cook, Will Everson, Charles Marble, and the admirable old Chief of the Crows, Plenty Coups.

The scope and general nature of the present survey of iron artifacts of the trader-trapper are such as to have necessitated help from numerous collaborators. The text, footnotes, and bibliography identify most of these allies, yet certain individuals and agencies have given assistance so basic in nature as to predicate further acknowledgment.

The National Park Service, the American Association of Museums, and the Oberlander Trust jointly sponsored my tour of museums in twenty European cities shortly before World War II.

In several of the repositories visited I was enabled to study numerous significant weapons and other iron objects constituting parts of the ancestral line of Indian trade goods. In the United States the American Association of Museums sponsored several trips to American museums, thereby giving me the opportunity to study many of the artifacts here reported upon. Museum directors, owners of private collections, and curators everywhere gave generously of their knowledge, their time, and their facilities; subsequent to my visits, many of them have corresponded with me, supplying copies of needed documents, translations of museum records, photographs of specified artifacts, and commentaries regarding identification and the history of the objects. Among the scores of collaborators who have contributed are the following to whom I am especially indebted: Douglas Adair, *William and Mary Quarterly;* John Barsotti, Columbus, Ohio; A. T. Bowie, Natchez, Mississippi; George R. Brooks, director, Missouri Historical Society; the late Dr. H. C. Bumpus, formerly of the American Association of Museums; Warren W. Caldwell, Missouri Basin Project; the late Dr. Robert Glass Cleland, formerly at the Huntington Library; Dr. Laurence Vail Coleman, formerly director, American Association of Museums; Dr. Cyril B. Courville, Cajal Laboratory of Neuropathology; Stuart Cuthbertson, Los Angeles; Clair M. Elston, president, The Collins Company; John C. Ewers, U. S National Museum; T. M. Hamilton, University of Missouri; Charles E. Hanson, Museum of the Fur Trade, Chadron, Nebraska; Dr. Kenneth E. Kidd, Trent University, Ontario; W. C. Lawrence, Museum of the Frontier, Jackson, Wyoming; Stephen R. Leonard, formerly with the Oneida Community; Harry E. Lichter, Oregon Historical Society; Dr. Philip K. Lundeberg, U. S. National Museum; Dr. R. S. Shankland, Case Institute of Technology; Dr. Carlyle S. Smith, University of Kansas; Dr. Cyril Stanley Smith, Massachusetts Institute of Technology; Dr. R. F. G. Spier, University of Missouri; Dr. Tracy I. Storer, University of California, Davis; Dr. H. J. Swinney, Idaho Historical Society; Charles Van Ravensway, formerly director, Missouri Historical Society; Thomas Vaughan, director, Oregon Historical Society; Dr. Waldo R. Wedel, U. S. National Museum; Arthur Woodward, formerly of the Los Angeles Museum; and Erwin Zepp, formerly head of the Ohio State Museum.

Since its inception, this fur-trade-history project has been nurtured by the National Park Service. Five directors, beginning with Horace M. Albright, have extended encouragement. There are today nineteen field areas within the National Parks system which have fur-trade significance because of historical events which transpired within them or in their immediate environs, or because they memorialize the trapper-trader and his activities. Bents Old Fort, Fort Laramie, Fort Vancouver, Grand Portage, Grand Teton, Scotts Bluff, and Yellowstone are particularly notable among these fur-trade sites. National Park Service personnel direct their studies upon fur-trade subjects in these parks and monuments and in central offices in Washington, D.C.; Santa Fe, New Mexico; Omaha, Nebraska; Philadelphia, Pennsylvania; and San Francisco, California. A great deal of this effort focuses upon the Jefferson National Expansion Memorial, St. Louis, and that unit has been very much a "home port" for the present writer's study project.

To name all National Park Service workers who have contributed to this study of iron weapons and tools would be listing a large part of the Service personnel engaged in administrative, historical, archeological, and museum work. There are several, however, who gave especially important assistance through a period of many years: Roy Appleman, Edward Beatty, the late Ned J. Burns, Louis Caywood, John Cotter, William C. Everhart, John C. Ewers, E. Raymond Gregg, the late Ansel F. Hall, Dr. J. C. Harrington, the late Dr. Alfred F. Hopkins, J. Paul Hudson, Dr. John Hussey, the late John Jenkins, Herbert Kahler, Ronald F. Lee, Ralph Lewis, John Littleton, William Macy, Merrill E. Mattes, James Mulcahy, Charles Peterson, Harold Peterson, Julian Spotts, Robert Starett, Hillory A. Tolson, Dorr G. Yeager. It is not exceeding the truth to say that this book could not have been written without the long-time cooperation of the foregoing associates.

Among the libraries, historical societies, government offices, and other institutions which have cooperated, several not mentioned in the preceding paragraphs have given extraordinary help. The Missouri Historical Society possesses one of the truly great collections of manuscripts pertaining to the mountain man and his predecessors in the beaver business. Also a wealth of three-dimensional materials representative of the Western fur trade is owned by the Society. These sources have been made available to the present study; archivists and curators gave of their help most generously, and a number of their artifacts were used in the illustrations here reproduced. It is to be acknowledged also that the *Bulletin* of the Missouri Historical Society published my "Picture Books of Fur Trade History," reprints of which proved useful as I solicited the cooperation of scholars, collectors, and other historical societies.

Among the distinguishing attributes of The New-York Historical Society is its ownership of the phenomenal collection of American Fur Company Papers, 1831–49. During years preceding the microfilming of these manuscripts, I benefited by the help of the Society's very patient librarians who wheeled out truckloads of the documents for my perusal. More recently I have made much further use of these materials, which now are represented in many libraries in microfilm copy.

During some years of residence in the Chicago area, I took opportunity to frequent the archives of the Chicago Historical Society, and there a staff of most courteous librarians saw to it that my needs for additional (and earlier) records of the American Fur Company were served. This involved some inter-library service, assistance which was cheerfully extended and for which my thanks are due.

In Berkeley, California, the University of California Library has been very much my home base for a good many years. Helpful librarians and the tremendous collections there, and at the Bancroft Library are never-failing, and auxiliary aid, such as photostatic services, have been important to my illustrations project.

The Inter-Agency Archeology Salvage Program conducted by the National Park Service has within it a number of historian-archeologists who have cooperated in appraising some problems of dating artifacts and who have advised regarding recent discoveries of fur-trade materials at Indian sites and trading posts in some of the Western river basins which are to be flooded when dams are completed. In this connection, it may be timely to mention that a veritable new congress of researchers has convened. A few years ago it was said quite truthfully that ordinarily only the records of men and of events received the scrutiny of students of fur-trade history—"The material things of the old-time beaver business are trivial, fugitive, mostly out of reach, and, at best, undecipherable. They are hardly worthy of serious investigation at this stage of the game." A comparatively few workers, having the antiquarian turn of mind, challenged this deprecation and, with federal, state, or local support, proceeded to create a new discipline among historians. The establishment of guidelines and demonstrations of the practicability of setting up datum points based upon excavated historic objects proved to be of great interest to some fieldworkers. Out of this interest grew numerous weddings between the Houses of History and Archeology. Now excavators and underwater investigators have developed a workable system of research, and they bring to the academic halls an important auxiliary school. Some of their raw materials constitute the substance of this book.

CONTENTS

[VI]
MISCELLANEOUS IRON TOOLS THAT WENT INTO THE WEST
312

[VII]
IRONS IN THE FIRE
357

[APPENDIX A]
Historic Objects as Sources of History
387

[APPENDIX B]
John Jacob Astor's Inventory of Tools and Blacksmithing
Equipment on the Columbia River, 1812–1813
402

[APPENDIX C]
Markings on Axes and Tomahawks
408

[APPENDIX D]
Representative Fur Returns, American Fur Company,
Indiana, 1839–1841
425

Bibliography / *427*

Index   *follows page 448*

CHAPTER I

The Mountain Men in American History

WHEN LEWIS AND CLARK RECRUITED THEIR PARTY OF EX-plorers in 1803–4, they selected and "signed up" nine young backwoodsmen from Kentucky and obtained the transfer of fourteen hardbitten soldiers from the Regular Army. Two French boatmen and the half-breed interpreter George Drouillard completed the permanent party. All these men had experience in wilderness life and Indian contacts. Like the two leaders, most of them were well schooled in the circumstances and causes of recurrent Indian wars, as they had occurred in Kentucky and the Old Northwest. A number of them were seasoned hunters thoroughly skilled in trapping beaver; inherently or intuitively they were already "mountain men," although the term had not yet been coined. This theory is not a figment; empirical demonstration of its validity was made a hundred times in the course of the great trek of 1804–6. Thomas Jefferson's initial orders regarding the purposes of the expedition are explicit in recognizing the nation's need for new and bigger beaver country; he instructed Meriwether Lewis to find such country, to determine the quantity of beaver it contained, and to submit a written report thereon.

Jefferson's concern with the future of the Western fur trade was paralleled by his anxiety for a sane settlement of some of the Indian problems which beset the infant United States. A certain British hostility still pervaded and adversely affected the states and territories just south of the Canadian border. To Jefferson and to

3

all perspicacious contemporary American statesmen, international competition in the fur trade, northern Indian threats, and Britain's American ambitions constituted one cohesive problem. Alexander Mackenzie's release to the world of his scheme for British expansion to the Pacific appeared in print in 1801. Mackenzie, the highly respected North West Company explorer, saw in the fur trade the vehicle by which Britain might gain commercial control all the way to the mouth of the Columbia River. He wrote: "By opening this intercourse [fur trade] between the Atlantic and Pacific Oceans and forming regular establishments through the interior and at both extremes . . . the entire command of the fur trade of North America might be obtained from 48° north to the pole. . . . Such would be the field for commercial enterprise and incalculable would be the produce of it." [1]

Subsequent to the publication of his book, Mackenzie went to England where he advocated establishment of a military base at the mouth of the Columbia, which could uphold the anticipated British sovereignty in Oregon. Thomas Jefferson and the U. S. Congress were further stirred by Mackenzie's polemic. As quickly as possible the Lewis and Clark Expedition was planned and launched.

From the beginning of their march, Lewis and Clark and their followers practiced the techniques of travel, trade, craftsmanship, and sustenance that later characterized the field activities of the Western beaver hunters. These were not new procedures; they were identical to those which most of the men had used all during their youth in Kentucky and north of the Ohio. Upon the return of the expedition, American trappers and fur traders in numbers occupied the Missouri, many of them going at once to the more promising beaver waters reported by the explorers. They accomplished their occupation of the new country by employing much the same methods that their progenitors had adopted in taking the trans-Allegheny region and the Mississippi Valley. Their purposes, their procedure in Indian intercourse—even their dress and personal equipment—were essentially the same. Our concept of the American fur trade is marked by this continuity of the trade as an institution.

During the late eighteenth century and in the opening decades

[1] Alexander Mackenzie: *Voyages from Montreal Through the Continent of North America* (New York, 1904), II, 358–9.

of the nineteenth century, it was determined by the British north of our then ill-defined boundary, as well as by the westward-facing Americans, that the length and breadth of the Rocky Mountains offered beaver in abundance. The "hairy bank notes" encouraged increasing numbers of adventurers, both British and American, to brave the dangers of the long, wild, and unmapped routes to the West. Financial returns were sufficiently promising to prompt the organization of a growing number of new trading companies to back the expanding field activities.

a   *b*

c   *d*

FIG. 1. *How Man's Hat Opened the American West.*

For three hundred years before Lewis and Clárk, the hatters of the civilized world had raised a cry for beaver. In the day of the mountain man, 100,000 beaver skins were consumed each year in the production of hats for men. Dandies of the boulevards were not the only buyers of the "beavers"; the armies of many nations wanted their own particular styles of beaver hats, and stalwarts in rural communities everywhere needed them for Sunday-go-to-meeting dress.

The tricorn or cocked hat (*a* and *b*) was widely used by the military in Europe and America in the eighteenth and early nineteenth centuries. Lewis and Clark carried into the West the U. S. Artillery version of the cocked hat, each adorned with a feather. Shown in *c* is a stylish model favored by the Beau Brummell during the 1820's and 1830's. The broad-brimmed type (*d*) was popular among country folk, some of the clergy, and a few military units, religious sects, and Southwestern traders and merchants. After long use the brim tended to soften and droop. It was not despised by some mountain men, as witness the occasional records left to us by contemporary artists who made on-the-spot drawings.

There were numerous additional models and styles, all having the same basic foundation—felt prepared from beaver fur. The beaver pelt as it came from the trader was a rough, greasy skin covered with coarse brown hair under which was the fine rich fur or wool. The first step in hatmaking was to shave both hair and wool from the skin. The bare skin was then sold to a maker of glue, and the wool and hair were separated by a blowing process. Only the wool found use in hatmaking. The soft, loose fur was applied in small quantities to a perforated copper revolving cone within which was a suction device that pulled the fur against the cone. A spray of hot water turned upon the fur-covered cone, together with manipulation of the fur with the hands, started the felting process. Repeatedly fur was added, and the manipulation continued until the felt became tough in texture. Then it was removed as a hood from the cone and placed in a mold where it was worked into the desired shape. While it was still soft and warm, shellac was forced into it from the inside.

Fine fur was then applied to the outside of the shaped hat. With the aid of hot water and careful handwork the outer surface was made to appear covered with a growth of fur. The final step in making the dress hat was to give it a high gloss and embellish it with a band and lining. By means of a revolving block and the application of brushes, irons, sandpaper, and velvet, a finish as bright as that of silk was obtained. Because of its long velvety "pile" or fur, the "beaver" was characterized by an exquisite beauty that never distinguished the silk hat.

Beaver-hat making is now a lost art. The introduction of silk in the 1830's gradually displaced beaver fur in the hatter's industry; today "beavers" are seldom found except in museum collections.

The transfer of the ownership of Louisiana from Spain to France in 1800–3 and then to the United States by purchase from France in 1803 doubled the size of the American nation but had little or no effect in curbing the English Indian trade on the upper Missouri. Lewis and Clark observed in 1804 the business being carried on between the Canadian companies and United States

Indians and reported on it in some detail. Montreal traders, united as the North West Company since 1787, were particularly active inasmuch as they regarded themselves the rightful successors to the old-time French interests on the Missouri. One of the partners, Alexander Mackenzie, was in 1807–9 already established in the trade on the upper Columbia and Pend Oreille Lake and in the Flathead country—the last two locations within the present boundaries of the United States.

The pioneer American trader in the Far Western fur fields was Manuel Lisa, who had gained a great deal of experience with tribes on the lower Missouri during the last years of the Spanish regime. In 1807 he built a post on the Yellowstone at the mouth of the Big Horn. From here he sent out John Colter on his remarkable journey of discovery in the Yellowstone–Grand Teton regions. Lisa's dealings with the Crows were so successful as to encourage the participation of other experienced traders who, in 1809, joined him in founding the "St. Louis Missouri Fur Company." Andrew Henry, a stock owner, led a strong party of trappers from Fort Manuel to the Three Forks of the Missouri, where in 1810 a post was built near the confluence of the Jefferson and Madison rivers. The Blackfeet broke up this business, and a year later Henry crossed the Continental Divide and established a post on Henry's Fork of the Snake, the first American establishment on the Pacific slope. The hostile Blackfoot Indians and the difficulties of procuring food in winter caused the Henry ventures to be short-lived indeed. This failure found reflection in the general lack of success of the St. Louis Missouri Company.

It is understandable that the investors in commercial enterprises in the distant wilds should ask for government protection for their field men. In St. Louis the interested parties expressed themselves emphatically, and the Louisiana politicians of the day found it necessary to declare themselves either for or against a federal underwriting, so to speak, of private business in the wilderness. At this time Thomas Jefferson, President of the United States, was the statesman most deeply interested in the development of the West. The constructive reports of Lewis and Clark had played into the hands of Jefferson and his collaborating Western expansionists, but Lieutenant Zebulon M. Pike's published appraisal in 1810 of the upper Great Plains gave ammunition to the New England Federalists and to other conservatives who feared the political effects of creating new Western states. Pike reported: "I saw in various places tracts of many leagues where the wind threw up sand in all the fanciful forms of the ocean's rolling waves and on which not a speck of vegetable matter existed. . . . Farms in the West will be limited to the banks of the Missouri and Mississippi, and the prairies, unfitted for cultivation, must be left to the wandering and uncivilized aborigines."[2] So started the myth of the Great American Desert, a legend that served to delay the arrival of overland Americans in California and on the Columbia.

The extension in 1808 of U. S. military authority to a new post, Fort Osage, in the vicinity of present-day Kansas City, was not wholly satisfying to the traders far up the Missouri, but this governmental concession did seem to be an indication that the War Department might go further in extending its protecting arms. John Jacob Astor, whose success in the East had already distinguished him as a highly competent fur trader, determined at this time to extend his business into the Far West. It is significant that Thomas Jefferson urged and assisted Astor in making this decision. In 1810 a subdivision of Astor's American Fur Company was established under the name Pacific Fur Company with the defined objective of conducting an American-China trade with a base at the mouth of the Columbia. Astor's ship, the *Tonquin*, laden with men and merchandise set out from New York in September 1810, convoyed for some distance by a U. S. naval vessel provided to forestall any search and seizure by British gunboats. The *Tonquin* entered the Columbia in March 1811, and the post, called Astoria, was constructed as rapidly as possible. An overland party of Astor men under Wilson Price Hunt started from St. Louis on March 12, 1811, and arrived at Astoria in January 1812.

It is unnecessary to dwell upon the ill-fated attempt of the Astorians beyond saying that the War of 1812 diverted it completely. From a promising American enterprise looking to the settlement of Oregon, it was converted overnight into a British business in the hands of the North West Company.

To say that the War of 1812 brought complications to the Western fur trade is something of an understatement. In June 1813 Fort Osage was abandoned in the face of threats from Great Britain's Indian allies. Thereafter the North West Company

[2] Elliott Coues, ed.: *The Expeditions of Zebulon Montgomery Pike* (New York: F. P. Harper; 1895), II, 525.

opened trading establishments as far south as the Mandan villages on the Missouri. Manuel Lisa suffered the loss of his upper Missouri trade but he is credited with having persuaded the Missouri tribes to desist from attacking the Americans on the lower Missouri. So far as fights were concerned, there were few in sharp contrast with the numerous bloody events on the Mississippi. But the American trade was at a standstill and so continued until American rights could be restored in accordance with the Treaty of Ghent signed in December 1814. This agreement did not influence affairs in the West for another year.

Pleas of the American traders finally brought response from the Congress. After the war a law was enacted that limited the Indian trade to American citizens and placed fourteen hundred troops in the West. At first there was little military activity west of St. Louis, but at least Fort Osage was reoccupied in October 1815 and gradually Americans returned to the upper Missouri. Notable among the military advances were the so-called Yellowstone Expedition of 1819–20 designed to "enlarge and protect our fur trade and to bring permanent peace to our North Western frontier." Both Major Stephen H. Long and Colonel Henry W. Atkinson held positions of command. The great bustle of military activity stirred the foes of westward expansion; they mustered sufficient strength in the Congress to balk the completion of the military project. Long was diverted from the Missouri to the Colorado Rockies, and his subsequent report only damaged the cause of the expansionists. Pike's "Great American Desert" of 1806 seemed all too real to the readers of Long's descriptions in 1823. The political factions who opposed expenditure of government funds for Western military purposes felt that they had gained another small victory, for, as they pointed out, there was no good sense in promoting citizen interest in a country that was fit only for wild Indians and wolves. These adverse circumstances notwithstanding, in the spring of 1822, Ramsay Crooks, agent for the American Fur Company, established a St. Louis headquarters for the Western department of his company. It was at this time that the political drive launched by Astor and other private interests against the government's twenty-six-year-old factory system of Indian trade culminated in the overthrow of that system. Thus in 1822 the way was opened wider for the American Fur Company's march to monopoly.

It should not be concluded, however, that the American Fur

Company had immediate undisputed sway in the Western fur trade. In fact, the vigorous resistance to that company's incursions resulted in a number of the Far West ventures upon which this chapter focuses. Before discussing the details of trapper affairs on the Pacific slope, we should identify the more important competing trading companies.

Along the lower stretches of the Missouri, the old-time traders responded quickly to the stabilizing influence of the military, and by 1819 Lisa's Missouri Fur Company was again dealing with the Pawnee, Oto, Omaha, Iowa, and some of the Sioux out of Fort Lisa near Council Bluffs. The Chouteaus served the Osage and Kansa. Robidoux and Papin overlapped upon the realm of Lisa, as did Pratte and Vasquez. The military posts, Fort Osage and Fort Atkinson, afforded the needed protection. The same year which witnessed the introduction of new blood by the American Fur Company (1822) also saw the coming of another new company, the Ashley-Henry group, which was destined to create a flurry of trade activity more flamboyant and at the same time momentous than any of its contemporaries.

Now present in the field or about to enter it were also several New Mexican groups, the Columbia Fur Company, Stone-Bostwick and Company, Bernard Pratt and Company, the French Fur Company, Nathaniel J. Wyeth, Captain B. L. E. de Bonneville, Sublette and Campbell, Gant and Blackwell, and a number of lesser lights. The Missouri could no longer contain them. The Missouri and Rocky Mountain fur trade entered upon that phase of its history in which the "mountain man" attained stature, overshadowing or displacing the traditional *voyageur* of the earlier day.

On the Columbia, the British North West Company, successor to Mr. Astor's enterprise, encountered no contest for eight years. It had extended its trapping operations southward on the Willamette and into the Snake River backcountry. After 1818 the Nor'westers forayed as far east as the Green River and south to the Bear. Generally, their affairs in the Oregon country were unchallenged by any rival, but in Canada the murderous trade war with the Hudson's Bay Company brought the North West Company and its rival to their knees, so to speak, and a merger of the two British companies was effected in 1821. Dr. John McLoughlin, a veteran employee of the Hudson's Bay Company, was placed in charge on the Columbia. In the spring of 1825 the headquarters establishment was moved from Astoria (Fort George) to a new post, Fort Vancouver, on the north side of the Columbia nearly opposite the mouth of the Willamette. Those outposts begun by the Astorians and developed by the Nor'westers were retained by the new operators, and the trapping expeditions eastward into distant fur fields on the Snake drainage and elsewhere in the direction of American enterprises were intensified. The anticipated impact of American interests upon the "private preserves" of the British in Oregon was not much longer delayed. There is a correlation between this American-British rivalry in the Great Basin and the story of trappers in California, but for the sake of chronology we will return for a moment to the Missouri fur trade.

The Ashley-Henry encounter with the Arikara Indians in 1823 precipitated the first battle on the Missouri in which a sizable body of U. S. troops engaged. Also, it was one of the causes of William Ashley's revolutionary change in field practices. To avoid further entanglements with hostile Indians and numerous rival traders on the Missouri, Ashley abandoned conventional trading-post methods and sent a mounted party of white trappers into the Rocky Mountains in the fall of 1823. Jedediah Smith led this expedition, which was to initiate procedures so novel and successful as to win fame and fortune for its promoters and at the same time make a vital contribution to the eventual acquisition of both Oregon and California. Smith's party traveled to the Sweetwater in the dead of winter and there, in March 1824 at a place later known as the Three Crossings, cached a part of their supplies and equipment. The trappers agreed to meet in this place on or about the first of June. They then proceeded through South Pass and thus became the first *westbound* white men known to have used it. Upon reaching the Green River, the party separated and had a highly rewarding hunt. By June 15 all the trappers had returned through South Pass to the appointed meeting place on the Sweetwater. So, in 1824, a new institution was foreshadowed, the "Annual Rendezvous" of the mountain men, a practice that superseded the fixed trading post so far as Ashley-Henry were concerned. In the next sixteen years fifteen annual meetings were held: on the Green, eight; the Wind, three; the Salt Lake Valley, two; the Bear, one; and the Snake, one. Most of the new country trapped by tramontane Americans was the range of the British fur brigades. Usually, the product of their hunts was packed down from the mountains to

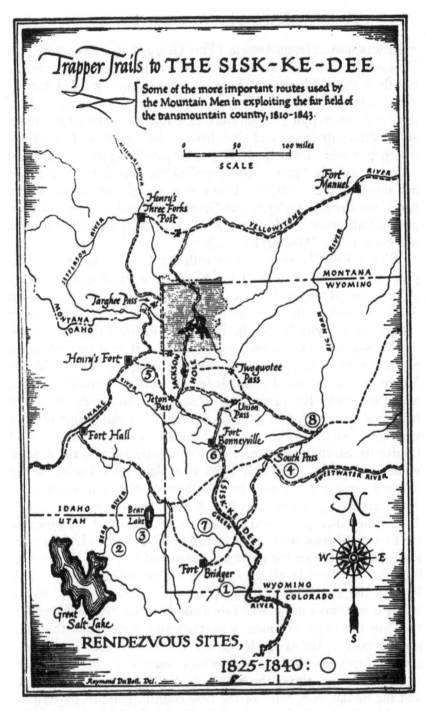

Raymond DaBoll drawing, *Westerners Brand Book*, 1944. Courtesy Chicago Corral, The Westerners.

Rendezvous Sites, 1825–40.

The great annual get-together of Far Western traders, trappers, and Indians for purposes of trade and hilarious revelry was initiated in 1825 and continued through 1840. These summer fairs, invented by William H. Ashley, brought about marked changes in the fur man's field methods west of the Rockies. Trade goods were packed in from St. Louis, usually, to the designated wilderness meeting places and there traded to Indians, deserters from the Hudson's Bay Co., free trappers, and company employees for beaver pelts and castoreum. Large villages of friendly Indians—men, women, and children—usually made up part of the assembly, which sometimes numbered several hundred persons. Hundreds of horses were required; so, of necessity, the meeting places were selected with an eye to availability of range grass. The combined business and carousel, in which liquor invariably figured prominently, continued for several days or several weeks. Ostensibly the traders who brought the merchandise to the rendezvous realized enormous profits, even as much as two thousand per cent on their investments. When the costs of the enterprise included the loss of numerous lives, as sometimes was the case, the conventional accounting of monetary gain became less meaningful. In any case, the mountain man's summer rendezvous was the "big doin's" in the life of a mountain man, and the story of the annual fairs contains some of the most dramatic episodes in fur-trade history. Part of that story, as related by participants, is to be found in Carl P. Russell: "Wilderness Rendezvous Period of the American Fur Trade," *Oregon Historical Quarterly* (March 1941), pp. 1–47.

The accompanying map indicates the locations of fifteen of the annual meetings held during a sixteen-year period. In 1831 the supply train failed, and there was no summer rendezvous.

No. 1 is the site of the 1825 fair on Henry's Fork of the Green. Ashley conducted this meeting, as he did the next, in 1826 in the Cache Valley vicinity near the location of present-day Hyrum, Utah (no. 2). The returns from these two trading ventures made Ashley a wealthy man. Site no. 3, at the south end of Bear Lake, marks the place of meetings in 1827 and again in 1828. On the upper Popo Agie, just east of South Pass (no. 4), the 1829 meeting was held. Various interpretations of the dim record of the 1830 rendezvous have been published by scholars, but the formal report by Smith, Jackson, and Sublette addressed to the Secretary of War in October 30, 1830, states that the meeting took place on the headwaters of the Wind River near South Pass. This was the first time wagons were used in transporting the trade goods. The written report implies quite strongly that the headwaters referred to was the upper Popo Agie, and that the 1830 rendezvous was held in the same general area as the site of the 1829 meeting.

In 1831 the supply train did not reach the mountains until fall, and no summer trade took place. No. 5 indicates the Pierre's Hole rendezvous site of 1832. In 1833 the summer assembly was held on the Green River at Horse Creek (no. 6), a locality which was to become celebrated as a popular place of meeting. No. 7 marks the site on Ham's Fork, where the rendezvous of 1834 was held. In 1835, 1836, 1837, 1839, and 1840 the meetings took place in the general area of site no. 6. The Wind River, at the mouth of the Popo Agie (no. 8) witnessed the 1838 rendezvous. There were no annual fairs after 1840.

the Platte and then shipped by water to St. Louis. The successful competition given to the English company by the mountain men was moderately applauded by the United States government; Thomas Forsyth, an official of the U. S. Indian Office, wrote to Lewis Cass, Secretary of War, October 24, 1831: "It is not exceeding the truth to say that half a million of dollars in furs are now annually brought down the Missouri River that formerly went to Hudson Bay, and it is the enterprising spirit of General Ashley which has occasioned the change of this channel of trade." [3]

Monetary gains were of course vital to the commercial companies engaged in the trade, but to certain statesmen the "geopolitics" involved were of greater importance. It can be shown beyond a doubt that the fur trade was not merely an incident in the fulfillment of the American destiny in the Oregon Country, it was an epoch. The mountain men not only hunted out the trails and passes which opened old Oregon to Americans, their industry and trade also provided the vehicle which took the American idea to the Columbia. American trappers had a similar influence on California history. That the United States government allowed such an important means of national expansion to wend its early way unassisted and without protocol is hardly conceivable; yet there are few recorded instances of direct support, but one looks in vain for a clear-cut chronicle of Washington's formal expressions of interest. The lack is more rumored than real, however. Many writers of history textbooks through the years have adhered to the point of view that during the 1820's and early 1830's apathy, indifference, or bitter opposition characterized the legislative handling of the

[3] MS, Forsyth Papers, State Historical Society of Wisconsin, quoted in Hiram M. Chittenden: *The American Fur Trade of the Far West* (2 vols.; Stanford: Stanford Univ. Press; 1954), II, 933.

westward-expansion question. There is reason for this stand-point—four bills for the establishment of a Territory of Oregon were defeated in 1821, 1822, 1823, and 1824. But during that early period the opponents of expansion managed to discourage support of a government-authorized westward movement by painting word-pictures of the futility of expending the taxpayers' money on Far Western projects; only an independent Pacific state or a colony in a "bleak and inhospitable" climate could be anticipated. "Possession of colonies is abhorrent to the principles of our political institutions," they said. The idea of a bona fide state or states in a land so distant was hard to accept.

On the other side of the ledger, however, were the cumulative results of work done by such exponents of westward expansion as Representative John Floyd of Virginia, Senator Thomas Hart Benton of Missouri, Senator John Tyler of Virginia, Senator Franklin Pierce of New Hampshire, Representative James Buchanan of Pennsylvania, and Representative James K. Polk of Tennessee. Their admonitions "made a lodgment in the public mind" which was bound to have some effect eventually.

The initial practical step toward a forcing of the Pacific Coast issue was the penetration of the old Oregon country by the Ashley-Henry-Smith Company of trappers, starting in 1824. "History by innuendo" wins no laurels for the entrepreneur, and I beg indulgence as I point rather arbitrarily to General William Ashley's long and intimate association with Senator Thomas Hart Benton as a likely place of origin of the plan for Jedediah Smith's Pacific Coast ventures. Similarly, I am of the opinion that the "adventures" of Captain Bonneville and the related expeditions to California led by Joseph Reddeford Walker in 1833 were agreed to if not instigated by Andrew Jackson and some of his Cabinet members. This last viewpoint is to some degree supported by existing contemporary documents.[4] Both these propositions deserve exposition, but for our present purposes they may serve "as is" for a starting point in the story of the mountain men on the Pacific slopes.

The first overland push in the direction of California was made by Santa Fe traders who, after Mexico gained independence from Spain in 1821, established a commerce between the Missouri River and New Mexico that depended upon pack animals and freight

[4] Carl P. Russell: *Guns on the Early Frontiers* (Berkeley, Cal.: Univ. of California Press; 1957), p. 149.

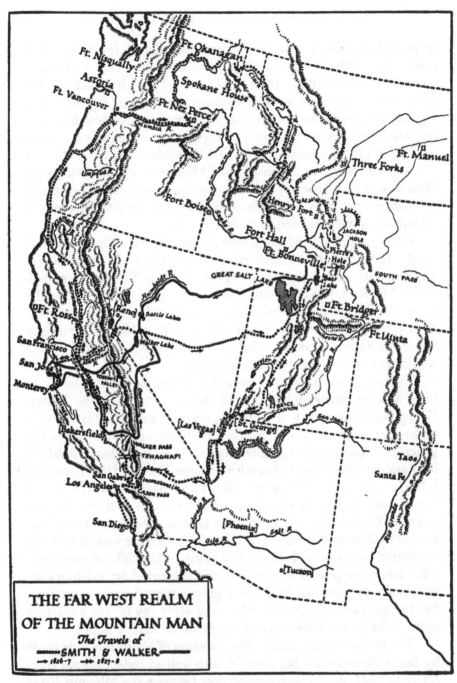

THE FAR WEST REALM
OF THE MOUNTAIN MAN
The Travels of
SMITH & WALKER
→ 1826-7 ⇢ 1827-8

From R. G. Cleland's *This Reckless Breed of Men* (New York: Alfred
A. Knopf; 1950), p. 83.

wagons. This activity in Spanish territory was not altogether distinct from the fur trade; the personnel of the two businesses overlapped or intermingled, many of the trade items were the same, some of the area tapped by the Santa Fe traders was also fur-trade country, and beaver pelts actually constituted an important part of the Santa Fe trade. But Santa Fe and its traders enter into the California story only because the Santa Fe Trail constituted a feeder route for one of the California trails and because the region of Santa Fe, Taos, and environs was a haven for Spanish traders and for mountain men, some of whom elected to move to California.

The real "breakthrough" to the Pacific occurred immediately after the fur traders' rendezvous of 1826, which was held on the Bear River some 40 or 50 miles from where that stream enters Great Salt Lake. On this occasion William Ashley sold his interests in the Ashley-Smith Company to Smith, Jackson, and Sublette. Upon the conclusion of trade and after Ashley had started for St. Louis (about the middle of August 1826), Jedediah Smith with 14 men sallied into the great unknown country southwest of Utah Lake. It is not inaccurate to say that he traced the route of our U. S. Highway 91 from the present day Ogden, Utah, to Barstow and Victorville, then over the mountains near Cajon Pass into the San Bernadino Valley and to San Gabriel. These employees of Smith, Jackson, and Sublette were the first white men to search out a Salt Lake–Colorado River route and the first Americans to enter California from the east. A great deal could be said here regarding hardships overcome, friendships won among Indians and padres, aid extended by American sea captains who vouched for Smith's documents and his innocent motives, and the cooperation of Captain William H. Cunningham, who sailed Smith from San Diego to San Pedro in his Boston ship *Courier*. However, this trapper party is but one of twenty-five that came to California during the period with which we are concerned. Due to space limitations, most of the dramatic incidents that occurred must be passed over so that the broader story of this "invasion" may be presented here. It is essential to my purpose, however, to continue with a very brief narration of Jedediah Smith's travels.

The disturbed governor of California sensed clearly enough that the coming of these Americans presaged disaster. Yet, since the visitors carried bona fide licenses and permits, he felt con-

strained to avoid arrests or other forced restraints. He issued instructions that they leave his country by the same route they had
come. Smith then led his men back to the San Bernardino Valley
and over the San Bernardino Mountains, whereupon he decided
that this was compliance enough. Instead of going east to the
Colorado, he made his way northward through the Antelope Valley
and over the Tehachapi Mountains into the San Joaquin Valley.
For three months the trappers worked the rich beaver streams that
they crossed as they moved northward. By the time they reached
American River, they were carrying 1,500 pounds of beaver.

About the first of May 1827, Smith attempted to go up the
American River and over the Sierra, but the snow was too deep.
With some loss of pack animals, the party managed to get back to
the valley. They then returned southward to a place they knew on
the Stanislaus River, where they settled down for a long, enjoyable
wait. Smith and two companions started up the Stanislaus on May
20 and in eight days were on the east side of the mountains. Their
route across the Nevada-Utah desert was approximately that of
present-day U. S. Highway 6. They crossed the Jordan River near
where it flows from Utah Lake, and then traveled northward along
the east shore of Great Salt Lake to Bear River and the appointed
rendezvous place at the south end of Bear Lake. One of the first
duties Jedediah performed at this encampment was to write a
report on California and the route thereto to General William
Clark, Superintendent of Indian Affairs at St. Louis. Included in
his interesting letter: "The Governor [of California] would not
allow me to trade up the sea coast towards *Bodaga* [seat of the
Russian trade]."

Implications of precursory understanding between Jedediah
and federal officialdom creep into his correspondence occasionally.
In the preceding instance one is reminded of the U. S. Congress'
formal recognition of the "Russian peril" on the Pacific Coast
during the 1820's. On January 25, 1821, Congressman John
Floyd, chairman of the Committee on the Occupation of the Columbia River, had written at some length regarding the determination of Russia

> . . . to make tributary the four quarters of the globe. . . . She
> sits not only in proud security as it regards Europe . . . she has
> also taken the opportunity of possessing herself of two important

stations on the American shore of the Pacific—one at a place called New Archangel, the other at Bodiga bay. . . . [The fort] at Bodiga is well constructed, supplied with cannon, and has a good harbor. They find the Indian trade very considerable. . . . The light articles destined for this trade are transported from St. Petersburg in sledges, which perform in three months that which would require two summers of water conveyance to effect. . . . The nation which can encounter such journeys to prosecute commerce must know its value. That the objects she has in view may not by any event be taken from her grasp, she has found it expedient to occupy one of the Sandwich Islands, which enables her effectively to maintain her position, and also to command the whole northern part of the Pacific Ocean.[5]

In 1822, the Czar's ukase sought to close the North Pacific to shipping, and the feared threat of a Russian California seemed real indeed. However, when Jedediah Smith departed on his expedition of 1826–7, there had been a recent formal assurance from the Czar that the Russians in western America would honor the Monroe Doctrine—a prohibitory precept that had been aimed quite directly at Russia. Whether or not Jedediah knew about the Russian disclaimer is uncertain, but, in any case, the Russians at Bodega and Fort Ross remained within their original limits and continued in their quiet agricultural and fur-trade pursuits for a total of more than thirty years. Never did the expanded occupancy and political aggression feared by some members of the Congress develop. Peacefully, Russian properties on the California coast passed by sale to the Sacramento colonizer John Sutter, a Mexican citizen, in 1840.[6]

Jedediah had promised the men he left on the Stanislaus that he would see them in four months or less. On July 13, 1827, he took leave of his partners in the Utah country, and with eighteen men and an outfit designed to last for two years he again set out for California. He followed almost the same route as he had in 1826, but his reception by the formerly friendly Mojaves was very different. While the party was preoccupied with crossing the Colorado, the Indians made a treacherous attack. Ten men were killed, and all Smith's goods and provisions were lost in a matter of

[5] *Oregon Historical Quarterly* (March 1907).
[6] Robert Glass Cleland: *A History of California: American Period* (New York: The Macmillan Co.; 1923), pp. 22–34; Earl Pomeroy: *The Pacific Slope: A History* (New York: Alfred A. Knopf; 1965), pp. 55–61.

minutes. The survivors made their way through the Cajon Pass but did not go to San Gabriel. They moved north through the Tehachapis over the identical route used in 1826 and rejoined Smith's men on the Stanislaus on September 18. Smith wrote: "I was there by the time appointed, but instead of bringing the promised supplies I brought to the men intelligence of my misfortunes."

Still further misfortunes were in store for Smith. He was held prisoner first at Mission San José; then Governor José Echeandía detained him at Monterey for six weeks. An American merchant, John Rogers Cooper, resident in Monterey, gave bond in assurance of Jedediah's good behavior if allowed to conduct his trappers out of California, whereupon the governor issued another passport which authorized the party to travel via Carquinez Strait and Bodega. Smith and his men were in San Francisco on November 15, when 1,568 pounds of beaver were sold to the captain of the ship *Franklin*. After outfitting in San Francisco, the party returned to San José, from where the cavalcade of twenty men and three hundred horses traveled northeast and arrived on the San Joaquin River on January 2, 1828. There is no evidence that Bodega figures in Smith's plan thereafter. All along the lower reaches of the river and the tributaries of the lower Sacramento a rich haul of beaver was made in spite of a shortage of traps. By the middle of April they were at the head of the Sacramento Valley, and Smith decided to veer northwest. With the greatest difficulty and a heavy loss of horses, the cavalcade pushed through to the coast near present-day Requa. Three weeks later the party was all but annihilated when about a hundred Kelawatset Indians attacked their camp on the Umpqua. Jedediah and two companions escaped the massacre because they were out scouting for a travel route at the time. Only one man in the camp escaped.

To make short this story of Jedediah's last disaster in the California-Oregon country, I will mention only that the four survivors made their way to the Hudson's Bay Company establishment at Fort Vancouver and there received every courtesy and aid from Dr. John McLoughlin, Chief Factor. A punitive party under Alexander Roderic McLeod of the Hudson's Bay Company was sent to the Umpqua to recover as much of the plundered Smith property as possible. During the next two months McLeod and thirty-six men, together with Jedediah and his three survivors, scoured the Umpqua country recovering some of the horses, beaver, equipment, and trade goods which had been scattered widely in various Indian camps. Perhaps the most significant recovery was the company records, including the journals of Rogers and Jedediah. At the end of December 1828 Smith accepted from the Hudson's Bay Company $2,369.60 in payment for horses and furs recovered by McLeod. As a guest, Smith prepared a map of the West for McLoughlin. He remained at Fort Vancouver until March 12, 1829, when with his employee Arthur Black he ascended the Columbia to Fort Colville, thence to Flathead Post and the Flathead River, where he joined his partner David E. Jackson. These two conducted a spring hunt on the upper Columbia, crossed the Rockies at Lemhi Pass, and met the third partner, William L. Sublette, in the vicinity of the Tetons in August 1829.

The record of the two Smith expeditions into California is replete with tragedy and the surmounting of terrific obstacles, both physical and political—the stuff of the theater. Yet the story has had little exposition by the dramatist and, its patriotic implications notwithstanding, has not received fitting recognition by the journalist and historian. Let us consider a few of the circumstances surrounding Jedediah's travels. Even prior to the start of the 1827 expedition, Daniel T. Potts, one of the men who intended to participate, wrote to his family from the Bear River rendezvous. "We are going into the country lying S.W. never visited by a white person. I expect my next letter will be dated mouth of Columbia River." [7] Obviously here is a hint that the Americans planned from the start to reach Oregon as well as California. A further reflection of the burden of thought carried by the men in the second party, that of 1827-9, is found in McLeod's report on his interview with the Chief of the Umpquas regarding the massacre of Smith's men:

> The old fellow expressed surprise at our interference by assisting people who evinced evil intentions toward us. He had been informed by the Indians who attacked the Americans that they [the Americans] talked about territorial claim, and that they would soon possess themselves of the country. . . . Mr. Smith when told of this said that he did not doubt of it, but the talk was without his knowledge and must have been intimated to the Indians by the slave boy attached to his party, a native of the

[7] Potts's letter of July 16, 1826, to his brother is quoted in Dale L. Morgan: *Jedediah Smith and the Opening of the West* (Indianapolis: Bobbs-Merrill; 1953), p. 193.

Wullamette who could converse freely with the Kelawatset Indians.[8]

In all statements either written or spoken by Jedediah Smith to Mexican and British authorities and in all recorded communications to American citizens in the ports of California, he maintained that his purpose in coming to the Pacific was (1) to obtain beaver and (2) to learn the truth regarding the mythical river, Buenaventura. On the other hand, his faithfulness in reporting so promptly to U. S. officials from the Bear Lake rendezvous after his 1926–7 explorations, and again from the Powder River on December 24, 1929, regarding experiences in 1827–9 rather belies the idea that only private business inspired his heroic labors.

In reporting to General William Clark on December 24, 1829, he minced no words in accusing the California governor, Echeandía, of instructing the Mojaves to massacre him and his men, and regarding his contacts in the North, he was quite outright in recommending that "British interlopers be dismissed from our territory." Lacking a Washington Irving, Smith's journals and letters received but little publicity in the 1830's and 1840's, but his map prepared for his old friend and partner, William Ashley, may well be regarded as an important contribution to the United States government archives and, ultimately, to the realms of business and politics. Ashley, recipient of the map, was a member of the U. S. Congress, 1831–7. His guide and mentor, the "Senatorial Paul Bunyan," Thomas Hart Benton, was then very much in the public view. These two missed no tricks in promoting the interests of the West. Notes from Smith's map were made available to Albert Gallatin, who published his map of the West in 1836. David Burr, Geographer to the House of Representatives, had access to the Smith map when he prepared his "Map of the United States," published in 1839. These maps, with the Bonneville map published in 1837, were of utmost importance to travelers in the West and to statesmen and geographers during the critical years of the accession of California and the settlement of the Oregon boundary question. A close approach to an original Smith manuscript map was found a few years ago in the collections of the American Geographical Society in New York. It is the George Gibbs copy of a map made by Smith for the Hudson's Bay Company during his

[8] Quoted in ibid., p. 277

stay at Fort Vancouver after the Umpqua massacre. The California Historical Society published the Gibbs copy some 103 years after it was made. The whereabouts of the original Smith maps continues to be a mystery.

Smith was still within California's boundaries on his 1827-8 expedition when the third party of American trappers entered the southern parts of the province. Annually thereafter additional groups came, the last arriving in 1838. The Hudson's Bay Company had tapped the extreme Northeast end of the province in 1827. It wasted no time in getting to California proper after hearing from Jedediah Smith about the abundance of beaver. The first British brigade came in 1829 and not less than a dozen parties came during the following fourteen years. Characteristically, they were large parties, often as many as two hundred people including women and children—so many as to cause John Sutter to beg the Mexican authorities to force the Hudson's Bay Company to reduce the traveling villages to thirty persons. Sutter, it may be explained, had his own company of beaver trappers.

Space does not permit discussion of the many companies, the individuals of high character, the renegades and undesirables, or the contacts made by the trappers with American sea captains and with American ranchers and merchants already established in California. Neither can more be told about conflicts with hostile Indians, rival Englishmen, and resentful Mexicans. Perhaps it is enough to outline the time scope of the industry and to compare the volume of activity engaged in by the fur hunters of the two nations. To that end the table on pages 24-5 is presented.

To summarize the story of the American push into the Southwest, there were in the dozen or so parties of American trappers that came to California prior to 1840 about a hundred discerning persons who elected to make their homes in the province. Most of these settlers did not desert their expeditions; they accompanied their parties back to the United States, then crossed the country again, sometimes as guides for emigrants but more often *as* emigrants, accompanied by old cronies, mountain men who had never before visited California. Practically all of them were staunch adherents of the idea that California must be a part of the United States. Many of them, thoroughly experienced in combat, fought

TRAPPER PARTIES IN CALIFORNIA, 1826–43
AMERICAN

Year	Leader	From	To
1826	Jedediah Smith	Great Salt Lake	San Gabriel
1827	Jedediah Smith	Bear Lake	San Jose
	R. Campbell	Santa Fe	San Diego
1828	S. Pattie	Santa Fe	San Diego
1829	Ewing Young	Taos	San Jose
1830	William Wolfskill	Taos	Los Angeles
1831	David E. Jackson	Santa Fe	San Francisco Bay
1832			
1833	J. R. Walker	Green River	San Joaquin Valley
1834			
1836			
1837			
1838	Richens (Dick) Wooten	Bent's Fort	Sacramento Valley
1839			
1840			
1841			
1842			
1843			

TRAPPER PARTIES IN CALIFORNIA, 1826–43
BRITISH

Leader	From	To
Peter S. Ogden	Ft. Vancouver	Mount Shasta
A. R. McLeod	Ft. Vancouver	San Joaquin Valley
Peter S. Ogden	Ft. Nez Percé (Walla Walla)	Sacramento Valley
M. Laframboise	Ft. Vancouver	Sacramento Valley
John Work	Ft. Nez Percé	Sacramento Valley
M. Laframboise	Ft. Vancouver	Central Valley
Tom McKay	Ft. Nez Percé	Pit River
M. Laframboise	Ft. Vancouver	Central Valley
M. Laframboise	Ft. Vancouver	Central Valley
M. Laframboise	Ft. Vancouver	Central Valley
M. Laframboise	Ft. Vancouver	Central Valley
* Gov. Simpson and A. R. McLeod	Ft. Vancouver	San Francisco
F. Ermatinger	Ft. Vancouver	Central Valley
† William Rae	Ft. Vancouver	San Francisco
F. Ermatinger	Ft. Vancouver	Central Valley
M. Laframboise	Ft. Vancouver	Central Valley
F. Ermatinger	Ft. Vancouver	Central Valley

* Governor Simpson and Dr. McLoughlin came to San Francisco via the ocean route. They arranged for a Hudson's Bay Company office and store in San Francisco, then returned to Ft. Vancouver via the Honolulu route.

† William Rae arrived on a ship bringing merchandise to the company's store in August 1841. Rae committed suicide in 1845, and the post was abandoned.

for this cause when the time for a "shooting war" came. Subsequently a number of them became leading citizens.

This influx of trapper-settlers was important to the ultimate solution of the acquisition problem, but of still greater significance was the role played by the fur men in defining the issues and in bringing to the American people a sense of the urgency of taking action. It is commonly said that the rank and file of the American fur brigades was made up largely of dissolute ruffians and bums who saw no future beyond the season of drunken revelry made possible by the annual rendezvous or a winter in Taos. Some present-day judges only credit the leaders of the trapper parties as having been responsible men, capable of envisioning the magnificence of a nation spread from ocean to ocean. It is only necessary to read the affidavits, letters, and journals of some of the underling mountain men to realize that this is not a realistic appraisal. It was no renegade spirit that pervaded the trapper organizations. Among the more literary men (other than leaders of the parties) who came to California and wrote of their purposes there were Kit Carson, James Clyman, Job F. Dye, Thomas Fitzpatrick, Josiah Gregg, Jacob P. Leese, Zenas Leonard, John Marsh, George Nidever, Sylvester Pattie, Daniel Potts, Harrison G. Rogers, Osborne Russell, the Sublette Brothers, J. J. Warner, John Wolfskill, and George C. Yount.

It will be observed that the foregoing list does not include the leaders of the American-California parties. To it may be added the better-known names: Richard Campbell, David E. Jackson, James Ohio Pattie, Jedediah Smith, Joseph R. Walker, William Wolfskill, R. Wooten, and Ewing Young. Some of these Chiefs of Party were more prolific in writing than were others, but only the enigmatic Davy Jackson failed to leave at least some small written record of his being. Generally, the gist of their message was: "California is a bounteous land; its Mexican claimants know not its worth, and they struggle futilely among themselves over selfish matters of personal concern. They lack a national spirit. The United States will do well to add this desirable province to our country before a foreign government steals a march."

I do not conclude that the Yankee merchants on the California coast failed to make an important contribution in shaping the statesmanship that resulted in the acquisition of California, but it was the presence of the knowledgeable mountain men in so many strategic places throughout the interior of California that had the greatest effect upon both the resident Mexicans and the designing Englishmen—not to mention the assistance and encouragement they gave to the American emigrants, that influential element already entrenched prior to the conquest.

Perhaps we may quite reasonably assert that the California cause was well on the way to success when Jedediah Smith escaped the slaughter at the Mojave villages, and was as much as won when the Indians on the Umpqua failed to kill him.

In the first instance, his attempted destruction was a defensive move on the part of Mexican officials; in the second, the murderous blow was struck on behalf of British interests, indirectly of course but nevertheless treacherously, by the simple savages who recognized only the Hudson's Bay Company as the Great Father.

Admittedly, this conclusion disposes of a number of important factors in perfunctory manner. It takes no cognizance of the long-time effects of the sea-otter trade, the New England whaling industry in the Pacific, and the hide and tallow trade, all three of which made fortunes for some Americans and at the same time enlightened the United States citizenry regarding California's coastline attractions. It ignores the results of internal strife among the California Mexicans, such as the Alvarado revolution of 1836 and Micheltorena's revolt in 1844. The role played by Johann August Sutter, feudal baron of the Sacramento, is omitted. The untimely seizure of Monterey in 1842 by our Commodore Jones is left out. The significant work of Thomas O. Larkin in reporting on English maneuvers and his plan for peaceful acquisition get no mention. There is no hint of the effects of instability in Mexico City upon negotiations attempted by our State Department, and the momentous results of the Bear Flag Revolt are slighted.

But I do want my conclusion to signify that the actions of Smith and his successors in the United States beaver business in California initiated the acquisition movement and influenced Andrew Jackson, John Tyler, James K. Polk, and their Cabinets in pursuing the California question right up to the crucial moment of war. In this connection it is pertinent to mention that the influence exerted by the trappers was not entirely long-range and indirect; some of them had a great deal to do with the Bear Flag Revolt, which constituted a decidedly direct action.

Nevertheless the political impact of the revolt was largely lost in the maelstrom of excitement accompanying the declaration of general war with Mexico. This long-anticipated break had occurred some six weeks prior to the independence proclaimed in Sonoma on July 4, 1846. Later that month the Bear Flaggers were apprised of the occupation of Monterey and San Francisco by U. S. naval forces. John C. Frémont and 150 men, assembled at Sonoma, reported to Commodore Robert F. Stockton in San Francisco. Later he led a larger party of Bear Flaggers and trappers to southern California.

Thus some of the mountain men were able to join in certain glorious fights in California, where local victories contributed to the general success of the Mexican War. Probably the big moment for a number of trappers came that December day in 1846 when a command under Stephen Watts Kearny engaged a force of Californians at the little Indian village of San Pasqual, near San Diego. In a few minutes of battle, eighteen Americans met their deaths and fifteen were wounded, but the Mexicans were driven from the field. A greater number of trappers were treated to an exhilarating experience when in the fall of 1846 they followed Frémont into Los Angeles to become a part of the conquering "army" under Kearny and Stockton. By January 1847 the fighting in California was ended, and the mountain men were quickly absorbed (and forgotten) in the swelling flood of humanity which inundated the Golden State.

In Oregon, the affairs of the mountain man included some sanguinary encounters, but these fights did not constitute a full-fledged war. Generally they were isolated encounters with Indians and, with the exception of the tragic Whitman massacre in which trappers featured only in the mopping up following the attack, they occurred in the earlier years of the American westward thrust. This is not to say, however, that the mountain men never confronted a major opponent in old Oregon. British aggression in the Western fur fields was the principal reason for the dispatch of Lewis and Clark to the Pacific, and the same British fur interests continued to exert pressure upon parts of the American Far West all through the mountain-man period. Provocative incidents sometimes flared in the intercourse, and the fact that there was no bloodshed reflects credit upon the civil instincts of the white principals, both British and American. The civilities, however, did not dull the commercial appetites of either side, and much of the mountain-man picture is colored by the competition offered by the traders from north of the boundary.

Mr. Astor's loss of his Columbia River enterprise during the War of 1812 enabled the Canadians to establish a peculiarly British pattern for the Oregon beaver business, which persisted for nearly thirty years. Our history books tend to be quite cavalier in crediting only the American emigrant and his political backers with the disruption of that pattern. Actually, the mountain men played an epochal role which sometimes receives too little attention. In 1818 Astoria was restored to the United States by treaty, but John Astor regarded the North West Company as too strongly entrenched there to permit a revival of the Astorian Columbia trade. The same agreement which returned Astoria to the United States also recognized the rights of the British as well as the Americans to trap and trade in the region. The Canadians began reaching out from the Columbia with the itinerant trapping brigades previously mentioned. At first the parties were called "Snake River Expeditions," but their operations were not limited to the Snake. At the mouth of the Walla Walla, Fort Nez Percé was built and from there the brigades ranged eastward and southeastward into country trapped by the Americans. The Nor'westers (after 1821, the Hudson's Bay Company) blanketed the whole Northwest from the Continental Divide in Montana, and in western Wyoming, Utah, Idaho, the Great Basin, and California. In 1827 the "joint occupancy" agreement was renewed but with the provision that it might be abrogated by either party upon a year's notice.

Rumors of the lively interest expressed by American citizens in the congressional debates of the early 1820's regarding establishment of a Territory of Oregon had reached Governor Simpson of the Hudson's Bay Company. When Jedediah Smith visited Fort Vancouver in 1828, the governor questioned him about the likelihood of American colonists' coming to the Willamette Valley. Smith put him at ease by expressing doubt that families from the United States could make the difficult journey in wagons. However, when Smith reported to the U. S. War Department in 1830, he was not at all pessimistic regarding the practicability of taking wagons overland to the Columbia. He also protested the British-American treaty of joint occupancy and reported: "The British do

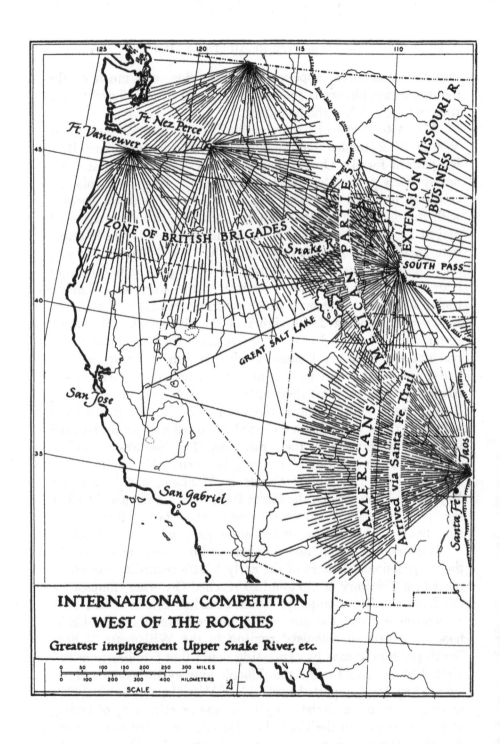

INTERNATIONAL COMPETITION
WEST OF THE ROCKIES

Greatest impingement Upper Snake River, etc.

SCALE

not trap north of latitude 49°, but confine the business to the
territory of the United States . . . if they are not stopped from
trapping, that country will soon be stripped of beaver." [9]

They were not stopped, but more and more American trappers
passed over the mountains to contend with them, and an increasing
number of American citizens became personally interested in what
was going on west of the Rockies.[1] Hall Jackson Kelley, an ardent
expansionist from Massachusetts, worked in the East for several
years, expending his personal funds to enlist citizen interest and
press for congressional action which might give financial help to
Oregon emigrants. The government support was not forthcoming,
but in 1832 Kelley went to San Diego, where he met the well-
known mountain man Ewing Young and persuaded him to accompany him to Oregon. Young, in turn, induced seven or eight
tried-and-true American trappers to accompany them to the Columbia. Young and his cohorts settled in the Willamette Valley not far
from the site of present-day Portland. Kelley, worn down by his
years of arduous efforts to establish the Oregon-for-America movement, was further sickened by untrue charges lodged against him
by Governor Figueroa of California. Figueroa had sent messages
ahead telling the Hudson's Bay Company officers that Kelley's
party were horse thieves wanted by the Mexican authorities. Kelley
departed for the Hawaiian Islands and thence to Boston in 1836.
His physical strength, like his money, was gone, and he died soon
after returning from his trip to Pacific shores. Young and his
mountain men, living the role of Oregon ranchers, made notable
demonstration of the American way on the Columbia—a life in
which the beaver business did not figure importantly. It was the
"new view" of Oregon values and, needless to say, Young did not
conceal from his compadres still in the fur fields the enthusiasm he
had for the Willamette. Young died in 1841 and even in death this
mountain man influenced the future of Oregon.[2] He left no will,
and, since his estate was of some consequence (it included a valu-

---

[9] The report of Smith, Jackson, and Sublette to the Secretary of War, sent
from St. Louis on October 29, 1830, is published in D. L. Morgan: *Jedediah
Smith*, pp. 343–8.

[1] Carl P. Russell: "Trapper Trails to the Sisk-ke-Dee," Chicago Westerners
Brand Book for 1944 (1946) and "Blue-eyed Men in Buckskin," *Corral Dust*
(December 1960, March and May 1961).

[2] Ewing Young's grave site in Chehalem Valley near Newberg, Oregon, is
now in the keeping of the Oregon Historical Society as a memorial to this
mountain man.

able herd of cattle), his immediate associates desired to arrange for formal distribution of the properties. No court existed; so one was set up, and a judge was named to handle proceedings in a manner corresponding to the New York laws for administering an estate. This was the first governmental action among Americans on the Columbia and it led to the creation of a committee to shape a constitution—a "flash in the pan." Not until 1843 did another committee succeed in drafting a code of laws acceptable to the community. A provisional Oregon government was adopted at Champoeg pending the day when the United States might extend its jurisdiction to the Columbia. Today there is a Champoeg State Park and History Museum, and in the Oregon State Capital, Salem, in the House Chamber is a beautiful and very lifelike mural by Barry Faulkner which depicts the historic voting at Champoeg on May 2, 1843. Also in the House Chamber emblazoned on the walls are the names of seventeen trappers and fur traders, some British and some American, who pioneered in establishing government and in attaining Oregon statehood. On the walls of the Senate Chamber appear the names of ten additional American mountain men, "prominent in the history, background and development of Oregon." These trapper-trader names are blended into the general record of all pioneers here honored, quite as the men themselves blended into the life of the new state they had done so much to create.

Similarly, almost everywhere across the American West, from the Missouri to the Pacific, the beaver hunters are to be credited with much of the basic pioneering that led to the expansion of the United States from coast to coast. In recent years historians and journalists have successfully defined and published this story of the men, events, and specific places involved in the beaver business, and very recently, indeed, historian-archeologists have applied themselves to the task of identifying and interpreting the material things, the three-dimensional objects, with which the fur men performed their daily work and which facilitated the conquest.

The present book pertains to iron objects primarily and, to a degree, to the iron men who used them. A survey of the fur man's iron leads one into many areas of study because the numerous ramifications of the story and because the roots of the Western fur trade must be traced in the history of American colonial trade, which had its beginnings more than two hundred years before Lewis and Clark.

The colonial trader invented much of his own paraphernalia and hit upon his own methods for their use; his equipment, trade goods, and successful processes became something of a legacy which he bequeathed to successors who moved on, penetrating the wild country west of the Mississippi. In the following chapters we shall focus upon Western-fur-trade artifacts, with such comment regarding their origins or predecessors as is discernible and pertinent. The history, so briefly outlined here, affords a thread upon which my antique beads are strung.

CHAPTER II

Firearms of
the Beaver Hunters

THE FIREARMS OF LEWIS AND CLARK

THOMAS JEFFERSON NEVER USED THE TERM "MOUNTAIN man," but there is ample documentary proof that Jefferson conceived of the Lewis and Clark Expedition as the prime move of the United States in launching the Western fur trade and thereby opening the era we call the "Mountain Man Period." [1] This was the glorious dawn of the nation's march to the Pacific.

It has been said, correctly, that the first mountain men of the American West were members of the Lewis and Clark Expedition. In the course of the explorations, 1803–6, the Lewis and Clark party introduced to the Far West many of the field practices which today we recognize as characteristics of the mountain man, and the impressive array of the known Lewis and Clark properties are, in truth, the same types of paraphernalia and trade goods which we now accept as marks of the mountain man. Furthermore, several members of the Lewis and Clark party went back to the Western

---

[1] "The activities of the aggressive North West Company convinced Jefferson that prompt American entry into the field was an absolute necessity to prevent ultimate British possession of the furs and permanent possession of the land on the basis of prior exploration and ultimate settlement. In his message to the Congress requesting funds to launch the expedition, Jefferson indicated the primary purpose was "to investigate a commercial opportunity of very great importance to the United States." (William C. Everhart: *"The Fur Trade,* Theme XV, Westward Expansion," *National Survey of Historic Sites and Buildings* [Washington, D.C.: National Park Service; 1960] [multilith edn.], p. 12; Ralph B. Guinness: "The Purpose of the Lewis and Clark Expedition," *Mississippi Valley Historical Review*, Vol. XX [June 1933].)

wilds immediately after the explorations and became principal figures in mountain-man history.

The Lewis and Clark party, so long and so far removed from civilized sources of supply, "lived off the land." Understandably, the meat of wild animals constituted a major item in the larder, and the skill of the hunter and the worthiness of his gun were much more than chatty after-supper topics. One of the many recorded incidents in the business of hunting during the winter of 1804–5 is revealing. A journal entry written at the wintering post, Fort Mandan, near the mouth of Knife River, North Dakota, tells that on February 13, 1805, Captain Clark and a party hunted some forty miles south of the fort. Captain Lewis and another party hunted in an area closer to the base. To bring in their kill improvised sleighs were used. Clark writes that on February 21, 1805, Captain Lewis returned to the post "with the meet which he killed [36 deer and 14 elk] plus that in the lower deposit [Clark's] amounting to about 3000 pounds, brought up on two slays. One drawn by 16 men had about 2400 pounds on it." [2] This meat had been boned at the time of kill to reduce the weight to be transported. The frozen supply of course constituted no problem of preservation. Forty-seven men and Sacajawea were usually at table during this winter at Fort Mandan.

Game was plentiful in the vicinity of Fort Mandan, and its procurement, as described above, was more a trial of physical strength and endurance than a test of guns and the hunter's skill. Later, during the expedition's long march, there were numerous occasions when game was scarce and it was then that the hunting prowess of certain backwoodsmen in the party came to the fore. Understandably, these occasions also pointed up the fact that some guns in the party's armament were superior to others.

The Lewis and Clark party was essentially a military organization. Captain Lewis was experienced in field service, familiar with the regulation armament of the U. S. Infantry, and prepared to specify what he wanted in the way of firearms and related accouter-

[2] Paul Allen, ed.: *History of the Expedition under the Command of Captains Lewis and Clark to . . . the Pacific Ocean, 1804–5–6*, 2 vols. (Philadelphia, 1814), I, 164, 254. Reuben G. Thwaites, ed.: *Original Journals of the Lewis and Clark Expedition, 1804–1806*, 8 vols. (New York: Dodd, Mead & Co.; 1905–6) (hereafter referred to as *Journals*); see entries February 10, 1805, through February 21, 1805.

ments. From the beginning of planning for the expedition, he benefited by the help of friends at the Harpers Ferry Armory. This new government gun factory had produced arms during the two preceding years. It extended an important service to Lewis in selecting and conditioning some of the pieces to be carried by the enlisted personnel of the expedition.

Muskets and Scatterguns

BASICALLY, the flintlock musket was the infantryman's arm of the day. The Lewis and Clark records of issues contain no reference to the U. S. musket; nevertheless, the *Journals* reveal that it was carried by some of the enlisted men. In 1803 the regulation musket was the U. S. flintlock, Model 1795 [3] (fig. 2*a*). It was capable of firing a death-dealing ball heavy enough for deer or elk (slightly less than 1 ounce in weight) [4] or its load could consist of shot, either buckshot or bird shot, for smaller game. Actually, because of its poor accuracy beyond 50 or 60 yards, the musket loaded with ball was not the favorite meat-getter.

Another scattergun in the hands of the explorers was the light "fuzee" (fig. 2*b*). Like the U. S. musket, this gun would fire a single ball or it could be loaded with fine shot. Because of their long-time familiarity with this type of gun, and because it was lightweight, it was a favorite of the French-Canadian boatmen, civilian employees of the Lewis and Clark party. Clark records the fact that Charbonneau, the interpreter, also had an "elegant" one. [5] Probably most of the light fusils of Lewis and Clark were nothing

---

[3] Captain Lewis on July 15, 1806, recorded that Hugh McNeal carried a musket; he broke it in two when he clubbed a charging grizzly. The U. S. flintlock musket, M. 1795, is described rather fully in Carl P. Russell: *Guns on the Early Frontiers* (Berkeley: Univ. of California Press; 1957), pp. 150–7.

[4] The results of earlier American trials are not recorded, but U. S. Army tests made in the 1820's and 1830's revealed that the regulation flintlock musket with the service load drove its ball 1 inch into white oak at 100 yards. At closer ranges the penetration was proportionately greater. From the standpoint of the meat-hunting explorers this penetration was fairly adequate, but the accuracy of the musket left much to be desired. "A soldier's musket will strike the figure of a man at 80 yards; it may even at a 100, but a soldier must be very unfortunate, indeed, who shall be wounded by a common musket at 150 yards." What was said of soldiers could have been said of deer with equal truth. Hanger, quoted by B. R. Lewis: *Small Arms and Ammunition in the United States Service, 1776–1865* (Washington, D.C.: Smithsonian Institution; 1960), p. 90.

[5] Bernard De Voto, ed.: *The Journals of Lewis and Clark* (Boston: Houghton Mifflin Co.; 1953), pp. 151–2.

more than the trade gun, which is treated elsewhere (pages 64–9).
When handled with regard for its limitations it was a fairly satisfactory gun; but the piece and its ammunition weighed much less
than did the U. S. musket. Long before the coming of Lewis and
Clark, Indians and French Canadians on the Missouri had become
enamoured of the light fusil; they liked its durability and its practical game-getting attributes. At this time the type was largely a
British product, so far as the Far West was concerned.

Rifles with Lewis and Clark

RIFLES get frequent mention in the *Journals*, and with good reason; "in the pinch" they were the dependable killers of big game.

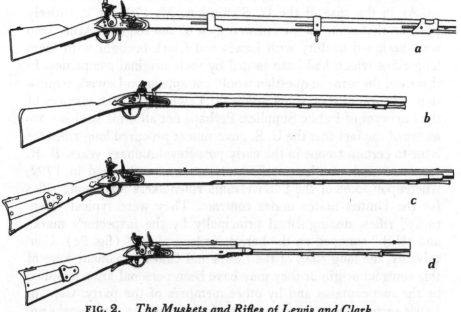

FIG. 2. *The Muskets and Rifles of Lewis and Clark.*

a, U. S. flintlock musket, M. 1795; barrel 44 inches. M. H. de
Young Memorial Museum, San Francisco. b, "elegant fusil"; barrel 34
inches. Made by P. Bond, London, 1776–1800. University of Kansas,
Lawrence. c, U. S. flintlock "Kentucky" rifle, contract of the 1790's;
barrel 42 inches. Similar pieces were made by Welshams, Augstadt,
Nicholson, Dickert, Ganter, Graff, and Morrow—all in Pennsylvania. d,
U. S. flintlock rifle, M. 1803; barrel 34 inches. Milwaukee Museum.
The drawing is by Glen Dines.

The numerous artists who during the past half century have busied themselves with interpretating the Lewis and Clark story seldom failed to give the long rifle (Pennsylvania-Kentucky rifle) prominent places in their paintings and sculptures. Their selection of such equipment seems to be justified. However, evidence of the presence of the long rifle in the armament of the Lewis and Clark party is more circumstantial than direct. For example, Clark in his journal occasionally refers to his "small rifle" in contrast with his "rifle." The phenomenally long shots [6] made with the "small rifle" when aimed at small game suggest very strongly that he was using the traditional squirrel rifle of his old Kentucky haunts. However, the requisitions, "Articles Wanted by Captain Lewis, May–June, 1803," do not list long rifles, and there seems to be no rumor even of the existence today of a long rifle of Lewis and Clark provenance.

As in the case of the U. S. musket, M. 1795, it is entirely possible that some of the enlisted men of the Regular Army who were assigned to duty with Lewis and Clark brought with them long rifles which had been issued by their original companies. In this case, the arms in question would not appear on Lewis's requisitions nor would they show up on the Lewis and Clark invoices of the Purveyor of Public Supplies. Perhaps not all arms students are aware of the fact that the U. S. government procured long rifles for issue to certain troops in the early post-Revolutionary years. B. R. Lewis reminds us that a rifle battalion was authorized in 1792, whereupon some of the Pennsylvania riflemakers made long rifles for the United States under contract. They were typical "Kentucky" rifles, distinguished principally by the inspector's marks and "U.S." stamped on the barrels or lock plates [7] (fig. 2c). Conceivably, the long rifles of the Lewis and Clark armament were of this contract origin or they may have been personal arms supplied by the two captains and by other members of the party. Captain Lewis seems to have been partial to the long rifle as a personal arm.

Two Kentucky rifles attributed to William Clark and now preserved in the collections of the Missouri Historical Society, St. Louis, are obviously of the post-expedition period.[8]

[6] Paul Allen, ed.: *History of the Expedition*, II, 93.
[7] B. R. Lewis: *Small Arms*, p. 49.
[8] Carl P. Russell: "The Guns of the Lewis and Clark Expedition," in *Historic Objects of Lewis and Clark Provenance* (MS in National Park Service Collection, Fort Clatsop, Oregon, 1959), p. 43. The illustrated gun section appears in print in *North Dakota History*, XXVII: 1 (Winter 1960), pp. 25–34.

Most noteworthy among the guns of Lewis and Clark was the brand-new U. S. rifle, Model 1803 (fig. 2d). The expedition put to trial the first specimens of this arm. The official requisition, "Articles Wanted by Captain Lewis, May–June, 1803," [9] lists 15 stands of this service rifle together with "15 powder horns and pouches complete; 15 pairs of bullet moulds; 15 pairs of wipers or gun worms; 15 ball screws; extra parts of locks; and tools for repairing arms." Conspicuous on the list are "200 lbs Best rifle powder," and "400 lbs lead." Unexplained is the request for "15 gun slings." The regulation U. S. rifle, M. 1803, as later issued to troops, has no swivels or other provision for attaching gun slings. Obviously, on such a trek as was the march of Lewis and Clark there was a most practical reason for "slinging" the shoulder arms. One conjectures that the Model 1803 issued to the expedition was not in every particular identical with the ultimate regular issue of the model.

The complement "15," mentioned in the previous paragraph, is repeated in connection with the requisition for government-issue clothing. Evidently, it was anticipated in the spring of 1803 that 15 men from the Regular Army would make up the unit of privates and noncommissioned officers, but by 1804 there were 31 men in the enlisted personnel of the permanent party, with 7 additional soldiers attached as far as Fort Mandan—38 men to be regularly armed by the U. S. Army.[1] No one has learned whether or not this expansion affected the original requisition and ultimate issue of the U. S. rifle, M. 1803. It should be said also that there is no known record of the existence in a present-day collection of a Lewis and Clark M. 1803.

The *Journals* reveal that this rifle gave a good account of itself throughout the expedition. Such breakage as occurred was always repairable with the extra parts and special tools that the farseeing Lewis had procured. In this connection, it is to be noted that the wilderness gunsmithing of John Shields was nothing less than phenomenal, considering the adversities with which he contended. Shields is to be counted as *first* among the American gunsmiths in the Western beaver country. Even the Indians of the Fort Mandan region handed down to us an expressive record of their opinion of

---

[9] Lewis's "List of Requirements," with many pertinent vouchers, appear in Donald Jackson, ed.: *Letters of the Lewis and Clark Expedition* (Urbana: Univ. of Illinois Press; 1962), pp. 69–99.

[1] For notes on personnel see De Voto, ed.: *Journals*, pp. 489–91.

him. The "One-Eye," LeBorgne, chief of the Minnetarees, declared to his white friends among the nearby British traders: "Had I these white warriors [of the Lewis and Clark party] in the upper plains, my young men would soon do for them as they would for so many wolves, for there are only two sensible men among them, the worker of iron and the mender of guns." [2]

The U. S. rifle, M. 1803, featured in the one and only accidental wounding by gunshot that occurred in the course of the explorations. Captain Lewis was the unfortunate victim. This blight on the expedition's remarkable safety record was inflicted by the fiddle-playing boatman Peter Cruzatte, when the party was on the Missouri en route home.

Lewis writes that on August 11, 1806, his detached party, traveling in boats, was at "the most northern point of the Missouri" (just north of the Little Missouri) when he saw "a herd of elk on a thick willow bar. I determined to land. I went out with Cruzatte only. We fired on the elk. I killed one and he wounded another. We reloaded and took different routs through the thick willows in pursuit of the elk. I was in the act of firing again when a ball struck my left thye about an inch below my hip joint, missing the bone and passing through my left thye and cutting the thickness of the bullet across the hinder part of the right thye. The stroke was very severe. I supposed that Cruzatte had shot me in mistake for an elk as I was dressed in brown leather and he cannot see very well. Under this impression I called out:

'Damn you, you have shot me!' "

Suddenly discreet, Cruzatte, who was only forty yards distant in the willows, said nothing. Lewis made his way to his pirogue on the shore and, as best he could, inspected his wounds. He found that "the ball had lodged in my breeches. I knew it to be the ball of the short rifles [U. S. M. 1803] such as that he had. . . . I have no doubt of his having shot me."

When Cruzatte was brought to the boats, he "seemed much alarmed and declared if he had shot me it was not his intention." [3] Lewis was incapacitated for a couple of weeks and spent his days

---

[2] Some of Lewis's testimony regarding wilderness gunsmithing is found in De Voto, ed.· *Journals,* entry for March 20, 1806, and Clark's testimony of April 8, 1806, pp. 335, 344. LeBorgne's appraisal as stated to Charles Mackenzie of the North West Co. was published by L. R. Masson: *Les Bourgeois de la Compagnie du Nord-Ouest,* 2 vols. (Quebec, 1889), I, 330.

[3] Lewis's entry of August 11, 1806, in De Voto, ed.: *Journals,* pp. 444–6.

as well as nights reclining in a boat. However, his poultices of "peruvian barks" afforded medication which eased pain and forestalled infection.

Perhaps the first M. 1803 rifles to find use by Indians were the pieces presented by Lewis and Clark to their Nez Percé guides. In May 1806 the eastbound expedition reclaimed its horses, which had been cared for through the winter by the friendly Nez Percé in the vicinity of present-day Kamiah, Idaho. There the Lewis and Clark party camped for a month waiting for high mountain snow to melt. On May 12, 1806, Clark recorded the presentation of a "gun," powder, and 100 ball to Chief Twisted Hair. At this time Clark was consistent in writing "rifle" when a rifle was meant. Late in June, Nez Percé guides, in return for one rifle given at the start and the promise of two more U. S. rifles, M. 1803, led the party into the mountains and over the packed snow of the Lolo Trail. Both Lewis and Clark regarded the Nez Percé to be the most generous and likable of the tribes. Only to these Indians were small arms given intentionally and willingly—a presentation of four pieces which made the Captains parties to the extension of the gun frontier. Prior to this time the Nez Percé did not possess firearms.

On the occasion of the final gift-making at Travellers Rest, east end of the Lolo Trail, Shields sawed off and filed a ruptured rifle barrel, M. 1803, which although "very short was made to shute tolerable well." This piece and one other went to the Indian guides [4] on July 2, 1806.

Breakage and failures notwithstanding, Lewis and Clark uttered no complaints regarding the U. S. rifle, M. 1803. Shields kept the arms in working order. What he may have thought of the short rifle is not recorded; if Lewis and Clark submitted formal report on their experiences with the new rifle, it is not known. The history of the ultimate disposal of the some 20,000 Model 1803 manufactured through the sixteen-year period (1803–19) is obscure. Understandably, the Army did not immediately drop the model when the U. S. rifle, M. 1817, became available; in 1836 the Model 1803 was still being issued to regular troops.[5] That it was not always favored by the Army in the West is indicated by Colonel Woolley's report on Fort Atkinson (Nebraska) in 1826:

[4] *Journals*, Clark's entries of June 18 and July 2, 1806. See also P. Allen, ed.: *History of the Expedition*, II, 317, 332.
[5] C. P. Russell: *Guns*, p. 182.

The arms of the regiment [6th Infantry] are old and of various patterns and are unfit for the Regiment, very probably inferior to those of any other Regiment in the Service. The Rifles of the Rifle Company are particularly bad, altho in firing order; they are old ones very hastily manufactured in the early part of the war [of 1812]. There are several hundred of this description in store. [Refers to the 1814 type, M. 1803.] If pains were taken *they could be sold at this post to Indians and traded for their full value.*[6]

Whether or not any of the 665 old rifles at Fort Atkinson were sold to Indians, as recommended, is not known, but material evidences of the deterioration of some of the stands is at hand; fragments of the U. S. rifle, M. 1803, were brought to light along with other gun parts dug up in a refuse dump at the Fort Atkinson site in 1956.[7] Kivett, in charge of the dig, determined that the Rifle Regiment, believed to have been armed with the Model 1803, was absorbed into the 6th Infantry in 1821, the rifles were turned in, and muskets were issued. This was the demise of the Rifle Regiment, but in the fall of 1825 Light Company B of the 6th Infantry was armed with rifles, and the unit was designated a "rifle company," the company referred to by Colonel Woolley in his 1826 report, previously quoted. Presumably the mutilated, broken, and surplus parts of the Model 1803 were consigned to the trash by the post armorer when Fort Atkinson was abandoned in 1827. This accumulation of remnants of worn-out stands occupied the very locality where Lewis and Clark held their celebrated Indian council (Council Bluffs) in 1804—an occasion for the parading of the first M. 1803 ever to come from the factory.

Records from 1803 through 1819 show that some 20,000 of the Model 1803 were manufactured; about 5,000 of them were produced at Harpers Ferry before 1808. To meet the demands of the three new regiments of riflemen created in 1813, a second period of production was initiated in 1814. The Springfield Armory contributed to this effort by manufacturing parts for the arm. Specimens in existing collections marked "Richmond, Virginia, 1821" and "Tryon, Philadelphia, 1815" reveal that private contractors contributed to the production. Writers often refer to the stands pro-

---

[6] Italics mine. Marvin F. Kivett: "Excavations at Fort Atkinson, Nebraska. Preliminary Report," *Nebraska History* (March 1959), p. 56.
[7] Kivett illustrates these gun fragments in his Pl. 1A, ibid.

duced after 1813 as the "U. S. rifle, M. 1814," but the distinction is thinly justified.[8]

Army officers with troops in the West during the 1820's and 1830's sometimes referred in their reports to the "half-stocked rifle" with which their rifle companies were armed, a positive identification of the M. 1803. Usually, these fieldmen commended the rifle. They liked its agreeable balance and favored its shorter barrel, characteristics which appealed to Henry Dearborn of the War Department when he ordered adoption of the Model 1803. He wrote: "I have such convincing proof of the advantage of the short rifle over the long ones (commonly used) in actual service as to have no doubt of preferring the short rifle with larger caliber than the long ones usually have. The great facility which such rifles afford in charging [loading], in addition to their being less liable to become foul by firing, gives a decided advantage to men of equal skill and dexterity over those armed with the common long rifle." [9]

It is not possible to prove that the M. 1803 was the progenitor of the mountain man's favorite gun, the mountain or "Plains" rifle, but the half-stock, short and partly round barrel, larger caliber, and the iron rib from tail pipe to muzzle, together with the "sporting" balance of the entire piece, suggest that this military arm did indeed lead the way in providing the mountain man with a distinctive arm.

Pistols

As in the case of military muskets, little is said by the Lewis and Clark journalists about the handguns carried by the party, yet there is evidence that pistols were included in the armament. At the time of the expedition it was quite usual for Army officers to carry personally owned pistols; so although we have Lewis's testimony regarding his use of a holster pistol on the occasion of his fight with the Piegans on July 27, 1806, we have no positive proof that the weapon was a military model. But if it were a regulation U. S. military piece, it could have been none other than the Model 1799 made by Simeon North, and supporting the theory that it *was* the

[8] C. P. Russell: *Guns*, p. 178. For the Tryon and Richmond specimens see J. G. W. Dillin: *The Kentucky Rifle* (Washington, D.C.: National Rifle Assn.; 1924), Pl. 24.

[9] James E. Hicks: *Notes on United States Ordnance*, 2 vols. (Mount Vernon, N.Y., 1940), I, 25–6.

M. 1799 is the invoice of "Arms issued from the public stores to Captain Lewis" recorded by Israel Whelen, Purveyor of Public Supplies. "1 pr. Horsemans Pistols" and "1 Pair Pocket Pistols" appear on Whelen's list. The horse pistols were delivered from the Philadelphia Arsenal on May 18, 1803, and the pocket pistols, with "secret" triggers, were purchased from Robert Barnhill for $10.00. Meriwether Lewis took delivery of them June 7, 1803.[1]

Surprisingly enough, the *Journal* entries for November 4, 1805, contain a reference to pistols in the hands of Indians on the Columbia near the outlet of the Willamette River. These handguns had been traded by the Yankee and English ships that trafficked at the mouth of the Columbia several decades prior to the arrival of Lewis and Clark.

Meriwether Lewis's Air Gun

INCONGRUOUS though it seems, an air gun proved to be one of the more valuable pieces in the Lewis and Clark armament. With purpose aforethought, Lewis procured it in Pennsylvania as one of the first items on his list of needs in 1803. His account of the accidental shooting of a white woman with this gun during the early stages of his journey from Pittsburgh is impressive testimony regarding the power of the arm.[2] Captain Lewis stopped with a friend, Dr. Felix Brunot, at the Brunot estate near Pittsburgh. During his visit some of the local people toyed with the air rifle, and one of them accidentally pulled its trigger. The ball, flying wild, grazed the temple of a woman forty yards away. She dropped in her tracks. The wound was superficial and the blow only stunned the victim, but the startling incident was the beginning of a succession of events which distinguished the air gun in the Lewis and Clark saga.

The novel gun was of no consequence as a game-getter, but all Indians regarded it to be "Big Medicine." It was a powerful agent in the "*public relations* program" conducted by Lewis among the

[1] C. P. Russell: *Guns*, pp. 199–200 and Fig. 37 a. Donald Jackson, ed.: *Letters of the Lewis and Clark Expedition* (Urbana: Univ. of Illinois Press; 1962), pp. 91, 98. It is to be noted that Lewis shot his Piegan victim "at the distance of 30 steps," not with a pistol but with his "gun," presumably the long rifle—*Journals*, July 27, 1806.

[2] Milo M. Quaife, ed.: *The Journals of Captain Meriwether Lewis and Sergeant John Ordway, 1803–1806* (Madison: Wisconsin Historical Soc.; 1916), p. 31.

tribesmen. The *Journals* record a score of instances when open-mouthed Indians from the Missouri to the Pacific were entranced by its multishot mysteries. Apparently Lewis had no difficulty in keeping it in working order. On August 7, 1805, at the forks of the Jefferson he wrote: "My air gun was out of order and her sights had been removed by some accident. I put her in order and regulated her. She shot again as well as ever she did."[3]

The much-appreciated air gun was still being displayed among the Indians at the mouth of the Columbia and among the Nez Percé in the spring of 1806.[4] Undoubtedly, it made the round trip with the explorers.

Blunderbusses

AT their camp below the Great Falls of the Missouri in June 1805 the expedition lightened its load in preparation for the long and difficult portage. On June 26 Captain Clark selected "2 blunder-butts" as part of the properties to be cached. Captain Lewis in his notes for the same day referred to these guns as "2 blunderbushes." Lewis's journal entry for May 29, 1805, makes it clear that these big pieces were swivel guns. In describing the havoc created by a berserk buffalo bull which charged through camp on the night of the twenty-eighth, he wrote: "A rifle was much bent. He had also broken the spindle, pivot, and shattered the stock of one of the blunderbusses."

In all likelihood these scatterguns were carried in the two pirogues as the party ascended the Missouri, but when trouble with the Sioux erupted on September 25, 1804, they were on the keelboat. Sergeant Ordway provides the information that they were "loaded well with buckshot" and brought to bear upon the hostiles as they tried to bully the explorers.[5] This is the only recorded incident of imminent trouble requiring use of the blunderbusses. At Fort Mandan the logical place for them was at the ends of the sentinel's "catwalk" on the roof of the storerooms, where in case of attack they could deliver an enfilading fire along the long outer walls of the fort.

In August 1806 the homeward-bound explorers dug up the

[3] De Voto, ed.: *Journals*, pp. 180–1.
[4] P. Allen, ed.: *History of the Expedition*, II, 136.
[5] De Voto, ed.: *Journals*, p. 37.

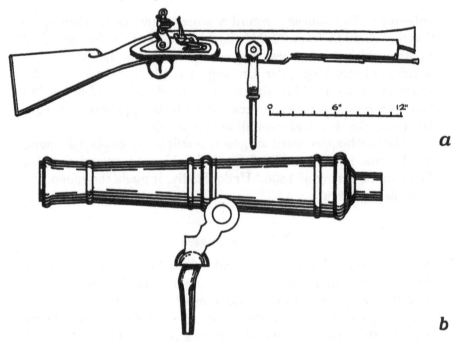

a

b

FIG. 3. *Swivel Guns of Lewis and Clark.*

a, swivel-mounted blunderbuss. Barrel 22½ inches; flared muzzle 2 inches in diameter. Milwaukee Museum (N7013). *b*, early U. S. swivel gun. Total length about 30 inches; bore 1⅞ inches; a one-pounder. Rock Island Arsenal. The drawings are by Glen Dines.

blunderbusses at Great Falls and again made them a part of their defensive armament as they prepared to pass through the Teton Sioux gauntlet. There was no occasion to repel an attack, but on September 21, 1806, "We arrived opposite St. Charles. We saluted the village by three rounds from our blunderbuts." On September 23 the guns were returned to St. Louis.

The Small Cannon of Lewis and Clark

FROM the day of departure from Wood River, Illinois, May 14, 1804, to the time of the Great Falls cache, June 26, 1805, the one small cannon, swivel-mounted on the keelboat, figured quite prominently in the journal entries. It was fired in farewells and in salutes. It found its most important use in discouraging the hostile Teton Sioux, when on September 25, 1804, those Indians threatened to disrupt the expedition. Sergeant Ordway tells us that on this occasion it "was loaded immediately with 16 musquet Ball." [6] This suggests that it had a bore of something less than 2 inches and fell in the 1-pounder class.

Swivel guns of this kind were not an innovation. Even on the lower Missouri they had been used by the Spaniards for a decade or more prior to the coming of Lewis and Clark. In the world's military circles they were an institution and had been for several centuries.[7] More is said about them in the section devoted to swivel guns of the mountain men (pages 78–84). Early in August 1806 Lewis and Clark lifted their small cannon from its cache at

FIG. 4.　*Swivel Gun Mounted in Prow of a Pirogue.*

Either the blunderbuss or the 1-pounder cannon could be mounted on the big skiff used by the explorers, but the 1-pounder was regarded to be more appropriate for the keelboat. The drawing is by Glen Dines.

[6] Ibid.
[7] C. P. Russell: *Guns*, pp. 251–7.

Great Falls and transported it to the Mandan villages, where on August 16 it was presented to the chief, "One Eye"—he who had said: "My young men would do for them as they would for so many wolves" (page 40). Regarding this gift Captain Clark wrote on August 16, 1806: "We concluded to make a present of it [the cannon] to the great chief of the Menitaras (the One Eye) with a view to ingratiate him more strongly in our favor." What befell thereafter is not told in legend nor history, but the curators of Great Plains history and the historian-archeologists who today dig cannon and cannon fragments from Missouri River sites do not forget the Minnetaree accession of 1806.

Ammunition

ONE of the evidences that Lewis's requisition of 1803 covers only a portion of the equipment and supplies is seen in the record for gun powder. In 1803 Lewis asked for "200 pounds Best rifle powder." Quite obviously he obtained more. As the party moved westward, caches of properties were made from time to time with the expectation of recovering them on the return trip; the amount of gunpowder deposited at Maria's River and in the caches at the Great Falls of the Missouri, at Shoshone camp on the Beaverhead, and at Canoe Camp on the Clearwater [8] (in present-day Idaho) would have made excessive drain had the total been only 200 pounds.

Further light is thrown on the gunpowder supply by Lewis's journal entry for February 1, 1806, in which he names as still on hand at Fort Clatsop: 27 canisters best rifle powder, 4 of common rifle powder, 3 of glazed powder, and 1 of musket powder. The canisters were made of sheet lead weighing 8 pounds each. Each canister contained 4 pounds of powder. "We have an abundant stock to last us back."

Lewis's "happy expedient" of sealing the gunpowder within leaden containers of the exact weight to complement the powder when loaded into their guns proved to be one of his triumphs in logistics. Quite frequently the cargoes carried in the dugouts were soaked while passing through rough water. According to Lewis, who wrote about one of these occasions when westbound, August 6, 1805: "We unloaded all our canoes and opened and exposed to

[8] De Voto, ed.: *Journals*, pp. 134, 150, 210, 243.

dry such articles as had been wet. A part of the load of each canoe consisted of the leaden canestirs of powder which were not in the least injured, though some of them had remained upwards of an hour under water. About 20 lbs. of powder which we had in a tight keg or at least one which we thought sufficiently so got wet and intirely spoiled. This would have been the case with the other had it not been for the expedient which I had fallen on—lead canesters well secured with corks and wax. In this country the air is so pure and dry that any [wooden] vessel however well seasoned the timber may be will give way or shrink unless it is kept full of some liquid."

Again, when settled for the winter at Fort Clatsop, Lewis wrote on February 1, 1806: "Today we opened and examined all our ammunition which had been secured in leaden canesters. We found . . . the powder in good order, perfectly as dry as when first put in the canesters, altho the whole of it from various accedents has been for hours under the water. . . . Had it not been for that happy expedient . . . we should not have a single charge of powder at this time. . . . We have an abundant stock to last us back and we always take care to put a portion of it in each canoe . . . our only hope for subsistence and defense in a rout of 4000 miles through a country exclusively inhabited by savages."

It may be presumed that ladles for melting lead were included in the field equipment, as well as the bullet molds which are accounted for in Lewis's requisition of 1803. "500 best gun flints, wipers or gun worms, ball screws, powder horns, and bullet pouches and extra parts of gunlocks" were also obtained. The mention in the *Journals* of "fixed ammunition" suggests that some prefabricated paper cartridges were on hand. Invoices indicate that "Cartouch Boxes," [9] in which such paper cartridges were carried, were issued to Lewis by the Purveyor of Public Supplies.

In summary, the following outstanding facts of the story of the guns of the first mountain men should be emphasized:

1. "Preparedness" was ever uppermost in the minds of the leaders. Formal inspection of the arms and ammunition was almost painful in its frequency and thoroughness.

2. The marksmanship of Captain William Clark, the hunter George Drouillard, and a number of the men was extraordinary.

---

[9] The paper cartridges and the cartridge box of the day are described and illustrated in B. R. Lewis: *Small Arms*, pp. 69–71, 172–4.

John Colter, John Shields, and the two Fields brothers get special mention in this connection.

3. The air gun, of no consequence as a game-getter, nevertheless was "Big Medicine" in dealing with Indians.

4. The flintlock weapons of the day were surprisingly effective in killing all game except the grizzly bear.

5. The threat of a blast from three swivel guns (one conventional small cannon and two blunderbusses mounted on swivels) probably "saved the day" on September 25, 1804, when the Teton Sioux attempted to bully the northbound party at the mouth of the present-day Bad River, opposite Pierre, South Dakota.

6. In providing the Nez Percé with a few guns, Lewis and Clark became a party to the extension of the gun frontier in the American West; in presenting their swivel gun to the Minnetarees in 1806, they made western Indians owners of a cannon for the first time. (It is to be mentioned that there were very few instances thereafter when Indians came into possession of cannon.)

7. The only instance in which an Indian was killed by gun play occurred when Captain Lewis shot an offending Piegan on July 27, 1806, "through the belly . . . at the distance of 30 steps." Lewis refers to his arm simply as "my gun," which, consistently, seems to have been a long rifle. Some writers have assumed that this Indian was not killed, but Indian testimony given in 1807 to the Canadian David Thompson, and Lewis's "Sketch of Voyage to the Pacific Ocean," October 14, 1806,[1] assert that this Indian, as well as the one knifed in this same fight by Private Reuben Fields, was in truth dead on the field of encounter.

8. There are no well-known, indisputable Lewis and Clark gun relics in present-day collections. One gun which may possibly be of Lewis and Clark provenance is a smoothbore, .58 caliber piece owned by the National Park Service and preserved in the Claud E. Fuller Collection at Chickamauga-Chattanooga National Military Park. Mr. Fuller handed down a document[2] expressing his belief that this gun was indeed carried by a member of the expedition, but the member is not named in the deposition. The

[1] J. B. Tyrrell, ed.: *David Thompson's Narrative of His Explorations in Western America, 1784–1812* (Toronto: Champlain Soc.; 1916), p. 375. D. Jackson, ed.: *Letters*, p. 342.

[2] C. P. Russell: "The Guns of the Lewis and Clark Expedition," *North Dakota History*, XXVII: 1 (Winter 1960), 25–34.

original flintlock mechanism of this gun has been replaced by the percussion system, and the later lock plate bears the name "A. W. Spies." The gunmaker Spies is recorded to have been active no earlier than 1820. The brass butt plate of the piece appears to be original and it is marked "T. Hill. Charlotte." T. Hill is known to have made guns in Carlotta, Vermont, during the first decade of the nineteenth century. There is then at least a bare possibility that this is a Lewis and Clark gun.

The rush of American trappers to the beaver country explored by Lewis and Clark began even prior to the expedition's return to civilization. Immediately after Captain Lewis suffered his gunshot wound, his detachment encountered two hunters from the Illinois, Joseph Dixon and Forest Hancock, who for two years had been trailing the Lewis and Clark party. Lewis wrote in his journal on August 12, 1806: "I gave them a short description of the Missouri, a list of distances to the most conspicuous streams and remarkable places on the river above, and pointed out to them the places where the beaver most abounded." A significant separation from the Lewis and Clark party occurred at this moment; John Colter was permitted to join Dixon and Hancock. The trio proceeded westward, so taking the first practical step in launching the Rocky Mountain fur trade. As the homecoming explorers spread the news regarding teeming beaver waters, numerous trappers and traders in the settlements organized to take far bigger steps; within a year a hundred individuals and companies were licensed to trade on the Missouri, and a great many others proceeded to trade without formal license.

Manuel Lisa's Fort Manuel, built at the mouth of the Big Horn, provided the first American anchorage for the mountain trade. Lisa, head of one of the more substantial companies, led some forty trappers upriver to this site in the spring of 1807. Four members of the Lewis and Clark expedition were in this field organization, and William Clark, by this time Brigadier General and U. S. Indian Agent, St. Louis, was a promoter and, ultimately, a shareholder in the Lisa company. In 1807–8 Lisa's men spread out among the tribes of the Rockies, and the mountain-man business was on its way. These trapper-traders were fully armed, of course; unfortunately there are no existent requisitions, invoices, or lists of the guns.

Firearms of the Mountain Men

Rifles

WHEN in 1806 John Colter was released by Lewis and Clark, he was presented with "several articles which will be useful to him on his expedition." Powder and lead are mentioned as included in the presents, but the firearm itself is not identified—an omission quite in keeping with the common failure of many old documents to satisfy the inquisitiveness of gun antiquarians. Occasionally the guns themselves stand solidly in the presence of the researcher, inviting criticism of the legend in which they are wrapped. Part of the time, at least, the touted pieces and their stories are unassailable. Probably it is no more disappointing to the antiquarian to lose a fugitive gun like John Colter's arm than it is to uncover the error or deceit in a cherished story and, in effect, thereby lose a piece actually in the student's hand.

If one wishes to conjecture regarding the firearm that John Colter carried as he returned to the wilderness in 1806, one can say with some reason that he kept his U. S. rifle, M. 1803. Time and again, Captain Lewis committed himself in the matter of objectives; his writings show clearly that he regarded the Western fur trade to be a principal reason for the "Corps of Discovery." Contributing a government-owned firearm to the cause would be quite consistent with the "ingratiating" gifts extended by Lewis and Clark to the Cheyenne, for example, who wished to learn how to prepare and market beaver pelts. In Colter's case the government gun would have been written off the record along with the Nez Percé and Mandan presents as "expendable."

After a year of hardship "on his own," John Colter in 1807 was disposed to give up his independence as a free trapper. While still in the Missouri wilds, he encountered the northbound Lisa party and signed up as an *engagé.* His experience and influence counted heavily for Lisa almost at once. Several scholars who have investigated his story agree that it was because of Colter's admonitions that Manuel Lisa placed his fort on the Yellowstone rather than on the Missouri.[3] As previously mentioned, there were in addition to

[3] Hiram M. Chittenden: *The American Fur Trade of the Far West*, 3 vols. (New York, 1902), I, 119; Burton Harris: *John Colter* (New York: Scribner's; 1952), pp. 69–70; M. O. Skarsten: *George Drouillard, Hunter and Interpreter for Lewis and Clark* (Glendale: Arthur H. Clark Co.; 1964), pp. 256–7.

FIG. 5. *The First American Trading Post on the Upper Missouri.*

Lisa's Fort Manuel under construction at the confluence of the Big Horn and Yellowstone rivers, fall of 1807. The trading services accorded by this first of American establishments delighted the Crow Indians and the Flatheads but aroused the bitter hatred of the Blackfeet. With guns traded by Lisa, the Flatheads waged successful war against the Blackfeet. The Blackfeet, in turn, waged war against the white traders—hostilities that persisted throughout much of the mountain-man period. Drawing by William Macy, Jefferson National Expansion Memorial, St. Louis.

Colter three more former members of the Lewis and Clark party with Lisa: George Drouillard, John Potts, and Peter Wiser. Presumably, Colter still carried his U. S. rifle, M. 1803. If this military arm found wider use in the Lisa expedition, probably it would have been in the hands of these veterans.

But there is no proof. Neither is there a record of a specific instance of Lisa's use of the long rifle. But, as was the case with the Lewis and Clark personnel, many of Lisa's men were born and bred to the use of the "Kentucky" rifle, and it is a foregone conclusion that the contemporary references to the "rifle" in the hands of Lisa's men usually meant that they carried the long rifle. One of these references is sworn testimony in George Drouillard's trial for murder. On the Missouri at the river Osage in 1807, under orders from Lisa to bring back a deserter "dead or alive," Drouillard gave chase and shot the fleeing Antoine Bissonnette. When Drouillard returned to St. Louis in August 1808, he was held for murder, tried, and found "not guilty." In the course of the proceedings one Ante Dubreuil deposed: "Manuel ordered, 'George, go and find this Bazine.' Mr. Drouillard took his rifle and went away in the company of Benito. Some time after they left I heard a rifle shot and about half an hour later Mr. George Drouillard came back and said that he shot Bazine but he did not die. He wanted men to bring the wounded man to camp." *The Missouri Gazette*, October 12, 1808, gives some further particulars: "The bullet penetrated his back near one of his shoulders. . . . Mr. Lisa procured him [Bissonnette] a canoe . . . and hastened him toward St. Charles . . . but he died in the canoe the next day." [4]

Manuel Lisa constituted a major force in the Western fur trade until his death in 1820. Thereafter, his company, the Missouri Fur Company, under the leadership of Joshua Pilcher, was active on the upper river for another decade. Its posts were substantial, its boats numerous, and its parties big. In its day it traded many guns to the Crow, Flathead, Pawnee, Omaha, Oto, Sioux, and Iowa particularly. The men in its employ numbered about 300 in the heyday of its action, and their armament, if described, would provide a good cross section of mountain-man firearms of the flintlock period. Sad to say, there is no description of them, and antique guns in present-day collections that can be traced to the Missouri Fur Co. are few indeed.

Lisa's contemporaries in the employ of John Jacob Astor provided some relief to this dearth of recorded information. The circumstances surrounding Astor's loss of Astoria to the North West Company in the fall of 1813 commanded such attention in the U. S. Congress as to result, belatedly, in hearings. The published account [5] includes Mr. Astor's personal statement (itemized invoice) regarding the firearms of the Astorians. This significant material receives some analysis in our Appendix B (pages 402–7). In the entire armament belonging to the Pacific Fur Company, valued at some $18,000.00 and transferred to the British North-

---

[4] The story of this killing and details of Drouillard's trial are well covered in Skarsten: *George Drouillard*, pp. 271–9.

[5] John Jacob Astor's testimony regarding properties delivered to the North West Co. at Astoria in Oct., 1813, *in* Message from the President of the United States [James Monroe] Communicating . . . Documents Relating to an Establishment at the Mouth of the Columbia River. Jan. 27, 1823. 17th Cong., 2d sess., H. Doc. 45 (Washington, D.C.: Gales and Seton; 1823), pp. 1–80 (invoice of Astor's properties, pp. 20–63).

westers by the Astorians, there is not one rifle, part of a rifle, nor a rifle accouterment. One might jump to the conclusion that the Astorians had an aversion to rifles. Such inference is wrong. Robert Stuart, Gabriel Franchere, Ross Cox, Alexander Ross, and Wilson Price Hunt have handed down to us eyewitness accounts of the affairs of the Astorians.[6] They wrote "rifles" into their narratives. They were not specific in mentioning the type of their rifled arms but it is clear that they did not mean smoothbores; logically, we accept their designations as meaning the long rifle.

Concrete support for the theory that the Astorians possessed long rifles is found in the very interesting relics raised from the bottom of the Snake River in the vicinity of Hunt's disaster of early November 1811. Hunt's westbound party fared badly after adopting dugouts; the turbulent Snake proved to be a veritable death-trap. Ramsay Crooks, who later put his name to the voluminous collection of manuscripts, The American Fur Company Papers, suffered the first sinking. His boat turned over in the "Caldron Linn," one of its occupants was drowned, and its cargo went to the

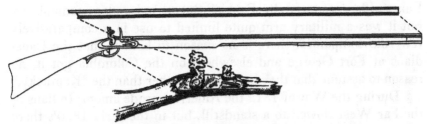

FIG. 6. *Astorians' Long Rifle.*

In 1938, the remains of two long rifles were recovered from the bottom of the Snake River near Murtaugh, Idaho. It was in this vicinity that several of Hunt's dugouts were overturned in the raging waters in November 1811. It is believed that these rusted fragments represent part of the armament of the overland Astorians. They are the property of the Idaho Historical Society, Boise. The relic with lock in place is a trade musket; locks for the rifles no longer accompanied their pieces when found. The drawing is by Glen Dines.

[6] Robert Stuart's narrative of his overland trip, Astoria eastward in 1812–13, and Wilson Price Hunt's diary of his overland trip westward to Astoria, 1811–12, appear in Philip Ashton Rollins, ed.: *Discovery of the Oregon Trail* (New York: Scribner's; 1935). Franchere's *Narrative* was first published in English in 1854; *Adventures on the Columbia River* by Ross Cox was published in London and in New York, 1831–2; *Adventures of the First Settlers* by Alexander Ross first appeared in London in 1849.

bottom. Some miles downstream in the vicinity of present-day Murtaugh, Idaho, four more dugouts were lost. The relics aforementioned are believed to represent some of the baggage of one of these canoes. Among the Astorian items salvaged during a period of unusually low water in 1938 are the rusted remains of three guns. Two of these flintlock arms have octagonal barrels, one of which, quite intact, is 44 inches long. The other octagonal barrel is rusted through, and the remaining portion is 33 inches long. The third gun is a light flintlock musket, perhaps a Northwest gun, with a short barrel.

These precious pieces were acquired by the Museum of the Idaho Historical Society, Boise. One of the rifles, no. 1886, Idaho History Museum, was lent to the National Park Service and is exhibited in the Fur Trade Museum at Moose, Grand Teton National Park, Wyoming (fig. 6); the others are in Boise.

Successors to the Astorians, employees of the North West Company, tell us that their hunters along the Columbia in January 1814 were using rifles to kill deer and elk.[7] For more than a decade certain British troops had used their .70 caliber short-barreled Baker rifle—produced by Ezekiel Baker, a London gunmaker—but it was a military arm quite limited to use in a comparatively few rifle companies; there is no reason to believe that the Canadians at Fort George and elsewhere on the Columbia got it, no reason to assume that they had any rifle other than the "Kentucky."

During the War of 1812 the American trade among Indians of the Far West slowed to a standstill, but in the early 1820's there was renewed and lively action. The several fur companies that sent parties up the Missouri and into the Rocky Mountains at this time were still fostering the use of the long rifle. The first major change in the traditional Kentucky rifle in the hands of Westerners was simply an increase in its caliber and a corresponding increase in the weight of its barrel. But, as was true of some other classes of trapper equipment (steel traps, for example), the long rifle very soon underwent some further drastic changes in the hands of the mountain men. The long-barreled, muzzle-heavy "squirrel rifle," even when enlarged to fire a heavier ball, was not at all the perfect arm for the mounted trapper-trader in the Western wilds. It was

---

[7] Henry's Astoria Journal, November 15, 1813–May 21, 1814, in B. C. Payette, comp.: *Oregon Country under the Union Jack* (Montreal, 1961), pp. 1–163.

difficult to load, clumsy to handle when in the saddle or on rough trails, and in its original design usually was too small of caliber for big game—or hostile Indians. To a small segment of the pioneer mountain-man fraternity the half-stock, short-barreled, .52 caliber U. S. rifle, M. 1803 (fig. 2d), already was known as a superior arm. Gradually a prevailing and widespread preference for a similar short rifle for civilian use was made known to gun manufacturers, and there came into being the half-stock arm which at first was dubbed the "mountain rifle." The birth of this weapon type occurred at about the same time that the percussion system began to supplant the flintlock. Typically, the mountain rifle differed from the Kentucky flintlock in that it had a shorter barrel, bigger bore, half stock, a heavier "wrist," and usually less drop in the butt stock. Frequently black walnut or another hardwood other than maple was used in the stock. The patch box, if any, was oval rather than rectangular. It consistently retained the shoulder-fitting butt plate of the long rifle, and the set trigger of the earlier arm was common.

It would be a mistake to assume that short-barreled rifles had not existed prior to the advent of the American "mountain" rifle. In 1702 Saint Remy described and illustrated in detail the full-stock rifled carbine with which the French military armed one company of *carabiniers* in each of its cavalry regiments. This piece had a 32-inch barrel "rifled from the breech to the muzzle with a rotary twist." [8] At this time also the sporting rifle in Central Europe was reduced generally to a relatively short arm (30- to 36-inch barrel of big caliber) always stocked to the muzzle. The German Jäger, immediate ancestor of the Kentucky rifle, is in this category. [9] By 1800 Britain had adopted a short rifle for her rifle brigades—the Baker, with full stock and a 30-inch barrel. [1] As we have seen, the

[8] Pierre Surirey de Saint Remy: *Memoirs D'Artillerie ou il est Traile des . . . Mousquets, Fusils, &c.* (Amsterdam, 1702). (Seventeen pages of text and 14 plates were translated, reprinted, and explained by James E. Hicks in *French Firearms, 1702* [Mt. Vernon, N.Y., 1939]. The rifled carbine appears on Pl. 95 of the orig. edn.)
[9] Henry J. Kauffman: *The Pennsylvania-Kentucky Rifle* (Harrisburg, Pa.: Stackpole; 1960), Chap. i, pp. 1–7. A compact but satisfying study of the short-barreled rifle and its relationships to the long rifle is Robert Held's "Kentucky Rifle Fact and Fiction," *Gun Digest* (1962), pp. 193–9.
[1] H. Ommundsen and E. H. Robinson: *Rifles and Ammunition* (London: Cassel & Co.; 1915), p. 20 and Pl. 7. A. M. Low: *Musket to Machine Gun* (London: Hutchinson & Co.; 1942), p. 29.

U. S. rifle, M. 1803, also was making its impress during the first decade of the century.

All of these short-barreled rifles are flintlock, and all except the Model 1803 have full stock. The half-stock rifle piece has a metal rib brazed to the underside of the barrel from the tail pipe to a point three inches from the muzzle. The ram pipes are fastened to the rib (fig. 2*d*). This structural feature ultimately became a constant characteristic of the mountain man's favorite, the "Plains" rifle, which emerged as a recognizable type for civilian use while the M. 1803 was still in use by the military.

The Plains Rifle

JOHN BARSOTTI, in his "Mountain Men and Mountain Rifles," [2] offers a thought quite pertinent here: "About 1807 Jacob Hawken arrived in the village of St. Louis. The population was small and Hawken, a gunsmith in his early twenties, arrived in time to have known a few Lewis and Clark veterans and he may have heard first-hand accounts of the Harpers Ferry rifle [U. S. M. 1803] that had served them so well. Its an interesting speculation." Some writers have taken exception to the idea of a relationship here, but I agree that it is an "interesting speculation."

Hawken's earliest St. Louis rifles were flintlocks made in the image of the traditional "Kentucky," except that sometimes they were massive in structure and big in caliber—powerful buffalo guns.[3] In time he reduced the length of his barrels and adopted the half-stock feature, but the flintlock mechanism persisted. Numerous other rifle makers of this period did the same thing,[4] but usually they adhered to the smaller calibers of the "Kentucky." Figure 7 shows an undated rifle of this type. The 36-inch octagonal barrel is marked "N. Kiles" in script. The patch box continues in the tradition of the "Kentucky" rifle. Mr. Kiles perhaps was the

[2] John Barsotti: "Mountain Men and Mountain Rifles," Part I, *The Gun Digest*, 8th edn. (Chicago, 1954), pp. 153–6. Charles E. Hanson, Jr.: *The Plains Rifle* (Harrisburg, Pa.: Stackpole; 1960), pp. 11–19, argues that Hawken full-stock rifles reflect the influence of Southern rifle makers.

[3] For Samuel Hawken's written testimony regarding his big rifles (.66 caliber) supplied to trapper-traders during the 1820's, see C. P. Russell: *Guns*, p. 307, n. 33.

[4] Short-barreled flintlock rifles made in the 1820's and 1830's are known from the shops of B. D. Gill, Lancaster, Pa.; John Krider, Philadelphia; S. Shuler, Liverpool, Pa.; and N. Kiles (?), Raccoon Creek, Ohio.

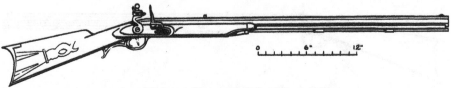

FIG. 7. *Midwest Version of the "Plains" Type.*

The 36-inch barrel is marked "N. Kiles" in script. The caliber is .33 and the patch box adheres to the "Kentucky" style. A number of Pennsylvania and Midwest makers produced these rifles of better balance in the 1820's and 1830's. Some years ago this piece was in the stock of James E. Serven, Santa Ana, California. The drawing is by Glen Dines.

Nathan Kile recorded as making rifles at Raccoon Creek, Jackson County, Ohio, in the early decades of the nineteenth century. At any rate, the maker of this arm did not cater to buffalo hunters; the caliber is .33, and it seems safe to assume that the prospective customer was not a Plains dweller.

Figure 8 shows the "standard" percussion Hawken rifle as distributed to the mountain men during the greater part of the period of beaver trade. This specimen, the personal arm of the noted Jim Bridger ("Old Gabe"), resembles in almost every particular the Hawken rifles once owned by Kit Carson, Mariano Modena, Edwin T. Denig, and James Clyman. These pieces of known mountain-man connections are preserved in public and private collections in widely separated parts of the United States.[5] In addition to these relics, the same Hawken model is represented in the collections of the Los Angeles County Museum; the State Historical Society of North Dakota; the Missouri Historical Society, St. Louis; the Society of California Pioneers, San Francisco; the John Barsotti Collection, Columbus, Ohio; the Gerald Fox Collection; and numerous other collections. Mr. Barsotti has surveyed some seventy-five Hawken rifles. One of the Hawkens in the Missouri Historical Society Museum is distinguished in having

[5] The Bridger Hawken is in the Montana Historical Society Museum, Helena, Montana; the Montezuma Lodge A. F. & A. M., Santa Fe, N. Mex., has one Kit Carson Hawken; and another is owned by the Boone and Crockett Club. Modena's Hawken is in the Colorado State Museum, Denver; and the James Clyman piece is owned by Clyman's descendants in Napa, Calif. Denig's Hawken was pictured by the artist Kurz at Fort Union, September 14, 1851. The drawing appears in Pl. 19 of the *Journal of Rudolph Friederich Kurz* (Washington, D.C., 1937).

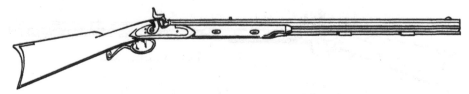

FIG. 8. *Jim Bridger's Hawken Plains Rifle.*

By the time that the percussion system was generally favored, the celebrated Hawken shop, St. Louis, had fairly "standardized" the model here shown. The caliber is big, and the weight of metal in the barrel sufficient to withstand the heavy charges used by buffalo-hunting mountain men. There are no projecting spuds or spurs to embarrass the hunter in a hurry, and in every way the arm is sleek yet sturdy enough to endure rough usage in rough country. It became famous as the mountain man's favorite. Specimen shown is in the Montana Historical Society Museum. The drawing is by Glen Dines.

with it the personal testimony of a gunsmith who contributed to its manufacture. In 1896 Horace Kephart purchased an unmarked Plains rifle in new condition from a dealer in St. Louis. Kephart recognized the Hawken characteristics in his find but sought confirmation. He visited the elderly Charles Siever, onetime gunsmith in the Hawken shop. Siever removed the lock.

"Ja, dot iss shenuine Hawken rifle. I make dot lock, py golly, mineself, more as forty years ago." [6]

Hawken rifle barrels may bear the name of either Jacob or Samuel Hawken or they may have no visible mark whatever. The brothers, Jacob and Samuel, were in business together from 1822 until Jacob died in 1849. Thereafter, Samuel conducted the business until he sold it in 1861 to one of the Hawken workmen, John P. Gemmer. Gemmer did not close out the business until 1915.

A typical Hawken Plains rifle of the late mountain-man period has a heavy 34-inch octagonal barrel, about .53 caliber (½-ounce round ball, 214 grains), low sights, set trigger, percussion lock with a peculiar basket of steel (the "snail") enclosing the nipple, half stock, ramrod carried under a metal rib, sturdy butt stock, crescent-shaped butt plate, and the total weight of the piece 10½ to 12 pounds. Because of its special qualities as a frontiersman's arm [7] it won the reputation as the *ne plus ultra* mountain-man gun.

[6] Horace Kephart: "The Hawken Rifle," *Saturday Evening Post* (February 21, 1920), p. 62.
[7] For some statistics regarding performance see pages 86–93.

FIG. 9. *Kit Carson and His Hawken Rifle.*

Washington Irving wrote: "With his horse and his rifle, he is independent of the World, and spurns all its restraints" (*The Adventures of Captain Bonneville*). The illustration is from an engraving in D. C. Peters's *Kit Carson's Life* (1873). The pen-and-ink adaptation is by Glen Dines.

"From William Ashley's first forays on the Missouri and beyond
the Rockies to the last days of Kit Carson at Taos, the name
Hawken on a rifle was one to swear by." [8]

Deservedly, quite a Hawken literature has built up. Fortunately Horace Kephart, St. Louis gun lover and man of letters,
became deeply interested in the Hawken while some of the principals were still alive. Kephart's first published report on Jake and
Sam Hawken and their works appeared in *Shooting and Fishing*,
October 1, 1896. He practiced scholarly method in recording ver-
batim transcript of interviews with Samuel and E. W. Hawken
and placed the resulting manuscript in the library of the Missouri
Historical Society, St. Louis. Subsequently he published on the
Hawken rifle in *The Saturday Evening Post*, February 21, 1920,
and in the *American Rifleman*, April 15, 1924. J. P. H. Gemmer,
encouraged by Kephart's work, procured a Samuel Hawken manuscript, "Memoirs," and published a firsthand account, "The Hawk-
en-Gemmer Story," in *The Gun Trader*, June 1940. Such primary
sources have provided a number of writers with basic material on
the Hawken enterprise. These writings have been published and
circulated widely. [9]

During the first twenty years of their St. Louis business, the
Hawken brothers had but little local competition. From the 1830's
to 1855 Christian Hoffman, first in partnership with a Mr. Huber
and later with Tristman Campbell, made fine half-stock rifles in St.
Louis. By 1840 J. F. Diettrich and Frederick Hellinghaus had
established factories. Diettrich became quite noted for his heavy
buffalo rifles. About the time of Jacob Hawken's death in 1849, H.
E. Dimick entered the St. Louis arena and in a few years he was
followed by F. Kerksroezer & Co. and Emanuel Kleinhenn. The
rifles made by these six men and their associates were not inferior,
and their combined output was of impressive volume—yet their
works have not left such lasting mark on history as have those of
Hawken. One reason for this circumstance was the "wedding"
during a critical period of the Hawken rifle to the ubiquitous
mountain man. It is also a fact that the Hawken business lasted

[8] Kephart: "The Hawken Rifle," p. 62.
[9] Noteworthy items on the Hawken rifle—Ned H. Roberts: *The Muzzle-
loading Cap-lock Rifle* (Manchester, N.H.: Clarke Press; 1944), pp. 309–14;
Hanson: *The Plains Rifle*, pp. 30–48 (portrait p. 24); James E. Serven, in
American Rifleman (April 1951 and December 1963); and Barsotti: "Mountain
Men and Mountain Rifles," pp. 153–6.

through a far longer period—about a hundred years of unbroken production, counting the Gemmer chapter. In Pennsylvania and New York numerous rifle makers produced creditable short rifles during the years of beaver hunting in the West. William Billinghurst, Rochester, New York, 1838– ; B. D. Gill, Lancaster, Pennsylvania, 1830–   ; Golcher & Butler, Philadelphia, 1830's; James Golcher, Philadelphia, 1833– ; John Krider, Philadelphia, 1820– ; J. Palmeteer, Poughkeepsie, New York, 1835– ; S. Shular, Liverpool, Pennsylvania, 1820– ; Patrick Smith, Buffalo, New York, 1835– ; Alexander Wright, Poughkeepsie, New York, 1835– ; and Andrew Wurffline, Philadelphia, 1835– , are among those made conspicuous because of the examples of their typical percussion, half-stock sporting rifles in present-day collections. Not all of these are "Plains" rifles from the standpoint of geography and use.

George W. Tryon, Philadelphia; Henry E. Leman, Lancaster, Pennsylvania; and J. Henry & Son, Philadelphia and Boulton, made Plains rifles for the Western trade at this time, but a notable part of their output was Indian rifles (often a thin distinction), and they are treated on pages 70–5. A dozen others could be named for the 1850's, 1860's, and later. Some European manufacturers also contributed to the supply of Plains-type rifles for Americans, i.e., C. Svendsten of Kiel; Morgenroth in Gernrode; C. Jaeckel a' Gustrow; James Purdey, London; and Delcomyn of Copenhagen. By 1845 the half-stock, muzzle-loading rifle was the accepted American sporting rifle, "a Plains-type adapted for use anywhere by anybody."

Not for long were the gunmakers satisfied to limit their production to the trim and efficient single-barreled rifle. Double rifles with round barrels side by side; double rifles with rotating, over-under barrels and a single hammer; revolving three-barrel combinations, rifle and shotgun; four-barrel rifles on the order of the "pepperbox"; and revolving-cylinder rifles and carbines, such as the Cochran and the Colt, all made bids for favor during the period of the Plains rifle. A number of the factories from which came the innovations were in New York State: B. W. Amsden, Saratoga Springs; B. W. Berry, Poughkeepsie (made Cochran revolving arms); Nelson Lewis, Troy; H. V. Perry, Jamestown; W. Roberts, Danville; and A. Selden, Whitehall. The old dependables, John H. Krider of Philadelphia, and John Shuler of Liverpool, Pennsylvania made some of the best double rifles, and the Paterson (New Jersey) Colt products at this time foretold a golden era in firearms development hardly sensed by the trapper-traders of the day. These "specialties" did not become popular among the mountain men, but some did come to trial in the Far West before the end of the beaver trade.[1]

Trade Arms: The Northwest Gun

A great splash in the Indian trade and in international politics was made wherever Colonial Americans shared their guns with the natives. The French began on a small scale to distribute guns to the Indians of the St. Lawrence as early as 1620; the English in Massachusetts were arming Indians in 1623; and the Dutch, destined to be leaders in the very early trade, were arming the Iroquois in the 1640's. The then-new Hudson's Bay Company did a sizable gun business in the North Country from the 1670's on, and in the early 1700's both the French and the English were sending guns to the Deep South and west of the Mississippi into regions some of which were to become mountain-man country. These beginnings [2] had a significant bearing upon nineteenth-century trade, but the story is too long to trace here.

It seems important at this point, however, to focus our attention on that vital entity in the gun trade, the Northwest gun. This interesting and truly consequential weapon type has received a good deal of consideration from arms historians during the past twenty years.[3] Many of the mysteries and misunderstandings which surrounded it have been dispelled.

[1] For Jim Bridger's superposed double rifle by Shuler see Dillin: *Kentucky Rifle*, Pl. 11, opposite p. 5; and Kauffman: *Pennsylvania-Kentucky Rifle*, 1960, pp. 334–6 and Pl. 269. Josiah Gregg's field experiences with the Cochran revolving rifle and with the Colt repeating rifle are quoted in C. P. Russell: *Guns*, pp. 76, 78, and 95.

[2] See C. P. Russell: *Guns*, Chap. i, pp. 1–61; T. M. Hamilton, comp. and ed.: "Conclusions," *Indian Trade Guns* (Columbia, Mo.: Univ. of Missouri; 1960), pp. 207–9.

[3] One of the first collectors to recognize the trade gun as something worthy of study was Edward A. Hawks in his paper "The Indian Buffalo Gun," *The Gun Report*, I:5 (1940), 1–2. The Muzzle Loading Rifle Association (E. M. Farris, ed.) in 1944 cooperated with the present author in obtaining the help of numerous owners of trade guns, bringing order to the extensive array of trade-gun specimens of various makes. This material found publication in C. P. Russell: *Guns*, Chap. iii, pp. 103–30. The Nebraska State Historical Society performed a major service in publishing the analytical *The Northwest Gun* by Charles E. Hanson, Jr., in 1955, and the University of Missouri in 1960 capped

The name "Northwest Gun" is not derived from the North West Company. As early as 1761 the internal correspondence of the Hudson's Bay Company contains references to "the N W Guns." In 1777–8 John Long, trading north of Lake Superior, wrote in his journal: "I gave . . . to eight chiefs who were in the band each a North-West Gun." (The enduring organization of the North West Company was not accomplished until 1783–4.) The true Nor'westers of the early nineteenth century continued to use the term; for example, David Thompson, who conducted trade for the North West Company in 1811, in inventorying the guns taken by him to trade west of the mountains, listed "8 N W Guns" valued at 16 beaver apiece.

At this time the names "Hudson's Bay Fuke," "London fusil," and "Mackinaw Gun," all referring to the same trade gun, also creep into the literature, but generally "Northwest Gun" prevails. As might be anticipated, English manufacturers produced the first of these trade guns, and the first were in many respects like the last. It is interesting to note that the last came off the bench only yesterday,[4] so to speak.

S. James Gooding's research in the Hudson's Bay Company papers enabled him to survey the recorded shipments of English trade guns procured by the company during the 107-year period 1674–1781—a total of some 46,000 guns made by 79 manufacturers, all London firms. After 1684 the greater number of these guns had 48-inch barrels; 40-inch barrels were a close second, with 36-inch barrels making respectable showing after 1717. No 54-inch barrels appeared after 1699.

Comparable statistics for the trade guns of the miscellaneous Montreal traders and of the North West Company (1783–1821) have not been assembled and published, but Hanson gives attention to the broad story of the guns of the "Canadian peddlers," and also provides data which extends the Hudson's Bay Company record referred to above.[5] Prior to the union of the Hudson's Bay Company and the North West Company in 1821, the gun manu-

the general project with T. M. Hamilton, comp. and ed.: *Indian Trade Guns*. This last volume contains a discerning study, "Trade Guns Sold by the Hudson's Bay Company," by S. James Gooding, which provides definite answers to several important questions.

[4] A cap-and-ball specimen by J. Hollis & Son, London, bears the date "1886." C. P. Russell: *Guns*, pp. 121–2, Fig. 26.

[5] Hanson: *The Northwest Gun*, pp. 15–20.

facturers who supplied the Montreal merchants were largely Birmingham firms, an entirely different set of gunmakers, apparently quite unrelated to the London industry which served the Hudson's Bay Company. After the union of the two trading companies, a number of the Birmingham firms received their first orders from the Hudson's Bay Company, but it is interesting to note that they were required to stamp "London" on their Birmingham barrels. By this time the barrel lengths for trade guns were fairly stabilized at 42 inches, 36 inches, and 30 inches, a "standard" scheme which with minor exceptions persisted through the era of the Northwest gun.

Not every particular within the history of the Northwest gun has been worked out, but some salient points are now quite well documented:

1. 1683, the convex outer surface of the lock. This feature was prescribed by Hudson's Bay Company order, December 5, 1683: Both "plaine" and fine guns are to have "round locks of 3 holes"—a style that persisted through two hundred years of trade guns.

2. 1700–15, the "dragon" ornament (side plate). Gooding shows that a certain Thomas Green, official Hudson's Bay Company gun viewer and maker of pattern guns to be used as guides by manufacturers catering to the company in 1715, was himself a manufacturer and that he had used a "dragon" side plate on some of his pistols. Mr. Gooding's sketch of this early eighteenth-century "dragon" shows it to have two supporting screws. It is flat, slender, relatively thin, lacks scales, and its head and neck are not curved back upon its body, but its general lines and configuration seem to be so much like the later "dragon" of the Northwest gun as to be more than a coincidence. Hanson, working independently, found that a thin, flat "dragon" ornament, similar to the Green pistol side plate, but with three screws, was characteristic of British Queen Anne all-purpose fusils of light-musket size. A good many of these were sent to America about 1700. A photograph of this 1700 side plate appears as Plate 1B in Hanson's *The Northwest Gun*. There can hardly be doubt that these flat "dragons" have affiliation with the scaled "dragons" that began to appear in the last half of the eighteenth century on a full-fledged Northwest gun of any and all makes.

3. 1740, the extra large bow of the trigger guard. Gun anti-

quarians were quick to recognize the big trigger guard as a distinguishing characteristic of the trade gun. It is an adaptation facilitating the hunter's use of his trigger finger even when encased in glove or mitten. Mr. Gooding reports that the Hudson's Bay Company minutes for December 24, 1740, instruct all company gunmakers to "make the guards larger than usual"—one more step toward a standard. The resulting big trigger guard persisted not only in the realm of the Hudson's Bay Company but throughout all sections of America where, during the coming century and a half, the trade musket found use.

Thus through documents of the day [6] we trace some earmarks to their origins within the Hudson's Bay Company. Such additional, universal characteristics as the approximately .60 caliber part-octagonal, thin-walled barrel, full stock, squared butt with flat brass plate, and the ribbed brass ram guides also were features of many of the earlier Hudson's Bay Company trade guns, but the contemporary documents do not show that they were accorded definition as "standard." Nevertheless they persisted and became part and parcel of the trade-gun tradition.

We arrive now at the subject of markings, something which received comprehensive study by Hanson. The core of Hanson's conclusions is that a distinguishing mark adopted by the Montreal merchants for their trade guns was "a sitting fox-like animal facing right and enclosed in a circle of 0.4 inch diameter." This "sitting fox" was stamped on the lock below the pan and often on the top of the barrel near the breech. Known specimens suggest that only the manufacturers serving the North West Company, 1783–1821, used this mark.

The Hudson's Bay Company, at the time of reorganization and union with the North West Company in 1821, had adopted another fox. It is commonly referred to as the "tombstone fox" because it appears in relief within an indented rectangular cachet shaped like a plain gravemarker. This sitting fox, facing left, has an upstanding tail. Beneath it are the letters "E B." The usual placement is on the lock just in front of the cock, and in the later guns it is found on one of the flats of the barrel also. From its earliest years the Hudson's Bay Company depended upon ap-

[6] Gooding: "Trade Guns . . . ," in T. M. Hamilton, ed.: *Indian Trade Guns* and Hanson: *The Northwest Gun* offer the major evidences and interpretation.

pointed viewers to inspect and approve the arms to be purchased. Various members of the Bond family of gunmakers, London, were for many years the official viewers for the company, and during the general period of reorganization Edward Bond was viewer. The "E B" on the trademark may, perhaps, be the viewer's initials. The fox's pose is identical to that of the fox on the Hudson's Bay Company's coat of arms. The "tombstone fox," variously placed, continued to be the mark of the Hudson's Bay Company in the cap-and-ball period and right up to the most recent company trade gun recorded, a Barnett of 1884.

Immediately after the War of 1812, John Jacob Astor redoubled his earlier efforts to obtain American-made trade guns which could compete with the European products to which our account so far has pertained. No one has succeeded in pinpointing many of the steps leading to Astor's success or failure, but Dillin [7] tells of Astor's 1816 contract with J. J. Henry, and there exists in The New-York Historical Society a "Memorandum of guns ordered [by the American Fur Company] from Mr. J. Joseph Henry of Boulton Gun Works near Nazareth, Penna," 1829, which refers to a contract of April 28, 1828, between Henry and the company. On this occasion 580 Northwest guns were ordered "to be fully equal to Barnetts." Kauffman shows the memorandum in photocopy. [8] Captain Bonneville reported that he witnessed the sale to the Blackfeet of American-made trade guns by the American Fur Company in the 1830's—possibly some of the Henry product here referred to. Further evidences have not been assembled which show conclusively that American Northwest guns were marketed in the West all through the heyday of the mountain man, but it is a matter of record that the Chouteaus in St. Louis got Northwest guns from the Henry firm in 1845 and from Edward K. Tryon, Philadelphia, still later.

The U. S. government was in the trade-gun business from the very beginnings of the U. S. Office of Indian Trade. In the earlier years, European Northwest guns were distributed almost exclusively, but Deringer of Philadelphia, George W. and Edward K. Tryon, Philadelphia, and H. E. Leman of Lancaster, Pennsylvania, through the years contracted to supply the Indian Office with

[7] Dillin: *The Kentucky Rifle.*
[8] Kauffman: *The Pennsylvania-Kentucky Rifle*, p. 259.

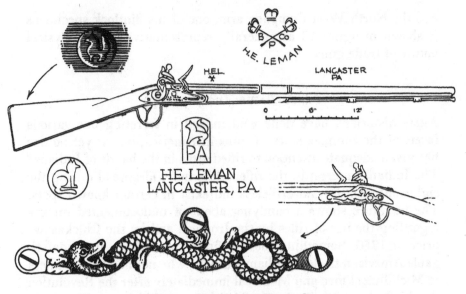

FIG. 10. *The Leman Trade Gun.*

H. E. Leman was one of the makers who demonstrated that the English trade gun could be imitated successfully in American shops. His barrels were mostly 30 inches, but some were longer. Birmingham proof marks appear on most of them, often differing from the genuine, and always they are accompanied by the name "H. E. Leman." The "tombstone fox" on the lock resembles the fox of the Hudson's Bay Company crest; it surmounts the initials "PA" in lieu of the usual European "E. B." The characteristic "fox in circle" (left center), mark of early Birmingham (North West Company) trade guns, is lacking on the lock and barrel, but the indented fox-in-circle (upper left) commonly placed on the stocks of Hudson's Bay Company guns appears on the Leman stocks. The traditional, scaled "dragon" side plate (bottom) as cast by Leman is of superior workmanship. In brief, Leman produced a high-grade imitation of the English trade guns distributed by the Hudson's Bay Company. These drawings are by Glen Dines.

the American version of the trade gun. Because of his long-time relationship with the government and because of his great output and superior product, H. E. Leman is probably the best known of the American manufacturers. He succeeded in producing a creditable imitation of the English Northwest gun, and since the basic structure and ornamentation of his trade guns simulate so many of the traditional features of both the Hudson's Bay Company gun and the North West Company arm, one of his flintlock specimens is shown in figure 10 as generally representative of the physical nature of trade guns.

Trade Arms: Indian Rifles

ARMS historians have done well indeed in ferreting out various facets of the complex story of guns in America, but as yet no one has given adequate attention to rifled arms in the hands of Indians.[9] The Indian's interest in the rifle, while not widespread during the eighteenth century, nevertheless did exist in certain known spots. The literature shows a bandying about of undocumented reports regarding the use of rifles by the Iroquois and by the Chickasaws prior to 1750. Something more definite comes from the indefatigable American trader William Burnett, who notified his suppliers in Michilimackinac and Montreal immediately after the Revolution that his Indians in what is now Michigan would have nothing to do with the Northwest guns; they demanded rifles.[1] Contemporary with Burnett's testimony are the records of the U. S. Office of Indian Trade, whose documents provide very satisfying information regarding the exact nature of the early Indian rifles, and they identify many, if not all, of the rifle makers who contracted with the government. During the first decade of the nineteenth century, fifteen Pennsylvania gunsmiths were occupied in this enterprise, as were two Maryland makers and one Massachusetts shop. Some of the daybooks and correspondence of the U. S. Indian trading posts or "factories" of this period have been preserved; they yield at least a few hints regarding the distribution and use of these first Indian rifles. The rifles themselves are very scantily represented in existing collections, although several thousand are accounted for in the contracts.

These arms were traded in order that the Indians scheduled for treaty making might have "meat-getters." That they found some use in intertribal warfare seems a certainty, and there are at least a few records of their use against the whites, notably in connection with the Creek War of 1813–14, General Jackson's invasion of the

---

[9] Approaches to the Indian rifle story are to be found in Hanson: *The Northwest Gun*, pp. 45–53, and in C. P. Russell: *Guns*, pp. 130–41, 317–22.
[1] Burnett's "Wilderness Letters and Accounts," in Henry H. Hurlbut: *Chicago Antiquities* (Chicago: Eastman & Bartlett; 1881).

Seminole, 1817–18, and the Sauk-Fox raids in Missouri, 1814–20.[2]

After the War of 1812 the number of independent fur traders increased mightily, and rifles became an important stock in the general trade. John Jacob Astor, one of the great promoters of the Indian rifle, branched out from his Great Lakes stronghold and in 1817 placed agents in the St. Louis region.[3] Within a few years the Astor influence resulted in the abolishment of the government factory system, but the government continued to buy rifles. They were needed to fulfill treaty obligations, and treaties were numerous as tribes of the Old Northwest and the South gave up their lands.

During the 1830's the extinguishment of Indian land titles went on apace and the business of Indian removal was advanced energetically—and heartlessly.[4] One of the steps taken by the government to assuage the injury felt by the Indian was the presentation of rifles—sometimes one to each warrior in the emigrating band. At this time, also, cash payments were made to the tribes, and the hanger-on traders, both independents and American Fur Company traders, garnered great harvest. Rifles were prominent in the merchandise offered at the treaty grounds, in the trading posts, and by itinerant traders.

Details of the gun business conducted by the lesser traders have not been assembled, but the meticulously kept records of the American Fur Company provide a rather complete picture of the big company's procedure in procuring and distributing the Indian rifle during the 1840's.[5] Cautious beginnings were made in 1830–1 in placing small orders with four manufacturers in Lancaster, Pennsylvania. By 1835 John Joseph Henry and his son, James, of the Boulton Works near Nazareth, Pennsylvania, had been selected as *the* suppliers of the company's Indian rifles. During the

[2] N. Bosworth: *A Treatise on the Rifle* . . . (New York: J. S. Redfield; 1846), p. 98; and Testimony, Louis Bissounette, regarding attack of May 21, 1820: 19th Cong., 1st sess., Sen. Doc. 55 (Washington, D.C.: Gales and Seton; 1826), pp. 80–1.

[3] Written instructions, August 20, 1817, from Ramsay Crooks and Robert Stuart, Michilimackinac, to Russell Farnham, American Fur Company Correspondence, May 30–August 28, 1817, items no. 48, 49, and 50. Photostat copies owned by Chicago Historical Society.

[4] C. A. Harris, Commissioner of Indian Affairs, Report of December 1, 1837, to Hon. Joel R. Poinsett, Sec. War. 25th Cong., 2d sess., Sen. Doc. 1, pp. 525–8.

[5] John E. Parsons: "Gun Makers for the American Fur Company," The New-York Historical Society *Quarterly* (April 1952), pp. 180–93.

next eight years some 2,300 Henry rifles are known to have been bought and distributed by the company. A typical example of the arm is shown in figure 11. Many Henry Indian rifles entered the realm of the mountain man, and some were carried as personal arms of the white trappers.

In government circles the year 1837 was a great rifle year. Large contracts for Indian rifles were entered into with four Pennsylvania manufacturers. Extant records show that at this time Henry Deringer, Philadelphia, agreed to make 2,500 rifles specified as "Indian rifles." Subsequently (1840) he contracted to

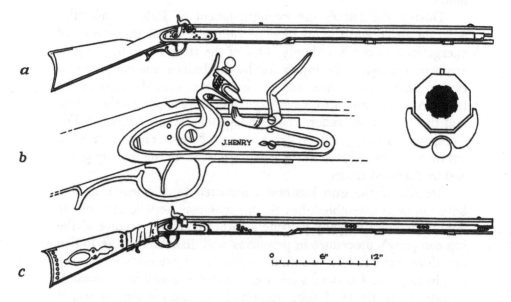

FIG. 11.   *Indian Rifles.*

The J. Henry rifle (*a*) has a heavy 35-inch barrel, .52 caliber, with eight grooves. It is sturdy but muzzle-heavy and awkward to handle. The conversion from flintlock utilized the original lockplate shown in *b*; superfluous screw holes were not filled and polished. This converted specimen is in Bright Angel Lodge, Grand Canyon National Park, and the original flintlock piece (*b*) is illustrated in Hanson: *The Northwest Gun,* p. 81.

The Leman rifle (*c*) also is a conversion from flintlock. It is so similar in all respects to the Henry just described as to indicate that its specifications were the same, although it is believed that Henry sold to the American Fur Company and Leman supplied the U. S. Indian Department. The Leman is owned by the Milwaukee Museum. The drawings are by Glen Dines.

make 6,000 rifles, some of which may have been Indian rifles.[6]
These are the largest orders of known record, yet the widespread
fraternity of gun collectors report few, if any, of these Deringers in
present-day collections. All told, the known contracts indicate that
the government procured from various makers some 11,000 Indian
rifles during this period.

H. E. Leman, Lancaster, is credited with one government
order for 500 Indian rifles. Because of the preponderance of Leman
pieces in present-day collections of Indian rifles, writers are unanimous in believing that Leman was given many more contracts and
that he was a major contributor to the supply. This belief is bolstered by the physical evidences of the Leman Rifle Works, a
three-story factory, and by the record of his employment of gunsmiths. Kauffman says of this: "The adoption of mass production
methods had a twofold effect. It thinned the ranks of individual
gunsmiths, for establishments like the Henry factory and the
Leman Rifle Works might easily have forced twenty-five to fifty
gunsmiths out of business or into the factories. . . . The second
effect was the uniformity in the quality of the rifles. . . . The bulk
of the factory output lacked the originality of earlier individual
makers."[7] In any event, the Sioux and Cheyenne who surrendered
in 1877 gave up 124 breechloaders and 160 muzzle-loaders. Of the
muzzle-loaders 94 were Leman rifles (all percussion), 6 were J.
Henry & Son rifles, 6 were Hawken rifles, and 3 were J. Golcher
rifles.[8] Other muzzle-loading rifles, unclassified as to make, were
taken from Sioux and Cheyenne bands in 1878, 1879, and 1880.
These relics are now conspicuous in museums and in the holdings
of private collectors all over the country.

The Indian rifle was not a shoddy piece of armament. Essentially, the earlier ones, 1800–20, were plain, sturdy Kentucky rifles
with flintlock mechanism, 48-inch barrels, .38 to .52 caliber, and
brought the gunsmiths about $12.50 each. In the 1830's the com-
mon length for a barrel was 40 inches or less and remained that
way "for the duration," except for a relatively few pieces made in
the half-stock model, which had still shorter barrels. The later
Indian rifles were made in both flintlock and percussion. Some

[6] Arcadi Gluckman and L. D. Satterlee: *American Gun Makers* (Harrisburg,
Pa.: Stackpole; 1953), pp. 48–9.

[7] Kauffman: *The Pennsylvania-Kentucky Rifle*, pp. 25–6, 159.

[8] John E. Parsons and John S. du Mont: *Firearms in the Custer Battle*
(Harrisburg, Pa.: Stackpole; 1953), pp. 33–9.

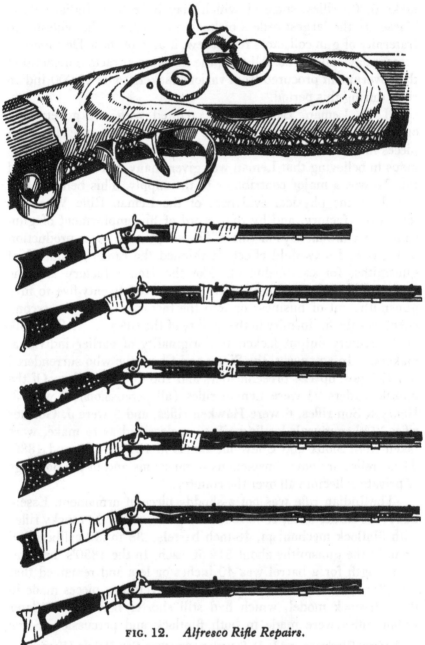

FIG. 12. *Alfresco Rifle Repairs.*

The top unmarked specimen is in the Bright Angel Lodge, Grand Canyon National Park, and its history is not known. The others, all by Leman, are captured or surrendered Indian rifles taken by the U. S. Army from the Sioux and Cheyenne in the 1870's. The bottom specimen is in the Missouri Historical Society, and the five above were once in the National Museum as parts of the U. S. Cartridge Co. Collection. Now they are owned by various collectors. All show the rawhide repairs so characteristic of used Indian arms. Splintered stocks and even loose lock plates were repaired, after a fashion, by the warrior far from gunshops. Wet rawhide was wrapped, tacked on, or well sewed around the broken parts. As it dried, it tended to shrink tight to the gun and became as hard as bone. The drawings are by Glen Dines.

makers supplied a patch box; some did not. Each rifle usually was provided with ball mold and wiper and was enclosed in a list cloth or cover. The price paid to the maker ranged from $11.00 in 1830 to $11.50, $12.50, $13.50, and $14.00 in 1835. The reasons for the disparity in price provided in the various contracts are conjectural. Representative pieces by Henry and by Leman are shown in figure 11.

Some of the testimony regarding the Indians' use of the rifle against white adversaries is contained in the writings of participants in the Seminole War, which started in 1835. Woodburne Potter, a staff officer in the U. S. forces under General Gaines, tells of examining the body of a hostile Indian killed on the Ouithlacooche River in February 1836. The Indian's rifle had been carried away by fleeing Indians, but "50 or 60 rifle bullets" were still on his body. "The U. S. rifle throws a ball nearly 400 yards, but even in the hands of good marksmen it does not often hit a man at 120 yards. The Indian rifles, generally, seem to be much more accurate." [9] Bosworth quotes General Gaines's report to the War Department declaring that entrenched U. S. sentries were wounded, even killed, by single shots from the Seminole rifles at 400 yards.[1]

The Plains Indian in the mountain man's day desired very much to possess the rifle and he got it in quantity, but the documentary evidences regarding his use of it are woefully lacking. In the form of old rifles themselves, there is voluminous evidence of his misuse of the arm. Figure 12 displays some of these and suggests the improvised "repairs" made by the warrior in the wilds.

Handguns on the Beaver Front

THE story of pistols in the hands of the mountain man is obscure, yet the handguns were there always. It has been shown that the

[9] Woodburne Potter: *The War in Florida* (Baltimore, 1836), p. 147 *n.*
[1] Bosworth: *A Treatise on the Rifle*, p. 21.

combat records of World War II and the Korean War are amazingly lacking in accounts of pistol play, but there were more than a million pistols in the hands of American soldiers at that time. The GI did not write or talk much about his use of the pistol against the enemy, yet upon his return to peaceful shores he voted for the issuance of handguns—"returning soldiers are almost 100% in their endorsement of the .45. . . . Soldiers who carry the .45 have confidence in their ability to fight it out in last ditch battle, and confidence is the difference between a stout defense or a retreat." [2] The same thesis may be offered for the pistol in the hands of the trader-trapper in the American wilds of the early nineteenth century. The handgun was a constant and necessary accessory in the fur trade, and as such it deserves study as a frontier institution.

The Hudson's Bay Company records reveal that small orders for pistols brought handguns to the Northern wilds on a number of occasions during the eighteenth century, and since the records state that they were "for the trade," it must be assumed that Indians took some interest at that early date. As has been mentioned, Lewis and Clark found a few Indians on the Columbia River armed with pistols in 1805 and 1806. No documentation has been found to suggest that pistols in any great numbers were traded to western Indians in the heyday of the mountain man, but Hanson located orders placed by the Chouteaus during the 1850's, which proves that at least a few Indians did want the muzzle-loaders in the percussion days. Apparently they did not last through to the period of the devastating Indian wars; at any rate, they are practically nil in the record of captured and surrendered arms of the 1870's.

The personal handgun of the mountain man varied with the whims of the individuals. Some were flintlocks, some were cap-and-ball, but the majority were single-barreled smoothbores of the horse-pistol ("dragoon") type. In later years a few were pepper-boxes, or revolving cylinder models of the Colt type. Ideally, the caliber of the pistol was the same as the rifle or musket carried by the owner, so that a single bullet mold would serve both guns. Even the big .69 caliber muskets often were accompanied by .69 caliber pistols. A more usual combination was the .52 caliber rifle

[2] Maj. James W. Campbell: *American Rifleman* (December 1953), quoted in C. P. Russell: "Some Handguns of the Mountain Man," Denver Westerners *Brand Book* (1962), pp. 149–59.

and a .52 caliber pistol. By hook or by crook, the trapper-trader sometimes acquired obsolete (or current) U. S. military pistols. The "Kentucky" or dueler type was also quite popular, and these were rifled arms usually with barrels seven to ten inches long. They were holster guns, but more often than not they were merely tucked into the trapper's waistband. Short-barreled, big-bore pocket pistols were not entirely lacking in the fur country but they were not numerous.

Some of the extant fur-company records contain orders and correspondence that shed light on certain trader-trapper pistols; occasionally travelers in the beaver country reported their observations on the trapper's pistol and its use; and a very few of the mountain men themselves wrote about their handguns. This rather scanty information is widely scattered in the literature and in manuscript collections in New York, Chicago, St. Louis, San Marino, Berkeley, etc. A part of it has been tracked down and may be read in the illustrated articles by Hanson and by Russell.[3] Fortunately, some pistols of known history in existing collections make possible a reconciliation of physical characteristics and documentary leads.

The Swivel Guns and Small Cannon of the Fur Brigades

It is possible to give an extensive account of the swivel guns used by the mountain men. They were practical from the standpoint of mobility and effective in impressing hostile Indians. During the early decades of the nineteenth century they were in general use in the fur fields by both American and British parties, and there are many reports and comments regarding them in the writings of the day.

On the lower Missouri they had been employed by Spanish authorities for many years before the mountain man's arrival. Lewis and Clark carried American swivel guns as far as Fort Mandan and the Falls of the Missouri (see pages 46–8). Manuel Lisa, Spaniard-turned-American-patriot, took swivel guns up the Missouri in 1807 and continued to use them throughout his thirteen years of activity in the trade. Practically all traders—large companies as well as the smaller independent groups—took swivel

[3] Hanson: *The Plains Rifle*, pp. 153–65; C. P. Russell: *Guns*, pp. 82–96, and "Some Handguns of the Mountain Men," Denver Westerners *Brand Book*.

guns wherever the Missouri and its tributaries permitted boats to go. The seagoing Astorians brought seven swivel guns to the Columbia; these with others of British origin found long continued use near the coast and well inland, first by the North West Company and later by the succeeding Hudson's Bay Company. In the Southwest the early wagon trains on the Santa Fe Trail regularly included them in their armament. Even the pack outfits bound for the rendezvous in the 1820's and 1830's took them overland to the beaver valleys on the Green, the Snake, and the Bear rivers. When posts were built in the tramontane country (Fort Bonneville, Fort Hall, Fort Uintah, Fort Bridger, etc.), swivel guns were brought in and given places on the palisades or parapets.

Both small cannon and oversize small arms could be equipped with swivel mountings. Figure 13 shows an 1812-model 33-pound flintlock, swivel-mounted rifle by William Moore, who made guns in London from 1790 to 1835. Its round barrel is bored ($1\frac{3}{16}$ inches) with eleven grooves to take balls weighing 8 ounces each. Maynard P. Buehler, owner of the piece, determined recently that a load of 28 drams of Fg powder gave 17,500 foot-pounds of muzzle energy, as against the 1,632 foot-pounds of the average muzzle-loading rifle of .525 caliber. The effective range would be much greater,[4] of course, than that of the usual rifle firing a half-ounce ball propelled by the standard 70 grains of rifle powder. Peterson reports that specimens of the early American swivel rifles are preserved in the Springfield Arsenal, Rock Island Arsenal, and in the West Point Museum.[5] The English specimen shown in figure 13 is in the Buehler Collection, Orinda, California.[6] A drawing by Peter F. Copeland shows one of the big swivel rifles in the arms of a Revolutionary soldier.[7] It goes without saying that the soldier is not likely to raise the piece to firing position at his shoulder. A half century after the Revolution, the U. S. War

[4] "On Feb. 4, 1776, Fielding Lewis, Commissioner of·the Fredericksburg Manufactury [Virginia], wrote to his brother-in-law George Washington that: '. . . I propose making a rifle next week to carry a quarter of a pound ball. If it answers my expectations, a few of them will keep off ships from our narrow rivers and be useful in the beginning of an engagement by land.'" Navigable "narrow rivers" in Virginia usually were a mile or more in width. (Harold L. Peterson: *Arms and Armor in Colonial America* [Harrisburg, Pa.: Stackpole; 1956], p. 207.)
[5] Ibid., p. 224.
[6] Maynard P. Buehler: "10 of the World's Most Powerful Rifles" (Orinda, Cal., n.d.), pp. 1–20.
[7] *Military Collector and Historian* (Winter 1963), p. 124.

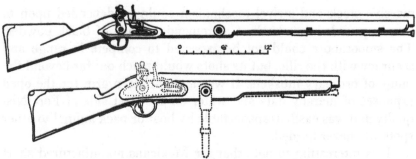

FIG. 13. *Rifle and Musket on Swivel Mountings.*

The massive rifle (top) has a bore of 1³⁄₁₆ inches and weighs 33 pounds. Maynard P. Buehler Collection, Orinda, California. The swivel musket is equally big of bore. Perhaps this is the one and only swivel musket of known history in America. It was used at the Hudson's Bay Company post Fort Nisqually and is owned by the Washington State Historical Society, Tacoma. The drawings are by Glen Dines.

Department made a few of the heavy swivel rifles with tripod mountings to be transported on a pack animal, but any records of their use seem to have disappeared. Two of the rifles are said to be in the Springfield Armory Museum.

Swivel-mounted muskets and blunderbusses found greater use on both land and water than did the big rifles. They were almost anywhere and everywhere in British precincts and in the realm of the mountain man. Accordingly, a great many have been preserved and are to be seen in numerous museums and private collections. The one shown in figure 13 is unique in that it is the only one known to the present writer which can be traced to its place of use in fur-trade days. It came from the Hudson's Bay Company post Fort Nisqually, south of present-day Tacoma, Washington, and is now exhibited in beautifully restored condition in the museum of the Washington State Historical Society at Tacoma. It is pictured here through the cooperation of Bruce LeRoy, director, and Fr. Andrew M. Prouty, curator of guns, who provided the photographs upon which the drawing is based.

Guns of this type could be heavily loaded with buckshot, devastating to human flesh at close range, or with a single big ball, if the target was distant. The Fort Nisqually piece has a bore slightly larger than the William Moore rifle previously mentioned; like the rifle, it used balls weighing 8 ounces each. The breech is 2½ inches in diameter—ample metal to withstand heavy charges—and the massive stock and swivel mechanism could be depended upon to stand up under the shock of a tremendous load of black powder. The smoothbore could not be expected to compete in range and accuracy with the rifle, but its shots would reach out far beyond the range of ordinary muskets. It was a well-chosen arm for the open expanses of marshy flats and water on the west side of Fort Nisqually and was easily transportable by boat or pack animal to other spots whenever needed.

It is interesting to note that the Mexicans manufactured short guns of one-inch bore to be swivel-mounted on pack saddles and fired from the back of a mule. Similar pieces were mounted in "gangs" of four each on wheeled carriages. In this case, the carriage itself pivoted on its wheels. Josiah Gregg observed them in Chihuahua in the spring of 1847. He declares in his *Diary and Letters* (Vol. II): "They were all captured by the Americans." One wonders: Where are they?

Swivel Guns of Small-Cannon Type

As mentioned earlier (page 46), the Lewis and Clark *Journals* reveal their small cannon to have been a notable piece in the explorers' equipment. It was swivel-mounted on the keelboat and led the way for scores of boat cannon which were to follow it up the Missouri. Practically every keelboat and some of the larger skiffs, which conveyed the trade during the next thirty years, carried a swivel gun. After the earlier years of the fur trade, the use of the small cannon in warfare was the exception rather than the rule, but its function in signaling and saluting was continuous and regarded to be necessary.

In the trading posts the swivel commonly was mounted on the palisade or perhaps on a roof bastion, from which strategic place it could command the entire length of one or more of the outer walls. The same tube that served as a swivel gun might be mounted on an improvised truck carriage and given the dignity of a gun emplacement within a blockhouse or might be stationed in the "parade ground" where, ordinarily, it would stand near the flagpole.

Few of the small cannon in existing collections can be identified with specific places or historic events. There are some exceptions, however. The Missouri Historical Society has the tube of one of the "boat cannon" of the American Fur Company that might well have

FIG. 14. *Swivel Gun on a Keelboat.*

Small cannon on the traders' boats became traditional. They sometimes were needed for defense and were continuously useful in signaling. The drawing is by Glen Dines.

served either on a swivel mounting or on a truck carriage, and in a
post or on a keelboat. The bronze tube in three places bears the
marking "A. FULTON PITTSBURGH." The Reference Department,
Carnegie Library of Pittsburgh, informs that Andrew Fulton was
a bell and brass founder in Pittsburgh during the 1830's and until
his retirement in 1864.[8]

An iron tube quite similar in size and shape to the above-
mentioned Fulton piece was recovered in fragments during the
recent excavation of the site of Kipp's North Dakota fur-trading
post built in 1826–7. Dr. Carlyle S. Smith prepared a reconstruction drawing based on the fragments of the tube. He found "the
caliber to be approximately 2⅛ inches, appropriate for a cast-iron

8 Personal letter, Mrs. Henry J. Palmieri, Pennsylvania Division, to C. P.
Russell, June 23, 1964.

FIG. 15. *Small Cannon of the Mountain Men.*

The tube is an iron gun which was recovered in fragments at the site of Kipp's Post, North Dakota. The illustration is taken from a restoration drawing by Dr. Carlyle S. Smith. A one-pounder cannon of this type might be mounted on a swivel or placed on a wheeled carriage. The specimens from Kipp's Post are preserved by the State Historical Society, Bismarck, North Dakota. The drawings are by Glen Dines.

ball weighing one pound or a handful of musket balls." Traditionally the iron tube would indicate manufacture somewhat earlier than that of the bronze tube more commonly used by the fur traders. In any case, the foundry job was not good. Figure 15 (top) follows Dr. Smith's drawing.[9] The specimens (fragments) are preserved in the State Historical Society, Bismarck, North Dakota.

Another ruptured iron tube of undisputed fur-trade provenance was brought to light in the course of archeological work at the site of Fort Berthold I, also in North Dakota. In this instance, the cylindrical breech end of the tube was found. A fragment of a

[9] Alan R. Woolworth and W. Raymond Wood: "The Archeology of a Small Trading Post (Kipp's Post) in the Garrison Reservoir, North Dakota." Bureau of American Ethnology *Bulletin*, No. 176 (1960), p. 267.

wrought-iron strap is attached to the cascabel, suggesting a handle which would have facilitated the handling of the gun if it were mounted on a swivel. Again, the bore is about two inches, which places the piece in the 1-pounder class. Dr. Carlyle S. Smith writes regarding this gun: "On the right side of the chamber a porous area has been covered with a wrought iron patch which must have been driven into place while hot, against a mandril pushed in from the muzzle. The porosity, the patch, and the fact that the gun must have exploded, suggest that the casting was not carried out in a skillful manner." [1] This specimen also is preserved by the State Historical Society of North Dakota.

In setting up his Columbia River trading establishment, John Jacob Astor shipped by sea four iron 4-pounders, two brass 4-pounders, two brass swivel guns "on carriages," and five iron swivels "without carriages." These guns are accounted for in the inventory of Astoria properties that were taken over by the North West Company in October 1813. Mr. Astor listed the swivel guns as being worth about $75.00 each. [2] In 1814, the Nor'westers were carrying these swivel guns up and down the Columbia as they serviced their interior trading posts. Much of this travel was done by boat, and at least some of the guns were mounted in the conventional manner. However, part of the journey involved travel on land. One might ask: "How were the swivel guns kept in readiness for use?" In attempting to answer, one turns to a specimen of "plank cannon" owned by the North Dakota State Historical Society. It is a 14-inch iron tube, 4 inches in diameter, with no trunnions, and having bore of 1¾ inches. The usual cascabel is present. A deep groove encircles the tube just in front of the vent, and an identical groove is just behind the vent. These indentations would accommodate ½-inch U-bolts or heavy strands of twisted wire that might be looped over the top of the tube and so bind it to a perforated flat piece of timber. The portable gun mounted in this manner could be fired from a makeshift position on the ground, or if circumstances permitted more deliberate preparations, the gun and its plank might be mounted on the top of breastworks and roped in position with a line around the cascabel.

[1] Carlyle S. Smith: "Analysis of Firearms from . . . Fort Berthold I," *The Plains Anthropologist* (July 1955), pp. 3–12.
[2] John Jacob Astor: Letters Regarding the Surrender of Astoria. 17th Cong., 2d sess., H. Doc. 45 (Washington, D.C., 1823), pp. 1–80.

Mr. Norman Paulson of the State Historical Society of North Dakota states: "We have no data on the piece [plank cannon] except that it was found very near the site of Fort Dilts. There are no markings on the cannon." [3]

Wheeled cannon of the 4-pounder and 6-pounder sizes were not totally lacking in the fur trader's realm. Usually they were on truck carriages and limited to the trading posts, but the Ashley cannon made history in 1827 by being the first wheeled vehicle to travel overland into the tramontane country, and the Hudson's Bay Company took a 4-pounder on wheels eastward over the Rockies and into Montana in 1824. Presumably this was a John Jacob Astor gun from Astoria. Smith, Sublette, and Jackson in 1831 camouflaged a cannon by mounting it on the rear axle of one of their Santa Fe-bound wagons. Documentary sources which might add to the story of wheeled cannon in the fur fields have been searched quite thoroughly, and the holdings of museums are now fairly well publicized. Perhaps the archeologist's approach offers the greatest promise of expanding knowledge of trader-trapper cannon. The U. S. military pushed westward during the opening decades of the nineteenth century, but its line of fortifications barely rimmed the eastern edge of the mountain man's domain. A total of fifty-six cannon are recorded for the Western military forts in the mid-1820's. This number increased during the succeeding twenty years, and military forays took wheeled guns, mostly 6-pounders, into parts of the beaver country. A good deal of the story of the impingement of the military upon the Indian world and upon commerce in the wilds from 1800 to the 1840's is told in this author's *Guns on the Early Frontiers*. [4]

PERFORMANCE OF THE FIREARMS OF THE PERIOD

Ballistics

QUITE evidently, the conscientious manufacturers of American guns of the early day tested their products for performance in firing as well as for safety. Records of the universal safety trials

---

[3] Personal letters, Norman Paulson to C. P. Russell, April 15 and May 26, 1964. I am indebted to Mr. Paulson for a photograph and a full-scale drawing of the "plank cannon."

[4] Pp. 251–82.

have been preserved, and there are numerous reports on the accuracy of rifles, but one looks in vain for contemporary accounts of experiments made by private interests to determine the velocity, penetration, shocking power, and related characteristics now classed as "ballistics." The U. S. War Department made beginnings in such scientific studies in the 1820's, focusing attention upon both the service rifle and the regulation U. S. musket. By 1837 the U. S. Ordnance Bureau had devised appropriate equipment and proceeded to conduct extensive investigations of small arms as well as cannon. Thereafter the printed record contains some particulars regarding ballistics of military muzzle-loaders.

Many of the models produced by private gunmakers for the trader-trapper and his Indian customers were similar to the military pieces insofar as barrels, bores, rifling, and weights were concerned. Such similar guns, when loaded with similar charges, could be expected to perform similarly. To test the validity of this assumption, a number of present-day admirers of the old muzzle-loaders in many parts of the country have made rather thorough tests. These tests and the testers are identified in the table following. The statistics offer fairly conclusive evidence as to just how well armed the mountain man was.

All else being equal, the smaller, round balls (lesser weights) are thrown with greater initial velocity. Reduction in length of barrel results in slight reduction of initial velocity, but sharp reduction in velocity does not occur until barrel length is less than 20".[5] Test number 11 (see table) seems to offer exception, but in this instance a part of the loss in initial velocity is due to gas leakage at the joint between the chamber and barrel of this pioneer military breechloader. The heavier balls of the larger calibers leave the muzzle with less force than do the smaller balls, but their loss of velocity in flight is notably less than that of the smaller balls.[6] In other words, the effectiveness of the heavier balls at longer

[5] Phil Sharpe: "Barrel Length and Velocity," *American Rifleman* (March 1950), p. 27.
[6] It is scarcely practical to offer comparison between the black-powder burners and the modern high-powered rifles, but it is interesting to note that the .35 caliber Remington firing a 200-grain soft-point bullet shows an initial velocity of 2,210 fps (foot-pound-second). Approximately 17.2 per cent of this force is lost in the first 100 yards of the bullet's flight. The .22 caliber Hornet with a 45-grain soft-point bullet develops a muzzle velocity of 2,690 fps, and loses 24.5 per cent of its force at 100 yards. (NRA Technical Staff: "Determining Muzzle Velocity," *American Rifleman* [May 1964], pp. 41–4.)

VELOCITY (RIFLES)

Arm	Barrel Length (inches)	Caliber	Ball Grains	Powder Grains	Foot-Pound-Second
1. Percussion rifle	40	.40	95	120 FFFg	2,463
2. Percussion rifle	40	.40	95	56 FFFg	1,884
3. Flintlock rifle, 1 turn, 48″	40	.45	127.5	56 FFFg	1,681
4. Percussion rifle	36	.40	95	75 FFFg	2,079
5. Percussion rifle, 1 turn, 64″	36	.55	249	155 FFg	1,907
6. Percussion rifle	36	.55	249	140 FFg	1,882
7. Percussion rifle	36	.55	249	120 FFg	1,794
8. Percussion rifle	36	.55	249	110 FFg	1,653
9. Percussion U. S. rifle, M. 1841	33	.525	214	70 musket powder	1,750
10. Flintlock Hall's rifle (issue 1826) —breechloader	35	.525	214	70 musket powder	1,490
11. Percussion Hall's carbine (1833) —breechloader	21	.525	214	70 musket powder	1,240
12. Percussion rifle —Sporter	20	.40	95	75 FFFg	1,818

VELOCITY (MUSKETS)

Arm	Barrel Length (inches)	Caliber	Ball Grains	Powder Grains	Foot-Pound-Second
13. U. S. flintlock musket, M. 1835	42	.69	411	110 musket powder	1,500
14. U. S. Cadet's musket, M. 1830	35.5	.57	219	70 musket powder	1,690

Numbers 1, 2, 4, and 12 were recorded with an electronic chronograph. Firing with increasingly heavy charges was discontinued when recoil became objectionable. Charles Haffner: "Muzzle-Loading Rifle Velocities," *American Rifleman* (July 1964), p. 45. See also P. P. Quayle: "Velocity of Muzzle-Loading Rifles," *Army Ordnance* (May–June 1930), pp. 60, 405–15.

Number 3 was recorded on a Potter electronic chronograph. Twist, one turn in 48 inches. O. H. McKagen made the test at Bel Air, Maryland; the figure represents average of ten shots. Manuscript report by McKagen to Harold L. Peterson; Letter, Peterson to Russell, March 17, 1964.

Numbers 5, 6, 7, and 8 were recorded on modern equipment. Twist, one turn in 64 inches. Carl Barrow conducted the tests. Manuscript report to John Barsotti; letter, Barsotti to Russell, March 17, 1964.

Numbers 9, 10, and 11 were recorded at Washington Arsenal by Major A. Mordecai with a ballistic pendulum in 1843. Report in Mordecai: *Ordnance Manual . . .* (Charleston, 1861), p. 367; in B. R. Lewis: *Small Arms*, p. 95. Musket powder (coarse grain) was regarded to be superior to FFg.

Numbers 13 and 14 were recorded with a ballistic pendulum in 1843. For number 13 see Mordecai: *Ordnance Manual*, p. 367. At the time of this test (1843), the standard ball for the U. S. musket was 18 to the pound, or 397.5 grains, and the musket powder charge was 120 grains. Upon the completion of his trials, Mordecai observed: "By reducing the windage with the larger ball (411 grs.) we obtain as great a velocity with a charge of 110 grs. as we get with the lighter ball (397.5 grs.) and 120 grs. of powder, and this without any increase in the force of recoil. . . . I propose that the changes [in the standard load] be adopted in service" (quoted in B. R. Lewis: *Small Arms*, p. 113). For information on test number 14 see ibid., p. 95.

ranges is much greater. Therein lies the explanation for some of the superiority of the big-caliber, slow twist Hawken rifles which compare with numbers 5–8 in the table.

The biggest powder load here indicated, 155 grains, is not the maximum within practical limits of the rifles of the Hawken type weighing ten to fifteen pounds. Horace Kephart loaded his 10½-pound .53 caliber Hawken with a round ball weighing 226 grains and with 205 grains of black powder.

This load gave great smashing power, yet the recoil was about the same as the 45–70 breech-loader with 70 grs. of powder, and the 500 gr. service bullet. Due to the slow twist of Hawken rifling, the ordinary powder charge (one-half weight of bullet, or about 108 grs.) gave recoil which was almost nil. The trajectory was almost flat up to 150 yards, and accuracy was excellent. With moderately heavier charges of powder, this rifle still shot straight and would kill at 200 to 250 yards with the round ball. With the sugarloaf [conical] bullet it was consistently accurate at 500 yards.[7]

It should be noted here, however, that the mountain men knew little or nothing about conical bullets and, during the heyday of the beaver trade, did not benefit in that regard from the full capacity of their rifles.

They knew full well, however, that their short-barreled .50 caliber (and bigger) slow-twist rifles shot practically "flat" up to 150 yards, and even at 200 yards with predetermined allowance in sighting they could readily compensate for the drop of the bullet.

[7] Horace Kephart: "The Hawken Rifle," *Saturday Evening Post* (February 21, 1920), p. 62.

Accuracy was good, killing power was great, and the recoil with such loads as is indicated in the table was hardly noticeable. They also found that the slow twist and the comparatively shallow grooves received little fouling. When greased linen patches were used, no cleaning was required during a full day of shooting. Occasionally while fighting Indians or stalking distant buffalo, the "double charge," some 200 grains of black powder, was used safely—but with less certain accuracy. The Hawken rifle was not alone in displaying these attributes, but it was one of the best and definitely the best known among the mountain men.

The trade muskets and other shotguns used by the mountain men varied in size and quality but, generally, they were well constructed and fell within the gauges represented by the two military arms detailed in numbers 13 and 14 of the table. A majority were of the size and weight of the Cadet's musket, but numerous well-made English trade muskets of .69 caliber were also used by the beaver hunters. They lacked some of the weight of the military musket (9.14 pounds), but the English pieces were sound products of conscientious manufacturers. When one of them was loaded as Mordecai loaded the U. S. military flintlock musket (number 13 in the table), an entirely comparable result could be expected. Similarly, the lighter trade muskets of any and all makes could be depended upon to handle the load shown for the Cadet musket (number 14) and yield a similar performance ballistically.

The initial velocity of the .69 caliber musketload (1,500 fps) is not spectacular, but the big, soft lead ball had a very respectable muzzle energy, and most of that heavy striking force was sustained as the bullet flew to its close-up target. Many records of the effectiveness of musket balls upon both game and the human anatomy were handed down by the mountain men. A fair example of this testimony is found in John Work's account of an attack by Blackfeet in western Montana, 1831, on which occasion two Hudson's Bay Company men, Cloutier and Letandre, were killed. "Cloutiers arms were broken below the shoulders and the balls passed through his breast; the savages were so near that from the appearance of the wounds the wadding as well as the balls entered his body. Letandre seems not to have died so soon. He received two balls; one passed through his left breast near his heart, and one through his back and belly." [8]

[8] William S. Lewis and Paul C. Phillips, eds.: *The Journal of John Work* (Cleveland, 1923), p. 97.

Sawyer observed a half century ago: "Whereas the modern rifle drills a small hole in a man so suddenly and cleanly that sometimes in the excitement of battle he barely feels it, the great round ball of the old musket smashed his bones, tore his flesh, let out his blood, and shocked him 'hors de combat.' " [9]

Penetration

ONE of the earliest recorded investigations of the penetrating force of American bullets was conducted in 1837 by the War Department at West Point, New York, which at that time was a U. S. arsenal. Dry white oak was used for the tests. In each trial 10 shots were fired to obtain the following averages:

CHARGE

Arm	Ball Grains	Powder Grains	Distance from Target (yards)	Penetration in White Oak (inches)
U. S. flintlock rifle, M. 1817	214	92	3½	2.10
			50	1.43
			100	.94
			200	.29
U. S. flintlock musket, M. 1816	411	134	3½	2.00
			50	1.43
			100	1.00
			200	.55
	411	90	3½	1.60

In 1839 similar tests were made with "improved" powder at Washington Arsenal:

CHARGE

Arm	Ball Grains	Powder Grains	Distance from Target (yards)	Penetration in White Oak (inches)
U. S. flintlock rifle, M. 1817	214	100	5	2.05
U. S. flintlock musket, M. 1816	411	144	5	3.00
U. S. flintlock pistol, M. 1836	214	51	5	.725

[9] Charles W. Sawyer: *Firearms in American History, 1680–1800* (Boston, 1910), p. 103.

The above experiments are reported in Mordecai: 1861 *Ordnance Manual*, p. 373. If any similar extensive tests of civilian arms of the day were conducted, there seems to be no record, but the above data are indicative of what the mountain man might expect of his comparable rifles and muskets when loaded with similar charges of powder and ball. The numerous testimonials written by the beaver hunters regarding the effectiveness of their bullets on man and beast bear out the fact that their arms, if knowledgeably and conscientiously loaded, could indeed be depended upon to execute within the range limitations imposed by the ammunition of the day. Even the muzzle-loading single barreled pistol was sometimes brought into play, successfully, in killing buffalo. For example, Francis Parkman on the Arkansas in 1846 carried a pair of rifled percussion pistols. He describes the pistol caliber as something less than the .52 caliber of his rifle; presumably, the handguns were about .44. We may believe that they were capable of slightly greater penetration than is indicated for the smoothbore U. S. pistol, Model 1836 (.725″ in white oak), listed in the table above. Parkman wrote regarding his use of the handgun on running buffalo:

> I shot one. The small bullet of the rifled pistol, striking too far back, did not immediately take effect. I began to load the empty pistol, still galloping by the side of the bull. By this time he was grown desperate. . . . I took to flight. . . . The pistol was soon ready, and then looking back, I saw his head five or six yards behind my horses tail. To fire at it would be useless. Inclining my body to the left, I turned my horse in that direction as sharply as his speed would permit. The bull did not turn so quickly. As I looked back, his neck and shoulders were exposed to view; turning in the saddle, I shot a bullet through them obliquely into his vitals. He gave over the chase and soon fell to the ground.[1]

Accuracy

THE touted accuracy of the long rifle is genuine and is still demonstrated daily by muzzle-loader devotees. That accuracy, of course, is not due to the long barrel itself; most of the advantage lies in the greater distance between the front and rear sights. The shorter,

---

[1] Francis Parkman: *The Oregon Trail* (New York: The Macmillan Co.; 1920), pp. 320–1.

big-bore rifles adopted by the mountain men also are accurate, and the muzzle-loading-rifle fraternity of today keeps that fact always before the eyes of the interested public. Some of the fraternity's gun antiquarians are now manufacturing new rifles made in the image of the mountain-man pieces.

John Barsotti, well-known student of mountain-man history, writes:

> We have collected data on the Hawken rifle and determined how rifles of the Hawken type will shoot. By "we", I mean Judge H. E. Resley of Fort Stockton, Texas, and me. The Judge is a most successful barrel maker and he has produced numerous copies of the J. & S. and S. Hawken rifles. I furnished him with one of his patterns—my J. & S. Hawken, St. Louis, full-stock. It is not easy to find Hawken rifles at this late day, with perfect, original bores. Also, the price of the Hawken is sky-high; it is usual to see them priced at $350, $500 and up to $1000, or more. For this reason the Judge made up faithful copies of certain old-time Hawken plains and mountain pieces, and used them in our tests. All have open sights. The calibers are .53, .55, .57 and a few others. The 8-groove rifling: 1 turn in 48", 1 turn in 50", 1 turn in 60", and 1 turn in 64". We ran our tests not to get gilt edge groups, but to show just what a big bore rifle of the Hawken type would do at 100 and 200 yards with open sights and a round ball propelled by big charges of black powder. Judge Resley wanted to know how well armed the mountain men were. His testing of his Hawken-type rifles extended over several years of shooting and gave the answers. Some of the shooting was done in the Texas Muzzle Loading Rifle matches; some on a range near Fort Stockton.
>
> I send herewith our data on representative tests of the Resley rifles and, also, a few targets made with original S. Hawken rifles at moderate ranges.

Mr. Barsotti's valued reports are incorporated in the following table.

Any formal experiments conducted by the U. S. Army on the accuracy of the regulation military muzzle-loading musket seem to have been devised to test the mass effect of fire upon big targets the size of a company front. An example of such testing in the 1830's is described in this author's: *Guns on the Early Frontiers.*[2] No old-

---

[2] P. 163.

ACCURACY

Arm	Barrel Length (inches)	Cal-iber	Ball Grains	Powder Grains	Range (yards)	Target
1. Hawken-type rifle, Resley copy, 15 lbs.	35	.54	247	165 FFFg	225	human silhouette
2. Hawken-type rifle, 11¾ lbs.	35½	.58	292	135 FFg	200	11″ groups
3. Hawken-type rifle, 13 lbs.	34	.53	226	187 FFg	200	9″ groups
4. Hawken rifle, 10½ lbs.		.53	226	82 FFg	200	(see below)
5. U. S. rifle, M. 1841 (percussion) 9.68 lbs.	33	.525	214	70	200	(see below)
6. Hawken-type rifle, 11¾ lbs.	35½	.58	292	100 FFg	100	4½″ groups
7. Hawken-type rifle, 11¾ lbs.	35½	.58	292	100 FFg	100	deer
8. Hawken-type rifle, 13 lbs.	34	.53	226	180 FFg	100	3″ groups
9. Hawken rifle, 12 lbs.	36	.52	214	75 FFFg	60	3¾″ groups
10. Hawken rifle, 10 lbs.	35	.50		80 FFFg	50	(see below)

Numbers 1, 2, 3, 6, 7, and 8 pertain to the shooting of exact copies of Hawken percussion rifles made by Judge H. E. Resley, Fort Stockton, Texas. Target, item number 1, was a silhouette of a human torso, 38″ x 24″; 17 hits out of 20 shots. In the instance of number 7, Judge Resley killed a large mule deer; 1 shot at 100 yards. The animal ran 30 yards. The targets indicated were shot by Judge Resley. Reporter, John Barsotti, Columbus, Ohio; personal letter, Barsotti to Russell, March 17, 1964 (12 pages with targets).

Number 4 was Horace Kephart's demonstration. He kept all shots within the 12″ bull. Horace Kephart: "The Hawken Rifle," *Shooting and Fishing* (October 1, 1896). See also Ned H. Roberts: *The Muzzle-loading Cap-Lock Rifle* (Manchester, N.H.: Clarke Press; 1944), pp. 312–13, quoting Kephart.

Number 5 was U. S. Ordnance tests, 1853–5. Of the 25 shots 22 were within group 12″ x 15″. Described by B. R. Lewis: *Small Arms*, p. 96.

Number 9 was the tests made by Dr. P. A. Matteson, Bennington, Vt., September 16, 1958. Original Hawken; barrel not recut. Dr. Matteson's target; 6 shots in this group of 10 can be covered with a 50-cent piece. Reporter, John Barsotti; Letter, Barsotti to Russell, March 17, 1964 (with target).

Number 10 was R. Wiedebush's tests, Muleshoe, Texas, using an original Hawken. R. Wiedebush's target; 5 shots at 50 yards—all 5 shots are grouped so close that they can be covered with a 5-cent piece. Reporter, John Barsotti; letter, Barsotti to Russell, March 17, 1964 (with target).

time records of accuracy tests of civilian arms of the musket class are known to the present writer other than those quoted from Hanson's 1959 "The Indian Fusial." [3] Here are described recent trials made by Hampton W. Swaine with an eighteenth-century shotgun and a trade musket. The guns were loaded with 150 grains of FFg powder and two balls, weight not mentioned. At 45 yards all balls struck within a 12-inch circle and penetrated 2½ inches into pine boards. With single, patched balls these smoothbores gave 6-inch groups. Swaine's modern demonstrations are quite in line with the firsthand accounts by old-timers who regularly shot their musket balls into living targets. The experienced English army officer R. G. A. Levinge, writing during the closing days of the mountain-man period, advocated that white hunters in Canada emulate the Indian in choosing the smoothbore "which throws a ball true at 60 yards. It is the best weapon for deer hunting, as most shots got in the woods are within that distance. . . . Patch the ball; in 99 cases out of 100 a patched ball will fly nearly as true at 60 yards as one fired from the best rifle." [4] Swaine's findings give some support to this assertion.

The foregoing statistics are at least suggestive of the scientific approach to performance studies that have been employed by some especially inquisitive present-day admirers of the muzzle-loaders. Not represented in the data are the earlier works of such well-known American investigators as Walter M. Cline, John G. W. Dillin, and Ned H. Roberts. These authors are not omitted because their works are inaccessible, but because they are not strictly pertinent. The sources cited in our tables bear directly upon the questions before us. Generally, the findings of the three authorities mentioned are broadly in line with the experiments here reported. [5]

A résumé of the particulars treated in this chapter brings several points clearly into focus:

1. The best-known manufacturers of trapper-trader muzzle-loaders, muskets, rifles, pistols, and small cannon produced arms of good grade. The scores of recorded incidents involving ruptured

[3] In T. M. Hamilton: *Indian Trade Guns*, p. 209.

[4] Capt. R. G. A. Levinge: *Echoes from the Backwoods; or, Sketches of Transatlantic Life*, 2 vols. (London: H. Colburn; 1846), II, 236.

[5] A notable exception, Ned H. Roberts, states: "The Hawken rifles [.50 caliber and bigger] . . . with 164, 180, 200, and 210 grains of powder would shoot nearly 'level sighted' at 200 to 250 yards." (*Muzzle-loading Cap-Lock Rifle*, pp. 313–14.) The experimenters cited in our tables found it necessary to sight upon points 17 to 30 inches above the bull's-eye at the 200-yard range.

barrels, broken locks, and splintered stocks could no doubt be multiplied were it possible to count the accidents which found no mention in print, but in the majority of cases of barrel failure the exploding guns blew up because of faulty loading or because of obstructions within the muzzles. Only rarely during the 1800's did defective barrels get out of the proving rooms and onto the assembly lines of the gunmakers. Failures of locks and stocks usually resulted from violent accidents or outright abuses in the field, not from careless gunsmithing or shoddy materials.

2. The comparatively inexpensive musket of the trade-gun class was distributed in greater numbers than were the rifles of the period (1800 to the 1840's). It was favored by the Indian and the metis hunter because of its traditional dual use—fine shot for small game, and a heavy ball for big game and for warfare; many white trappers swore by it also. It was highly useful in running buffalo, and most other occasions for shooting involved close-up targets. The trade gun was reasonably accurate and quite as effective as a big-caliber rifle, up to 50 yards. See the comparative statistics on "velocity" and "penetration" given earlier in the chapter. Quite a crowd of trapper-traders testified in writing regarding the satisfactory performance of the musket in the field.

3. The advent of the "Plains" rifle was momentous in the history of mountain-man armament. This weapon set the mountain man upon a peak of shooting perfection never attained by his beaver-trapping predecessors of the seventeenth and eighteenth centuries. Its big caliber, heavy charges, and slow twist of rifling resulted in comparatively flat trajectory, great smashing power, and consistently fine accuracy up to 150 yards, and yet the recoil was slight. The capacity of the rifle could be increased greatly through the use of the "double charge," yet such loading was not accompanied by impracticable side effects. Because of the Plains rifle, the hostile Indian acquired a new respect for the white trapper's ability to reach out into the far distance with lethal shots, and its killing power made it *the* arm of the meat-getter when stalking buffalo.

The "Indian rifle," obtained by the Western tribesmen through trade, emulated the "mountain rifle" and the "Plains rifle" in many mechanical respects, but often its red owner gave it anything but loving care. His disregard for the finish, mechanical structure, and the niceties of loading frequently reduced the arm to a broken ghost of the original, and the onetime precision machine became something less than positive and accurate.

4. The seldom-mentioned handgun was not the nonentity that its absence from fur-trade literature might imply. It was the arm of final resort in the "last-ditch stand," and in that connection it receives rare recognition in the records of the trade. But it was also ever-present on the trapper's person and was brought into more frequent unspectacular uses seldom mentioned in the journals. Ballistically it could not compare with the long arms carried by the trapper, but occasional contemporary trapper testimony and the published contemporary records of military tests indicate that even the smoothbore pistol of .525 caliber could inflict deadly wounds at short range. The rifled pistols of the day were still more effective.

Everything considered, we may conclude that the mountain man looked upon the brighter side of his armament problem. Wails of complaint are few and far apart, yet his guns were actually much like those of his predecessors who had contended with the wilderness two hundred years earlier. The invention of the percussion cap yielded advantages that were seized upon during the later years of the mountain-man period, and the development of the Plains rifle brought a competence never known to the *coureurs de bois*, *voyageurs*, and the earlier British and Yankee fur traders. Yet from the standpoint of defense against an Indian's sudden treachery or a wounded grizzly's ponderous charge, the single-shot, muzzle-loading guns then in hand were puny. To make them more nearly equal to demands put upon them, their users developed special skills, "know-how," and cunning—attributes that spelled the difference between the successful life of the trader-trapper or his death. The zest of such contending may well have been one of the factors that held "this reckless breed" to wilderness ways.

The firearms industry was just on the verge of introducing epoch-making improvements in its guns and in gunpowder when the mountain man moved off the Wild West stage. Had the well-loved Jedediah Smith followed up his single rifle shot with a fusillade from a pair of Colt revolvers on that fateful day on the Cimarron, he might have evened the odds which a small group of murderous Comanches levied upon him. A few years after Smith's death the revolver was in the West. And the vicious grizzlies—those beasts who took a terrific toll in maimed and dead trappers

throughout the mountain-man period—would not have been so im-
mune to lead, had the balls come to them in the form of heavy,
elongated "pickets," or the later hollow-based cylindroconoidal bullets. The superiority of these bullets had been demonstrated before
the end of the mountain-man period, but there is little evidence that
the mountain man had adopted them. While we are inserting these
"ifs," it is appropriate to mention that the appearance of the successful sporter breechloader was just in the offing (early 1850's).
Hard on its heels came the repeating breechloaders and the hol-
low-point expanding bullets. Many a mountain man lived to witness these phenomenal improvements and to mourn the quick dev-
astation of the living things in his old haunts brought about by the
better guns of his successors.

CHAPTER III

Beaver Traps and Trapping

ABORIGINAL HUNTING AND TRAPPING METHODS

THE TRAPPING OF BEAVER FOR WORLDWIDE TRADE HAD BEEN an American wilderness enterprise for two hundred years before the mountain man stepped into the scene. By the time the mountain man arrived, steel traps were all-important in the business of catching beaver, but there is abundant evidence that great quantities of fur were obtained in America, by Indian and white hunter alike, during the seventeenth and eighteenth centuries without benefit of metal traps.

The pre-Columbian beaver hunter did not have the incentive of trade with the white man, but we know that he did prize his beaver robe and that beaver flesh was an appreciated item on his bill of fare. Nowhere within the extensive range of the beaver did the demands of the precontact Indian make great inroads upon the beaver population, yet the big rodent was sought for and special methods were devised for conducting the hunt. Those primitive methods were demonstrated to the invading white man eventually, and during the early stages of the trade both white hunters and Indians practiced the ancient ways of capture. In some instances the white man introduced crude wooden traps of European lineage to the Indian.

The contemporary, specific accounts of primitive beaver hunting cited below pertain to the Canadian wilds and to regions east of the Mississippi River, but some of the journals of the earliest Western explorers indicate that the same or similar practices were

97

FIG. 16.   *The Old-Time Indians' Winter Hunt.*

This Mulcahy drawing is in the Jefferson National Expansion Memorial, St. Louis, Missouri.

also followed by the tribes of the Plains and the Rockies. This "winter hunt" was brutally successful and at the urging of the white trader-trapper, quickly decimated the beaver colonies in many parts of the country that later became the eastern United States.

The essential steps in the Indians' winter beaver hunt are depicted in figure 16. Captain John Smith [1] reported on the method practiced by the Virginia natives in the early years of the seventeenth century, and Lahontan [2] told of what he witnessed while with the Fox Indians of the Wisconsin country during the later decades of that century. One of the best accounts is in the "1723 Manuscript Memoire," which has been preserved in the Public Archives of Canada. [3] That the ancient method was still in vogue

[1] Captain John Smith: *A Map of Virginia with Description of the Country* (Oxford: ptd. Joseph Barnes; 1612), pp. 59–60.

[2] The account is carried in Baron de Lahontan: *New Voyages to North-America*, ed. Reuben Gold Thwaites (2 vols.; Chicago: McClurg; 1905), II, 482–5.

[3] Harold A. Innis: *The Fur Trade in Canada* (New Haven: Yale Univ. Press; 1930), pp. 411–12, quotes from the account.

in some northern sections even during the mountain-man period is revealed in an article in *Penny Magazine* in 1833.[4]

The ice chisel and a strong net made of sinew or cordage figured importantly in the winter beaver hunt—a hunt that required the cooperation of several men or women. A first move of the hunters was the locating of beaver burrows along the shores of a beaver pond. This could be done by thumping the banks with long-handled ice chisels. The hollow sound produced by a blow directly above a burrow guided the hunter; with ax and ice chisel he cut through the ice above the mouth of the burrow, making an elongated opening big enough to permit the passage of a beaver's body. The net was pushed into this hole and spread upon the muddy bottom immediately below in such a way as to leave pull strings or handholds on top of the ice at both sides of the opening. The attendant Indian then stood at "ready," prepared to jerk the net upward the moment a beaver swam over it. All other beaver burrows in the vicinity received the same treatment.

Other members of the hunting party gave attention to the beaver houses in the deeper water of the pond. Ordinarily each house is served by two entrances, both well below the underside of the ice cover. It was a common practice of the hunters to locate at least one of these "doorways" at certain houses during the summer or fall before ice formed, and in order that an outer narrow passage to and from the house should be defined, two parallel lines of several stakes were driven into the muddy bottom to make an aisle at the hut's entrance. At the beginning of the winter hunt, a hole like the one described in the preceding paragraph was cut through the ice above the outer opening of the aisle and a net was placed on or near the bottom of the pond at the entrance to the aisle. An attendant stood guard here prepared to pull the net. Other houses in the pond were given the same preparation, and always hunters stood guard at the nets.

The final step was the hunter's attack upon the frozen walls of the beaver houses. With ax, hatchet, or ice chisel the organized

[4] "The Beaver," *The Penny Magazine for Diffusion of Useful Knowledge* (April 6, 1833), pp. 129–31. Louis R. Caywood excavating Fort Meductic in 1964 found beaver harpoons among the recovered artifacts. He reports that documentary sources present the picture of Malecite and Micmac Indians hunting beaver with these harpoons. Letter, Caywood to C. P. Russell, February 16, 1965.

hunters chopped into all huts simultaneously. The beaver inmates, routed by the demolition, fled via their usual exits under the ice. At least one animal from each house would pass over a waiting net at the door. The expectant hunter at that door snatched his net upward at the critical moment, pulled the struggling animal onto the ice, and dispatched it with a club. It was quite important that the fatal blow be struck instantly, because the web of the net would not long withstand the chisel-like teeth of the beaver. Also, it was necessary to reset the net quickly because another victim could be expected momentarily, this time headed into the house from the outside waters.

Under such attack, the entire beaver population in the pond made a wild dash toward the havens that they habitually had depended upon during previous alarms. Some sought refuge in neighboring houses and some swam to burrows in the nearby banks. If the Indians had been thorough in locating the burrows, there could be no escape, for a beaver could only remain under water without air for a few minutes. In its distress, the beaver would try to enter either a burrow or a house. If it were the Indians' determination to kill the entire colony, such was within the realm of possibility, but, traditionally, the tribes never sought annihilation. The white trader was often less conscientious in the matter. At any rate, the French and English in Canada, the Dutch on the Hudson and Connecticut rivers, and the colonists in New England and Virginia procured some two million beaver skins during the 1600's and the first half of the 1700's. A notable number of the pelts were taken in winter hunts of the kind described.

There were of course other aboriginal methods of killing beaver. Deadfalls, underwater pens, and devices for drowning had been in use among the Amerinds through the ages. As might be expected, the earliest observations of these primitive traps were made by white men in the North. The Pilgrims left a record of what they saw in the early seventeenth century, Frenchmen wrote about their observations in New France in the early eighteenth century, and the English fur trader and explorer David Thompson reported in some detail on his findings in the North and West during the period from 1784 to 1812. In more recent times not less than forty anthropologists have studied the cultures of the northern tribes as they exist today, thereby bringing up to date the story of pre-Columbian types of beaver traps. A valuable compilation of many of these findings, together with a fully illustrated report on his own extensive field studies, was published by Father John M. Cooper.[5]

Cooper states that beaver were not taken in snares, and only certain types of deadfalls were used for this animal—the "kicker" deadfall with a tread-bar release (a conventional type), and the unique "beaver spear downfall," a device akin to the African and East Indian "harpoon downfall." It is a notable fact that the American Indian trapping devices, with the above single exception, were designed to strangle, crush, or drown the fur bearers in a manner that would cause no breaks in the skin and no soaking of the fur with blood.

Pens built in the water were equipped with vertical sliding doors which, when triggered, might be dropped shut by a swimming beaver that had entered the pen or by manual operation by the attendant hunter standing guard near the pen. A fourth type of trap, a drowning device, the "funnel" trap, found use by some Montagnis and James Bay Indians. The funnel, made of small poles lashed to hoops, was placed in a break in a beaver dam. The larger opening of the funnel extended into the waters of the pond, and the small end reached downstream with its opening underwater. A beaver investigating the break in the dam could enter the funnel from the pond and proceed downward to its small end, which was big enough to permit the animal's head to pass. Once the head was through the small opening, there could be no backing up because the pliable ends of the poles caught behind the skull. There the animal drowned.

These and comparable primitive traps were adopted by some of the white trappers throughout those parts of America which yielded marketable furs in pioneer times. Even the advent of the steel trap did not relegate the snares, deadfalls, etc., to complete discard. As a matter of fact, the primitive devices continue in limited use today; published "trapper guides" and the current "survival manuals" for military personnel devote much space to in-

[5] John M. Cooper: *Snares, Deadfalls, and Other Traps of the Northern Algonquins and Northern Athapaskans* (Washington, D.C.: Catholic Univ. of America; 1938), pp. 1–150. For information on beaver traps see pp. 94, 109–21.

struction for their preparation and use,[6] and factory-made snares are now on the market.

EVOLUTION OF THE STEEL TRAP

EXACTLY WHEN THE FIRST STEEL TRAPS WERE BROUGHT TO America is not recorded, but it seems reasonable to believe that the very first colonies established by France in Nova Scotia and on the St. Lawrence River during the first decade of the seventeenth century had some of the small machines. It is unlikely that they were brought for the purpose of catching beaver, but they would have been useful indeed in eliminating pests and in taking small mammals and birds needed for food. Similarly, there is reason to think that the Englishmen who in the early 1600's settled along the Atlantic Coast also had steel traps. Such conjectures find some support in the published accounts of sixteenth-century traps in Europe.

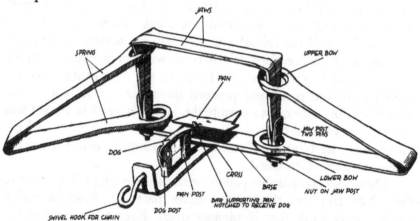

FIG. 17. *The Steel Trap and Its Parts.*

The 5-pound beaver trap pictured is a bona fide relic of the mountain man. It was found on the Green River near present-day Daniel, Wyoming, and is now in the author's collection—a gift from Mr. and Mrs. Wallace Hiatt. The nomenclature is derived from published records of the old-time trapmakers. Drawing by Glen Dines.

[6] See Bibliography: Andersch Bros. (1903); Craighead and Craighead (n.d.); W. H. Gibson (1881); A. R. Harding (1907); S. Harding (1875); W. B. Lord and T. Baines (1871); O. T. Mason (1900); E. L. Palmer (1943); G. A. Petrides (1946); H. Thrasher (1868); F. Tose (1928).

Figure 18 shows a double-spring trap pictured by the agricul-
turalist L. Mascall in 1590.[7] It is quite advanced mechanically and
rather belies the idea that it is in a beginning stage of development.
As one studies its parts, the notion is inescapable that many traps
must have preceded this one. The scholar who delves deeply into
the early history of the Iron Age probably will find evidences that
iron traps existed long prior to the 1500's.

Regarding his "griping trappe made all of yrne," Mascall
wrote:

> The lowest barre has a ring or hoope with two clickets, which
> ring is set fast to the sides of the barre.
>
> More unto it is a plate round in the middell with a sharpe yrne
> pinne in the middell, which plate hath a [little] springe on both
> sides under the edge, and they stirre not of ioyntes up and down.
>
> When the two shutting hoopes are opened abroade and holde
> down, it is to be shewed as hee standeth tyied with the two [big]
> springes downe flat to the long barre on both sides, which
> springes are made of good steele. As soon as the clickets which
> holde them downe be stride, the two springes shuts them sud-
> denly together. There is in the two shutting hoopes sharpe pinnes
> of yrne set one contrary to the other, with holes made for those
> pinnes to goe through and shut close together that it will holde
> anything, if it be but a rush or straw, so close they shut together.
> The two hoopes on both sides outward are made bigger and
> bigger upwarde, to holde more close when they come together, as
> ye may perceive by the hoopes within the springes, on both sides.
> Then there is at the ends of the long barres two square holes,
> which holes are made to pinne the long barre fast to the ground,
> where yee set or tyie him in any place at your pleasure. His
> clickets may so be made, that if any otter, fox, or other, do but
> tread thereon he shall be soone taken. Or ye must bind a piece of
> meate in the middell, and put it on the pricke, and so bind it fast.
> In pulling the baite, the clickets will slippe and the springes will
> rise, and so it will take him. Thus much for this kind of trappe
> shall be sufficient to understand the order thereof.

Figure 18a shows a top view of Mascall's sixteenth-century
trap when set. A circular base underlies the long basal bar to
which two springs are riveted. The ends of the toothed jaws are

---

[7] L. Mascall: *A Booke of Fishing with Hook and Line . . . Another of
Sundrie Engines and Trappes to Take Polecats, Buzards, Rats* (London: John
Wolfe; 1590), pp. 52–93.

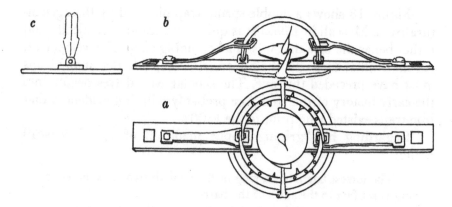

FIG. 18. *English Steel Trap of the Sixteenth Century.*

"The griping trappe made all of yrne, the lowest barre, and the ring or hoope [base], with two clickets [dogs]."

supported in jaw posts, each with a single pin. When the springs are depressed, the jaws may be opened. A pliable, circular pan has a central mounting and receives at its edge the two "clickets" or dogs which restrain the open jaws. Meat or other bait may be impaled on a sharp iron pin which projects upward from the center of the pan. Since the pan rotates on its central mounting, the dogs may be released either by the tread of an animal's foot or by the disturbance caused when an animal tugs at the bait. Movement of the pan in relationship to the delicately adjusted dogs permits the jaws to snap shut under the force exerted by the released springs. If the trapper is lucky, the jaws close upon the animal's foot or upon its head.

Figure 18*b* shows a side view of the trap, with jaws closed. "There is at the ends of the long barre two square holes, which holes are made to pinne the long barre fast to the ground, when yee set or tyie him in any place at your pleasure."

The strap-like springs, "made of good steele," persisted through four hundred years as a characteristic of the English rattrap, many of which in single-spring models were brought to America. Some are shown in the succeeding figures.

Figure 18*c* is an end view of the jaws, with springs removed. "The two hoopes on both sides outward are made bigger and bigger upwarde to hold more close when they come together, as ye may perceive by the hoopes within the springs" (*b*). This style of jaw construction became a characteristic of the mountain man's beaver trap and is still a feature of present-day factory-made traps of most types. Figure 19 shows steel traps of "jump" type. The steel spring mounted on the base inside the enclosing jaws exerts a sudden downward force when "sprung." The comparatively light trap tends to rebound or jump upward because of the impact of force against the ground. Some trappers are convinced that the jump trap grips higher on a fur bearer's leg than does the trap with a bowed spring. (For the nomenclature of the parts of the steel trap see figure 17.)

Curators of the Natural History Museum, Salzburg, Austria, credit their fur-hunting countrymen of the seventeenth century with the invention, manufacture, and use of the specimen shown in figure 19a. It is the most ancient trap examined by the author. Present-day traps made prior to World War II by the firm "C. Steiner and Schider, Salsburg," adhere to the general design of the old trap as do the modern jump traps made in Germany. The specimen was exhibited in the Natural History Museum of Salzburg in 1936. Dr. H. V. Jedina, Salzburg, wrote to me in 1952: "Our Natural History Museum was completely destroyed by bombs during the war." The antique trap vanished in the debris.

Figure 19b is a circular double-spring jump trap of the British type. It was still in use in 1847 on Gales Creek near Gales City, Oregon. The pan is missing (restored in our drawing). It was presented to the Oregon Historical Society (No. 235) by its last owner and user, Mr. S. W. Iler. The trap manufacturer, E. Aurouze, Paris, France, featured a single-spring trap of this model.[8]

Figure 19c shows a modern jump trap made by the Animal Trap Company of America in sizes ranging from No. 0, for barn rats, to No. 4, which is "large enough to hold the mountain lion." The evidences of its evolution from types exemplified by the ancient Austrian trap (a) are obvious. For an interesting portrayal of this and other modern traps, see the catalog *How To Catch More Fur.*[9]

The genesis of the modern coil-spring trap (fig. 19d) with double jaws made by the Animal Trap Company of America is

[8] See André deLesse: *Chasse Elevage et Piegeage* (Paris: J. B. Baillière & Fils; 1905), p. 535.
[9] Harold McCracken: *How To Catch More Fur* (Lititz, Pa.: Animal Trap Co.; 1945), pp. 1–48.

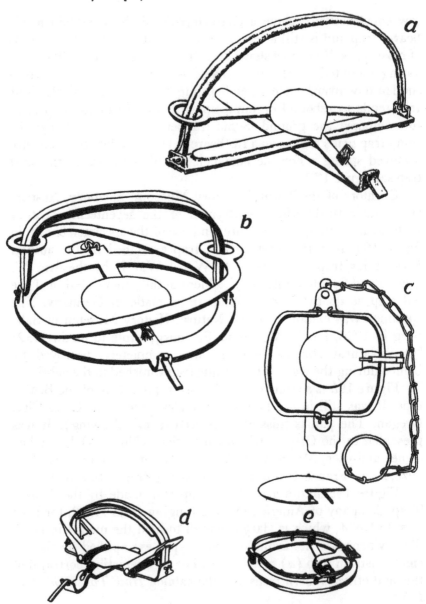

FIG. 19.   *The Modern "Jump" Trap Has Long Lineage.*

This Mulcahy drawing is in the Jefferson National Expansion Memorial, St. Louis.

discernible in the mechanism of the old French trap shown in figure 19*e*, which shows a coil-spring trap made and used in France in the eighteenth century. The detachable pan, shown above the trap, is of such size that it occupies most of the space between the spread jaws when the trap is set. The pan pivots on a transverse rod, the ends of which can be mounted in the frame of the trap. A small protuberance shaped like an inverted L mounted on the edge of the pan engages a horizontal protuberance, or lug, mounted on the jaw, thereby holding the jaws open. When the pan is stepped on by a small animal, it tilts (if the trapper is lucky) and the protuberances are disengaged, thus allowing the jaws to fly together under the force of the released spring. A similar system of setting and springing was employed in the traps shown in figure 20*b* and figures 21*e* and 21*f*.[1] Unquestionably there were many failures in the operation of this imperfect mechanism, and it is quite understandable why the system is obsolete.

Early Traps with Circular Bases

FOR a time it was the usual practice of European trapmakers to provide ample foundation for their products by giving them full round or oval bottoms. Later the style was followed in America. Even after the highly efficient type exemplified by the modern "Newhouse" (fig. 26) was well established, some smiths adhered to the old model of base, as shown by the 1851 Kenosha trap (fig. 22).

Figure 20*a* shows a trap from Southern Russia—"Karnton, Carinthia oder Krain." It is the product of a country blacksmith, weighs two pounds, and displays most of the characteristics of steel traps made throughout Europe in the eighteenth century. It is quite possible, however, that this specimen was in use prior to the eighteenth century. The device for setting and springing this trap apparently employed the conventional pan and dog, but unfortunately the pan and pan post are missing. The U-shape feature at the left side of the frame is a safety device for holding the jaws open while the trap is being placed in the "set." It is now in the Museum für Völkerkunde, Vienna, Austria.

[1] Jean Diderot and Denis d'Alembert: *L'Encyclopédie ou Dictionnaire raisonné des sciences* . . . (Geneva, 1778–81), Vol. XXXIX, Pl. XX, Figs. 5 and 6.

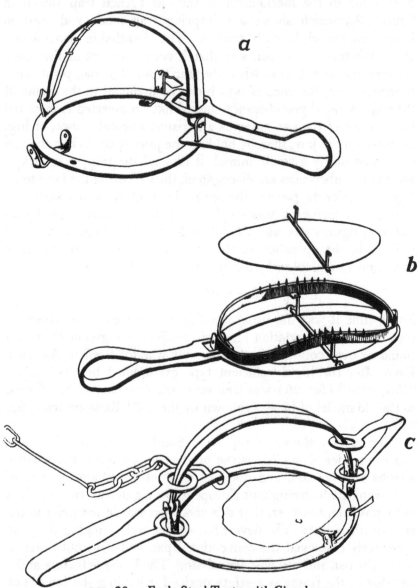

FIG. 20.   *Early Steel Traps with Circular or*
Oval Bases.

This Mulcahy drawing is from the Jefferson National Expansion
Memorial collection, St. Louis.

Figure 20*b* shows a French trap of the eighteenth century. Diderot describes its mechanism as follows:

This is how it operates: one lowers the two toothed hoops [jaws] which pivot in pierced openings [in the jaw posts] and open toward the circular band [which constitutes the bottom, or base, of the trap]; that can not be done without forcing down the upper part of the spring. The two toothed jaws are held in spread position by means of two barriers [or projecting lugs] mounted on the inner curves of the jaws. Over these lugs are adjusted the protruding ends of the L-shaped members of the transverse beam which holds the platform [pan]. This beam pivots in pierced openings in the base of the trap. The platform [or pan] is fastened rigidly to the beam. What happens when the animal comes? The animal steps on the pan which turns the beam on its pivot. The L-shaped posts are thus caused to swing off of the lugs of the jaws, so freeing them; the spring is released and in flying upward it drives the two jaws one against the other, because they are enclosed in the opening (bow) in the end of the movable part of the spring. The animal finds himself caught between the teeth of the jaws.[2]

Obviously, a slight depression or pit must have been prepared under the pan in order that it might be depressed when stepped on—an uncertain procedure which added to the over-all uncertainty of this, a most questionable trap type. Nevertheless the model was still being manufactured in the early 1900's.[3]

Note the unique relationship of the dog to the pan post in the handmade trap used in Pennsylvania shown in figure 20*c*. Examined in July 1935, the drawing was prepared from the author's sketch and photograph of trap No. 3887, Bucks County Historical Society, Doylestown, Pennsylvania.

The old bear trap in figure 21*a* has a jaw spread of 16 inches; it is attributed to the Hudson's Bay Company. It was found several feet below the surface of the ground near Astoria, Oregon. In all likelihood it was manufactured locally. This specimen is No. 379 in the old Fort Dalles Historical Museum, Dalles, Oregon (1948).

Figure 21*b* shows a very old trap of unknown origin. It was equipped with a pan mounted on a transverse beam and, like *c* below, depended on a lug mounted on one of the jaws to hold it in

[2] Ibid., Pl. 16, figs. 5–7.
[3] See deLesse: *Chasse Elevage*, p. 535.

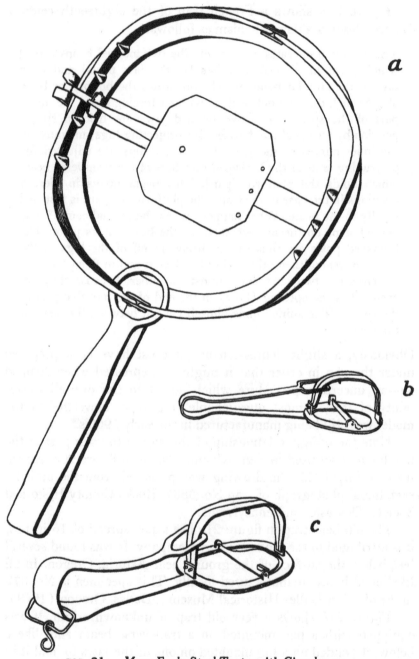

FIG. 21.   *More Early Steel Traps with Circular or
Oval Bases.*

The circular base made for strength of frame and stability when the trap was set, but it added greatly to the weight, a disadvantage not long tolerated by trappers in America.

The device for setting and "springing" the traps shown in *b* and *c* are relics of a mechanism that was never widely adopted by American trapmakers. Mulcahy drawing, Jefferson National Expansion Memorial, St. Louis.

set position. This lug engaged a projection of the pan. When the pan pivoted under the weight of an animal's tread, the lug and the projection were disengaged, the spring shot upward, and the jaws snapped shut. The specimen now lacks the pan and that part does not appear in the picture; it is No. 23863, Bucks County Historical Society. Diderot's eighteenth-century descriptions (*Encyclopédie*) have led students to class this style of trap as French. Its objectionable features notwithstanding, it is still being manufactured.[4]

Figure 21*c* shows a trap with an oval base that has retained all parts of the mechanism described under *b* above. Note the projection on the right margin of the pivoted pan and the lug attached to the right jaw, features which hark back to the inefficient French trap (fig. 20*b*). This specimen is in the Fort Ticonderoga Museum, Fort Ticonderoga, New York.

A Bear Trap with a Circular Base

THE inventive genius of American blacksmiths perfected the finish and improved the action of trap models devised in Europe but developed few innovations of basic design and mechanism. One of the rare examples of American originality in trap design is the Crossett trap presented in figure 22.

Figure 22*a* gives a general view of this exceptionally powerful and well-made trap, which has a unique device for releasing the spring. The single spring, incidentally, is of such proportions and tension that it can resist the full weight of a 200-pound man. The trap could be set only with the aid of a lever or a screw clamp.

Figure 22*b* is the same trap as *a* above, but it is in set position. The hammer-like dogs have been laid back against the open jaws, which are held down against the heavy pressure of the spring by the wedge effect of a slim rod of hardwood placed between the opposed dogs.

Figure 22*c* is a sectional view showing the relationships of

[4] See deLesse: *Chasse Elevage*, pp. 314, 335.

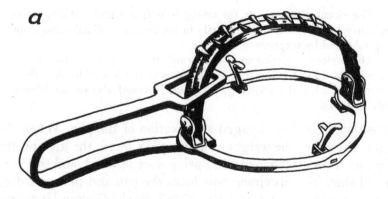

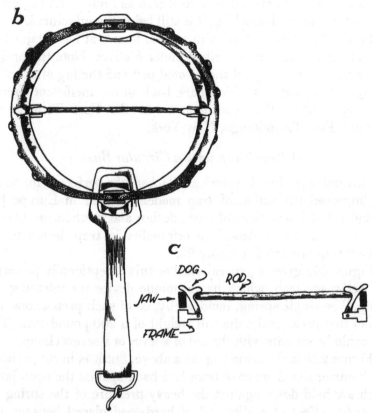

FIG. 22. *A Wisconsin Bear Trap with a Circular Base.*

This Mulcahy drawing is in the Jefferson National Expansion Memorial, St. Louis.

jaws, dogs, and the rod. Note the curved backs of the dogs in contact with the jaws and the method of mounting the dogs to give them free play on their pins. The backs of the dogs are of such shape as to assure the instantaneous release of the jaws when the wedging force of the rod is removed. This removal comes about, of course, when the weight of an animal's tread breaks or displaces the rod. It is possible that a small pan was fitted to the central portion of the rod.

The trap is credited to Mr. D. Crossett, pioneer craftsman of Kenosha, Wisconsin, in the 1840's and 1850's. It is owned by the Kenosha Historical Society (1946).

The English Rattrap

"The ordinary gin" of the Englishman is well represented in American trap collections. Generally the preserved specimens are of the small, single-spring variety used in the capture of barnyard pests, but larger traps of the same design were manufactured to serve the fur hunter. Contemporary realism in picturing the larger English traps is displayed in the early nineteenth-century painting of a Micmac Indian camp in New Brunswick reproduced as a two-page color spread in *American Heritage*.[5] The "rat" traps in this instance have two springs and appear to be approximately of No. 4 size—big enough for beaver. Pictured with the traps are stretched and dried skins of the fox and the river otter—implied bounty of the trap line. The original of this trap collector's document is owned by the National Gallery of Canada.

The small trap with bar-type spring in figure 23a is said to have been made prior to 1840 at Fort Vancouver on the Columbia River by Thomas Moore, a Hudson's Bay Company blacksmith. The maker followed the English design in every particular. The trap is now No. 233 in the collections of the Oregon Historical Society, Portland.

Figure 23b shows a British rattrap collected in "Vorderindien" (western India) by Austrian anthropologists. In 1936 this specimen was exhibited in the Museum für Völkerkunde, Vienna. It was designated as No. 31057 in the records of that institution.

Figure 23c is a small trap of English design now in the Museum of the Bucks County Historical Society. It bears the

[5] December 1965 issue, pp. 16–17.

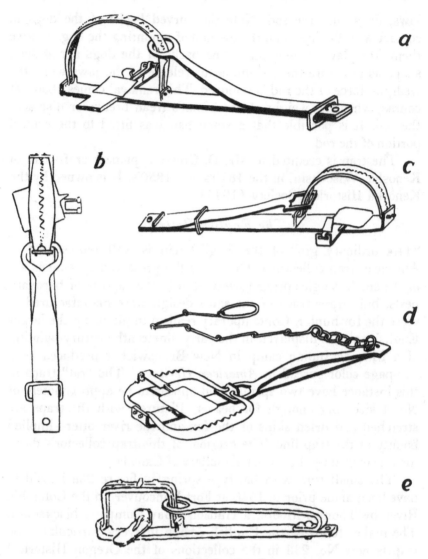

FIG. 23. *The English Rattrap.*

The antiquity of the small English rattrap can only be conjectured, but its relationship to Mr. Mascall's trap of 1590 seems quite obvious (fig. 18). The rattrap was in use in Salem, Massachusetts, in the 1650's, in York County, Virginia, in 1709, and in all probability had been used for centuries prior to these dates in the British Isles. Traps of this style, "the ordinary gin," accompanied English colonists to many parts of the spreading British empire, and in Europe it met with sufficient favor to induce French manufacturers to produce it (see deLesse: *Chasse Elevage*, pp. 316, 535). Occasionally this type of trap was made big enough to catch beaver. The Provincial Museum, Quebec, has one, the open jaws of which measure 7 by 8 inches; the single spring is 13½ inches long. R. S. Shankland has a Virginia specimen, total length 48 inches, with jaws 13 inches long—a "wolf trap." Robert M. Ballantyne (in *Hudson Bay . . .*) testifies regarding his observations of Canadian Indians catching beaver in oversize English rattraps. Mulcahy drawing, Jefferson National Expansion Memorial, St. Louis.

number 9265. The sliding iron ring on the spring constituted a safety device commonly used to prevent a trap from snapping while being adjusted in the "set."

An old English rattrap complete with chain is shown in figure 23*d*. Fort Ticonderoga Museum collection.

Figure 23*e* is a badly rusted steel trap of English style that is recorded to have come from the old iron house on the Hock Farm of General John A. Sutter ten miles from Yuba City, California. In structural details it is similar to the usual small British trap, except for the reverse curvature of the spring and the coarse teeth mounted on the jaws. This specimen is No. 138 in the Los Angeles Museum.

Miscellaneous Traps of "Beaver" Size

IN the middle of the nineteenth century the white man's method of catching beaver in a steel trap had been adopted by many Indians. The demand for steel traps throughout much of the continent north of Mexico brought about a sharp increase in the number of trapmakers, and at the opening of the nineteenth century the character of the beaver trap was fairly standardized in both Canada and the United States. Figures 24*b* and 24*c* represent typical beaver traps finally demanded by the trade.

The history of the eighteenth-century trap used by members of the Chew family in Atison Meadows, Burlington County, New Jersey (fig. 24*a*) was known and reported upon by William Chew, who at the time of his testimony in 1920 was ninety-four years old. Note the overlap of the jaws at the jaw post and the single pin upon which both jaws play—a mechanical feature which was thought to be objectionable by some beaver trappers. However, the single pin persisted all through the mountain-man period. This specimen is No. 3886, Bucks County Historical Society.

Figure 24*b* shows a forerunner of the mountain man's beaver

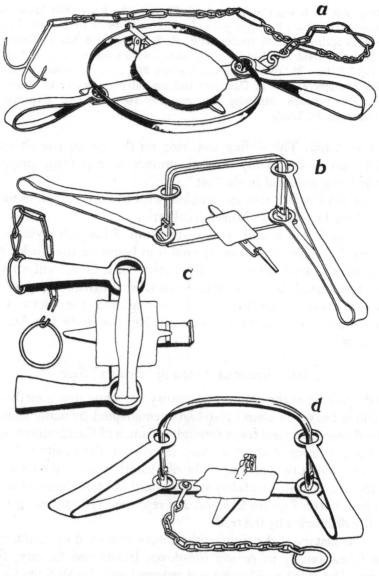

FIG. 24. *Miscellaneous Traps of "Beaver" Size.*

This Mulcahy drawing is in the Jefferson National Expansion Memorial, St. Louis.

trap; it bears the inscription "A. G. 1755." The jaw posts are not split. The artist has supplied the pan which is missing from the specimen. Many traps of this form, designed especially for beaver, were taken to the Far West in the opening decades of the nineteenth century. It is from the collections of the Valley Forge Museum of American History, 1936.

Typical of the well-made beaver traps of the early nineteenth century is the specimen in figure 24c. At this time the design and finish of such traps were fairly well standardized in the United States. Some Canadian leaders recognized the superiority of the beaver traps from south of their national boundary and asked that they be imported.[6] It is listed as No. 4839, Château de Ramezay, Montreal (1938).

Like figure 24c above, the specimen in figure 24d reflects the care of a skilled workman in following a proven design. Note that the chain is fastened to the bottom of the trap. It is in the collection of the Spring Mill State Park Museum, Indiana.

BEAVER TRAPS ACTUALLY USED BY THE MOUNTAIN MEN

ON THE LONG TREK INTO THE PLAINS COUNTRY, TO THE ROCKIES, and into the tramontane regions, traps, like other paraphernalia, were conveyed in boats, wagons, and carts, or packed on the backs of horses and mules. It was important that they be as light as possible, yet durability and effectiveness were not to be sacrificed in order that they might be portable. The specimens in figure 25 are representative of the American traps that followed Lewis and Clark into the West and for nearly half a century constituted a principal implement in the exploitation of the lands beyond the settlements.

Figure 25a shows one of N. M. Pryor's traps cached by him on the Colorado River in 1828 and later taken by him to Los Angeles.[7] It is considerably smaller and lighter than the average beaver trap brought into the Far West, but otherwise it is typical. Without its chain it weighs 1¾ pounds. One jaw has rusted through at the jaw

[6] "As the American steel traps are much superior to any we can get made I would be much obliged if you would get a case of beaver traps for this place." (Letter, December 20, 1859, W. Sinclair, Norway House, to W. McTavish, quoted by Innis: *The Fur Trade in Canada* [1930 edn.], p. 297.)

[7] "I present to your Society an old beaver trap [fig. 25a] that belonged to N. M. Pryor, and was used by him in trapping on the Gila and Colorado rivers the winter of 1827–1828, and brought by him to Los Angeles. It was given to me by Pryor in 1848 and has been in my possession ever since." (Stephen C. Foster: "A Sketch of Some of the Earliest Kentucky Pioneers of Los Angeles," *Publications of the Historical Society of Southern California* [1887], pp. 30–5.)

post, a defect not shown by the artist. The trap is preserved in the History Department of the Los Angeles County Museum.

An unusual single-spring beaver trap that was once the property of Jim Bridger is shown in figure 25*b*. It was purchased by Dr. F. M. Fryxell in August 1934, and presented by him to the Jenny Lake Museum, Grand Teton National Park, Wyoming. It is now exhibited in the Fur Trade Museum at Moose, Grand Teton. The identity of the trap is attested to by members of the family who received it from "Old Gabe" (Bridger) in 1847.[8] The mechanism for setting and springing this trap is ingenious. The dog has been dispensed with; the notch in the extension of the pan engages the jaw. This provides for a very delicate adjustment of the pan but makes for difficulty in setting the trap. The spring is powerful, and all parts of the trap are ruggedly yet accurately made. It is as serviceable today as it was a hundred years ago. Since Bridger was himself a capable blacksmith, it is possible that the trap represents his own handiwork.

The specimen of a beaver trap characteristic of the handmade traps brought to the Rocky Mountains by the fur brigades of the 1820's and 1830's (fig. 25*c*) had long been in the possession of "Trapper" (J. P. V.) Evans of Livingston, Montana, when in 1934 it was obtained by this writer for the history collections of the Yellowstone museums. It is now exhibited in the History Room of the Mammoth Hot Springs Museum, Yellowstone National Park. A trap that appears to be an exact mate to this one was found

[8] [AFFIDAVIT] *Walter J. Woosley of Wilsall, Montana, being first duly sworn, deposes and says:*

THAT, about the year of 1847 Jim Bridger gave to one James H. Carroll a certain large Beaver Trap.

That, sometime later this trap was given to my grandfather Samuel Maddox.

That, upon the death of my grandfather the trap came into my father's possession, his name being Joshua Y. Woosley.

That, upon the death of my father the trap came into my possession, and I then disposed of it to Mr. J. P. V. Evans of Livingston, Montana, who is disposing of it to the party who is donating it to the Museum in Teton National Park.

WALTER J. WOOSLEY

State of Montana
County of Park

SUBSCRIBED *and sworn to before me by Walter J. Woosley in my office in Wilsall, Montana, this 22nd day of September, 1934.*

F. L. Kistner

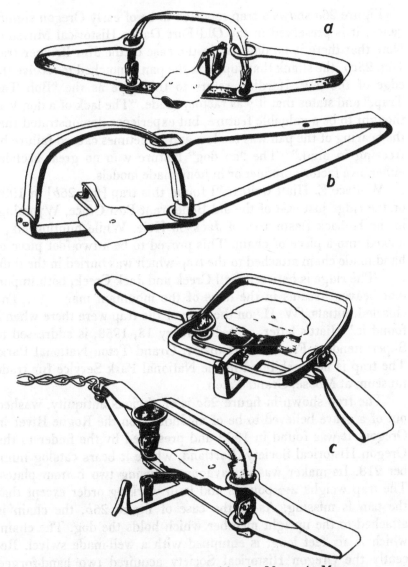

FIG. 25. *Beaver Traps Used by the Mountain Man.*

This Mulcahy drawing is in the Jefferson National Expansion
Memorial, St. Louis.

several years ago a few miles from the site of old Fort Hall, Idaho.
Three photographs of this specimen were published by Stanley P.
Young.[9]

[9] Stanley P. Young: "The Evolution of the Steel Wolf Trap in North
America," *Western Sportsman* (February 1941), pp. 10–11, 30.

Figure 26*a* shows a trap reported to be of early Oregon significance; it is preserved in the Old Fort Dalles Historical Museum. Note that there is no dog. As in the case of the Jim Bridger trap (fig. 25*c*), the shank that supports the pan is notched to receive the edge of the jaw. Harding refers to this type as the "Bob Tail Trap," and states that it was factory-made. "The lack of a dog was thought to be a valuable feature, but experience demonstrated that the bearing of the pan was too low and sometimes caused failure by freezing in mud." [1] The "no dog" feature won no great acclaim either as a factory product or in homemade models.

Wallace E. Hiatt writes: "I found this trap [fig. 26*b*] in 1920 on the ridge just east of the old Bondurant Post Office, Wyoming, in the Hoback Basin area of Jackson Hole. While hunting elk, I kicked into a piece of chain. This proved to be a two-foot piece of hand-made chain attached to the trap which was buried in the duff. . . . The ridge is between Dell Creek and Jack Creek, both important beaver streams in the days of the mountain man. . . . The chiseled initials, 'W. H.' on the base of the trap were there when I found it." Hiatt's letter, dated January 13, 1958, is addressed to Superintendent Frank Oberhansley, Grand Teton National Park. The trap is now exhibited in the National Park Service fur trade museum at Moose, Grand Teton.

The trap shown in figure 26*c* is of obvious antiquity, washed out of a grave believed to be of an Indian, on the Rogue River in Oregon. It was found in 1903 and presented by the finder to the Oregon Historical Society, Portland, where it bears catalog number 218. Its maker was extravagant in using two bottom plates. The trap weighs 2½ pounds and is in working order except that the pan is missing. As in the case of figure 26*b*, the chain is attached to the upright member which holds the dog. The chain, which is six feet long, is equipped with a well-made swivel. Recently the Oregon Historical Society acquired two hand-forged beaver traps that were found on the Siuslaw River near present-day Florence, Oregon. This is a locality in which Hudson's Bay Company brigades under Alexander Roderic McLeod trapped during the 1820's. It is highly speculative to assume that these traps were once used by McLeod's men, but it is no idle surmise to say that they are of Hudson's Bay Company origin. In size and structural design they resemble the Rogue River specimen (fig. 26*c*), and

[1] A. R. Harding: *Steel Traps*, p. 33.

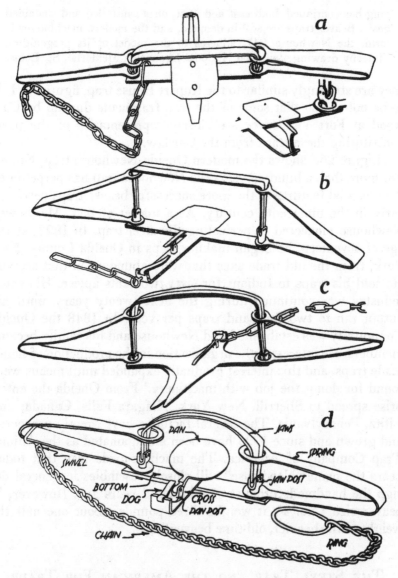

FIG. 26.   *More Beaver Traps Used by the Mountain Men.*

From approximately 1750 through the 1850's, the standard hand-made beaver trap remained constant in design and the general method of its use remained unchanged. Only the locale in which it found greatest use changed. During this period both Canadian and American fur interests shifted their activities westward until they covered the entire Pacific slope. By 1850 many of the wilderness fur fields had been stripped of beaver. Subsequent to that denudation, beaver trapping has continued, both east and west, on a controlled and sustained basis. Beaver traps are still in demand, and the modern machine-made form, the Newhouse (*d*), adheres to the model of its progenitors. Mulcahy drawing, Jefferson National Expansion Memorial, St. Louis.

they are strikingly similar to the Rupert House trap, figure 31. It is to be noted also that some of the trap fragments dug up by Caywood at Fort Vancouver are closely representative of the parts constituting these traps from the Siuslaw.

Figure 26*d* shows the modern Oneida Newhouse trap, No. 4.[2] For more than a hundred years the Newhouse trap has perpetuated the essential features of the more successful beaver traps perfected early in the nineteenth century. As a matter of fact, Mr. Sewell Newhouse pioneered in perfecting the steel trap. In 1823, at the age of seventeen, he began making traps in Oneida County, New York, from the old trade axes that were abundant in that section. He sold his traps to Indians for sixty-two cents apiece. His small industry was continued during the next twenty years, until his output ran to two thousand traps per year. In 1848 the Oneida Community was established and Newhouse and his family became members. He interested the organization in the production of hand-made traps, and this interest gradually expanded until means were found for doing the job with machinery.[3] From Oneida the enterprise spread to Sherrill, New York; Niagara Falls, Canada; and Lititz, Pennsylvania. The several factories have greatly prospered and grown and since 1925 have been amalgamated as the Animal Trap Company of America. The machine-made trap that today bears the name "Newhouse" still closely resembles in general design the handmade product of a hundred years ago. However, in beaver size (No. 4) it weighs three pounds, about one half the weight of the heavier, old-time beaver traps.

THE STEEL TRAP AND THE AMERICAN FUR TRADE

THE DEVELOPMENT IN EUROPE OF THE LITTLE MACHINE KNOWN as the steel trap had its beginnings long before the eighteenth-century use of the trap in America. The earliest trap examined by

[2] McCracken: *How to Catch More Fur*, pp. 27, 29.
[3] S. Newhouse: *The Trapper's Guide* (Wallingford, Conn.: Oneida Community; 1867), pp. 208–12.

this author is the specimen represented by figure 19*a*, a seventeenth-century Austrian "jump" trap. The claims for antiquity propounded by the museum curator, who in 1936 exhibited the specimen in the Natural History Museum of Salzburg, could not be checked for verity, but there is no good reason to doubt them. The Austrian Alps were a noted source of regal furs in ages past and continue to yield fine peltry. Trapping has long been a calling there, and the trapmakers of Salzburg continue to produce steel traps,[4] some of which are strikingly similar to the seventeenth-century specimen that they saved as a relic.

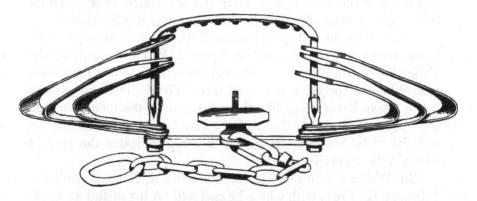

FIG. 27.   *Handmade Multi-Spring Trap from Idaho.*

Found near the head of Conant Creek and tentatively credited to "Beaver Dick" Leigh, much publicized trapper of pioneer times in the Grand Teton–Pierre's Hole region, this specimen in all its parts is rugged and big enough for wolves, puma, and bears. The jaws, when open, spread to 10 by 11½ inches. A screw clamp is necessary for depressing the springs. Six-spring bear traps identical in all particulars with this Idaho specimen were manufactured by John Wickham, New York, during the closing years of the mountain-man period (see Nick Drahos: "Evolution of Steel Traps," *The National Humane Review* [December 1951], p. 19). W. C. Lawrence, owner; specimen in the Jackson Hole Museum, Wyoming. Glen Dines drawing.

In America the known documentary record of the steel trap begins with the inventories of the Thomas Trusler properties, Salem, Massachussetts, 1650's, and the lists of Captain Daniel Taylor's effects used by him in Virginia in the late seventeenth and

---

[4] A. R. Harding, in his *Steel Traps*, p. 38, pictures a "German Fox Trap" which in almost every respect is like the Austrian jump traps of modern make.

early eighteenth centuries. The inventories are preserved in the Records of the Quarterly Courts, Salem, and in Book 14, Orders-Wills, York County, Virginia, 1709–1716, Williamsburg, Virginia. The traps are listed as "steele trapes," as distinguished from "mouse traps," which also are listed. In all likelihood, the "steele trapes" refer to the English rattrap shown in figure 23.

A "facsimilie" of a broadside advertising a pioneer shooting match, December 15–16, 1727, appears in John G. W. Dillin's *The Kentucky Rifle*. The advertisement announces: "There will be more prizes, such as traps, robes, knives, and skins. . . . Lead, powder, and flints to be sold. Bear and wolf traps to sell." Dillin fails to give a source for the broadside; possibly it is fictitious?

Next in the chronological outline of American steel-trap history is the dated trap represented in figure 24*b*. The records of the Valley Forge Museum, in which institution the trap was preserved, referred to the specimen as a "wolf trap." To all intent and purpose it is a heavy beaver trap like those favored by the mountain men after 1800. Presumably the "A. G." on the trap refers to the owner, and the "1755" also engraved on the trap indicates the year in which A. G. marked it.

Sir William Johnson addressed a letter to General Amherst, February 12, 1761, with which he enclosed "A list of Indian goods as are usually wanted and bought" for the trade at Detroit. "Beaver and fox traps" were included in the list. On May 7, 1761, Amherst received and approved this list.[5]

In 1762, Thomas Gage, Military Governor of Montreal, issued a pass, "Permit the bearer, Lucas Van Vachten and Compy. 4 Englishmen, 2 negroes, 12 Canadiens in 3 canoes to pass from hence to Toronto or elsewhere on Lake Ontario, and to carry on a furr trade with the savages, being provided with merchandize as stated on the back of this for that purpose in which they are not to be molested. Signed Thomas Gage at Montreal." Included in the list are "41 steel traps."[6]

Sir William Johnson, as Superintendent of Indian Affairs in North America in 1764, included 5,000 beaver traps at 10 shillings apiece, a total of 1,458 pounds, 6 shillings, 8 pence sterling, in a list of objects deemed most desirable for the Indian trade. In 1765,

[5] James Sullivan, ed.: *The Papers of Sir William Johnson* (Albany, 1921–33), III, 335, 388.
[6] Ibid., 755.

when some of these traps had been supplied, they were traded to Indians "for 2 beavers middle sized, or 2 bucks" per trap.[7]

The distribution of beaver traps during the mid-eighteenth century was not limited to the North country. In the *Virginia Gazette* (Purdie and Dixon, editors) of April 11, 1766, appears the advertisement: "To be sold at John Greenhow's store, Williamsburg,—vermine and beaver traps."

A maker of beaver traps in or near Philadelphia in 1767 was Baltzer Geere, who supplied the firm of Baynton, Wharton and Morgan with 100 traps for which he was paid 50 pounds.[8] Ac-

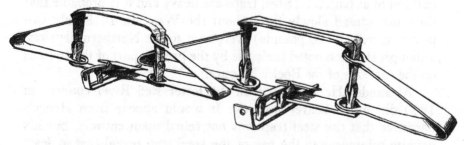

FIG. 28. *Two Sizes of Beaver Traps Used by the Mountain Men.*

The trap to the left was dug up in the vicinity of Fort Hall, Idaho (S. P. Young: "The Evolution of the Steel Wolf Trap," p. 11). Without the chain it weighs about 2½ pounds and is to be classed with the "lightweight" beaver traps exemplified by the N. M. Pryor trap (fig. 25a), and the Yellowstone trap (fig. 25b). Two of the Astorian traps from the Hunt wreck of 1811 (Idaho Historical Society) are also "lightweight."

The 5-pound trap at the right was found in a cache on the divide between the Green River and the Hoback. It is typical of many of the earlier hand-forged traps used by the mountain men. The National Park Service Museum, Jefferson National Expansion Memorial, acquired the specimen as a gift from Mr. and Mrs. Wallace Hiatt. Drawing by Glen Dines.

[7] *Illinois Historical Collections*, X, 339, 403. It is probable that New York Indians at this time were fairly well supplied with steel traps, but archeologists who have explored many of the sites occupied by the Iroquois and other tribes find little or no evidence of the trap. W. M. Beauchamp, in his *Metallic Ornaments of the New York Indians*, New York State Museum *Bulletin* (Albany, 1903), p. 74, quotes Mr. S. L. Frey, writing of the Mohawk Valley, "I never heard of a single steeltrap being found" in an Indian site. Beauchamp adds: "Steel traps were commonly used at a distance from the towns and were not likely to be lost at home. The writer has found but one small one on an Indian site."

[8] Personal letter, Arthur Woodward to Carl P. Russell, September 13, 1937, quoting from the Account Book of Baynton, Wharton and Morgan (1760's), p.

cording to a list of goods sold in August 1768 by Baynton, Wharton and Morgan to three white hunters who were to descend the Mississippi, the retail price of three beaver traps was 37 shillings, 6 pence [9]—a reasonable profit of about 25 per cent.

David Thompson testified that the use of steel traps and castoreum by beaver trappers on the lower Red River (in the present Manitoba) began in 1797; he regarded the use of castoreum for baiting to be an invention of northeastern Indians.[1] Innis attributes, in part, the rapid exhaustion of the beaver fields of this section "to the use of steel traps and the discovery of the use of castoreum as bait. . . . Steel traps are heavy and it is probable that their use spread slowly throughout the West. In 1818 only two pieces of traps (180 pounds) were sent to the Northern districts, although Harmon noted their use by the greater part of the Indians on the east side of the Rocky Mountains." [2]

Alexander Henry's party in the lower Red River country in 1800 did much beaver hunting. It would appear from Henry's narrative that the steel trap was not relied upon entirely, but his definite references to the use of the steel trap reveal that at least some of the hunters were equipped with it. In the spring of 1801, one of Henry's trappers was out two days and returned with twenty-five beaver.[3]

Lewis and Clark, intent upon sampling the natural resources of the unknown Western country through which their expedition passed, carried and used steel traps. They reported their catches of

200. In 1937 this manuscript material was preserved in the archives of the Historical Commission, Harrisburg, Pennsylvania.

[9] Baynton, Wharton and Morgan papers (MS), Harrisburg.

[1] J. B. Tyrell, ed.: *David Thompson's Narrative of His Explorations in Western America, 1784–1812*, Champlain Society Publication No. 12 (Toronto, 1916), pp. 204–5. Also see John C. Ewers's "Iroquois Indians in the Far West," *Montana, The Magazine of Western History*, XIII: 2 (October 1962), 5.

[2] Innis: *The Fur Trade in Canada*, p. 266. The Harmon item to which Innis here refers is Daniel W. Harmon: *A Journal of Voyages and Travels in the Interiour of North America* (Toronto, 1904). The book first appeared under the editorship of D. Haskel and was printed by Flagg and Gould (Andover, 1820). Also see Edward Umfreville: *Present State of Hudson's Bay* (London, 1790), pp. 56 ff. "The principal things necessary for the support of an Indian and his family, and which they usually trade for, are the following: a gun, a hatchet, an ice chisel, Brazil tobacco, knives, files, flints, powder and shot, a powder horn, a bayonet, a kettle, cloth, beads, and the like." The steel trap is conspicuous by its absence.

[3] Elliott Coues, ed.: *New Light on the History of the Greater North-West*, a vol. in *The Manuscript Journals of Alexander Henry and of David Thompson . . . 1799–1814* (3 vols.; New York: F. P. Harper; 1897), I, 175.

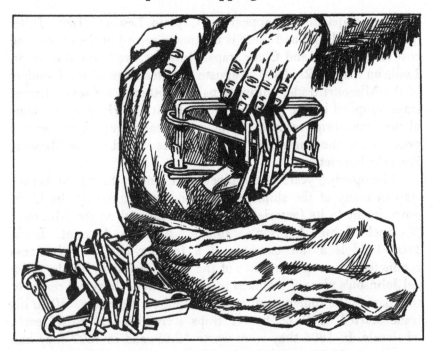

FIG. 29. *"Folded" Beaver Traps.*

When large shipments of traps were sent out by the blacksmiths to the fur companies, pine boxes or barrels served as the containers. When individual trappers transported their personal traps from one camp to another, via horse or canoe, it was usual to "fold" the traps and to wrap the chain around the fold, thus conserving space. Each complement of six or eight traps (total weight, 50 or 60 pounds) was carried in a leather bag. The Astorian traps recovered from the Hunt wreck of 1811 were folded and the chains wrapped (Idaho Historical Society). One specimen from this lot is exhibited in the National Park Service Museum, Moose, Grand Teton National Park. Glen Dines drawing.

beaver in the *Journals*.[4] That other white men also busied themselves with steel traps in the Mandan country in 1804 is evidenced by the fact that on October 31, 1804, a Mandan chief turned over to Captain Clark two steel traps that the Indians had purloined from some Frenchmen who had complained to Clark about their loss.[5]

[4] Reuben G. Thwaites, ed.: *Original Journals of the Lewis and Clark Expedition, 1804–1806* (8 vols.; New York: Dodd, Mead & Co.; 1904–5), I, 97 *passim*.

[5] Ibid., I, 214; B. De Voto: *The Journals of Lewis and Clark* (Boston: Houghton Mifflin; 1953), p. 61.

Steel traps do not appear on Captain Lewis's "List of Requirements," 1803, and there is no known record of the origin and cost of the Lewis and Clark traps. However, we know that in St. Louis on August 21, 1807, Auguste Chouteau, one of the founders of the Missouri trade, willingly paid $7.50 each for seven beaver traps supplied by the pioneer jobbers Hunt and Hankinson. Some of the manuscript records of Chouteau's early trap purchases are preserved in the Auguste Chouteau Papers owned by the Missouri Historical Society.

The opening years of the nineteenth century found the beaver trap in many of the shipments of goods consigned by the U. S. government to its factories in the Midwest and on the Missouri. "Colonel John Johnson's Indian Agency Account Book, 1803–11" [6] is a fair example of a frontier record of business conducted by a representative of the Office of Indian Trade. Colonel Johnson's place of business was Fort Wayne, business center of that part of the Indian country called Indiana Territory. When his trade started in 1802, beaver traps were listed at $1.67 each, wholesale. In 1806 they were worth $2.25, and in 1807 they had gone up to $3.00 each. [7] Steel traps, however, constituted a very small item in the trade at Fort Wayne, and beaver pelts were so few as to be almost negligible. In this country raccoon were traded in amazing numbers, as were deerskins. At that time traps ordinarily were not employed in taking raccoon.

Uncle Sam's prime movers in conducting the business of the headquarters, Indian Factory Office, George Town, D.C., were from the first keenly aware of the potential importance of the steel trap in the trade and were alert in screening out the faulty products of smiths who, though conscientious in their workmanship, perhaps had themselves never put their traps to practical use. The following letter [8] of 1808 is enlightening:

[6] Bert J. Griswold, ed.: *Fort Wayne, Gateway of the West, 1802–1813* (Indianapolis: Indiana Library and Historical Dept.; 1927), pp. xi–690.
[7] Ibid., pp. 418, 470, 483.
[8] The letter appears in Memorandum Book, Indian Factory Office, George Town, 1808 (MS). This book and other documents pertaining to the Indian Factory System are preserved in the National Archives, Washington, D.C. A summary of the contents of these original documents with abstracts from especially significant items was made by Dr. Alfred F. Hopkins in 1941–2 and is now filed in the library of the Branch of Natural History, National Park Service, Washington, as "Report on Indian Trade Objects Purchased by the United States

Mr. George C. Sibley
Baltimore, Md.

I have before me yours of the 14th and have seen and examined the Beaver trap. It is well made and shows the marks of a good workman, but it is unquestionably defective. You or the maker could not have tried it by the only test to set it and spring it. I have tried to set it three times. Neither time did it spring when the plate fell. It not only creeps, but hangs. I think the defect to be in the manner of fixing the points of the jaws to the upright pieces in which they play. These [the jaw posts] are split. The point of the jaw is introduced flat-wise between, and a round piece inserted and riveted on each side. This occasions too much friction and when rust takes, it will be much worse. The same is the fault with the manner of hanging the kicker [dog], and the plate. The springs are too stiff as you say, but that is easily remedied. The jaws are remarkably well-made, but not quite high enough because when expanded and the trap set, they don't give space enough for the chancers to take the animal; for the same reason the plate is too narrow, and holes should be punched in it to attach the bait when requisite. There is no doubt, however, from the sample, Mr. Lamb can execute the traps completely and at $3.25 each with the chain, I am willing he should immediately make fifty to be delivered by the fifteenth of April if he will. After those hints, he can go the price he asks, twenty-five cents higher than heretofore paid and than I give for same now making here, but as his are well finished, I will give it. I can't now wait for more than fifty from him, but I have no doubt I shall frequently give him orders. The jaw should work in the upright piece attached to the frame thus on a pivit, engaged a little at the extremity. [Here a diagram was inserted by Mason portraying a jaw post like those of the English traps shown in figure 23.] The friction is much less, and the obstruction to the play by rust much less feared, but warn him of one thing whenever he finishes a trap, test it by setting and springing it several times. I have written you a long chapter I find on a small subject, and am yours in haste,

Respectfully,
John Mason.

Government through Its Several Superintendents of Indian Trade at Philadelphia, Penn., and George Town, District of Columbia, from 1801 to 1822, Inclusive" (MS), pp. 1–56.

Additional trial traps made by Mr. Lamb were also defective, and further exchange of correspondence and the submission to the blacksmith of a model trap made in George Town were necessary before the Philadelphia traps were satisfactory. The admonition "Tell Mr. Lamb that the Beaver Trap, when set, the jaws should be open and flat" suggests again that the trapmaker was unacquainted with the practical use of his product.

Alexander Ross, the Astorian turned Nor'wester, records in his *Fur Hunters of the Far West:* "Six traps is the regular allowance for each hunter, but to guard against wear and tear, the complement is frequently ten." [9] Ross referred specifically to Mackenzie's 1819–20 expedition in the Snake River country. The style of the beaver traps carried by the Canadians at that time differed in no basic way from the conventional beaver traps used by Americans and shown in figures 25 and 26. A set of American traps which (with good reason) are believed to have been used by Astorians in 1811 were recovered from the bottom of the Snake River in 1938. We may assume that they are contemporary with the Mackenzie traps and similar to them in weight and design. They are owned by the Idaho History Museum and are given some attention in our figure 28. Two of the Astorian traps are quite like the five-pound beaver traps of figures 25 and 26; two are lightweight and more closely approximate the size of the N. M. Pryor trap (fig. 25a). If these actually are Astorian traps, it is possible that they came from Canada orginally, for at this time John J. Astor drew upon Canadian sources in part for equipment and trade goods, just as he did for manpower. This fact is brought forth in a letter of January 18, 1818, from Ramsay Crooks to William W. Matthews, Montreal, in which one Jean Baptiste Macon is named as a prospective maker of traps for the Astor Company.

According to an Invoice Book, 1822–3, now in the National Archives, the United States Office of Indian Trade found it desirable in 1822 to turn to British manufacturers to obtain a part of its steel-trap supply. The noted gunmaker Henry Deringer also contributed to the supply of traps at this time. Both the Deringer and the British product brought $3.00 apiece. These traps were shipped in casks (the "tierce," a 42-gallon container) holding 28 to 36 traps each and in hogsheads (63 gallons) holding 85 traps each.

[9] 1924 edn., p. 219.

Information regarding the Indians' use and purchase of these government-procured beaver traps is scanty indeed. It is to be noted, however, that traps were sometimes consigned to the tribesmen through treaty provisions. For example, the Treaty with the Cherokee in 1817 stipulates in its Article 6: ". . . To all warriors who may remove to the western side of the Mississippi River, one rifle gun with ammunition, one blanket, and one brass kettle, or in lieu of the brass kettle, a beaver trap. . . ." [1]

Muskrat traps also were made for the Office of Indian Trade during its early years of activity and shipped to some of the government's establishments in the northern Indian country. At this time, also, the raw materials from which steel traps could be made or repaired were purchased for the use of blacksmiths at the "factories" or posts. [2]

Other private interests in the United States, notably the St. Louis Missouri Fur Company, John Astor's organization, and the North West Company of Canada, were pushing westward into the tramontane regions, carrying with them the steel trap. The enterprise of the United States companies was sharply curtailed by the War of 1812, but trapping activities in the Far West became ever more extensive immediately upon the cessation of hostilities, and the demand for traps induced many smiths, east and west, to expand their manufactories. New trading companies entered the field, and posts came into existence at strategic spots on the Missouri and its major tributaries. Some of these posts maintained blacksmith shops of considerable productiveness; however, the greater number of steel traps came up the Missouri from the smithies in St. Louis or, as in the past, were transported from the shops on the eastern seaboard via Pittsburgh, the Ohio River, and the Mississippi-Missouri routes.

The American Fur Company's emporium at Michilimackinac distributed large numbers of beaver traps during the 1820's to its outposts in Wisconsin, Michigan, Minnesota, Illinois, and the lower Mississippi regions. Most of these trading posts were reached by boat from Lakes Superior and Michigan and via por-

[1] Charles J. Kappler, ed.: *Indian Affairs, Laws and Treaties* (Washington, D.C.: Gov't Printing Office; 1904), II, 143.

[2] In the Account Book, opening with an entry of April 13, 1805, Office of Indian Trade, George Town, D.C., an order is recorded: "100 lbs best German steel for springs for traps," to be purchased from J. Goetz, Philadelphia, December 17, 1808. (Hopkins: "Report on Indian Trade Objects," p. 7.)

tages from the Mississippi and its tributaries. The headquarters at Michilimackinac obtained its supplies from Montreal and New York. A revealing account of the business transacted is found in the great American Fur Company Invoice Book, Michilimackinac, 1821-2 (MS), preserved in the Chicago Historical Society Library. The beaver traps contained in this record range in value from $1.60 to $4.00 each. Some came from Montreal, but many were made in the Mackinac shops. The wide range in prices cannot be attributed to differences in the costs of materials over a period of years, for the records all pertain to 1821-2. Both the cheapest and the most costly grades are traced to their origin in Montreal. Those classed as "Mackina" are consistently listed at $3.50 each, with chain. We may assume that these were the five-pound type which after 1830 seems to have been preferred by most of the mountain men.

By 1835 the "management" of the American Fur Company, New York City, took exception to the cost of the Mackinac traps. Ramsay Crooks wrote to the Mackinac agent, Samuel Abbott, February 19, 1835: "Your beaver traps cost too much. I can get as good, if not better, made here [New York] for $1.50, six months credit. So we had better break up the Mackinac shop if our blacksmiths cannot produce more work than they have done thus far." Abbott replied on April 9, 1835: "When I set up the record of costs of the 100 beaver traps made by our blacksmiths I was fearful that my figure would be too low, and I charged a large price for the use of the shop and tools. Reducing this shop charge to a proper one, each trap costs $1.58. . . . I remind also, that the wages of the mechanics are paid in goods at a profit to the Company of 50%."[3]

The watchful Mr. Crooks also observed in the accounts of the company's Detroit establishment some evidences of wastefulness in trap transactions. On January 20, 1835, Crooks addressed the Detroit agent, William Brewster: "Do not make more contracts for traps, tomahawks, axes, or grubbing hoes, and the like. We can get better beaver traps here than up the country, and cheaper too. Let me have the list of iron works you want next year." Brewster

[3] American Fur Company Papers, 1831–49, MS Collections, The New-York Historical Society, Letter Book 1, items No. 245 and No. 373.

conformed; his order for "iron works" to be manufactured in New York is dated February 14, 1835.[4]

Individual design of trap mechanism promoted by various blacksmiths engaged in making traps gradually yielded to a preponderant demand for the standardized beaver trap of demonstrated effectiveness. By the early 1820's, when enterprising American trappers and traders advanced in numbers upon the Rocky Mountains and to the river systems west of the Rockies, a purchaser could be reasonably confident of obtaining a satisfactory beaver trap of given weight in response to his written order.

Yet even the standardized design permitted of some originality in proportioning and shaping the working parts of the trap. The preference shown by some trappers for single-pin jaw posts instead of two pins (one for each jaw) is a case in point. Pratt, Chouteau & Company, St. Louis, in 1834 desired that the head office of the American Fur Company, New York, procure Eastern-made traps for its Missouri River trade, but no chances were taken regarding full understanding of the details of trap structure wanted; pattern traps were sent with the order.

Upon receipt of the order, Ramsay Crooks invited his favored blacksmith, Miles Standish, to confer with him. The personal interview was then confirmed in writing:

Specifications of traps to be manufactured for the American Fur Co., by Mr. Miles Standish, no. 93 Perry St., and to be ready for

shipment 1st Feb. 1835 under marginal marking P C & CO.

35

A

| 200 beaver traps St. Louis pattern | @ $1.50 |
| 800 muskrat traps with two springs | @ .75 |

Note: These articles are to be of your very best work and fully equal in quality to any you ever made. They are to be packed carefully and securely in good strong pine boxes. The beaver traps 25 in a box, the muskrat traps 50 in a box. . . . Your packing boxes have not heretofore been as good as they ought to be, and I wish to see one before you pack the goods. Payment in 6 months

---

[4] Ibid., items Nos. 162 and 230.

after delivery to store no. 45 Liberty Street, or in cash less 3½% discount at option of the Company.[5]

Not always did the fur companies supply a pattern in ordering traps. In January 1832 Nathaniel J. Wyeth, then embarking upon his venture in the Western fur trade, wrote to his brothers in New York and to the firm of A. Norris and Company, New York, asking them to "ascertain if Beaver Trapss can be had in your city. Those wanted should weigh 5 lbs. [with chains], have double springs, jaws without teeth, and chains 6 feet long, with two swivels in them. Of these I want 40 dozen." On February 13, 1832, Wyeth ordered from Davenport and Byron, New York City, "20 dozen of the traps such as you name and such as used by Mr. Astor." Apparently the traps in this batch were satisfactory, and to make sure that the next lot would be like them, one trap was held as a

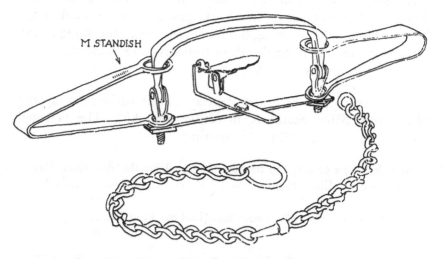

FIG. 30. *Beaver Trap by Miles Standish c. 1835.*

Reasonably, we may assume that this is one of the beaver traps of "St. Louis pattern" procured by Pratt, Chouteau & Co., St. Louis, from the New York trapmaker Miles Standish. The specimen is owned by the Museum of the Fur Trade, Chadron, Nebraska, and the sketch is based upon a photograph lent by Mr. Charles E. Hanson. Another "M. Standish" beaver trap is at Chadron (No. 568), which "was found on the site of a Pawnee village recorded as burned by the Delaware in 1844." (Letter, Hanson to Russell, November 11, 1964.)

[5] The order (MS) is found in the file "MEMORANDUMS, Vol. 1, 1834–40," American Fur Company Papers. The microfilm copy of the Papers provides it in Reel 20.

model. On February 4, 1834, Wyeth wrote to Tucker and Williams, Boston, Massachusetts: "They [beaver traps] should be equally well finished with the pattern, and by contract, are to be set for one week, and then be rejected if the springs do not come up fair or are broken." The price agreed upon was $165.00 for 100 traps of proven quality.[6] Traps of this general character are shown in figures 25, 26, and 27. As might be expected, the value of the trap increased mightily when it reached the Western fur fields.[7]

Sometimes the beaver hunters did not fare as well as Wyeth in procuring dependable traps. Even the experienced Ewing Young was caught napping when he purchased traps for his 1831 expedition bound for California. Young, then a veteran with ten years' successful trapping behind him, bought New Mexico traps in Taos or Santa Fe with which to outfit his firm, Jackson, Waldo and Company. Practical trial of the traps apparently was not a part of Young's inspection procedure. Young personally led a party of thirty-six trappers from Taos to the Gila River, thence to the Colorado. En route it became obvious that beaver were not being held by the new traps, but it was not until the expedition had passed the Colorado that the failure was explained; the upper eyes, or bows, of many of the trap springs were too large to close the jaws tightly. J. J. Warner, employee of Jackson, Waldo and Company records the incident.[8]

A somewhat similar en masse trap failure is brought to light in the American Fur Company correspondence preserved in The

[6] F. G. Young, ed.: *The Correspondence and Journals of Captain Nathaniel J. Wyeth, 1831–1836* (Eugene, Ore.: Univ. Press; 1899), pp. 28, 33, 39, 107.

[7] John Colter at the Minataree villages on the Missouri in 1809 sold a "set" of traps, presumably six, to Thomas James for $120.00. See Walter B. Douglas, ed.: *Thomas James, Three Years among the Indians and Mexicans* (St. Louis: Missouri Historical Soc.; 1916), p. 35. On July 9, 1832, Fort Union (American Fur Co.) billed Johnson Gardner for 16 traps at $12.00 each. Gardner turned in 16 beaver traps at Fort Pierre in 1833 and was credited by the American Fur Co. with $192.00. See Hiram M. Chittenden: *The American Fur Trade of the Far West* (2 vols.; Stanford, Cal.: Stanford Univ. Press; 1954), II, 943, 945. Beaver traps were included in the surplus merchandise sold by William H. Ashley to Smith, Jackson, and Sublette after the 1826 rendezvous in Cache Valley, Utah. They were inventoried at $9.00 each. Chittenden: *American Fur Trade* (3 vols.; New York, 1902), I, 5; Maurice S. Sullivan, ed.: *The Travels of Jedediah Smith* (Santa Ana, Cal., 1934), p. 26, identifies the site of the rendezvous.

[8] Warner was not with Young during the trip west, but the two were associated in Los Angeles as soon as Young reached that town. Young was still voicing exasperation. J. J. Warner: "Reminiscences of Early California, 1831–46," *Annual Pubs. of the Hist. Soc. of S. Cal.*, VII (1907–8), 186. See also Warner's MS "Reminiscences" in the Bancroft Library.

New-York Historical Society's Manuscript Collections. Samuel Abbott, writing from his post (Mackinac) on June 28, 1841, informed Ramsay Crooks, head of the company in New York: "This day some of my Indian hunters have arrived and brought back all the beaver traps of last year which were sold to them here. They state that the traps are entirely too small. The springs are good but the jaws are not in proportion. They are too small for the springs and otter and beaver escape from them." Abbott added that John Lawe, agent at Green Bay, Wisconsin, experienced the same loss due to the same fault in the traps of 1840.

Contemporary accounts of field experiences with trap mechanisms are very few in the existing records. Trappers did much better in handing down to us their notes on the use of traps in taking beaver. The picture of faulty construction, breakage, deterioration, and the raw materials for manufacture and repair of traps is for the most part hidden except as partially revealed through current archeological studies. Outstanding among these investigations are the excavations of historic fur-trade sites in the Columbia River Basin conducted under the supervision of Louis R. Caywood, Thomas R. Garth, Donald Collier, Alfred E. Hudson, Arlo Ford, and a few others. Much of the more recent work was done under the auspices of the National Park Service in cooperation with the University of Washington, the Washington State Parks and Recreation Commission, various state and county offices, and other Washington and Oregon institutions. The Coulee Dam locality, Fort Clatsop, Fort Spokane, Fort Walla Walla, Fort Okanogan and, most important, Fort Vancouver, were excavated and reported upon.[9]

At these historic centers the "junk" of the fur traders was dug from the earth. Shop floors, old garbage dumps, trash piles, and

[9] Louis R. Caywood: "Excavating Fort Vancouver," *The Beaver* (March 1948); *Exploratory Excavations at Fort Spokane.* (Vancouver, Wash.: Nat'l Park Serv.; 1950); *Archeological Excavations at Fort Spokane, 1951, 1952, and 1953* (Nat'l Park Serv., Region Four; 1954); *Excavations at Two Okanogan Sites, 1952* (Nat'l Park Serv., Region Four; 1954); *Final Report Fort Vancouver Excavations* (Nat'l Park Serv., Region Four; 1955); John A. Hussey: *Preliminary Survey of the History and Physical Structure of Fort Vancouver* (Nat'l Park Serv., Region Four; 1949); *The History of Fort Vancouver* (Tacoma: Washington State Historical Soc.; 1957); Thomas R. Garth: "Archeological Excavations at Fort Walla Walla," *Pacific Northwest Quarterly*, XXXXIII: 1 (January 1952), 27–50; Donald Collier, Alfred E. Hudson, and Arlo Ford: "Archeology of the Upper Columbia Region," *Univ. of Washington Publications in Anthropology*, IX: 1 (1942), 1–178.

the pits of privies yielded the broken or worn-out relics of the life and works of the beaver hunters. Seldom are the crafts of artisans in the trading posts described in fur-trade documents, but to him who is prepared to interpret, the three-dimensional objects speak volubly on many aspects of this subject.

Fort Vancouver was the great cultural focal point and the central depot for supplies to be distributed to the outlying posts; so quite naturally the big finds were made there. In the tons of artifact material recovered during four years of digging at Fort Vancouver are 95,846 pieces of iron. Steel traps are well represented; in fact, more trap fragments were found here than have been unearthed at any one historic site on the continent. Caywood provides drawings and an interesting analysis of this unique trap material.[1]

Since Fort Vancouver was the emporium of the Hudson's Bay Company for the entire Far West from 1824 to 1860, it might be assumed that the recovered trap fragments invariably are representative of Hudson's Bay Company traps. Such a conclusion might be criticized, however, because some worn or damaged traps from Okanogan, Spokane, Walla Walla, and the old Fort George (Astoria) localities in all probability were brought to the base at Fort Vancouver, thus introducing trap parts of the North West Company and of U. S. origin. Generally, however, the traps (fragments) dug up at Fort Vancouver display a few fairly constant characteristics that seem to distinguish them. The chains, for example, consist of smooth, uniform links slightly more than one inch long. These chains contrast sharply with the long, hand-forged links on many of the mountain-man traps of U. S. origin (see fig. 29). Possibly, the small-link trap chains at Fort Vancouver were received in the voluminous shipments of ironworks that the Hudson's Bay Company imported from England.

The jaws of many of the Fort Vancouver traps show a gentle curve like the curve of the modern Newhouse jaws; a majority of the older mountain-man beaver traps of U. S. origin are sharply rectangular in silhouette (figs. 26e and 26f). However, the foregoing characteristics cannot be accepted as diagnostic. As Caywood observed, "After 4 seasons' excavations it is still difficult to determine from broken parts the exact kinds of traps made at Fort Vancouver. The finished traps probably were moved to outlying posts and as time passed were broken, lost, buried, stolen, and

[1] Caywood: *Final Report*, pp. 42–4 and fig. 11.

discarded until now it is very difficult to find a complete trap dating from the fur trade period. . . . In the museums of the northwest, I failed to find any trap identical to the beaver trap parts found at Fort Vancouver. A few traps now in museums have been catalogued as being Hudson's Bay Company traps, but the specimens do not compare closely to the Fort Vancouver specimens. . . . Analysis of the iron in old traps known to have been made in the United States as compared with an analysis of the iron in Fort Vancouver traps might provide a determination." [2] Caywood estimates that the number of traps on inventory at any one time for all the Hudson's Bay Company posts on the Columbia "must have been several thousand." [3] The senior blacksmith responsible for the production and maintenance of this hardware, William Cannon,[4] a Kentuckian who came to the Columbia with the Astorians, must have been very familiar with the characteristics of the beaver traps made and used by the Americans. It does not follow, however, that he did not adopt a trap of somewhat different detail when he became an employee of the Hudson's Bay Company.

Whatever be the perplexities arising from the tremendous array of detailed evidences offered by the small parts of Fort Vancouver traps, it may be said rightly that the fur brigades of the Hudson's Bay Company, Columbia District, used a well-made beaver trap of medium weight which in its basic design was like the traps made in Philadelphia, Baltimore, New York, and Boston since the 1750's. The Rupert House trap (fig. 31), provides an excellent example of the Hudson's Bay Company model.

Of the scores of blacksmiths who manufactured steel traps during the period with which we are concerned, only a very few are identified in the fur-trade documents. As a step toward gathering information on more of these craftsmen, it seems worthwhile to list chronologically the known trapmakers, fragmentary though that itemization may be. All these men have been previously mentioned.

1767. Baltzer Geere, Philadelphia, supplied beaver traps to the firm of wholesalers, Baynton, Wharton and Morgan.

C. 1800. The father of William Chew, Atsion Meadows, New

---

[2] Caywood: *Final Report*, pp. 42–3. It is to be noted that Mr. Caywood did not see the traps from the Siuslaw River now in the Oregon Historical Society collections (pages 120, 122).

[3] Ibid., p. 42.

[4] William Cannon receives some further notice on page 140.

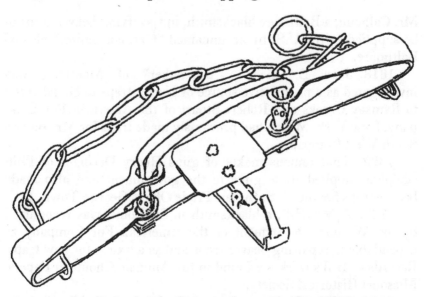

FIG. 31. *Hudson's Bay Company Beaver Trap from Vicinity of Rupert House.*

Hand-forged and marked on the cross under the pan "Kenneth McLeod." Weight of trap, 3 pounds, 8 ounces; with chain, the total weight is 4 pounds, 7 ounces. The jaws are 7¾ inches long and they stand 5½ inches above the base. In size and general style this Hudson's Bay Company trap resembles the early handmade Newhouse beaver trap, and many of its parts are similar to corresponding trap fragments recovered at the historic Hudson's Bay Company site, Fort Vancouver—similar but not identical. The Rupert House specimen stands as another testimonial to the proposition that in the later day of individual hand-crafting a standard design for beaver traps was recognized, north and south. That standard design persisted after the advent in the 1850's of machine-made traps and continues in the No. 4 trap of today. This specimen is in the Dr. R. S. Shankland Collection. The sketch is based upon a photograph and detailed description provided by Dr. Shankland.

Jersey, is reported to have manufactured steel traps of beaver size for the Mullica River trade. Specimens of his work are preserved in the museum of the Bucks County Historical Society, Doylestown, Pennsylvania.

1808. A Mr. Lamb of Baltimore made traps for the U. S. Indian Trade Office, George Town, D.C.

1809. The U. S. Indian Office used a model trap made by a

Mr. Calhoun, a Baltimore blacksmith, in specifying beaver traps to be supplied to the U.S. by an unnamed "German Smith," also of Baltimore.

1818. Jean B. Macon, "trapmaker" of Montreal, was investigated as a prospective source of beaver traps to be delivered to Ramsay Crooks and Robert Stuart of the American Fur Company, New York. Macon had previously made traps for Mr. Astor's South West Company.

1822. That famous maker of guns Henry Deringer of Philadelphia supplied trade guns to the government and also made beaver traps for the U. S. Indian Trade Office, George Town, D.C.

1823. A Mr. Hill, a blacksmith in St. Louis, was recognized by the Western Department of the American Fur Company as dependable in repairing beaver traps and as a source for new traps. Records of Hill's work are found in the Auguste Chouteau Papers, Missouri Historical Society.

1834–5. The Chouteau firm of St. Louis (subsidiary of the American Fur Company) believed so strongly in the merits of their "St. Louis pattern" beaver trap as to demand of Ramsay Crooks that any traps made for them in the East be exact copies of models submitted by them. The trapmaker Miles Standish, 93 Perry Street, New York, was brought into conference with Crooks when such special orders were placed with Standish. In some particulars, the Standish traps are much like the undated Hudson's Bay Company trap by Kenneth McLeod (fig. 31).

1840's. Thomas Moore, a Hudson's Bay Company blacksmith at Fort Vancouver, is reported to be the maker of certain traps of the English rattrap style now preserved in Oregon collections. However, the master blacksmith of the Hudson's Bay Company, for Fort Vancouver and the entire Columbia District, was the Kentuckian William Cannon, who had come to the Columbia in 1811 with the overland Astorians. In other words, Cannon had worked for Mr. Astor and for the North West Company at Fort George (Astoria) for thirteen years prior to his participation in the establishment of Fort Vancouver by the Hudson's Bay Company in 1824–5. For more than thirty years he directed the big program of ironworks done at the several forges at Fort Vancouver, and when the company withdrew from the place in 1860, he retired to French Prairie. He died there about five years later. The National Park

Service archeologist Louis Caywood, appreciative of the big and very revealing collection of iron artifacts dug from the ground at Cannon's principal seat of action, remarked: "Mr. Cannon must have been a busy blacksmith! An interesting story of his life and works should be researched and written. At any rate, an instructive diorama showing him at his forge could be made for a museum."

1848. Among the trapmakers of the early decades of the nineteenth century only one established himself so firmly in the minds of his contemporaries and in the history of the industry as to perpetuate his name in the modern trade. Sewell Newhouse, as a boy in New York State in 1823, made traps for his personal use and for sale to his Indian friends, some of whom were moved by the government to Wisconsin. These traps went with them. During the next twenty years, Newhouse expanded his industry until his output was two thousand traps per year, and the fame of the quality of his hand-forged product spread widely through the land. In 1848 the Newhouse family became members of the Oneida Community, which identified itself with the Newhouse trap. The industry was converted from the hand-work stage to the machine-enterprise with no change in the design of the trap which is still on the market. The name Newhouse continues to be synonymous with the best of steel traps.[5]

Machine-made traps of the period following the establishment of the Oneida Community that attempted to compete with the Oneida Newhouse trap appear in a very few museum collections. These are later than the mountain-man period but they deserve mention.

The Colorado Historical Society, Denver, has a double-spring trap (catalog no. OH 113), upon the pan of which is stamped "S & W Co. No. 3" or "P S & W Co. No. 3." Its construction seems to be identical with that of the Newhouse trap. It is said to have found use in Colorado in the 1860's by J. B. Donovan. A trap of average beaver size and design bears No. $\frac{27937}{6629}$ in the Milwaukee Public Museum. Stamped in the metal is "Bonner and Hedges." It is reported to have come from Canada. The W. C. Lawrence Collec-

---

[5] A. R. Harding: *Steel Traps*, p. 26. See also Newhouse: *The Trapper's Guide* (1867 edn.), pp. 208–12; S. P. Young: "The Evolution of the Steel Wolf Trap," pp. 10–11, 30; and McCracken: *How to Catch More Fur*, pp. 27, 29.

tion, Jackson, Wyoming, contains a trap in excellent condition that is marked on the pan "Sargent & Co. No. 4." The specimen differs in no visible way from a Newhouse No. 4. It was found in 1915 near the north end of Jackson Lake on ground that is now underwater.

Mr. S. R. Leonard,[6] long-time official of the Oneida Community, identifies two additional competitors: Hart Brothers, of Unionville, Connecticut, and Peck, Stowe and Wilcox, another New England firm. Traps by Hart Brothers (early Blake & Lamb) do not seem to be in any collections examined by the present author. Mr. Leonard also tells of five brand names other than Newhouse used by the Oneida Community for different types and grades of traps produced by its factories. Beginning in 1874 the "Hawley & Norton," named for Alfred Hawley and John Norton of the Oneida organization, was manufactured for many years and in great numbers, until January 1915. In quality it was in its time second only to the Newhouse. Beginning in 1886, the "Victor" was made and it continues to this day to be the best-known trap. The "all steel" (no malleable iron) was manufactured from 1890 through 1896. The "jump" trap appeared in 1896 and is still on the market. In 1905, and for a few years thereafter, the "Blake" made a bid for favor.

The relative popularity of these several brands of Oneida Community traps is suggested by the following sales records for a twenty-five-year period, exact years not known to the author.

Type	Total Number Manufactured
Victor	13,278,023
Hawley & Norton	5,696,719
Newhouse	2,123,120
All steel	1,387,714
Jump	687,328
Blake	214,195

[6] Personal letters, S. R. Leonard to C. P. Russell, January 29, February 29, and March 14, 1960. Mr. Stephen R. Leonard of Oneida, New York, made a career within the Oneida Community, Ltd. In 1895 he graduated from Cornell University and immediately went to work in the Oneida shops in Sherrill, New York. He continued with the Oneida Company until his retirement. At the age of eighty-seven he provided the National Park Service and the present author with valuable unpublished notes on Newhouse and the trap industry as developed by the Oneida Community. Accounts of early procedures in trapmaking were obtained by Mr. Leonard from some of his predecessors in the pioneer trap industry. The statistics herewith of production were assembled by Mr. Leonard and are used with permission.

Sportsman's magazines and trade journals of the past half century reveal the onetime existence of a number of additional steel-trap manufactories:

W. A. Gibbs and Son made the "Gibbs" and "Triumph" traps. The business was sold to the Animal Trap Company of America in 1936.

Lester A. Beardsley made the "Diamond" trap; sold to Animal Trap Company of America in 1944.

Pratt Manufacturing Company, Joliet, Illinois; sold to Animal Trap Company of America, 1937.

Charles D. Birdell, Crisfield, Maryland; sold to Animal Trap Company of America in 1939.

Lovell Manufacturing Company, Erie, Pennsylvania; sold to Animal Trap Company of America in 1947.

"Currently the Hawkins Company, South Britain, Connecticut, manufactures the historic Blake and Lamb long-spring and jump traps. Samuel S. Hart of the Hawkins Company states that there was interruption of the early series of long-spring traps, but that manufacture was resumed in 1929–1930, and continues today."

Traps bearing the brand names "Eclipse," "Kangaroo," and "Arros" (origins not known to the writer) are sometimes seen in collections. Occasionally steel traps of foreign makes, such as Maison Moriceau, Bourdon & Benoit, and E. Aurouze, all of Paris, France, appear in American museums. A few products of skilled American blacksmiths, who made no pretense of competing in the trade but took pleasure in making a limited number of hand-wrought traps for friends or for their personal use, have been preserved. Such is the rugged specimen with 11-inch jaws by Mathias Luppold, which is owned and exhibited by the Missouri Historical Society, St. Louis. Another example in this category is the D. Crossett trap, Kenosha Historical Society, pictured in figure 22. Both Luppold and Crossett were active in the 1850's.

Exclusive of unnumbered recent traps and innumerable trap fragments, seventy-six intact, old, handmade steel traps were handled, sketched, and photographed in making the present study. The specimens are preserved in twenty-four repositories in the United States and in four museums in Montreal, Quebec, Salzburg, and Vienna.

Outstanding among the collections in the United States are eight which seem to the present writer to be especially noteworthy because of great size or because of special significance of their holdings:

Animal Trap Company of America, Lititz, Pennsylvania
Bucks County Historical Society, Doylestown, Pennsylvania
Fort Vancouver Museum, National Park Service, Vancouver, Washington (archeological recoveries)
Museum of the Frontier (W. C. Lawrence), Jackson, Wyoming
Museum of the Fur Trade, Chadron, Nebraska
Great Smoky Mountains History Museum, National Park Service, Great Smoky Mountains National Park (handmade bear traps)
Professor R. S. Shankland, Cleveland, Ohio (private collection; about 1,000 traps)

There are, of course, additional collections of traps that have not come to the author's attention. Some of the unidentified lots may deserve place among the "outstanding." As yet the business (or pleasures) of assembling historic steel traps has not become widely popular among American antiquarians.

How the Steel Trap Was Used by the Mountain Men

THE fur trade as conducted by the Americans in the Far West in the day of the mountain man was peculiarly a business in beaver. Along the lower Missouri, throughout the Mississippi Valley, and everywhere eastward, this was not so. In the appendix (p. 426) is a facsimile copy of the American Fur Company's detailed statement of fur returns for the State of Indiana for the winter of 1839–40. Seven agents and their sub-agents in Indiana collected 550,351 pelts and skins valued at $452,450.51. In this sizable "take" were 892 beaver pelts valued at $4,558.13, about one per cent of the whole. Business of this character could be cited for many of the states in the Mississippi Basin.

It should not be understood that only beaver existed on the high plains and in the Rockies. The records of American companies that maintained trading posts on the upper Missouri and the records of business conducted by the Hudson's Bay Company in

Far Western establishments show that fox, lynx, marten, muskrat, otter, etc., as well as beaver, were purchased from Indian and white trappers who brought such peltry to the trading posts. The standard to which all these other furs were reduced and by which the trappers were paid was the beaver. In 1821, for example, the Hudson's Bay Company adhered to the following scale: [7]

Type	"Made Beaver"
Beaver, full grown	1 = 1
Beaver, cub	1 = ½
Otter, prime, large	1 = 2
Otter, prime, small	1 = 1
Fox, black, prime	1 = 2
Fox, red, prime	1 = ½
Marten	1 = ⅓

The sale of merchandise—all manner of trade goods—was accomplished through pricing in the terms of "made beaver." In other words, the beaver pelt was the base for the Far Western system of settling debits and credits without the actual transference of money.

The mountain man in his haunts on the upper Missouri, the Colorado system, the Snake, and the Columbia, worked the beaver waters rather than the dry uplands. The beaver was his special quarry, his consuming interest; his packs were filled with beaver pelts, not with a mixed collection of furs. To this end, his traps were set in beaver habitat—the willow-fringed streams and ponds and the boggy meadows in cottonwood country.

The published testimonials of the mountain men are replete with descriptions of their method of trapping beaver.[8] There are minor differences in the descriptions, but generally one basic method of placing the steel trap was used by all. It is shown in figures 33 and 34. It is the good fortune of students of fur-trade

[7] From the diary of Nicholas Garry, 1821, quoted by Innis: *The Fur Trade in Canada* (1962 edn.), p. 319.

[8] Frances Fuller Victor: *The River of the West* (Hartford, 1870), pp. 64–5 (Joseph Meek's experiences); Washington Irving: *The Adventures of Captain Bonneville, U.S.A.* (New York, 1849), pp. 226–77; J. S. Campion: *On the Frontier* (London, 1878), pp. 156–65; William Baillile-Grohman: *Camps in the Rockies* (1882), pp. 249–54 (description based on interviews with old-timers). Recent writers have published interpretations of the contemporary accounts of trapping: Chittenden: *The American Fur Trade* (1954 edn.), II, 820–1; Bernard De Voto: *Across the Wide Missouri*, pp. 156–60.

FIG. 32.   *The Beaver and Its Green River Habitat.*

To the uninitiated, the large expanses of sagebrush country west of the Rockies may not appear to be wet enough to attract the water-loving beaver. In reality, however, the sage-filled basins are often laced by numerous small streams, and the small streams unite to form rivers. Along all of the "forks" and rivers are abundant growths of willow, and often the level terrain also supports groves of cottonwood. Both willow and cottonwood provide food favored by the beaver. In the earliest days of the mountain man some of these vast valleys held such concentrations of beaver as to encourage the hunter to kill his quarry with a club.

The Green River country shown here, and scores of similar basins in the Snake River drainage, along the Humboldt, the Bear, the Uintah, the Virgin, the Sevier, and the Central Valley of California, to mention but a few, offered rewarding trapping grounds frequented by the mountain men in the Far West. Glen Dines drawing.

history to have at hand the works of an accomplished artist who journeyed to the heart of the mountain man's realm during the heyday of the beaver business. Alfred Jacob Miller, a youthful Baltimore artist, accompanied the 1837 caravan of Pratte, Chouteau and Company from Independence to the Green River rendezvous, Tom Fitzpatrick in command. Miller sketched and painted during his every waking hour, capturing on his sketch pads an amazing record of any and all details of trader-trapper activities in the fur

FIG. 33. *Making the Set.*

This Mulcahy drawing is in the Jefferson National Expansion Memorial, St. Louis.

fields. To him we are indebted for an eyewitness depiction of two mountain men "making the set" for beaver. Miller's original sketch was in the care of the Peale Museum, Baltimore, for many years.[9] It was there that Macgill James, director, made it available for reference to Mr. Mulcahy, National Park Service artist, who prepared the pen-and-ink drawing for figure 33. Regarding his original, Miller wrote: "In hunting the beaver two or more trappers are usually in company. . . . With all the caution the poor trappers take, they cannot always escape the lynx-eyes of the Indians. The dreadful war-whoop with bullets or arrows about their ears, are the first intimations of danger. They are destroyed in this way from

[9] Miller made and brought home more than two hundred field sketches, most of them in watercolor. After 1933, 163 of them were lent by the Miller family to the Peale Museum, Baltimore. A large part of this collection of originals was purchased by Mrs. Clyde Porter, Kansas City, in 1936. She made them available for public viewing in a number of cities, east and west. The collection now is owned by the Joslyn Memorial, Omaha. In addition to the numerous large oil paintings made by Miller from these field sketches, several sets of copies of the small, on-the-spot drawings were also prepared by him in his Baltimore studio. One set is owned by the Walters Art Gallery, Baltimore. It provided the substance of the valuable work *The West of Alfred Jacob Miller*, ed. Marvin Ross (Norman, Okla., 1951).

time to time, and 'lost' until by a mere chance their bones are found bleaching on the borders of some stream where they have hunted." [1]

The diagram in figure 34 clarifies the picture of setting and baiting the trap and drowning the captured prize. The trapper, having found the "sign" of fresh activities of beaver, concentrated his trap-setting along the waters where the animals were "using." To avoid disturbing the animals, the search for suitable places to "set" was made, so far as possible, while wading along the banks of stream or pond. Thus little or no human scent was left at the set.

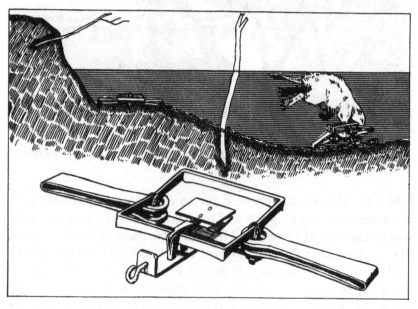

FIG. 34.　*The Beaver "Set."*
This drawing is by Glen Dines.

When a likely spot was found, a bed for the trap was prepared underwater in such a manner as to assure that the pan and spread jaws of the trap would be about four inches below the surface of the water. This may have involved cutting into the mud or sand to make a depression, or it might have been necessary to scrape up a mound. The springs of a beaver trap are readily depressed by the

[1] No. 140 in Alfred J. Miller: "Rough Draughts for Notes to Indian Sketches" (n.d.) (MS), 66 typed pages copied in 1935 from Miller's long-hand notes for 166 drawings (Washington, D.C.: National Park Service).

weight of a man standing with a foot on each spring. This implies that the base of the trap rests on firm ground or upon the hard bed of a stream or pond in shallow water. On those occasions when the trap could not rest on a solid surface, the springs were generally depressed with a "squeezer" device made with two strong sticks about eighteen inches long that the trapper carried for this special purpose. The sticks were held side by side and a thong, strong cord, or a leather strap with buckle was wrapped around one end. The other ends of the sticks were then pulled apart and the bow ends of one of the steel springs were placed between the sticks. Using both hands on the free ends of the sticks, the trapper squeezed the spring until it was fully depressed, whereupon he wrapped and fastened a second strap or cord around the free ends of the sticks, thus holding one spring in depressed position. With another pair of sticks and a third strap or cord, he squeezed the other steel spring, spread the trap jaws, and engaged the dog in the pan notch. Thus the jaws were held open in set position, and the sticks were then removed. When the set trap had been adjusted on the underwater bed, the trap chain was extended its full length outward to deeper water, and a trap stake, or "float stick," was passed through the ring at the end of the chain, and driven deep into the bottom. A dry, hard pole of dead wood always was selected to serve as trap stake because a freshly cut, succulent piece with the bark on it might have been gnawed by the beaver for food. Usually precaution was taken by tying the chain ring to the stake with strong cord, thus making sure that the stake would be a float stick attached to the trap even though it would be pulled up from the muddy bottom by a captured beaver.

A final and important step was the placement of "bait." A wand or switch of willow or other pliable wood was cut to a length that would permit its small end to extend from the stream bank directly over the pan of the trap. The bark was scraped from this stick and castoreum from the bait bottle carried by the trapper was smeared on the small end of the switch. The bait stick was then jammed into the earth of the stream bank and adjusted so that its odoriferous end hung six inches or more above the trap. Thus the set was complete. The trapper then waded from the water some distance from the set.

The odor of castoreum wafting on the air in beaver country is not discernible to the human olfactory system, but the beaver's nose picks it up at a distance. In the breeding season it is especially compelling to the animal and the mountain man's bait surely attracted any beaver that came into the vicinity. In most cases, the animals made their approach from the water. The swimming beaver came to the bait and in lifting his nose toward the hanging attraction put down one or both front feet upon the pan of the trap. The released springs snapped the trap jaws shut upon the beaver's leg, and the frightened animal plunged for deep water, taking the trap with him. The weight of the trap held him in the depths, and there his drowned body awaited the trapper when next he made the rounds of his sets. A number of mountain men left contemporary testimony regarding their use of this set as regular practice (see page 145). Their statements, of course, do not mean that other sets were not in vogue.

Six traps generally made up the complement for a trapper and his helper. It usually took a full day to find suitable places to prepare the set, to make the rounds of the traps, to skin the captured animals, and to flesh the pelts. Under favorable conditions, a skilled trapper could be sure of taking a beaver at each set. Under some circumstances, certain traps could be visited twice in one day, thus improving the average of six pelts per day. If the trapper was working out of a large central camp in association with numerous trappers, clerks, cooks, and handymen organized under a company system, he could turn over his freshly skinned pelts to a camp employee for stretching and drying. If the party was small, the work of stretching pelts was done by the same men who caught the animals. In either case, the skinning was done in the vicinity where the animal was trapped and, unless meat was in short supply, only the pelt and perhaps the castoreum glands and the tail were carried to camp. Roasted beaver tails were one of the delicacies of the trapper's mess, and the entire carcass was decidedly edible, if needed.

Indians "caught on" to the white man's method of preparing beaver pelts readily enough upon being shown what was wanted. Frenchmen from St. Louis and English and French traders from the North West Company and the Hudson's Bay Company posts in Canada had instructed such Missouri River tribes as the Assiniboin, Minnetaree, Mandan, and Arikara long prior to the arrival of Lewis and Clark at the Mandan villages in 1804. Steel traps had been acquired through trade and by theft by a few of these Indians,[2] and they followed the conventional method of preparing beaver pelts for trade. The arrival of Lewis and Clark at the Mandans stirred the officers of the North West Company to extend their influence and their beaver trade to some other tribes not yet indoctrinated in the white man's art of trapping and skinning beaver. François Antoine Larocque, a leader of North West Company parties from the British post on the Assiniboine, paid several visits to Lewis and Clark at Fort Mandan during the winter of

FIG. 35.   *The Nor'wester Larocque on the Yellowstone (1805) Demonstrating to Crow Indians the Method of Skinning Beaver and Stretching the Pelt.*

The prescribed procedure was to slit the skin down the length of the animal's belly, with transverse cuts along the inside of each leg. The feet were cut off; the tail remained with the body, unless it was to be removed to serve as a tidbit on the trapper's supper plate. When the pelt had been removed from the carcass, it was scraped with a sharp knife or ax blade to free it from fat and shreds of flesh. In order to dry it quickly and uniformly, it was stretched smoothly on a hoop made by bending a willow withe of proper length held in circular form by binding the ends together. The edges of the beaver pelt then were sewed with sinew or cord to the hoop, thus making a flat, round plew which, when dry, resisted insect attacks. Mulcahy drawing, Jefferson National Expansion Memorial, St. Louis.

[2] Paul Allen, ed.: *History of the Expedition under the Command of Captains Lewis and Clark* (2 vols.; Philadelphia, 1814), I, 123.

1804–5. He requested and was refused the privilege of accompanying the explorers on their expedition westward. In June 1805, weeks after the Lewis and Clark party had moved up the Missouri, Larocque and a few white companions left the Mandan villages in the company of a party of Crows. They proceeded overland to the Yellowstone near the mouth of the Big Horn. This was the first white contact in the Crow country and the beginning of the North West Company's push to the Far West. Larocque encouraged the Crows to trap beaver and, as suggested in figure 35, instructed them in the method of preparing beaver pelts for the trade.[3] There must have been numerous occasions for similar lessons given to friendly Indians by white trappers on the high Plains and in the Rockies during the first decade of the nineteenth century, but the teachers did not write about their teaching. We do have Captain Wm. Clark's account of his confab with chiefs of the Cheyenne, who met the homeward bound expedition when it stopped at the "second" Arikara village, August 21–2, 1806. "As I was about to leave, the chief of the Cheyenne requested me to send some traders to them, that their country was full of beaver and they would then be encouraged to kill beaver, but now they had no use for them as they could get nothing for their skins and did not know well how to catch beaver. If white people would come amongst them they would learn how to take the beaver. I promised the Nation that I would inform their Great Father the President of the U States, and he would have them supplied."[4] Some of Manuel Lisa's mountain men, particularly John Colter[5] and George Drouillard,[6] made long marches into unknown Indian country on the Big Horn, Tongue, and the upper reaches of the Shoshone, Wind, and Snake rivers, 1807–8, for the express purpose of exploring the fur resources and, where practicable, encouraging the natives to catch, skin, and trade beaver. Lisa's post at the mouth of the Big Horn was, of course, the principal receiving point thus advertised. Neither Colter nor Drouillard wrote about their experiences, but in oral reports to William Clark in St. Louis they were sufficiently specific regard-

---

[3] L. J. Burpee, ed.: *Journal of Larocque from the Assiniboine to the Yellowstone, 1805*, Publications Canadian Archives, No. 3 (Ottawa, 1910).

[4] Allen, ed.: *History of the Expedition*, II, 413; Lewis and Clark *Journals*, quoted in De Voto: *Journals*, p. 463.

[5] Burton Harris: *John Colter* (New York: Charles Scribner's Sons; 1952).

[6] M. O. Skarsten: *George Drouillard . . .* (Glendale, Cal.: Arthur H. Clark Co.; 1964).

ing their travels to enable Clark to map their routes.[7] Apparently, most of the Indians contacted were scattered bands and established villages of Crows and Shoshone. The Shoshone later became a chief reliance of the mountain men as they conducted their trade via the rendezvous system. A number of Alfred J. Miller's sketches made in 1837 feature the first generation of Shoshone descended from Colter's friends of 1807. In thirty years many of them had become past masters of the beaver trap.

Figure 36 shows some of the personnel of a large American trapper party in camp on the shores of one of the upper Green River lakes. It was common practice for trappers attached to large parties to bring their freshly skinned beaver pelts to the clerk of the camp, who credited the trapper. "Camp-keepers" then stretched the pelts on willow hoops and hung them up to dry. Dried skins were carefully marked with the identifying sign of the company to which they belonged. This precaution sometimes "paid off" in important ways. In 1828 Jedediah Smith's party suffered a murderous attack by Umpqua River Indians at his camp on the Umpqua, a site now proposed for recognition as an Oregon State Historic Monument.[8] All but four white members of Smith's party were killed, and all properties, including the packs of furs, were seized and carried away by the Indians. Smith made his way to the Hudson's Bay Company establishment, Fort Vancouver, where Chief Factor John McLoughlin declared that the American properties would be recovered and the guilty Indians punished. Alexander Roderic McLeod was sent out at the head of a punitive expedition. Smith and the other three survivors of the massacre accompa-

---

[7] Colter's route appears on Clark's map of 1810. The final version of this map went from Clark to Nicholas Biddle, editor of the Lewis and Clark *Journals*, December 10, 1810. Biddle had it engraved, and it was distributed both as a separate and as a part of some sets of the 1814 *History* (Allen). Donald Jackson, ed.: *Letters of Lewis and Clark Expedition, 1783–1854* (Urbana: Univ. of Illinois Press; 1962), p. 564, concludes that Clark's original draft of the map is preserved in the Yale University Library. Merrill J. Mattes: "Jackson Hole, Crossroads of the Western Fur Trade," *Pacific Northwest Quarterly* (April 1946), pp. 91–3, analyzes the geographical problems posed by Colter's route. See also Merrill J. Mattes: "Behind the Legend of Colter's Hell," *Mississippi Valley Historical Review* (September 1949), pp. 258–9. In conference with George Drouillard in St. Louis, August and September 1808, William Clark made a map of Drouillard's travels of 1807–8. This manuscript map became the property of the Missouri Historical Society. M. O. Skarsten reproduced it in his *George Drouillard* as a large folded insert following p. 338. See Skarsten's analysis of Drouillard's route in ibid., pp. 259–70.

[8] National Park Service: *Parks for America* (1964), p. 445.

FIG. 36. *Stretching, Drying, and Marking Beaver Pelts.*

The American Fur Company clerk Warren Angus Ferris provided an excellent eyewitness description of such a camp scene as shown above. On May 15, 1832, "in a narrow bottom beneath the walls of Grays Creek [near the sources of the Blackfoot River, Idaho] we found a party of trappers, headed by Bridger, one of the partners in the R. M. F. [Rocky Mountain Fur] Company. Their encampment was decked with hundreds of beaver skins, now drying in the sun. These valuable skins are always stretched in willow hoops, varying from eighteen inches to three feet in diameter, according to the size of the skins, and have a reddish appearance on the flesh side, which is exposed to the sun. Our camps are always dotted with these red circles in the trapping season when the weather is fair. There were several hundred skins folded and tied up in packs laying about their encampment." (*Western Literary Messenger*, June 28, 1843, p. 406.) Mulcahy drawing, Jefferson National Expansion Memorial.

nied the party.[9] At the village where the greater number of the guilty Indians were camped, 588 beaver, 43 land otter, and 4 sea otter, together with steel traps and other equipment including 26 horses and mules, were surrendered. At other villages along the coast more equipment, including traps, and a few additional beaver were recovered. The half-breed Thomas McKay, McLeod's lieutenant on this expedition, is quoted as saying that the identification

[9] Dale L. Morgan: *Jedediah Smith and the Opening of the West* (Indianapolis: Bobbs-Merrill; 1953), pp. 274–9.

and recovery of the furs was made easier "as the American trappers mark all their skins." [1]

Another example: in the fall of 1833, Thomas Fitzpatrick of the Rocky Mountain Fur Company transported fifty-five packs of beaver skins from the Green River rendezvous. His pack train moved over South Pass to the Big Horn River, where other officers of the Rocky Mountain Fur Company loaded the beaver into bullboats destined for St. Louis via the Yellowstone and the Missouri. Fitzpatrick with his followers took their herd of horses to the Tongue River Valley, where he sought out a Crow village, intending to obtain permission to trap in the Crow country. Trapping proceeded while search was made for the Indians. Before Fitzpatrick could parley as planned, a band of Crows "robbed me and my men of everything." The plunder was traded by the Indians to agents of the American Fur Company at the Crow village. Sir William Drummond Stuart, who had traveled with Fitzpatrick, entered a written document into this story when he informed Kenneth McKenzie: "Fitzpatrick was robbed of 100 horses, all his merchandise, some beaver and traps, his capote, and even his watch." McKenzie, in charge at Fort Union, transmitted the news to Pierre Chouteau.[2] Fitzpatrick was well aware of the fact that the robbery had been arranged by his rivals in the American Fur Company.[3] The Crows confessed that they had been influenced by them and a local agent of the company admitted the truth of it. McKenzie, writing to that agent on January 8, 1834, proposed: "The 43 [stolen] Beaver skins traded [by the Crows] marked 'R. M. F. Co.', I would in the present instance give up if Mr. Fitzpatrick wishes to have them, on his paying the prices the articles traded for them were worth." [4] This was not exactly a benevolent gesture on the part of the American Fur Company, but McKenzie's letter serves to document the field practice in marking pelts.

The independent trapper Osborne Russell contributed another shred of evidence regarding marking. On the Big Horn River in

---

[1] Harrison Clifford Dale: *The Ashley-Smith Explorations . . . 1822–29* (Cleveland: A. H. Clark Co.; 1918), p. 275.

[2] Chittenden: *American Fur Trade* (1954 edn.), I, 301–2.

[3] Letter, Thomas Fitzpatrick to W. L. Sublette, November 13, 1833. Sublette MSS, Missouri Historical Society. Cited by Sunder: *Bill Sublette, Mountain Man* (Norman: Univ. of Oklahoma Press; 1959), p. 132.

[4] Chittenden: *American Fur Trade*, I, 302.

November 1837, a band of Crows relieved Russell's party of horses, most of their equipment, and their catch of beaver skins. Lucien Fontenelle of Fort William (Fort Laramie) connections encountered the Crows and forced them to surrender the horses, but he learned that the beaver had been traded at Portuguese Houses on the Powder River. Fontenelle went to this place and ordered the trader Antonio Montaro "to give me the key to his warehouse, which he reluctantly did. I then ordered my clerk to go in and take all the beaver skins he could find with your names [Russell's] marked upon them, and to have them carried to my camp, which was done without further ceremony." [5]

As the accumulating dried beaver pelts piled up in camps, they were pressed into compact bundles to facilitate handling. Dried pelts of the usual size weighed about 1½ pounds each. They were

FIG. 37. *A Fur Press in the Field.*

Even in the trapper camps far from the trading posts, crude presses were devised for compacting large accumulations of beaver pelts so that they might be packed on the backs of horses or mules or stowed in the bullboats, flatboats, or other small vessels used on the tributaries of the Missouri. Drawing by Mulcahy, Jefferson National Expansion Memorial, St. Louis.

[5] Osborne Russell: *Journal of a Trapper* (Boise, Idaho: Syms Fork Co.; 1921), p. 83.

folded once, fur side in, and pressed into a pack encased within a wrapper of dry deerskin. In the field, the camp attendants commonly employed the "chain, pole, and sapling press" [6] as pictured in figure 37. However, these presses were not as efficient as the large ones in the trading post, but nevertheless they compressed the furs sufficiently to permit their transportation in handy "pieces" on pack saddles or in small boats. About sixty pelts went into each pack; thus a pack weighed from 90 to 100 pounds and was worth between $300 and $600, depending upon the market at the time. Under normal circumstances two packs constituted a load for a pack animal. The pack trains carried their valuable cargoes to points on one or another of the Missouri tributaries served by dugouts, bullboats, scows, or other small craft that could descend to the river where larger boats plied. If the furs in question were owned by a large company that maintained a trading post on the Missouri, the travel-worn packs often received attention at the post. For example, the American Fur Company establishment Fort Union, at the mouth of the Yellowstone, sometimes received the cargoes of the company's boats which had come down the Big Horn and Yellowstone rivers. The packs of beaver skins were opened; the pelts were reconditioned and thoroughly dried, when necessary, then repacked. The fur press employed at the post was a far more powerful machine than the improvised pole-and-chain device used by the fieldmen at their backcountry camp. Two types of big presses [7] are shown in figure 38.

The wedge press could be made from raw materials available in the local countryside. To put the contrivance together the workman needed nothing more than hammer, saw, brace and bit, drawshave, and ax—tools that were always at hand in any trading post.

[6] This was a small edition of the press later employed by the buffalo-hide hunters. See Theodore Davis: "The Buffalo Range," *Harpers Monthly Magazine* (January 1869).

[7] For illustration of a screw press dating to 1805, see Elizabeth L. Gebhard: *The Life and Ventures of the Original John Jacob Astor* (Hudson, N.Y., 1915), p. 74. Contemporary accounts of pressing furs are found in: Henry Dee, ed.: *The Journal of John Work, 1835*, Archives of British Columbia, Memoir 10 (1945); E. H. Oliver, ed.: *The Canadian Northwest*, Publications of the Canadian Archives, No. 9 (2 vols.; 1914), II, 812; E. Coues, ed.: *The Expeditions of Zebulon Montgomery Pike* (3 vols.; New York: F. P. Harper; 1895), I, 284–5; Isaac Cowie: *The Company of Adventurers* (Toronto: W. Briggs; 1915), p. 105. Present-day procedure in pressing raw furs is described and illustrated in *The Beaver Magazine* (December 1937), p. 18; (September 1938), p. 66; (December 1945), p. 39; (December 1948), pp. 28–9.

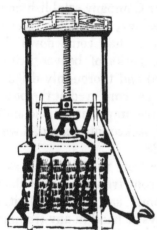

FIG. 38.   *Pressing Furs in the Trading Post.*

The wedge press (top) could be made from raw materials available in the countryside. The workman needed nothing more than hammer, saw, brace and bit, drawshave, and ax—tools that were always at hand in any trading post.

The screw press (bottom) was a factory-made machine, very powerful and heavy. It employed the same principle of operation that characterized the ancient massive fruit and wine presses of Europe; however, its screw, levers, frame, and plate were iron. William Macy drawings, Jefferson National Expansion Memorial, St. Louis.

Pressure was exerted upon the stack of some sixty pelts to be compressed by the simple process of driving wood wedges between the movable slabs placed above the furs within the frame of the press. Thongs or lengths of small rope encircled the pelts, passing through open channels in the base and in the block right above the pelts. When the furs were sufficiently compacted, the ends of the thongs were pulled tight and knotted securely. Removable stops above the series of slabs were then knocked out of the frame, thereby releasing the pressure, and the tied bundle of skins was removed from the press. Dried deerskins were folded tightly around the bundle and were laced or sewed to make a smooth cover. The "pack" was thus completed.

The heavy, powerful screw press was the ultimate in mechanical efficiency sought by the warehouse men in such great emporiums of the trade as St. Louis, Michilimackinac, Detroit, Sault Sainte Marie, and Grand Portage, all on waters navigable by sizable boats. The screw press of the old days was machine-made and very heavy. It usually was transported at great expense from the industrial city where it was manufactured to the fur centers mentioned.

The St. Louis Circuit Court records of 1821[8] throw interesting light upon the screw press as it was used in St. Louis. Michael E. Immel, clerk of the Missouri Fur Company, onetime officer in the U. S. Army, and an experienced fur trader, testified: "I know of three iron [screw] fur presses in this town of St. Louis—one at Berthold & Chouteau Company, one at Mr. Kennerly's (a public press), and one at Col. Auguste Chouteau's. One [out of town] is the property of the Missouri Fur Company." The ultimate accomplishment of the attorneys who questioned Immel in the course of this fur trader's law suit was the jury's favoring the Missouri Fur Company. Immel's testimony regarding marks left by his company's screw press upon beaver pelts, and regarding individual marks of ownership recognizable in a certain collection of pelts, was decisive in swaying the jury.

This trial grew out of a constable's seizure by search warrant of a quantity of beaver held in the William Easedale warehouse in St. Louis. The Missouri Fur Company had suffered a loss by theft

[8] "Trial of a suit between William Easdale, Plaintiff, and Thomas Hempstead, Defendant," St. Louis Circuit Court File, April Term, 1821, No. 71. A copy of the depositions in this court case was obtained by Charles E. Peterson, Jefferson National Expansion Memorial, who made them available to me.

of 500 pounds of beaver pelts and found reason to believe that the stolen skins were in the Easedale storage rooms. After the search-warrant action, Mr. Immel examined the seized furs and recognized them to be the stolen property. The entire lot was then retained by Thomas Hempstead of the Missouri Fur Company, and this seizure caused Easedale ("plaintiff") to bring suit against Hempstead and the company ("defendant") in an attempt to re-cover the seized pelts. The deposition by Immel in the course of the trial placed in the record some details of old-time procedures in marking and pressing beaver skins that are not to be found else-where. The record is extensive and interesting but much too long to be quoted here in its entirety. However, the following fragment is given because of its immediate significance:

A Mr. Bates in behalf of the defendant questioned: "What is the difference between a pack pressed at an iron press, and one pressed at a wooden press?"

Immel answered: "I find a very great difference. I can bring a pack in an iron press to half the size of one pressed in a wooden press. . . . The impression made on the skins by an iron press is such that it can not come off unless the skins are dampened with water. I found a good many skins among the parcel [seized from the plaintiff] that had the impression [made by the press of the Missouri Fur Company]."

Immel's damaging testimony in this connection was somewhat negated by his later statement that the screw press owned by the Berthold & Chouteau Company made a pack similar to that made by the Missouri Fur Company press—"the two presses were bought at the same time." However, the explicit and extensive testimony given by Immel regarding the trappers' or traders' marks on many of the seized beaver pelts seems to have convinced the jury that the 500 pounds of pelts in question were indeed the stolen furs. "The Jury find for the Defendant [the Missouri Fur Company]."

In conclusion, it should be said that a number of mountain men and their contemporaries in trading posts and central offices in St. Louis and New York handed down to us rather satisfying written accounts of procedures and processes pertaining to trapping and the handling of pelts. Less explanatory are their notes regarding the traps themselves. Yet the three-dimensional objects (old traps and parts of old traps) that survive, plus the fragmentary documentary evidences, make possible the reconstruction of parts of the steel-trap story.

It is a story that began earlier than has been generally assumed by antiquarians. As we have noted previously in the chapter, Englishmen in their homeland used a double-spring steel trap of sophisticated design in the 1500's, and it seems probable that the little machine had its beginnings long before that period. We may believe that elsewhere in Europe the steel trap found wide use during the same period, and we have concrete evidence that a "jump" trap fully comparable to the modern jump trap was in use in Austria during the 1600's.

Thereafter a great variety of devices were invented for the capture of animals. Most of these machines were iron and were designed to catch animals by the leg or legs, although some were of the "killer" type—so constructed that they would snap big jaws around the victim's neck or rib cage. Predominant were the smaller traps needed to kill pests around farm homes and to catch the fur bearers of wood lot and forest. Europeans who came to America sometimes brought these traps with them. Seventeenth-century records preserved in Virginia and Massachusetts testify to the use of steel traps by English colonists, and early eighteenth-century documents reveal that steel traps were then in general use by beaver trappers north and south. The early beaver traps were of various designs, but by the middle of the eighteenth century, a double-spring trap of a certain style and weight had become the favored trap for beaver. It was but little different from the present-day No. 4 trap still used for beaver.

During the first years of the nineteenth century, a few American blacksmiths in Baltimore, Philadelphia, New York, and Montreal perfected the details of the mechanism of this trap and improved their techniques in producing this "best" beaver trap, adhering to the style that during a half century of use had demonstrated its worth and had received the expressed preference of many professional trappers. In effect, the beaver trap was "standardized," although it was still handmade. Blacksmiths in a number of places in addition to those mentioned then did their best to meet the growing demand for this style of beaver trap. Not always did the American smithies keep up with the demands; in the beginning years John Jacob Astor called upon Montreal shops to supplement his supply of traps.

Lewis and Clark carried and used beaver traps throughout their trek across the continent. On the upper Missouri they found steel traps already in use among French trappers and Indians. Some of these traps came from St. Louis and some from Canada; any differences are not revealed to us. On the heels of Lewis and Clark came Manuel Lisa's men. They took American beaver traps to the Big Horn, to the Three Forks of the Missouri, and over the Continental Divide to the upper Snake drainage. A couple of years later the overland Astorians carried beaver traps all the way to the lower Columbia. A few examples of these Astorian traps still exist; they belong in the class of "standardized" traps of the late eighteenth century. The North West Company's coup on the Columbia in 1813 brought about the demise of the Astorians and caused the intermixing of Canadian traps with those of the Astorians.

By the time the early mountain men first plied their trade in the Far West, the Americans among them were unanimous in their selection of beaver traps of the conventional design, the "standardized" trap. However some of these men adopted a lighter trap, one that weighed about half as much as the big five-pound trap yet resembled it in all structural relationships. Specimens of both weights still turn up in the wake of the old-time trappers.

The British subjects who competed with the United States mountain men in old Oregon and along the Pacific slope south into California procured a tremendous number of beaver traps. The far-ranging fur brigades of the Hudson's Bay Company carried these traps into country that is now Washington, Oregon, Idaho, Montana, Wyoming, Utah, Nevada, and California. Some of the English company's traps were left with Indians or dropped in the field, of course. It would be satisfying to say that the Hudson's Bay Company's traps can be recognized readily whenever and wherever they are recovered by archeologists or other present-day searchers, but, in truth, the traps of English or Canadian origin cannot always be differentiated from the United States product.

The classic site for the study of English and Canadian beaver traps in the United States is Fort Vancouver, Washington, where archeologists of the National Park Service have been systematic in taking from the ground an extensive collection of trap parts that were discarded by blacksmiths as they repaired and replenished the company's trap supply over a thirty-five-year period. The recovered materials show a few characteristic minutiae that under some circumstances may be diagnostic, but the Hudson's Bay Company's beaver traps came from several sources; some were "Columbia-made," some were imported from England, some were brought from Canada, and a few were of American origin—thus making a mixture not readily unscrambled when only a great array of rusted fragments constitute the source material. Certain sites in Canada—i.e., Ruperts House—have yielded intact Hudson's Bay Company traps of the Fort Vancouver period. These functional specimens present the same characteristic structural features that appear in many of the trap fragments recovered along the lower Columbia River. One may confidently conclude that in general the Hudson's Bay beaver trap was comparable in weight and design to the ubiquitous double-spring trap of No. 4 size, popular throughout the beaver country since the mid-eighteenth century and still on the market today as the Newhouse No. 4.

A very few of the many blacksmiths who produced the handmade beaver traps of the eighteenth and early nineteenth centuries are identifiable in the records of the old-time fur trade. Only one so distinguished himself as to make his trap a present-day symbol and his name a living memorial—Sewell Newhouse.

As yet, the collecting and studying of historic steel traps is not widely popular among antiquarians, but a new surge of popular interest is predicted. Public concern with the modern beaver trap is not likely to fade into nothingness because the famous fur bearer is still very much with us and continues to be the quarry of American trappers in many localities. H. Raymond Gregg writes regarding the status of the beaver in the United States:

> By World War I, stringent or total protection was provided by law almost everywhere. Widespread efforts were begun to restock depleted territories, or even to extend the known range of beavers. The ensuing years have brought fruitful results. Today, relatively few Americans live more than a day's drive from a wild-beaver colony. . . . [A quarter of a century ago] surveys of eleven Pacific Coast, Rocky Mountain, and Great Basin states [the historic realm of the mountain man] reported a beaver population of 324,000. In one year removal of "nuisance" beavers in those states produced 53,936 pelts, worth $1,096,659.[9]

[9] From H. Raymond Gregg: "The Magnificent Rodent," *The Scientific Monthly* (August 1948), pp. 73–82.

CHAPTER IV

Knives of

the Frontiersmen

KNIVES, DAGGERS, AND HISTORY

I N THE ADOPTION OF HIS HANDY BLADE, THE MOUNTAIN
man differed very little from his predecessors anywhere on the
raw margins of civilization. Surprisingly, the design of the hunter's knife in 1800 often closely approximated the style of knives
used throughout the greater part of Europe one thousand years
B.C.[1] The materials that prehistoric European knives were made of,
usually bronze, were not the same as the iron knives of the first
American frontiersmen, but the over-all style, proportions, and
"balance" were very similar. This was especially true in the categories of "dags" and daggers.

When that indeterminate day of the "Early Iron Age" came,
the European wielder of iron knives adhered closely to many of the
preferred designs that had characterized the preceding bronze
knives. Again, the knives, the daggers especially, copied the earlier
form,[2] and as a favored type the dagger seems to have taken ever
deeper root in the consciousness of man. Down through more than
a thousand years of successive stages of human culture, particularly within the higher ancient civilizations, the "dag" and the
dagger persisted in their early forms. They came to the New
World with the first white adventurers and were still a feature of

[1] Reginald A. Smith, ed.: *Antiquities of the Bronze Age, British Museum*
(Oxford, Eng., 1920), pp. 30, 41, 48, 89, 121, 128, 129, 134, 161, 162,
179.
[2] R. A. Smith, ed.: *Early Iron Age Antiquities, British Museum* (Oxford,
Eng., 1925), pp. 33, 34, 54–7, 59, 67, 74, 89, 109–10.

the armament of the American Indian and the white trader-trapper in the period with which this book is concerned (figs. 40–1, 43–5).

Even the big knives and the bowies (figs. 48 and 49) of the American frontiersmen have an impressive lineage traceable back to the Middle Ages and earlier. The Scandinavian skramasax (scramasax), sometimes classed as a sword but in the Völkerwanderungzeit definitely a big knife, seems but slightly removed from the great iron knives found in the chariot burials of the Marne. These burials are thought to date from a century or two before Christ,[3] and the men and the hardware that they contain are not Scandinavian.

One style of the legendary American Bowie knife finds its counterpart in literally hundreds of existing European specimens that were manufactured during the fourteenth, fifteenth, and sixteenth centuries. An impressive assemblage of these Renaissance "bowies" is owned by the Schweizerisches Landesmuseum, Zurich, and there are many smaller collections elsewhere.[4] The accompanying sketches (fig. 39) suggest the sizes and shapes of some of these ancient forerunners of the American pieces.

A fortunate set of circumstances resulted in the preservation of some of the first professionally made pictures produced in America. The French Huguenot Jacques LeMoyne de Morgues, an accomplished artist, accompanied René de Laudonnière's expedition to Florida in 1564. Spanish forces massacred the Frenchmen in 1565, but LeMoyne and his drawings and paintings escaped. LeMoyne started for France but landed in England. There Theodore deBry made engravings from the original illustrations, and they were published in 1591.[5] LeMoyne captured the human element in his Florida experience as well as the natural scene. In picturing the French military personnel, he gave attention to dress and accouterments including the knives. Figure 40a, based on LeMoyne's drawing,[6] shows a French soldier with his small sword-hilted dagger carried horizontally on his belt at his back. A well-

---

[3] R. A. Smith: *Iron Age Antiquities*, p. 55; J. B. Himsworth: *The Story of Cutlery* (London: Ernest Benn; 1953), pp. 41–2.

[4] E. A. Gessler: *Waffensammlung, Schweizerisches Landesmuseum* (Zurich, 1928), pp. 19–20, 32–5, 143, 144, Pls. 3, 9, 10; Carl Schuchhardt: *Deutsche Vor- und Frühgeschichte in Bildern* (Munich and Berlin, 1936), p. xi, Pl. 67.

[5] Stefan Lorant: *The New World: The First Pictures of America* (New York: Duell, Sloane & Pearce; 1946).

[6] Ibid., p. 105.

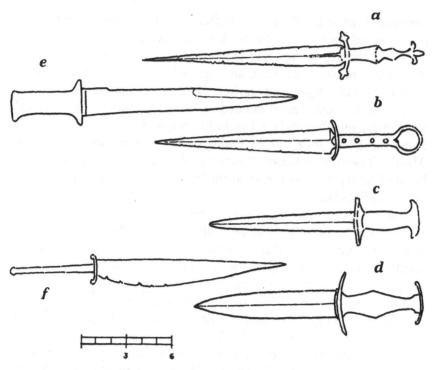

FIG. 39. *European Daggers and Fighting Knives, Fourteenth–Fifteenth Centuries.*

These specimens suggest the ancestry of certain of the knife types used by American frontiersmen some five hundred years after the European prototypes "went to their rest." There is nothing very conclusive about this circumstance; it would be quite possible to prepare another chart showing very similar iron knives that have been recovered from European sites dating back five hundred years earlier than these Swiss finds. The point to be made: any and all fighting knives used in America were descended from similar knives developed in the Old World long before America was discovered. *d* is a sixteenth-century Swiss dagger; it is in clean condition and comes from a museum collection. The others shown are recoveries from archeological excavations.

The specimens shown are owned by Schweizerisches Landesmuseum. The sketches are from photographs in Gessler's *Waffensammlung, Schweizerisches Landesmuseum.*

FIG. 40. *Sixteenth-Century Dagger.*

Shown in *a* is LeMoyne's on-the-spot drawing of a French soldier in Florida, 1564–5. A sheathed dagger is carried horizontally on the belt at the back. *b* shows a well-preserved dagger of the sixteenth century now in the Harold L. Peterson Collection. The drawing is by Glen Dines.

preserved dagger of this type and general period is shown in some detail in figure 40*b*.[7] An almost identical knife of the same period is in the collection of rusted daggers in the Schweizerisches Landesmuseum (fig. 39). This style of slender, brittle dagger did not become enormously popular in the New World,[8] but it did persist in small numbers in the personal armament of U. S. Army and Navy personnel of the late eighteenth and early nineteenth centuries and among Indians (fig. 41*c*) and Indian traders throughout the fur-trade period. During World War II it had a rebirth as the official United States Marine Corps stiletto (fig. 41*d*).

Meriwether Lewis testified to the fact that a dagger on the order of a "Navy dirk" (fig. 41*b*) had been procured by him for his personal use on the Lewis and Clark Expedition, but inadvertently it was left behind when he went to Pittsburg in July 1803. President Jefferson, apprised of the oversight, notified Captain Lewis that the dirk would be forwarded. Lewis replied: "The dirk can not well come by post, nor is it of moment to me, the knives that were made at Harper's ferry will answer my purpose equally as well and perhaps better; it [the dirk] can therefore be taken care of until my return."[9] The Harpers Ferry knives mentioned by Lewis are presumed to be the ancestors of the U. S. rifleman's knife, the first model of which appeared a quarter of a century after Lewis and Clark (fig. 49*e*). No specimen of the 1803 Lewis and Clark Harpers Ferry knife is known.

In the course of their epoch-making round trip through unknown Indian country, the blacksmiths of the Lewis and Clark party won high acclaim among many of the tribes because of the practical usefulness of their products. It is likely that the knives they made and traded were of various types and styles, but with a single known exception those knives are not to be seen today. The exception is a stag-handled dagger that was acquired and cher-

---

[7] The specimen is owned by Harold L. Peterson and is here pictured with the owner's permission. See Peterson: *American Knives* (New York: Scribner's; 1958), p. 11.

[8] A goodly number of "plug bayonets" consisting of specialized forms of this dagger-type found use in America during the last half of the 17th century. Peterson: *American Knives*, pp. 17–19, 118.

[9] Reuben G. Thwaites, ed.: *Original Journals of the Lewis and Clark Expedition, 1804–1806* (8 vols.; New York: Dodd, Mead & Co.; 1904–5), VII, 260; Donald Jackson, ed.: *Letters of Lewis and Clark Expedition, 1783–1854* (Urbana: Univ. of Illinois Press; 1962), pp. 107, 111.

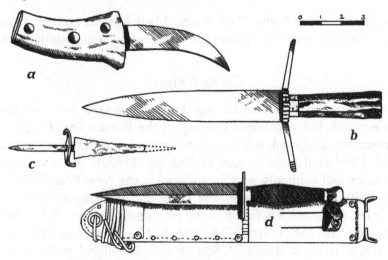

FIG. 41. *American Daggers.*

a, dagger by a Lewis and Clark blacksmith, presented to the Nez Percé. National Park Service, Fort Clatsop Museum, Oregon. *b*, Stephen Decatur's dirk, now in the U. S. Naval Academy, Annapolis. The drawing is after Peterson: *American Knives*, p. 95. *c*, stiletto taken from an Indian grave, Prairie du Chien, Wisconsin, part of the Bureau of American Ethnology Collection, 1882–3. It was obtained as a gift from Paul Goeke. The specimen is catalogued as item No. 88092, U. S. National Museum. *d*, U. S. Marine Corps stiletto and scabbard of World War II, now in the West Point Museum, New York. These drawings are by Glen Dines.

ished through the years by the Nez Percé.[1] Not until recently did it pass to a white person, Mrs. Joe Evans, at the old Mission center, Spalding, Idaho. The National Park Service investigated the history of the piece and obtained it for exhibit purposes at the Lewis and Clark Memorial, Fort Clatsop, Oregon (fig. 41*a*).

The history of the Prairie du Chien dagger (fig. 41*c*) is not recorded, but it was taken from an Indian grave in western Wisconsin, and is now item No. 88092 in the United States National Museum. The comparatively long tang once was enclosed within a

[1] Lewis and Clark stopped with the Nez Percé both going to and coming from the Columbia, a total of six weeks with these friendly natives. When westbound, the explorers were with them in late September and early October at the forks of the Clearwater ("Canoe Camp") where dugouts were built for the journey down the Columbia. Here thirty-eight horses were left with three of the Nez Percé for safe keeping. On Oct. 5, 1805, Clark wrote: "To each of these three Indians, one of them the son of a chief, I gave a knife." (Bernard De Voto, ed.: *The Journals of Lewis and Clark* (Boston: Houghton Mifflin; 1953), p. 242.

handle of wood or antler. The slender blade has lost an inch or two of its sharp-pointed tip. Obviously the weapon was country-made.

Clasp Knives

How long ago the first folding knives appeared has not been conjectured, but specimens turn up in the Roman site, Corinium, Cirencester, England, which archeologists date as the first century A.D.[2] They continued in use in Europe through the succeeding centuries and evidently were introduced in the New World not less than 250 years ago. One of the early documentary evidences of their use in America is found in the records of the French Fox War expenses for the years 1715 and 1716—"horn handled clasp knives, 6 livres a dozen."[3] Setzler and Jennings[4] write of one from the Cherokee site, Peachtree Mound and Village, near Murphy, North Carolina. Quimby[5] states that one recovered from an Indian grave in Michigan may be as early as 1781–1809. In the small museum at Tadoussac, Quebec, is a specimen of French lineage in "fresh" condition (fig. 56e), and Maxwell[6] reports numerous disintegrated specimens recovered at Fort Michilimackinac, most of which are "indigenous to the earliest French features" (early 1700's). He recognizes others of English origin that were brought to the fort by victorious British forces in 1761 and later. All these clasp knives were considerably larger than the jackknives that were also recovered in the course of the excavations mentioned. Regardless of nationality, they have in common the single folding blade controlled by a spring, but they were not "switchblades" in the modern sense. Often there are protruding catches on the tangs of these blades that engage the spring and ensure that the blades shall remain open when in use. The protruding knobs, or pins, which constitute the catches also facilitate the releasing of the "lock" when the knife is to be closed.

The French clasp knife almost always has a one-piece horn

[2] Himsworth: *Cutlery*, p. 127.
[3] Charles E. Brown: "Indian Trade Implements and Ornaments," *Wisconsin Archeologist*, XVII: 3 (1918), pp. 77–8.
[4] Frank M. Setzler and Jesse D. Jennings: "Peachtree Mound and Village Site," Bureau of American Ethnology Bulletin, No. 131 (1941), Pl. 12.
[5] George I. Quimby: "Dated Indian Burials in Michigan," *Papers*, Michigan Academy of Science, Arts, and Letters, Vol. XXIII (1937), p. 67.
[6] Moreau S. Maxwell: *Excavations at Fort Michilimackinac, 1959 Season* (East Lansing: Michigan State Univ.; 1961), pp. 105–6.

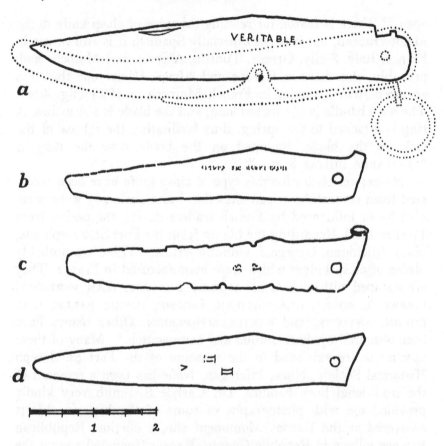

a

VERITABLE

b

c

d

1   2

FIG. 42.   *French Clasp Knives, Blades.*

a, recent—from French Morocco, 1923. The traditional one-piece
horn handle and modern steel-spring arrangement are shown in dotted
lines. *b*, blade recovered at site of Fort St. Joseph, Niles, Michigan.
French marking. It is thought to have been used about 1700–60
(Quimby: "European Trade Articles," pp. 25–7, Pl. II). *c*, recovered
at Kansas Monument Site, Republic County, Kansas. Marked "B/F,"
it is probably not earlier than 1777. *d*, recovered at site of Fort St.
Joseph. The date is the same as for *b* above.

handle with no lining. Often it has been referred to as "Spanish."
Even some of the early nineteenth-century American traders took a
liking to the term. On February 28, 1832, Nathaniel Wyeth addressed the New York jobbers, Davenport and Byron: "What I
now want is 3 dozen Spanish knives of best quality for personal
arms, 5½ inch blade with a set to prevent its shutting when

open."[7] There is reason for relating this type of clasp knife to the Mediterranean, but it is not especially Spanish; it is still in use in France, Italy, Sicily, Greece, Tunisia, Algeria, and Morocco and, probably, elsewhere in Europe and Africa. I have one that was acquired from a vendor in French Morocco in 1923 (fig. 42*a*). The horn handle is 6½ inches long, and the blade is 5¾ inches. A ring is attached to the spring, thus facilitating the release of the lock on the blade. Stamped on the blade near the tang is "VERITABLE DUMAS & CIE."

Numerous blades for this type of clasp knife have been recovered from several American sites that quite obviously were occupied by or influenced by French traders during the period from 1700 to 1760. Regarding the blades from the Fort St. Joseph site, Niles, Michigan, George I. Quimby writes: "These are probably blades of clasp knives which were manufactured in France. They are stamped with such names as IEAN B. TIVET, IEAN PERRIOTT, PIERRE, I. ROVET, CLAUDI, IEAN ARCONE, HUGUE PALLE, I. C. DORON, ANTOINE, and BARTELEMY PERRIN. Other names have been obscured by deterioration and encrustation."[8] Many of these specimens are exhibited in the museum of the Fort St. Joseph Historical Society, Niles, Michigan. None has even a remnant of the traditional horn handles. Dr. Carlyle S. Smith very kindly provided me with photographs of some of the historic objects recovered at the Kansas Monument site, a onetime Republican Pawnee village in Republic County, Kansas. Included among the artifacts is a clasp-knife blade of the kind under discussion. Regarding it, Smith states: "The blade has a perforation [for the pin] and a thickened button [slips into a spring lock] to keep it straight when open." Tentatively, he dates these Kansas objects as no earlier than 1777 and suggests that they may have come from Spanish sources in St. Louis, a circumstance which would not have precluded a French origin for some of the objects.[9] The nature of these eighteenth-century blades is compared with a typical French Moroccan clasp knife of recent manufacture in figure 42*a*.

[7] F. G. Young, ed.: *Correspondence and Journals of Captain Nathaniel J. Wyeth, 1831–1836* (Eugene, Ore.: Univ. Press; 1899), p. 42.

[8] George I. Quimby: "European Trade Articles as Chronological Indicators . . . ," *Papers*, Michigan Academy of Science, Arts, and Letters, Vol. XXIV, Pt. IV (1939), p. 27, Pl. 2.

[9] Carlyle S. Smith: "European Trade Material from the Kansas Monument Site," Plains Archeological Conference *News Letter*, III:2 (1950), p. 3.

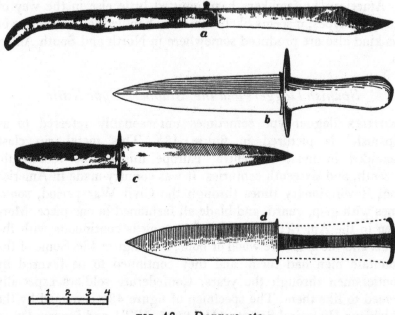

FIG. 43. *Daggers, etc.*

a, big clasp knife, English type, formerly in the Philip Medicus Collection, New York. *b*, "Spanish" dagger found in Oklahoma. It is item No. 3396, JBT, Oklahoma Historical Society. *c*, horn-handled dagger, formerly in the Philip Medicus Collection. *d*, Bavarian Reitergrab relic *c*. A.D. 400, now in the Naturhistorisches Museum, Vienna. This drawing by William Macy is in the Jefferson National Expansion Memorial, St. Louis.

The English clasp knife is represented by figure 43*a*, an especially large specimen formerly in the Philip Medicus Collection, New York. The 10-inch bolstered handle has a central metal divider between two pairs of horn scales. Unlike the French clasp knives, it has a lining. Maxwell, during excavations in 1959, found such knives at Fort Michilimackinac associated with English artifacts. One of these is marked on the blade, "ALLO FOLD." Maxwell identifies these as British and he concludes that they came to Michigan in 1761 and later.[1] Additional eighteenth-century English clasp knives at Michilimackinac are illustrated in Petersen.[2] None has the one-piece horn handle.

[1] Maxwell: *Excavations*, p. 126, Pl. X.
[2] Eugene T. Petersen: *Gentlemen on the Frontier* (Mackinac Island, Mich., 1964), p. 58.

American knifemakers have omitted little else in the way of European types; it seems likely that horn-handled folding knives of this kind also are produced somewhere in North and South America.

Spanish Daggers and the "Stabber"-Type Knife

ANOTHER dagger-type sometimes unreasonably referred to as "Spanish" is pictured in figure 43b. This metal-grip class abounded in most of central Europe during the fourteenth, fifteenth, and sixteenth centuries. It was country-made in America from Revolutionary times through the Civil War period, sometimes with grip, guard, and blade all fashioned in one piece. More often in the American version only a tang is continuous with the blade, and the grips are wood or bone, as in figure 43c. Some of the mountain men had them, and they continued to be favored by frontiersmen through the years. Confederate soldiers especially seemed to like them. The specimen of figure 43b is owned by the Oklahoma Historical Society (No. 3396, JBT) and is recorded as having been found near Kenton. Its 7½-inch blade is double-edged with a pronounced median rib; its wide guard encourages one to class it as a "bowie knife." The dagger (fig. 43c) is from the Philip Medicus Collection. Its riveted grip is horn. A notable number of these spear-pointed bowie-like knives are in American collections. Some of them have fur-trade connections, and they antedate the James Bowie generation by several decades.

A great many ancient specimens of spear-pointed iron daggers can be pointed to as evidence that this type of knife has found favor among fighting men for more than fifteen hundred years. The example in figure 43d was taken in 1906 from a Teutonic Reitergrab in Bavaria. The archeologists who studied the remains of the horse and the man with his equipment there excavated attributed the specimens to about A.D. 400. The knife (fig. 43d), together with the skeletons of the horse and the rider, were on exhibit prior to World War II in the Naturhistorisches Museum in Vienna. Similar daggers that scarcely vary from the Bavarian piece are seen in the large collections of fourteenth-, fifteenth-, and sixteenth-century weapons owned by the Schweizerisches Landesmuseum, Zurich.[3]

[3] Gessler: *Waffensammlung*, Tbls. 3, 9, and 10.

The broad-blade "dags" shown in figure 44 had wide distribution in the northern districts of the American fur fields. Like the spear-pointed daggers that precede (fig. 43), the dags have an impressive history extending back at least into the Roman period.[4] Presumably they persisted in the Old World, since they were supplied to the Indians by the early European adventurers in America, where they attained a lasting popularity, especially in the northern belt from coast to coast. Perhaps they were at first seized upon by the savages because their basic form was so very close to the aboriginal knife with blade of flint or obsidian.

The specimen in figure 44a is owned by the Museum of the American Indian, Heye Foundation, New York, and was obtained from an unnamed northern Plains tribe. Its blade, like most dag blades, originated in the shops of the white man. It is the same trade piece that on occasion served the Indian as spear point and as a spike for the war club. The silhouette of the blade accompanying the knife picture reveals the nature of the crossbars and notches that allowed firm anchorage in hilt or handle. Ordinarily these blades were traded just as they came from the blacksmith. Handles were made and affixed by the Indian. In the present case, however, an unusual handle was used, made from heavy russet leather that also must have come from the trader. Twenty-three brass tacks, of the kind often used by the Indian in ornamenting his gunstock, hold together the edges of the two stiff layers of leather that constitute the knife handle. Four heavier rivets pass through the leather and through the notches at the end of the tang. One assumes that this dag is a fairly recent relic, a supposition that is supported by the blade maker's mark stamped upon it, "Jukes Coulson & Co.," a Sheffield cutlery exporting company active during the first half of the nineteenth century.[5]

In the Maryhill Museum on the Columbia is an old-time dag (fig. 44b), that was used by Northwest Coast Indians. The handle is the characteristic pair of polished bone plates fashioned by the Indian to fit the tang, and to afford a good hand grip. By far the greater number of dags now in collections have this type of bone handle. Many Indians who carried dags drilled the handles of their

---

[4] Gustav F. Klemm: *Das Alte Vorchristliche Europa* (Leipzig, 1850), Pl. VI, Fig. 1.

[5] Himsworth: *Cutlery*, pp. 197–8; Arthur Woodward: "The Knife on the Frontier," New York Westerners Posse *Brand Book*, II: 1 (1955), p. 11.

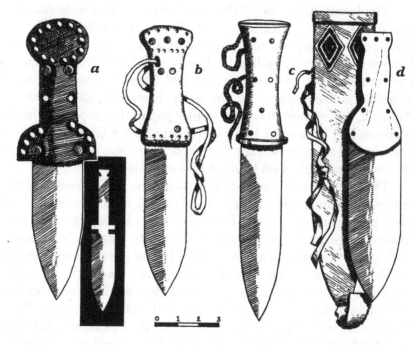

FIG. 44. *Dags.*

a, Northern Plains dag, Museum of the American Indian, New York. *b*, Northwest coast dag, Maryhill Museum, Washington. *c*, Columbia River dag, Maryhill Museum, Washington. *d*, Blackfoot dag with beaded sheath, item No. 729, U. S. National Museum. Glen Dines drawing.

knives so that a wrist cord could be attached. In the present instance, the wrist cord is a rawhide thong. Six metal rivets are in evidence. The rows of small holes at the ends of the hilt are shallow, incised decorative pits, the owner's concession to ornament.

Another "stabber"-type knife from the Maryhill collection is shown in figure 44*c*. It is similar to the preceding dag, but a brass flange, or collar, encloses the tang and separates the bone hilt from the blade. A single brass rivet passes through the collar and into the iron. The wrist cord is made of twisted strands of sinew. Essentially the dag was a fighting knife; the northern Indian traditionally kept it "at hand." Journals written by early-day mariners on both coasts frequently tell of Indians in canoes or swimming in the immediate vicinity of the visiting ship displaying their naked dags attached to their wrists. White observers in villages of the northern tribes in the interior state that the "stabbers" commonly dangled from the warrior's left wrist, and both knife and wrist usually were kept concealed under the enfolding buffalo robe or blanket. When Governor Simpson of the Hudson's Bay Company passed down the Columbia River in 1824, he was impressed by the dags (his term) "which hung by a thong to the wrist of nearly every male." This observation was made in the upper Dalles country.[6]

Sheaths were used by some owners of dags, however. The specimen shown in figure 44d is item No. 729 in the National Museum. It is recorded as being from the Blackfoot country, where it was collected in the 1840's. The hilt is Indian-made, from two plates of bone riveted to the tang with nine copper rivets. The bead-decorated leather sheath is so constructed as to receive the entire knife, handle and all. The soft leather thong attached to the sheath's upper end suggests that the knife may have been suspended from the neck of the owner, a practice not uncommon among northern Indians. Among the drawings and watercolor paintings made by Frederick Whymper[7] in the Yukon River country during the 1860's is a portrait of a Tanana Indian carrying a dag in a sheath suspended from his neck. Also shown[8] is a Whymper drawing of an Indian in a canoe dispatching a swimming moose with a "stabber."

Evidences presently available seem to point to the British trading companies as the only sources for the supply of dag blades. They have been found in various conditions of oxidation at historic sites from New York State all the way across the country to Puget Sound, almost always in the northern tier of states. In Canada and Alaska they have a general distribution. Comparatively few of those collected are still intact within the handles that made them knives instead of spear points or war clubs.

The dag was obviously not a general-purpose knife. The Indian as well as the white trader-trapper needed a big knife that

[6] *Forest and Stream* (May 6, 1899), quoted by Woodward: "The Knife," p. 11. For Simpson's comments see Frederick Merk, ed.: *Fur Trade and Empire* (Cambridge, Mass.: Harvard Univ. Press; 1931), pp. 61–2.

[7] Terry Pettus: "Expedition to Russian America," *The Beaver* (Winter 1962), pp. 8–19. Here, among other Whymper pictures, are reproductions of several engravings from Whymper's *Travel and Adventure in the Territory of Alaska*, including drawings of Tanana Indians.

[8] Ibid., p. 18.

would serve as a butcher's cleaver as well as a weapon of war; celebrated Indian chiefs needed special knives as symbols of their station. There were such knives in nearly every camp, of course, and some of the identifiable specimens are shown in figure 45. Figure 45a represents "Tecumseh's dagger" now owned by the Château de Ramezay, Montreal, where it bears catalog number 10. The magnificence of this swordlike knife is quite in keeping with the great generosity of the British government's policy for assuring the allegiance of the tribesmen destined to fight the United States in the War of 1812. Tecumseh's Shawnees were recipients of this largess, and it may be reasonable to accept the purported history of this knife as it is recorded in Montreal. It is not reported that it was carried by Tecumseh at the time of his fatal fight on the Thames on October 5, 1813. Yet it seems likely that it, like the next specimen (fig. 45b), was as much a symbol of rank and distinction as it was a practical weapon or tool.

The "broadsword" (fig. 45b) was presented by Governor George Simpson of the Hudson's Bay Company to his piper, Colin Fraser, who as a young man made the canoe trip with him from York Factory to the Columbia in 1828. Subsequently Colin Fraser was placed in charge at Jasper House, 1835–49; at Fort Assiniboine, 1850–3; at Lesser Slave Lake, 1854–62; and then was given a final five-year tour of duty in charge at Lac-Sainte-Anne. With him through this lifetime of service to the fur trade went this big knife, badge of his friendship with the governor. If it ever functioned in anything other than symbolic capacity, we find no mention of the occasions. Today the ornamented relic is in the Fraser Museum, Winterburn, Alberta, owned and operated by Robert and Mrs. Fraser.[9]

In the museum of the Michigan Historical Commission, Lansing, is a big knife (fig. 45d) deeply rusted and devoid of the wood or other plates that were once riveted to the massive iron tang. This rugged piece, a part of the Edinger Collection of Indian relics, is referred to as "Indian Knife found in Thornapple River, Nashville, Barry County, Aug. 14, 1901, by H. R. Hayes." The locality was the scene of quite continuous early Indian trade, French, English, and finally American. It seems likely that the relic is contemporary with or a trifle earlier than the "Tecumseh dagger" (fig. 45a) and

[9] Iris Allan: "Colin Fraser Lives On," *The Beaver* (Winter 1959), pp. 38–43.

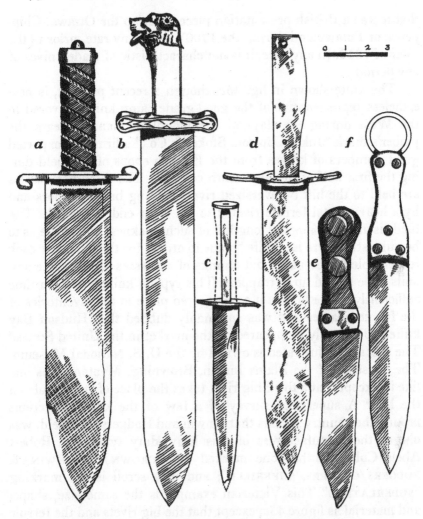

FIG. 45. *Miscellaneous Big Knives.*

a, "Tecumseh's dagger," No. 10, Château de Ramezay, Montreal. *b,* Colin Fraser's broadsword, Fraser Museum, Winterburn, Alberta. *c,* Greenville Creek (Ohio) dagger, John Barsotti Collection, Columbus, Ohio. *d,* Thornapple River (Michigan) big dagger, Michigan Historical Commission, Lansing. *e,* "Hudson Bay campknife," U. S. National Museum. *f,* Twanah Indian dagger, Museum of Northwest History, Walla Walla, Washington. Drawing by Glen Dines.

that it was a British presentation piece given to the Ottawa, Chippewa, or Potawatomi during the 1780's or, at any rate, prior to the War of 1812. In any case, it is not characteristic of trade knives of any period.

The knife shown in fig. 45e, though a recent product, is nevertheless representative of the good-grade camp knives favored in the West during the days of the mountain man. It bears the jobber's mark "Jukes Coulson, Stokes & Co.," a firm that exported great numbers of knives from the English shops of Sheffield during the first half of the nineteenth century.[1] The thick horn scales are held to the hilt by oversized rivets holding brass washers and by a heavy metal ferrule riveted to the front end of the hilt. The blade is about 8½ inches long but of such thickness and shape as to be quite stiff. Here is a knife "made to order" for the hunter or cook responsible for breaking out chunks of carcasses of the game animals to be served up to trappers. This type of knife was for a time sufficiently stable to give it a recognized place in the inventories of the fur companies and was commonly dubbed the "Hudson Bay knife." Ultimately it appeared on the market in the United States.[2] The specimen illustrated is owned by the U. S. National Museum. The Museum of the Plains Indian, Browning, Montana, has one like it, except that a third big rivet takes the place of the ferrule on the hilt.[3] A superficial survey of a few of the knife collections around the country reveals that Unwin and Rodgers, Sheffield, was one of the manufacturers of this heavy-duty type. The Robert Abels Collection has one marked "v (CROWN) R/UNWIN & RODGERS/CUTLERS, SHEFFIELD"; and in a scroll is the marking "SUPERLATIVE." This Victorian example is the same size, shape, and material as figure 45e, except that the big rivets and the ferrule at the end of the hilt are nickel-plated and there are no rivets in the ferrule. Other specimens are owned by the Museum of the American Indian and the North Dakota Historical Society.

The smaller daggers (fig. 45c and fig. 45f) are stiff of blade and equal to general duty. The specimen of figure 45c was found by Fred Cline, Ohio antiquarian, in 1894, buried in the bank of historic Greenville Creek on the onetime bloody terrain that is now

[1] Woodward: "The Knife," pp. 10–11; Himsworth: *Cutlery*, pp. 197–8.
[2] Woodward: "The Knife," quoting Emerson Hough's article in *Forest and Stream* (February 4, 1899), p. 89.
[3] John C. Ewers: "The Story of the Blackfeet," *Indian Life and Customs*, U. S. Indian Service, Pamphlet 6, p. 17.

Drake County, Ohio. It is plausible to accept the piece as a relic of the repeated desperate conflicts that occurred during the 1790's when confederated Indians, encouraged by the British, resisted the advance of American settlers upon the "Indian State" propounded by the English fur interests. The knife is now in the collection of John Barsotti, Columbus, Ohio.

The Twanah Indian knife (fig. 45f) is an elongated dag. We learn from eyewitness accounts of the early nineteenth century and from on-the-spot drawings that northwestern Indians regularly made practical use of such knives in hunting and warfare.[4] The brass ring suggests the use of the wristcord so characteristic of the shorter dags. Renaissance European daggers sometimes were provided with such rings, but they were iron continuations of the iron tangs.[5] This ring is brass and is held to the pommel by two of the rivets that fasten the bone scales to the tang. The specimen is in the collections of the Museum of Northwest History, Whitman College, Walla Walla, Washington.

THE COMMON TRADE KNIVES

Butchers and Scalpers

FROM the earliest days of the U. S. Indian Trade Office (late eighteenth century to the final period of the American Fur Company, 1840's, the Orders Outward, invoices, and other business records of the fur traders are replete with references to "scalping knives." The nonchalance with which the term was tossed around might lead one to believe that it meant something fairly specific. Actually, in the trade, any cheap butcher knife might be a "scalper." This had been as true in the early colonial trade as it was in the days of the mountain man. Some indication of the wholesale cost of a scalping knife to the nineteenth-century trader is found in the following abstracts from the American Fur Company Papers:

1839. Apr. 15. [Letter, Pierre Chouteau, Jr., St. Louis, to American Fur Company, New York, regarding previously placed

[4] P. D. Baird: "Expeditions to the Arctic," *The Beaver* (June 1949), pp. 41–7. It reproduces the engraving "Franklin's Second Expedition attacked by the Western Arctic Eskimos [1826]," showing those daggers in the hands of dozens of natives.

[5] Gessler: *Waffensammlung*, p. 144, Pl. 9. See also fig. 39 at the beginning of this chapter.

order for scalping knives.] "We want an article of good appearance, but cheap, to offer to the U. S. Indian Office [to be included in treaty goods]."

1840. Feb. 19. Memorandum of sundry goods to be furnished by Hiram Cutler, Sheffield, England, to American Fur Co., N. Y. 60 doz. warranted scalping knives @ $10.75 [approximately 9¢ each].

1840. Aug. 13. [Order, American Fur Company, New York, to Hiram Cutler, Sheffield.] To be shipped by the packet of Nov. 25, 1840, or earlier, 200 doz. warrented scalping knives @ $10.75; 500 doz. common scalping knives @ $8.12 [about 7¢ each]. You will please pack the knives in casks of 100 dozen.

Even when dealing in wholesale lots, the American Fur Company demanded nearly 100 per cent profit on scalping knives:

1835. April 24. [Ramsay Crooks, American Fur Company, New York to Colonel Henry Stanton, Washington, D.C., submitting his bid to supply Indian goods to be delivered at Indian Treaty Grounds, Chicago, August 15, 1835] agreeable to your advertisement of 25th ult. 700 scalping knives like sample No. 1 at 18¢ each; 700 scalping knives like sample No. 2 at 15¢ each. If it is impracticable for us to obtain the whole 700 of the No. 1 scalping knives, the deficit will be made up with the No. 2 description at the lower price.[6]

The company was awarded this contract on May 21, 1835.

In the field the price charged the mountain man who purchased a butcher knife was about ten times greater than the figures just quoted. On July 9, 1832, Johnson Gardner, free trapper, paid $2.00, each, for butcher knives purchased at the American Fur Company post Fort Union.[7] A full description of these scalpers on the Missouri is not given, but it is reasonable to put them in the same class with the knives distributed by the company in 1835. In other words, the selling price exceeded the cost by about 1,000 per cent. A further gain to the company was realized in that the merchandise was paid for by Mr. Gardner with beaver pelts, a commodity which the company, in turn, sold at a notable advance over the price allowed to the trapper. If one attempted to determine

---

[6] The American Fur Company Papers preserved by The New-York Historical Society are now represented in microfilm copies owned by many large libraries. The items quoted above are found in Reel 1 and Reel 12.

[7] Hiram M. Chittenden: *The American Fur Trade of the Far West* (Stanford: Stanford Univ. Press; 1954), II, 944.

the net profit made in the sale of knives or other goods in the field, it would be necessary to consider, of course, the cost of transportation and the varied expenses of "overhead" in maintaining one or more establishments in the wilderness. The gain then shrinks to something much less than the gross 1,000 per cent.

Some statistics are available regarding butcher knives distributed by William H. Ashley at his Green River rendezvous in 1825. Twenty free trappers at this meeting bought knives of several different kinds and grades, paying from 40¢ to $2.75 apiece. The ordinary butcher knives sold to the trappers brought $1.50 to $2.00 each. In 1826 Ashley again took an "outfit" to the rendezvous, this time held in the Cache Valley of the Bear River. His retail price for scalping knives at this get-together is not recorded, but he sold out, lock, stock, and barrel, on this occasion to his friends and co-workers Smith, Jackson, and Sublette. In so doing, he committed himself in writing to bring merchandise from St. Louis to his successors at the 1827 rendezvous to be held at Bear Lake. His formal agreement bound him to sell trade goods to the new firm, and only to that firm, at specified wholesale prices. The specified price for butcher knives was 75¢ each.[8]

It is unrealistic to picture any Indian as reserving one particular knife for scalping. His all-purpose butcher knife, usually carried in a sheath on his belt or waistcord, found constant use, but the "lifting of hair" was not one of its daily practices. When there was occasion to take scalps, the same knife which pared tasty morsels from hump ribs at mealtime loosened the scalp of the victim destined to provide the trophy. Usually the victim was dead when the scalp was taken, but not always. The grisly process of scalping has been analyzed and described by various anthropologists,[9] and there are numerous published eyewitness accounts by frontiersmen.[1] In a few instances mountain men, not to be outdone

[8] Dale L. Morgan, ed.: *The West of William H. Ashley* (Denver: Old West Pub. Co.; 1964), pp. 118–29, 150–2. In 1841 when wagon trains gave the traders great advantage in transporting merchandise, the retail price for ordinary butcher knives traded on the Kansas River still was $1.00 to $2.00, each, so observed Rufus B. Sage: *Wild Scenes in . . . the Rocky Mountains . . . and the Grand Prairies* (Philadelphia, 1855), p. 29.

[9] Gabriel Nadeau: "Indian Scalping Technique in Different Tribes," *Ciba Symposia* (January 1944), pp. 1676–81; illus. in G. Friederici: "The Business of Scalping," in *When Peoples Meet* (New York and Philadelphia, 1949).

[1] George F. Ruxton: *Life in the Far West* (Norman: Oklahoma Univ. Press; 1951), pp. 21–2, 26, 102, 126; Robert Glass Cleland: *This Reckless Breed of Men* (New York: Alfred A. Knopf; 1950), pp. 35–6.

by their red-skinned enemies, did some scalping of their own, a revival of a practice that was common during colonial Indian wars in the East.[2] The recorded observations in these connections are quite comprehensive and convincing, but seldom if ever did the writers see fit to tell anything about the knife with which the scalping was done. Artists of the day supplied a few authentic pictures of the knives, and some of the knives have also been preserved.

In figure 46 appear six specimens, the earliest of which dates back to the period of Iroquois supremacy in the Northeast, and the most recent of which is representative of the mountain man in the Rockies. The 11-inch blade (fig. 46*a*) is item No. 116 in the collections of the Washington State Historical Society, Tacoma. This handleless specimen, according to the acquisition record, rotted and rusted for many years within the grave of a Wisconsin Indian. So far as its characteristics are concerned, it might have come from any locality where white traders contacted the American Indian. It is entirely representative of the cheapest butcher knives distributed by the thousands throughout the period of United States trade from the Revolution to and including the day of the mountain man. Evidence that at least some of the earlier eighteenth-century trade knives of the French and English were also like this is seen in the blades recovered at Fort Michilimackinac, Michigan.[3]

The simple style of the cheap butcher-knife blade persisted all through the days of the Western fur trade and into the period of the professional buffalo hunter. The specimen shown in figure 46*b* was found in 1895 by J. P. V. Evans near Glendive, Montana, among the skeletons of fifty buffalo left by hide hunters. Its handle is buffalo horn, probably improvised by its former owner.[4] Today the knife is catalogued as item No. 7169 in the Yellowstone Museums, National Park Service.

---

[2] John C. Ewers: *The Role of the Indian in National Expansion* (Washington, D.C.: Nat'l Park Serv.; 1938), pp. 183–4. Ruxton: *Far West*, pp. 21, 31, 65, 83, 88, 120, 124, 140. Fairfax Downey: *Indian Wars of the U. S. Army, 1776–1865* (New York: Doubleday; 1963), pp. 1–10.

[3] Maxwell: *Excavations*, p. 42, and Pl. X; Petersen: *Gentlemen on the Frontier*, p. 58.

[4] It is to be noted, however, that the English cutlery works imported American buffalo horns in quantity. Himsworth: *Cutlery*, pp. 73–4: "It was a common sight, and one within my recollection, to see truck loads of black buffalo horns passing through the streets of Sheffield, having arrived from the United States."

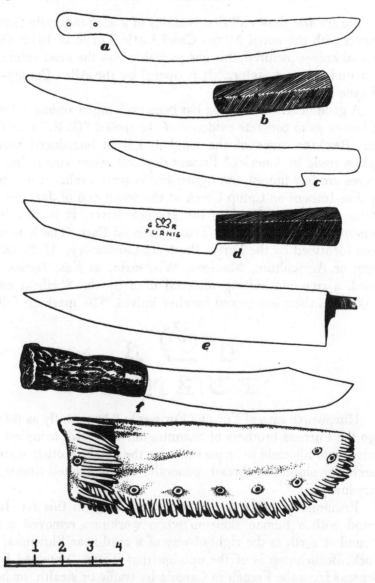

FIG. 46. *"Scalping Knives."*

a, Washington Historical Society, Tacoma, No. 116. *b*, National Park Service, Yellowstone Museums, No. 7169. *c*, Allen County–Fort Wayne Historical Society, Indiana. *d*, National Park Service, Grand Teton Museums, Wyoming. *e*, from Fluvanna, New York. It was done after Beauchamp: *Metallic Implements*, p. 72, Pl. 35, Fig. 170. *f*, Wyoming State Museum, No. C-1231/1. Drawing by William Macy, Jefferson National Expansion Memorial, St. Louis.

Figure 46c shows all that remains of a scalping knife that was buried with the noted Miami Chief Little Turtle in 1812. Of the several knives pictured, this one probably lays the most valid claim to actual use as a scalper.[5] It is owned by the Allen County–Fort Wayne Historical Society.

A good deal of discussion has been exch.nged among collectors of knives as to concrete evidence of the touted "G. R." (for Georgius Rex) on some of the English knives introduced into the Indian trade in America.[6] Present-day collections containing such knives are few indeed, but figure 46d is such a relic. It was found by Jim Imeson on Camp Creek at the south end of Jackson Hole where the creek flows into the Hoback River. It is now in the museum exhibits of Grand Teton National Park. The handle has been identified by the Forest Products Laboratory, U. S. Department of Agriculture, Madison, Wisconsin, as East Indian rosewood, a common hafting material used by the Sheffield cutlery makers on their low-priced butcher knives. The marking follows.

G ♡ R

F U R N I S

Himsworth says of Furnis (Furness): "As recently as 60 years ago the Furness brothers of Stannington were still bringing their knives into Sheffield to be packed with the goods of other manufacturers for shipment abroad, generally to the United States, at a very low price."[7]

Presumably figure 46e is the oldest knife in this lot. It was found with a human skeleton when workmen removed a large mound of earth in the right-of-way of a road near Fluvanna, New York. Beauchamp is of the opinion that it was "obtained by the Senecas from the French in Canada by traffic or stealth, or buried in this mound with some deceased French hunter."[8] The mark "Sabatier, Rue St. Honore, 84A, Paris" lends a possible clue to its

[5] A vivid account of the Miamis scalping propensities appears in Downey: *Indian Wars*, pp. 55–69.

[6] Lt. William Digby's *The British Invasion from the North* (Albany, 1887) provides a contemporary reference to English trade knives marked "G. R. for Georgius Rex" among the rampaging Wyandot Indians in New York, 1777.

[7] Himsworth: *Cutlery*, pp. 54–5.

[8] Beauchamp: *Metallic Implements*, p. 72, Pl. 35.

age. In any case, this is a typical French carving knife of the design that persists today in varied sizes as the "French knife," favorite of professional cooks and restaurateurs.[9] It would indeed serve as a "scalper," and seventeenth-century invoices show that it was traded in some quantity in New York;[1] but it never "caught on" in the trade of the day with which we are especially concerned, probably because it is high-quality, expensive, and rather foreign to the general market which supplied the Western fur trade during the early nineteenth century.

Jim Baker, mountain man, lingered on in some of his trapper haunts well into the modern period.[2] Personal mementos of his experiences in the fur fields are preserved in several Western museums. The country-made knife and its sheath (fig. 46f), no. C-1231/1 in the Wyoming State Museum, are documented as "made and used by Jim Baker. Received from Mr. Frank G. White, Palo Alto, Calif." The specimens are good examples of the clever workmanship of frontiersmen who made the best of the crude and limited materials that could be had in the wilds. Another Jim Baker knife made from a file is owned by the Colorado State Historical Society (No. 322F) and is illustrated in figure 51c.

A country-made blade, heavy enough for the chopping block yet small enough to be used as a scalper or a general-purpose knife, is shown in figure 47b. It was found in 1924 at the site of a trappers' camp at the mouth of Curtis Canyon, five miles north of the present-day town of Jackson, Wyoming, by William McInelliy, who passed it on to the Roy Van Vleck Collection of Jackson Hole relics.

William M. Beauchamp, a pioneer among American antiquarians, presents the Iroquois knife (fig. 47c) as "more suggestive of a true scalping knife than most others. . . . It was found at East Cayuga in 1888. The rough handle is of antler, probably made by the Indian owner."[3] A very similar scalping knife with handle of reindeer antler is preserved in the Royal Ontario Museum, Toronto.[4] This specimen was taken from an Indian grave.

[9] Elizabeth Sweeney: "Better Cutting with the Right Knife," *McCalls Magazine* (December 1947), pp. 88–9.

[1] A. J. F. Van Laer, ed. and tr.: *Documents Relating to New Netherland, 1624–1626* (San Marino: Huntington Library; 1924), p. 220.

[2] Nolie Mumey: *The Life of Jim Baker, 1818–1898* (Denver, 1931).

[3] Beauchamp: *Metallic Implements*, p. 71, Fig. 105, Pl. 25.

[4] Himsworth: *Cutlery*, pp. 196–7, Fig. 65, reproduces Mrs. Arthur Woodward's photograph of the Ontario knife.

FIG. 47. *More "Scalping Knives."*

a, bowie knife, formerly in the Philip Medicus Collection. *b*, handmade scalper blade, Van Vleck Collection, Jackson Hole, Wyoming. *c*, Iroquois scalping knife, East Cayuga, New York; the drawing was done after Beauchamp: *Metallic Implements*. *d*, Creek scalping knife, Oklahoma Historical Society. *e*, Onondaga scalping knife; drawing done after Beauchamp: *Metallic Implements*. Illustration by William Macy, Jefferson National Expansion Memorial, St. Louis.

The Oklahoma Historical Society owns the crude blade shown in figure 47*d*, that is accessioned as a "Creek scalping knife obtained from Mrs. Alex. Posey, Talequah, Oklahoma in 1925. Catalog No. 1166 ccc."

The Iroquois, long conversant with the white man's ways, have enjoyed a continuity of residence upon ancestral lands and, perhaps more than any other Indians, have cherished and preserved their old-time properties and held to certain ancient traits. One of the old-time properties handed down through generations of Onondaga Indians is the scalping knife pictured in figure 47*e*. In the late nineteenth century it was given to Albert Cusick, an Indian, by another Onondaga who declared that it had seen use in warfare. For some two hundred years it received care in the hands of succeeding Iroquois generations, always sheltered in camp or cabin or on the person of its owner. Both the blade and the wooden handle are in perfect condition. It is of more than passing interest to find that this same knife type was supplied by the British to some other Indian allies before and during the French and Indian War, especially the Cherokee and Chickasaw.[5]

These eighteenth-century English knives are remarkably similar in style to the "Hangiar" of the 1700's shown in figure 50a.

THE BOWIE KNIFE

IN THE LATE 1820's A MAN-KILLING SOUTHERN FRONTIERSMAN won such a reputation with his big handmade "bear knife" that it directed the attention of both his friendly associates and his enemies upon the blade which did such execution. The man was James Bowie, and his lethal weapon quickly became known locally as the "bowie knife." There was little really new about the design of the bowie knife. Similar styles had been in vogue among warriors in Europe for hundreds of years (see fig. 39, p. 166). But to many American patriots and to a small army of roisterers in the South and Southwest it was new—and magical. Actually, it was the personality and the prowess of James Bowie that was magical, but lesser men wanted to emulate him. A demand was placed upon James Black, the Arkansas blacksmith who made James Bowie's knife, and upon other country blacksmiths who might be expected to produce the superior blade. Within a period of a few years bowie knives of various sizes were in the hands of numerous habitues of the South and Southwest. Both the users of the knives and the blacksmiths experimented with changes in the weight, balance, edges, point, guard, and shape of hilt. A goodly number of double-edged, spear-pointed, dagger-like bowies came into use, ultimately, but the preponderance of choice rested in the clipped point and the ever-present cross guard.

The tragic events at the Alamo, Texas, in February and March

[5] Beauchamp: *Metallic Implements*, p. 71, Fig. 11, Pl. 27; John R. Swanton: *The Indians of the Southeastern United States*, Bureau of American Ethnology, *Bulletin* 137 (1946), Pl. 10, No. 2, and *passim*.

1836 witnessed the death of James Bowie and gave immortality to Davy Crockett and his knife-wielding compatriots. The carnage wreaked upon the attacking Mexicans by the besieged Americans was, and still is, indelibly remembered as a blazing chapter in bowie-knife history. The worldwide publicity given to the Alamo heroes also spread the word regarding the bowie knife. Thereafter it was not possible for country blacksmiths to supply the demand for the celebrated knife. Several cutlery makers in Sheffield, England, received orders for bowies in 1836, and presently an enormous segment of the English cutlery industry engaged in making the famous weapon for the American trade.[6] Peterson [7] identifies and illustrates a great series of bowie knives representative of thirty-three Sheffield shops. Keener,[8] in picturing the bowie knives in the Robert Abels Collection, identifies thirty-two additional Sheffield manufacturers. There were, of course, some English sources not known to the two writers mentioned, which could be added to their sixty-five firm names. Seasoned judgment or individual whim caused some of the English cutlers to inflict various changes upon the bowie design. By the 1840's a number of factories in Baltimore, Philadelphia, Shelburne Falls (Massachusetts), and Baton Rouge supplied American versions of the bowie knife. The number of American factories increased just before and during the Civil War; at least forty United States manufacturers are represented among the marked specimens in present-day collections. Unnumbered individual blacksmiths, most of them unidentified, added their output to the general supply.

The demand for the bowie fighting knife fell off after the Civil War, and by the 1880's comparatively few manufacturers produced it. Smaller hunting knives made in the image of the bowie continued in some demand, and in a few instances pioneer firms,

[6] Raymond W. Thorp: *Bowie Knife* (Albuquerque: Univ. of New Mexico Press; 1948), pp. 136–41. This is an exhaustive treatment of the "bowies"—family and knife; authentic of background and well indexed. J. Frank Dobie: "Jim Bowie's Knife," *Saga* magazine (May 1956), pp. 12–15, 85–8. See also Dobie's *Tales of Old-Time Texas* (Boston: Little, Brown; 1955). Himsworth: *Cutlery*, p. 54: "The first large fortunes made in Sheffield sprang from the American trade."

[7] Peterson: *American Knives*, pp. 25–70. Here is a most satisfying account of the bowie knife.

[8] William G. Keener: *Bowie Knives from the Collection of Robert Abels* (Cleveland: Ohio Historical Soc.; 1962). Excellent illustrations of 93 bowie knives in the Abels Collection, New York.

such as the John Russell Green River Works and the Collins Company,[9] maintain to this day a production that has been continuous since the heyday of the bowie. A few newcomers in the field also produce bowie knives equal to or better than those of a hundred years ago.[1]

In the autumn of 1836, after the fall of the Alamo and after the early orders for bowie knives had reached England, Hiram Cutler of Sheffield sent to Ramsay Crooks of the American Fur Company a sketch of a "Texian knife that would probably suit Indians." Crooks replied: "We have the drawing of the Texian Knife for which we thank you. The article is not wanted yet in our region." [2] There is small evidence that the true bowie knife found favor in the northern Plains and the Rockies until after the day of the mountain man; it did come into limited use among trappers and traders in the Southwest and among emigrants in the North [3] before the close of the 1840's.

The unidentified bowie knife shown in figure 47a is not traceable to the beaver country, but it has the 10-inch heavy blade of the early models, heavy enough to cleave a human skull, and rugged enough to disarticulate the joints of a bull elk—or dig the grave of a fallen comrade. Its stout ivory grip is mounted with copper. The scabbard is black leather. Formerly the specimen was in the Philip Medicus Collection, New York City; its present whereabouts is not recorded.

Travelers on the overland trails in the first years of emigration sometimes armed themselves with bowie knives, and the U. S. War Department adopted bowie-style knives that were used during the late 1830's and the 1840's in both the Regular Army units and the militia. These last were of three regulation styles and were manufactured under government contracts by Andrew G. Hicks of

[9] Collins Company: *Catalogo Illustrado de Herramientas* . . . (Hartford, Conn., 1919), pp. 31, 34, 35, 37, 49; *Catalogo M. Facoes* . . . (Collinsville, Conn., 1958), pp. 6, 8, 9, 12, 14, 15. Richard Wilcox: "The Long Knives of Collinsville," *Steelways* (January 1948), pp. 8–11.
[1] Peterson: *American Knives*, pp. 149–54; Al Buck: *Knife Know-How* (San Diego, 1964), pp. 1–12 and suppl.
[2] American Fur Company Papers, letter, Cutler to Crooks, September 24, 1836; letter, Crooks to Cutler, November 23, 1836. *Letter Book* 4, p. 106; reel 2, microfilm.
[3] J. G. W. Dillin: *The Kentucky Rifle* (Washington, D.C.: Nat'l Rifle Ass'n; 1924), Pl. 99.

Cleveland, Ohio, and by the Ames Manufacturing Company of Cabotville, Massachusetts.[4] The Ames "rifleman's knife" of 1849 especially was carried into the Far West (see fig. 49d). The civilian bowies that featured in early Far West history were varied in style and in origin; they were anything but "regulation."

The bowie knives pictured in figure 48 all came from the same maker, William F. Jackson, Sheffield, England. The rusted, handleless blade (fig. 48a) is owned by the Oregon Historical Society, where it bears catalog number 1349. It appears to have been through a fire, and both the scales of the handle and the cross guard are lacking. Stamped in capital letters on the blade is RIO GRANDE CAMP KNIFE; at the tang end of the blade (above the choil) is the maker's name, WM. JACKSON & CO. This battered and incomplete specimen affords an example of the deceptive nature of some dilapidated iron artifacts; under casual glance it is a nondescript butcher knife, but in its original condition it was like the bowie knife pictured in figure 48b.

The staghorn-handled Rio Grande camp knife (fig. 48b) has had the benefits of continuous care. Its spear-pointed blade, 10 inches long, is edged along its upper margin for about one half its length. As on the preceding specimen (fig. 48a), the words RIO GRANDE CAMP KNIFE are stamped longitudinally upon the blade, and transversely just in front of the guard appears:

WM JACKSON

SHEAF ISLAND WORKS

SHEFFIELD

The Lincoln Museum, Ford's Theatre, Washington, D.C., owns John Wilkes Booth's Rio Grand camp knife, which he brandished on the occasion of Lincoln's assassination and with which he stabbed Major Rathbone after the shooting. Booth's knife is like the one illustrated, except that it lacks the escutcheon plate, the blade is 8 inches long, and RIO GRANDE is spelled RIO GRAND. A second Rio Grande camp knife owned by the Lincoln Museum also was one of the conspirators' weapons the night of the assassination. It is a "dead ringer" for figure 48b, except that there is no escutch-

[4] B. R. Lewis: *Small Arms and Ammunition in the U. S. Service* (Washington, D.C.: Smithsonian Inst.; 1960), p. 84, Pl. 22; Peterson: *American Knives*, pp. 73–4.

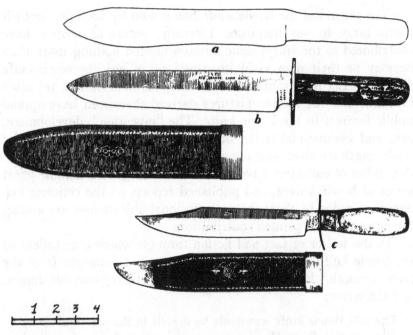

FIG. 48. *Rio Grande Camp Knives.*

a, rusted blade of a Sheffield bowie knife made by William F. Jackson; now in the Oregon Historical Society. *b,* intact bowie knife of the same origin as specimen *a;* formerly in the Philip Medicus Collection. *c,* lightweight bowie knife made by W. F. Jackson, Sheffield. Drawing by William Macy, Jefferson National Expansion Memorial, St. Louis.

eon plate.[5] The knife illustrated in figure 48*b* has a silver guard. Its total length is 15 inches, and the staghorn scales are held to the tang by five rivets. The leather sheath has red finish, embossed with gold; the throat is silver. Formerly the specimens were in the Philip Medicus Collection.

The William Jackson knife (fig. 48*c*) is characteristic of the smaller bowie knives once in vogue among American gentlemen anywhere and everywhere. Its 8-inch blade bears pictures of the hunter and the chase, and the slogan "I surpass. Try me." The leather sheath is ornamented in gold and silver. The specimens were once included in the now-scattered Philip Medicus Collection.

[5] I am indebted to the National Park Service for opportunity to examine the specimens and for photographs of the "conspirators' knives" in the Lincoln Museum.

The legend of the bowie knife has grown by accretion until it looms large in our literature. Literally, scores of writers have contributed to the story; some authors needed nothing more than hearsay or their own vivid imaginations in writing bowie-knife "history." Let it be said to their credit that their stories are often brilliant, and the motion pictures derived therefrom have spread public interest in the bowie knife. The "invention," development, use, and commercialization of the knife constitute subjects for book-length treatises, and some such volumes have been published. A number of collectors have followed their urge to assemble great series of bowie knives, and published reports on the concrete evidences afforded by these three-dimensional objects now are among the more valuable printed contributions.

In the welter of fact and fiction through which the student of the bowie knife may wade are some assertions "straight from the horse's mouth." Rezin P. Bowie, brother of the redoubtable James, in 1838 wrote:

> The first Bowie knife was made by myself in the parish of Avoyelles, in this State [Louisiana], as a hunting knife, for which purpose, exclusively, is was used for many years. . . . Following are the facts respecting the manner in which Col. James Bowie first became possessed of this knife. He had been shot by an individual with whom he was at variance; and as I presumed that a second attempt would be made by the same person to take his life, I gave him the knife to be used as occasion might require, as a defensive weapon. Some time afterwards it was resorted to by Colonel James Bowie in a chance, rough fight between himself and certain other individuals with whom he was then inimical . . . it was the means of saving his life. The improvement in its fabrication and the state of perfection which it has since acquired from experienced cutlers, was not brought about through my agency.[6]

Rezin Bowie wrote more, but most of his comments had to do with men and events rather than with the knife. Raymond W. Thorp, in his book *Bowie Knife*, has weighed the bulky evidences advanced by the Bowie brothers, by miscellaneous historians, and by the romancers. Briefly and incompletely, the sequence follows:

---

[6] Rezin P. Bowie, Iberville, Louisiana, writing to the editor of *The Planters Advocate*, August 24, 1838; quoted by Raymond W. Thorp in *Bowie Knife* (Albuquerque: Univ. of New Mexico Press; 1948), pp. 99–102.

Rezin Bowie's hunting knife in the hands of James Bowie was the first to arouse interest.[7]

An Arkansas blacksmith, James Black, made a number of knives for James Bowie and for frontiersmen who wanted weapons "like Bowie's." Black took occasion to modify the design of the original and succeeded in attaining a temper and finish which excelled.

With one or another of these knives, James Bowie engaged in several bloody encounters in the late 1820's and early 1830's that received wide publicity and popularized the bowie knife. Demands for the weapon came from many parts of the country, and the cutlery makers of England received the bulk of the orders.

James Bowie became a notorious citizen of Texas in the early 1830's. He was commissioned a colonel in Sam Houston's forces in the fight for independence, was placed in command at the Alamo at a critical moment, and there died at the hands of attacking Mexican forces on March 6, 1836. His demise only intensified the popularity of the "bowie knife," which by this time existed in a variety of shapes and sizes.

It is next to impossible to define realistically one knife type as *the* bowie knife. This was not always the case. An observer in 1838, identified only as "P. Q.," gave a clear description of the bowie known to him: "The blade measures twelve inches. . . . Observe its edge—keen and smooth, and so perfect that a barber might use it in his trade. Its point is curved and hollowed at the back, cutting both ways, like a two-edged sword. It is two inches broad at the heel and of proportionate thickness. The weight, alone, is sufficient to give effect to a descending blow." [8]

Obviously this is the type of knife exemplified by figure 47a. Just as obviously, it is not the type shown in figure 47b; yet a few years after "P. Q." wrote his letter, both knives were widely advertised and accepted as "bowie" knives. Keener states: "As the bowie knife gained in popularity, variations in form increased. . . . The Sheffield cutlers were largely responsible for the wide variations in blade, hilt, and guard design that characterized the knives made after 1840. . . . Knives marked with the magic Bowie name often

[7] Peterson: *American Knives*, p. 28, illustrates an early bowie knife that was made for Rezin Bowie and presented by him to a friend, H. W. Fowler.

[8] Thorp: *Bowie Knife*, p. 95, quoting "P. Q.'s" letter published in *Baltimore Commercial Transcript*, June 9 and 11, 1838.

bore little resemblance to large fighting knives, but they sold just as well." [9]

H. V. Wilkinson & Co. ("American bowie knife") and Unwin & Rodgers ("cast-steel bowie knife") were among the Sheffield manufacturers who marked their spear-pointed blades with the Bowie name. By the time of the Mexican War, the term "bowie knife" was applied to almost any big fighting knife, and during the Civil War the confusion was multiplied. Harold Peterson takes a step toward clarification by recognizing the bowie-type knife described by "P. Q.," above, and pictured in figure 47a as "the classical form." [1]

Miscellaneous Big Knives

It is unlikely that the eighteenth-century Turkish knife shown in figure 49a has any lineal relationship to the eighteenth-century scalping knives that the British supplied to the Iroquois in New York, yet the style is remarkably similar to the shape, size, and structure of those "scalpers" (see fig. 47e). Diderot, who in his *Encyclopédie* presents the Turkish knife, says of it: "A type of poignard which the Turkish soldier carries in Constantinople." Presumably neither it nor the English scalper had sufficient commendable features to warrant perpetuation of the model; it finds no continuing niche.

The battered and rusty big butcher knife illustrated in figure 49b was taken from an Indian grave. It is now in the U. S. National Museum, where records refer to it merely as "Bone-handled Knife; J. H. DEVEREUX." The haft is 5 inches long; the blade is 11 inches long and 1½ inches wide. The broken point has been rounded. In 1822–3, the U. S. Indian Trade Office, George Town, D.C., invoiced 224 dozen scalping knives at $1.37 to $2.50 per dozen. Included were 50 dozen "white bone" knives like this one.

In the Wells Fargo Museum, San Francisco, is the fine quality camp knife shown in figure 49c. A false edge extends for 4 inches along the back of the blade; the true edge is razor-sharp. The *ricasso* is ⅝ of an inch in length, and the stout blade is 9¼ inches long and ¼ inch thick for several inches forward from the tang. The wide tang is conspicuous, and the visible metal parts of the

---

[9] Keener: *Bowie Knives*, p. 3.
[1] Peterson: *American Knives*, p. 34.

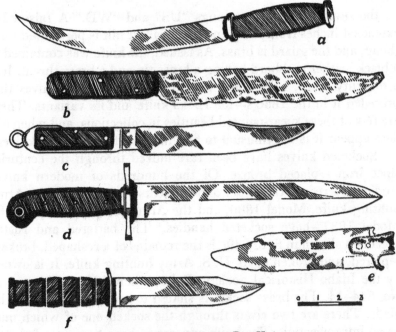

FIG. 49. *Miscellaneous Big Knives.*

a, hangiar; 10-inch blade. The drawing is after Diderot: *Encyclo-pédie*, Vol. III of Pls., Pl. 2A. *b*, butcher knife from an Indian grave; 11-inch blade. U. S. National Museum. *c*, fine-quality camp knife; 9¼-inch blade. No. 220, Wells Fargo Museum, San Francisco. *d*, "Ames Riflemans Knife of 1849"; 11¾-inch blade. The drawing is after B. R. Lewis: *Small Arms*, Pl. 22*d*. *e*, U. S. Army hunting knife; 8½-inch blade. No. 344–14, Idaho Historical Society, Boise. *f*, U. S. Marine Corps knife, 1942–3; 7½-inch blade. The drawing is after *American Rifleman* (May 1944), pp. 26–7. These drawings are by Glen Dines.

handle, including a terminal ring, are of a white metal. Three larger rivets and four small pins penetrate the wood scales which constitute the 3¾-inch grips. Such superior knives seldom went to Indians in any ordinary trade. The owner of this one was Martin Colman, reported to have been a 49'er at Murphys Camp, California. The specimen bears number 220 in the Wells Fargo Collection.

One thousand "Ames Riflemans Knife of 1849" (fig. 49*d*) were made under a government contract of March 8, 1848, for the U. S. Regiment of Mounted Riflemen; price, $4.00 per knife. The 11¾-inch blade is marked "Ames Mfg. Co. Cabotville 1849," and on the reverse are the markings "US" and "WD." A false edge extends 4 inches from the point. The walnut hilt is perforated for a thong, and the guard is brass. As issued, the knife was contained in a black leather scabbard having a brass tip and a brass throat. It is a doughty piece, longer and heavier than the Army knives that preceded it in the 1830's—the Hicks knife and its variants. There are few of these spear-pointed beauties in collections, and when one does appear it is not unusual to find it classed with bowie knives.[2]

Socketed knives have been rare indeed through the centuries since iron replaced bronze. Of the hundreds of modern knives studied by recent collectors and students, two—the U. S. Army hunting knife, Model 1880, and the Army Hospital Corps knife, Model 1887—have socketed handles.[3] The battered and rusted specimen shown in figure 49*e* is the remains of a reshaped, broken, repaired, and broken again U. S. Army hunting knife. It is owned by the Idaho Historical Society, Boise, where it is catalogued as No. 344–14. The brass socket is slotted to receive the base of the blade. There are two rivets through the socket, one of which may be an improvisation. The knife appears to have been in a fire; the upper finger guard (brass) seems to have been melted. The small notch in the lower finger guard, next to the blade, is a constant feature of the model. The Idaho museum records indicate that a related artifact was "dug up in a garden of the old Russian fort, Wrangell, Alaska." Presumably the knife came from the same place. Whether or not U. S. troops ever occupied the site has not been determined.

The all-purpose Marine Corps knife illustrated in figure 49*f* is another descendant of the frontiersmans' arm. It is a modified bowie knife with some of the characteristics of the modern hunting knife. It was made to supply the U. S. Marine Corps in the South Pacific, 1942–3, and its rugged makeup places it in the category of big knives, even though its blade is 7½ inches long. Some of the attributes of a good fighting knife were sacrificed by its designers in order to give it stout qualities; it was expected to stand up under the strain of chopping jungle growth and digging foxholes. The blade is double-edged for two inches back from the point, may be

[2] Keener: *Bowie Knives*, No. 134; B. R. Lewis: *Small Arms*, p. 84, Pl. 22 d; Peterson: *American Knives*, p. 74, Fig. 98.

[3] Peterson: *American Knives*, p. 74, Fig. 99, and p. 77, Fig. 101. Through the cooperation of H. J. Swinney, director, Idaho Historical Society, I have full-size photographs and a thorough description of the Idaho knife.

bent deeply without causing permanent deformation, and by virtue of its well-tempered, high-carbon steel retains a sharp edge under considerable abuse. The mark "USMC" is stamped on the blade or on the guard. In 1943 and 1944 some 2½ million of these "Mark 3" knives were procured by the U. S. government for parachute troops and rangers.[4] This model resembles the Marine Corps knife in some respects, but it is lighter in weight and has a blade 6.7 inches long. Ultimately, the leather grips of all of these models had to be treated with a fungicide to obviate rotting of the leather washers, and, in the case of the Mark 3, the all-leather scabbard originally devised was replaced by a plastic scabbard.[5] This current Army knife finds place in our account because of its unmistakable lineage.

THE FAMOUS GREEN RIVER KNIFE

PROBABLY NOTHING IN THE PROPERTIES OF THE MOUNTAIN man had greater connotation of trapper life and the gusto of the *dramatis personae* in the fur fields than did the "Green River knife." The name had nothing to do with that tributary of the Colorado, the Green River, to which so many mountain men gravitated; it pertained to a Green River in Massachusetts, upon the banks of which John Russell of Deerfield built a factory in 1832–4. His earliest products were not knives, but by 1836 the firm was organized on a solid financial basis, and one of the first American cutlery enterprises was launched in Russell's expanded factory. Surprisingly enough, J. Russell and Company competed successfully with the age-old cutlery makers of England. Mechanization, then little thought of in Sheffield, became the watchword at Greenfield, the home of the Green River Works. Drop hammers and great stamping machines, driven by waterpower, hurried the processes of forging and shaping the Green River blades. Presently, J. Russell and Company made knives equal in quality to the Sheffield product, and the price compared favorably with the Sheffield price. Butcher knives and kitchen knives constituted

[4] Mark 1 and Mark 2 knives were issued to U. S. Navy personnel during World War II. The Mark 2 is quite similar to the Mark 3, but the blade has a short, wide fuller and is stamped "USN. MARK 2."
[5] *American Rifleman* (May 1944), pp. 26–7; Peterson: *American Knives*, pp. 87–9, 110–11, fig. 139.

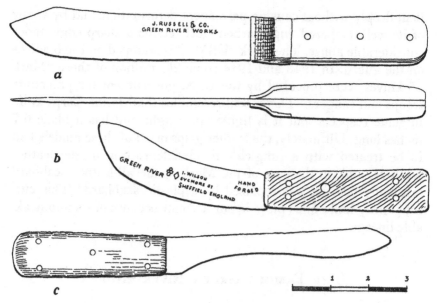

FIG. 50. *Green River Knives.*

a, J. Russell and Company butcher knife of the 1840's, Missouri Historical Society, St. Louis. *b*, English imitation of a Green River skinning knife, National Park Service, Grand Teton National Park. *c*, a much-used Green River knife, Missouri Historical Society, St. Louis.

major items in the production. Upon the blades of these early Russell knives was stamped "J. RUSSELL & CO./GREEN RIVER WORKS," as shown in figure 50*a*.

The desire of Americans to patronize home industry, coupled with the demonstrated worthiness of this Massachusetts product, quickly placed the Green River Works in the forefront. Substantial orders came from wholesalers who supplied the Far Western trade, and in no time at all the mountain men on Green River adopted the Green River butcher knives as their own. Ultimately the Sheffield industry felt the competition, and some of the makers imitated the Green River knives. One example of the English version of a Green River skinning knife appears in figure 50*b*. It has a superior-grade blade, bright and shiny, by I. Wilson of Sheffield, which bears the stamp "GREEN RIVER." The tang extends through the full length of the light-colored, natural-finish wooden handle. The rivets are polished, shiny brass. This specimen, made in the image of one of the J. Russell popular models, is in new (unused) condition and quite possibly came from the Sheffield shops at a comparatively recent date. It is exhibited in the National Park Service History Museum at Moose, Grand Teton National Park.

I. Wilson's "Green River" mark on this recent imitation is stamped near the point of the blade, a placement which tends to nullify the old-time trapper's cryptographic "Up to Green River." Two of the more successful writers, contemporaries of the mountain men, who left imperishable records of trapper behavior and trapper speech, clinched this particular euphemism in frontier literature. George Frederick Ruxton, in his *Life in the Far West*, tells of a brawl during a Taos fandango:

> Sweeping them [broken chair legs] round their heads, down came the heavy weapons amongst the Mexicans with wonderful effect—each blow, dealt by the nervous arms of Wooton and LaBonté, mowing down a good half-dozen of the assailants. At this the mountaineers gave a hearty whoop, and charged the wavering enemy with such resistless vigor, that they gave way and bolted through the door, leaving the floor strewed with wounded, many most dangerously; for, as may be imagined, a thrust from the keen scalp-knife by the nervous arm of a mountaineer was no baby blow, and seldom failed to strike home—up to the "Green River" on the blade.[6]

Lewis H. Garrard, in his *Wah-to-Yah and the Taos Trail*, quotes Louy Simonds reminiscing with Long Hatcher:

> "Mind the time we took Pawnee topknots away to the Platte?" questioned Simonds. Hatcher replied, "Wagh! ef we didn't, an' give an ogwh-ogwh longside that darned screechin', I'm a niggur. This child doesn't let an Injun count a coup on his cavyard always. They come mighty nigh rubbin' me out tother side of Spanish Peaks—woke up in the mornin' jist afore day, the devils yellin' like mad. I grabs my knife, keels one, an' made for timber, with four of thar cussed arrows in my meatbag. The 'Paches took my beaver—five packs of the prettiest in the mountains—an' two mules, but my traps was hid in the creek. Sez I, hyar's a gone coon if they keep my gun, so I follers thar trail an' at night crawls into camp, an' socks my big knife up to the Green River, first dig.

[6] Ruxton: *Life in the Far West*, Hafen edn. (Norman: Univ. of Oklahoma Press; 1951), p. 189.

. . . I got old bull thrower [the stolen rifle], made medicine over him, an' no darned niggur kin draw bead with him since." [7]

Of course, the expression "Up to Green River" had been in common use among the mountain men for some years before Ruxton and Garrard publicized the usage. It had come to mean "good job done"—a metaphor for perfection applicable to admirable *things* as well as to doughty *deeds*.

The misshapen blade shown in figure 50c is a Green River butcher knife deformed through repeated grinding and sharpening. A notable number of J. Russell knives now in Western collections are like this one. The specimens in both figures 50a and 50c are in the Missouri Historical Society Museum, St. Louis.

Records show that some 5,000 dozen Russell butcher knives were shipped to the West each year for many years. Understandably, old Green River knives are well represented in both private and public collections. Some of the existing specimens can be identified with certain Indian tribes, and a few are accompanied by the handmade sheaths provided by their last users. Practically all have undergone long years of handling by the greasy hands of men (and Indian women) who converted the wild bounty of the plains and mountains into food for human consumption, or made hides and pelts ready for local use or for the fur trade; the hilts are saturated with animal fat, and many of the blades bear little resemblance to their original shapes.

The several aspects of the history of the J. Russell and Company Green River Works are analyzed by Woodward.[8] Harold L. Peterson provides a comprehensive account in his *American Knives*.

The English butcher-knife blade illustrated in figure 51a is a relic of the beaver business in the Rockies. The marking "V(Crown)R" suggests that the maker of the blade was busy during the reign of Queen Victoria, who ascended the throne in 1837. As will be seen (p. 204), during the late 1830's and early 1840's, the Chouteaus of St. Louis were importing thousands of such knives from England. Most of the purchases were ar-

[7] Garrad: *Wah-to-yah and the Taos Trail* (Norman: Univ. of Oklahoma Press; 1955), p. 163. (Orig. publ. in 1850.)

[8] Woodward: "Those Green River Knives," *Indian Notes*, IV: 4 (October 1927), pp. 403–18; "Up to Green River," Los Angeles Westerners *Brand Book* (1948), pp. 141–6; "Green River Knives," *Western Folklore* (January 1950), pp. 56–9.

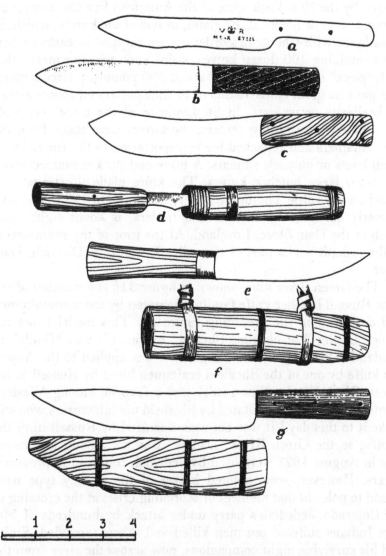

FIG. 51. *Butcher Knives and Wooden Scabbards.*

a, English blade, Loveland, Colorado. *b*, Green River "Dadley"; drawing after Woodward: "Those Green River Knives," pp. 411–12. *c*, Jim Baker handmade knife, Colorado Historical Society, Denver. *d*, Winnebago wooden sheath, State Historical Society, Wisconsin. *e* and *f*, Puget Sound wooden sheath, Washington State Historical Society, Tacoma. *g*, Wyoming wooden sheath, Rawlins National Bank, Wyoming. Drawing by William Macy, Jefferson National Expansion Memorial, St. Louis.

ranged by the New York office of the American Fur Company, and Hiram Cutler of Sheffield, England, provided the knives, which, in accordance with Chouteau's orders, were shipped in casks or barrels containing 100 dozen knives, each. Such packing meant that each "piece" of freight weighed about 300 pounds, a circumstance that gave no great embarrassment to transporters on routes served by keelboats or wagons. In St. Louis or at the more accessible backcountry distributing centers, the knives were taken from the big containers and repacked for transportation to the fur fields in small boats or on pack animals. A 90-pound pack contained about 30 dozen large butcher knives. The knife blade illustrated was found on the Little Thompson River, Colorado, in 1933. The site, formerly occupied by Indians and traders, is about eight miles south of the Dam Store, Loveland. At the time of my examination of the relic, it was a part of the collectionof D. R. Dietrich, Dam Store.

The Green River knife shown in figure 51*b* is a member of the John Russell butcher knife family celebrated by the mountain men and described in the preceding figure 50. This model bears the name "Dadley," of old-time Sheffield origin. (It was "Dadly" in England.) Presumably the designation was applied to the American knife by one of the Sheffield craftsmen hired by Russell in his Green River Works. The model was a favorite among Western frontiersmen and was imitated by Sheffield manufacturers who still make it to this day.[9] It was not manufactured by Russell until the 1830's; so the Green River "Dadley" was not among the knives that in August 1827 were used by Jedediah Smith in improvising spears. However, spear-pointed knives of the Dadley type were bound to poles in that moment of scorching crisis at the crossing of the Colorado. Jedediah's party under attack by hundreds of Mojave Indians suffered ten men killed and others wounded. Smith and his surviving eight companions, now across the river from the dead men, found that they had remaining to them five guns and their butcher knives. Jedediah wrote: "With our knives we lopped down the small trees in such manner as to clear a place in which to stand. The fallen poles formed a slight breastwork, and to the ends of some of the lighter poles we fastened our butcher knives with cords so as to form a tolerable lance. Thus poorly prepared we

[9] Woodward: "Those Green River Knives," pp. 411–12; Peterson: *American Knives*, p. 69.

waited the approach of our unmerciful enemies. On one side the river prevented them from approaching us, but in every other direction the Indians were closing in."[1] Two shots at long range downed two of the attackers and wounded another, whereupon the Indians gave up the attack.

The Jim Baker knife illustrated in figure 51c, is another example of a mountain man's handiwork.[2] The specimen is No. H322-F in the Colorado State Historical Society, Denver, where it is recorded as "made by forging a common file. Used for many years by Jim Baker."

SHEATHS AND SCABBARDS

A MIDDLE SIXTEENTH-CENTURY MANUSCRIPT, QUOTED BELOW, provides one of the earliest references to knives in America; it pertains to a knife encased in wood. Some Dutch, French, and English colonial inventories of the seventeenth and eighteenth centuries also recognize wooden scabbards; and wooden sheaths are still featured in catalogues and advertisements issued by some present-day manufacturers. Thus the documentary evidences of the use of wooden sheaths in America are rather continuous through a period of four hundred years, and the sheaths themselves are quite numerous in collections. Often the knives they contain are light-weight butcher knives. The wooden sheaths encountered in the present study were mostly "country-made."

As has been mentioned, the Frenchman Jacques LeMoyne de Morgues, wrote a priceless account of his experiences in Florida with the ill-fated Huguenot party of Laudonnière in 1564–5. Regarding the appalling slaughter inflicted upon the Huguenots by Spanish forces, LeMoyne wrote of a man who had been bound, slugged, and left in a pile of dead: "The sailor coming to his senses in the night, found himself among dead bodies. He remembered a knife he wore in a *wooden sheath*, and he managed to twist himself around little by little until he could get the knife out and cut his fetters. He then slipped away, walking throughout the night." Friendly Indians succored him.[3]

[1] Dale L. Morgan: *Jedediah Smith*, pp. 239–41.
[2] A second knife by Jim Baker is shown in figure 46f.
[3] Lorant: *The New World*, p. 84.

Indians usually made their own knife sheaths. They favored leather scabbards, and rarely was it reported that a wooden sheath was being used by Indians. One of the rarities is the specimen pictured in figure 51d. This knife and its wooden case are recorded to have been used in 1845 by a Winnebago Indian in what is now Dodge County, Wisconsin. The sheath is wrapped tightly at its ends with finely cut rawhide thongs. A further wrapping with thin strands of sinew appears between the fine bindings. The wooden-handled knife has undergone repeated sharpenings until the blade is little more than a sliver. Mrs. Emma House is credited as donor; see catalogue number 3821, State Historical Society of Wisconsin.

The blade and the wooden handle of the knife shown in figure 51e fit snugly in the wooden sheath (fig. 51f), as does a cork in the mouth of a bottle. These specimens, not accompanied by data, are strikingly similar to Finnish hunting knives with metal ferrules and wooden scabbards currently imported to the United States from Finland.[4] The large thongs encircling the scabbard enable it to be attached to the user's belt or elsewhere on the person. Henry Sicade is credited as donor of this specimen, now in the Washington State Historical Society, Tacoma.

The knife and wooden sheath illustrated in figure 51g is reported as having been used by a member of an Austrian labor crew employed in railroad construction near Rawlins, Wyoming, at the end of the nineteenth century. In this example, the binding around the sheath is soft, iron wire, tightly twisted. In the 1930's the specimen was among the local history exhibits displayed in the Rawlins National Bank. A knife and wooden sheath so like these specimens in every particular as to suggest that the source was the same is owned by the Montana Historical Society (No. 2225).

The assortments of small knives that might be brought together in the storage rooms of museums and in the cabinets of private collectors are almost endless in variety. The specimens shown in figure 52 constitute a small sampling of improvised knives that reflect the special needs, whims and, in some instances, the crudities of their onetime makers and owners. Most of the pieces pictured are from Western sites.

[4] Finlandia House, Portland, Oregon. This type of knife and wooden scabbard with stopper-like fitting was in use among the California Argonauts. Patrick Breen of the Donner Party had one, and it is now exhibited by the State of California in the Old Custom House, Monterey.

The iron knife shown in figure 52a was discovered in a Chumash Indian grave in Santa Barbara County, California. The deeply rusted blade is of early trade origin, and the wooden handle, one may assume, was fashioned long ago by an Indian owner. The specimen is No. 18330 in the U. S. National Museum, where it is credited to "Bowers and Schumacher."

Pride of workmanship is apparent in the Spanish knife illustrated in figure 52b. The clipped-point blade is more than two inches wide and is etched lightly with a branching design along the midrib. The deeply grooved wooden hilt does not have a ferrule. Presumably the slender tang that passes through the hilt is threaded to receive the ornamental pommel, a gargoyle-like head of metal. Examples of oldtime knives of this design are discussed in Klemm.[5] Records in the Los Angeles Museum, where this specimen bears No. L-580, state: "Knives of this sort probably were carried by the men who rode with Portola in 1769. They were well made to withstand hard usuage, yet they were ornamented. The Spanish loved to decorate everything they used. Mary Parker Collection." In Mexico, backcountry smithies still make knives in the image of the eighteenth-century models, somewhat similar to this one. Even the present-day Mexican bowie knives are in the Spanish tradition and feature some of the distinctive characteristics of this blade and hilt.[6] The etching of modest designs on the blades also persists on the modern product.

The small handmade skinning knife shown in figure 52c was found during the earliest days of settlement in an old cabin in Nampa, Idaho. It was preserved as a treasured relic of wilderness ways by the family of the finder, a first settler. The Idaho Historical Society, Boise, now owns the knife.

A Russian site, Taral, on the Copper River in Alaska, yielded the problematical iron blade shown in figure 52d. Vanstone[7] recognizes it as native-made "because of its general resemblance to Eskimo and Athabascan end-bladed knives." The present-day Indians in the Taral locality are known as Ahtena. A Russian post existed there during the early 1800's, but apparently it was not occupied when a visiting party of Russians called there in 1843. It

[5] Gustav F. Klemm: *Allgemeine Kulturwissenshaft* (Leipzig, 1854–5), Vol. II.

[6] "Imports," *American Rifleman* (May 1960), p. 94.

[7] James W. Vanstone: "Exploring the Copper River Country," *Pacific Northwest Quarterly*, XLVI: 4 (1955), p. 122.

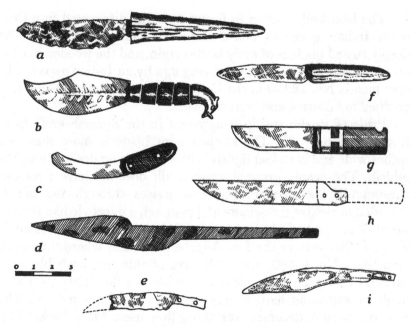

FIG. 52.   *Miscellaneous Small Knives.*

a, Indian-made California knife, U. S. National Museum. *b*, Spanish knife, Los Angeles Museum. *c*, Idaho skinning knife, Idaho Historical Society, Boise. *d*, problematical blade from Alaska; the drawing is after Vanstone: "Exploring the Copper River Country," p. 122. *e*, Pawnee blade with sheepfoot point, Museum of Natural History, University of Kansas, Lawrence (Dr. C. S. Smith). *f*, Iroquois knife, New York; the drawing is after Beauchamp: *Metallic Implements*, p. 71. *g*, rifleman's knife of the flintlock period, John Barsotti Collection, Columbus, Ohio. *h*, Jaco Finlay's knife, Spokane House, Washington State Parks Commission. *i*, Virginia plantation blade with sheepfoot point, Hume: "Excavations at Roswell," p. 223. Drawings by Glen Dines.

is said that Americans did not come to the place until 1885. Because of archeological considerations, including dated contexts, this blade is regarded by its finder to be earlier than the American period, "probably an example of early 19th century trade iron of Russian origin." In shape, the artifact is not unlike that of a present-day fish-filleting knife, but it also resembles some projectile points.

The incomplete blade illustrated in figure 52*e* was recovered at the onetime Pawnee place, Kansas Monument Site, Republic County, Kansas.[8] Numerous blades of "kitchen-knife" size were found at the same site, many of which bear the marks of French makers. Originally this specimen had the sheepfoot point favored by some Indian artisans for scribing, perforating, mortising, and carving wood and stiff rawhide. Literally hundreds of small knife blades made in France have been taken from the ground at such historic places as Michilimackinac and Fort St. Joseph, Michigan; the Stansbury Site, Texas; the Bell Site, Big Lake Butte des Morts, Wisconsin; the Angloa Farm Site and the Bayogoula Village Site, both in Louisiana; the Fatherland Plantation, Mississippi; the Kansas Monument Site, Kansas; and at other places not readily named by the author. All of the locations once had Frenchmen in residence, or French traders supplied merchandise more or less directly to the Indian inhabitants of the places. A surprising number of the rusted blades, some of which remained in the ground for two centuries or more, still show trademarks or the names of the makers. These makers and the periods of their works often are a matter of record in the commercial documents preserved in France. Altogether, it appears that the existing extensive collections of French trade knives offer occasion for collaboration on the parts of the archeologist and archivist in establishing a useful chronology, a tool to be used by the archeologist-historian.

The stag-handled iron knife shown in figure 52f was found in an Indian site at Fleming, New York. Geographically, it is a continent apart from figure 52a, the California knife, yet the primitive needs of the savage who made it were much the same as those of the California Indian. The knives (figs. 52a and 52f) are quite similar in structure, just as were the prehistoric chert and obsidian knives of New York and California. The stone blades frequently were the same size and shapes as are these hand-forged iron blades, as evidenced by a great many stone specimens from precontact sites all over the country. The two crude iron tools (figs. 52a and 52f) are existent examples "in hand" of a change in a native institution brought about by the electrifying touch of the white man's fur trade. The advantages of trade iron very quickly caused

---

[8] Carlyle S. Smith: "European Trade Materials," p. 2. I have the photograph from which the sketch (fig. 52e) was prepared through the cooperation of Dr. Smith.

the trading Indian to look upon iron as an urgent necessity; almost overnight he was caught up in a cultural revolution. The sudden change from stone to iron knives provides just one of the several discernible evidences of the quick disappearance of the pre-Columbian Indian world. The specimen figure 52*f* is from Beauchamp.[9]

Fred Cline of Arcanum, Ohio, was a firearms expert who specialized in flintlocks. The sketch in figure 52*g*, represents a rifleman's knife from a pouch that accompanied a flintlock rifle in the Cline Collection. Mr. Cline made the sketch, and it is used here through the kindness of Mr. John Barsotti. The knife is entirely handmade. The blade is forged from a rasp, and the polished hickory hilt features a block-tin or "white-metal" inlay very neatly made. The inlay technique is the same as that often employed in molding block tin in grooves cut in catlinite pipe bowls. A polished steel bolster separates the handle from the blade, and a "bullet starter" appears in the butt. Usually, the mountain man who carried a muzzle-loading rifle also carried a knife of this kind in a sheath attached to the strap that supported his rifleman's pouch. A sharp knife was quite essential in cutting patches and in shearing the surplus of the patch material after the patched bullet was forced into the muzzle.

John Work, a chief trader of the Hudson's Bay Company, left a contemporary account of the burial of Jaco Finlay, caretaker at the abandoned Spokane House in 1828. In 1954 Louis Caywood,[1] National Park Service archeologist, reported on the exhumation of human remains believed to be Finlay's. With the skeleton was the knife blade (fig. 52*h*) within a disintegrated light metal scabbard. No part of the knife handle remained. Spokane House was established by the North West Company in 1810, taken over by the Hudson's Bay Company in 1821, and vacated by that company in 1826. Jaco Finlay, whose employment dated back to North West Company days, remained at the post until his death and was there buried. His unprepossessing knife offers fair testimony regarding one type of knife carried by a trapper, and we have it straight from his hand, so to speak. Interestingly enough, Jaco's half-breed son, Jacques, is identified as the purchaser of two of the knives sold by

[9] Beauchamp: *Metallic Implements*, p. 71.
[1] Louis R. Caywood: *Archeological Excavations at Fort Spokane, 1951, 1952, 1953*, p. 23 and Pl. VII.

William H. Ashley at the 1825 rendezvous on Henry's Fork of the Green.[2]

To the Virginia blacksmith who hammered out the small blade shown in figure 52i, it would have seemed a far cry from the plantation use of his knife to the Pawnee use of the similar blade illustrated in figure 52e. Actually, however, the big differences were in the users and in the places of use. The buckskin-garbed Pawnee needed the beak-pointed blade to cut his "whang" leather and to incise and carve the hickory-hard rawhide of his parfleche and other decorated bags. The Virginian, black or white, needed this type of knife to cut the dressed leather with which harnesses and other horse gear were made and repaired. Both knives were made at about the same time, both served during the last half of the eighteenth century, both were relegated to refuse, and both were recovered by archeologists in approximately the same period. This Virginia knife went into a trash pit at Roswell on the York River, Gloucester County, sometime between 1763 and 1772.[3] Its sheepfoot point is decomposed but recognizable, and the rough lapping or folding of the tang and the blacksmith's hammer marks are still plainly in evidence, as are the three holes through which passed the rivets for the wood or bone plates of the handle. As in the case of the Nebraska knife, oxidation has been extensive, but enough remains to indicate that this stout blade never broke under use.

SPECIALIZED KNIVES OF THE MOUNTAIN MEN

Skinning Knives and Fleshing Tools

It is a foregone conclusion that the mountain man did not stand on any particular propriety or listen to possible dictates of the fraternity when skins were to be removed from carcasses; if he lacked a proper skinning knife, he used any knife most readily at hand. Nevertheless, special skinning knives were procured and, usually, they were available to the man responsible for skinning. After the wholesale slaughter of the buffalo was initiated, the

[2] D. L. Morgan, ed.: *William H. Ashley*, pp. 118–29, states that Jacques was one of the deserters from Ogden's Hudson's Bay Company party on Weber River, May 1825. However, Jacques is said to have rejoined the British later.

[3] Ivor Noël Hume: "Excavations at Roswell, Gloucester County, Virginia, 1957–59," U. S. National Museum, Bulletin 225 (1962), p. 223, Fig. 36, Item 4.

manufacture of skinning knives became a major enterprise in the cutlery works of Sheffield, England, as well as in America. It was quite customary for Indians and whites alike to regrind the knife to be used for skinning so as to place the bevel on one side only. This change in edge reduced the danger of slashing the hides. A number of knives suitable for the special skinning task already have been shown in figures 42, 44, 46, 47, 49, and 52, and many of the jackknives that follow are well adapted to the skinning of beaver, for example.

The specimen shown in figure 53a obviously was made by some old-timer expressly for skinning. It was hand-forged from a file or from similar tool steel. Possibly it once had plates of wood, bone, or horn riveted to the tang but, when found, it had fragments of a leather hand grip pinned through the rivet holes. The knife was collected by Robert Nymeyer in Dark Canyon on the eastern slope of the Guadalupe Mountains a few miles north of Carlsbad Caverns, New Mexico. It was buried under four feet of sand and gravel that had been washed into a cove by flash floods. Erosion had cut the deposit of earth in a way that left one vertical face, and the handle of the knife protruded from this bank. Regarding the depth of burial, Mr. Nymeyer observed: "This, of course, means nothing, as flash floods periodically roar down the canyon, shifting and relocating all movable soil and stones. One flood carried the knife from some location up canyon and buried it deep in the gravel, then a later one slashed away a part of the deposit and again exposed the relic." [4] The specimen is preserved in the Museum of the Historical Society, Carlsbad, New Mexico.

The skinning knife illustrated in figure 53b, was made from a circular saw blade for the use of a buffalo hunter. It is documented as "made in the early 1870's." Accompanying it in the Colorado Historical Society Collections is a 14-inch "ripping knife," a usual complement in the professional buffalo hunter's knife kit. The curved skinning knife of this size was used by the mountain man and by his Indian contemporaries in those parts of the beaver country where buffalo robes were an item in the trade. It did not meet really big demand, however, until the day of the organized hide hunters, beginning in the 1840's. During the period of whole-sale slaughter, Canadians of the prairie provinces were quite as

---

[4] Letter, Nymeyer to Russell, January 1, 1949.

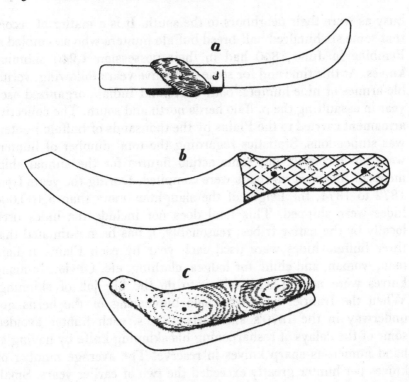

KNIFE TERMINOLOGY

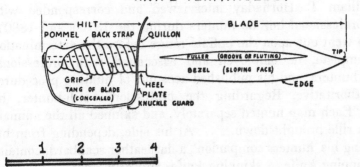

FIG. 53. *Skinning Knives and Fleshing Tools.*

a, hand-forged skinning knife, Historical Society of Carlsbad, New Mexico. *b,* hand-forged skinning knife, Colorado Historical Society, Denver. *c,* handmade fleshing knife, Bart Lynch Collection, Grand Junction, Colorado. Drawing by William Macy, Jefferson National Expansion Memorial, St. Louis.

busy as were their neighbors to the south. It is a matter of record that some six hundred half-breed buffalo hunters who assembled at Pembine in June 1840 had in their possession 1,240 skinning knives. At this time and for some thirty-five years following, veritable armies of hide hunters, both white and Indian, organized each year in assaulting the buffalo herds north and south. The collective armament carried to the Plains by the thousands of buffalo hunters was stupendous. Statistics regarding the total number of hunters were not recorded, but some actual figures for the annual shipments of robes via railroads were compiled. During the years from 1872 to 1874, the height of the slaughter, more than 5,100,000 hides were shipped. This total does not include the hides used locally by the native tribes; reasonably, it has been estimated that three buffalo hides were used each year by each Plains Indian, man, woman, and child, for lodges, clothing, etc. Obviously many knives were needed with which to do the big job of skinning. When the frantic, final wholesale butchering of the herds got underway in the 1870's and early 1880's, each hunter avoided some of the delays of resharpening his skinning knife by having at hand numerous sharp knives in reserve. The average number of knives per hunter greatly exceeded the two of earlier years. Small wonder that numerous skinning knives are still extant in collections.

William T. Hornaday interviewed and corresponded with many professional buffalo hunters during the 1870's and 1880's. He also went out upon the buffalo range before the extermination was complete, he employed and associated with professional buffalo hunters, and his published accounts of hunting procedures are authoritative. Regarding the professional still-hunter, he wrote: "Each man hunted separately, and skinned all the animals that his rifle brought down. . . . At his side, depending from his belt, hung his 'hunters companion', a flat leather scabbard, containing a ripping knife, a skinning knife, and a butcher's steel upon which to sharpen them." [5] The artist J. H. Moser in 1888 painted a revealing picture, "Still-hunting Buffaloes on the Northern Range," in which a close-up of the reclining hunter shows the

[5] William T. Hornaday: *The Extermination of the American Bison* (Washington, D.C., 1887), pp. 467–8, Pl. XIV. James McNaney, one of Hornaday's employees, testified that he and one partner carried 60 Wilson skinning knives on their 1881 buffalo hunt in Montana.

details of the scabbard. Seemingly few specimens of the "hunters companion" have been preserved. One is owned by the Yellowstone National Park Museums. Regarding it, park naturalist Merrill D. Beal writes: "It is a three-pocketed sheath now containing one knife, and was found beside a buffalo carcass in eastern Montana in 1884. The other knife and the steel have never been in our possession, nor do we know that they were ever found. The sheath measures 5″ x 11″. It is of tanned leather. The pockets measure 6½″ x 1⅛″, 6½″ x 1″, and 6½″ x 2¼″. The belt-slits are three inches long. The knife is 10″ long. The 6″ rusted steel blade extends into the 4″ wooden handle. There are no identifying marks." [6]

A rather full account of the buffalo-skinning procedure is given by Hornaday. He explains that after the carcass was rolled on its back, the sharp-pointed "ripping knife" was used "to make all the opening cuts in the skin. Each leg was girdled to the bone, about 8 inches above the hoof, and the skin of the leg ripped open from that point along the inside to the median line of the body [belly]. A long straight cut was then made along the middle of the breast and abdomen, from the root of the tail to the chin. . . . The opening cuts having been made, the broad [curved] skinning knife was used to detach the skin from the body in the shortest possible time. The tail was always skinned and left on the hide." The now-famous picture by the pioneer photographer L. A. Huffman, "Buffalo Skinners at Work," accompanies Hornaday's published description. [7]

The removal of shreds of flesh remaining on the hide received little attention from the hide hunter intent upon drying and piling his product with the least possible delay. But in the Indian camps, where fine robes and tipi covers were prepared, the hides were put through a thorough process of scraping and rubbing. This was also the case with deer, elk, and antelope skins that were destined for tanning and manufacture into moccasins and garments. A notable number of trapper camps witnessed the same industry; the work was done by Indian women. One type of fleshing tool is shown in figure 53c. The roughly shaped, dull-edged iron blade is

[6] Letter, Beal to Russell, October 30, 1959.
[7] Hornaday: *American Bison*, p. 442, Pl. IX. See also M. H. Brown and W. R. Felton: *The Frontier Years* (New York, 1955), pp. 70–6, for hide-hunting and other buffalo-skinning photographs by L. A. Huffman.

held between two polished plates of mountain-sheep horn, which make a handle. Six iron rivets pass through the handle and blade. The relic was found about 1890 in a caved-in underground shelter in the mountain range between the Moffit Tunnel and Redcliff, Colorado. The site of the find is at the timberline. With the scraper was a small trade ax and a single cracked wooden sandal held together by sheet iron fastened with square-cut nails. The Bart Lynch Collection, Grand Junction, contains the specimen.

The Crooked Knife

THE bowie is often referred to as a New World invention, distinctively American—an unsupported declaration, as we have seen. There is yet another knife which to many collectors seems to be uniquely American, the crooked knife, or *mocotaugan*. Never did this crooked knife sweep the continent in its popularity, but to certain segments of the northern Indian population it was, and still is, of prime importance. It should be said at once that it, like the bowie type, had a history before the white man arrived in America. "It is circumboreal in distribution; i.e., northern peoples of both the Old and New Worlds use it."

In the trade, it seems to have been distributed always as a blade, only; the Indian or Eskimo prepared and fitted the handle according to individual whim. In the author's observation, the earliest record of the crooked knife in Western fur-trade documents appears in a bill submitted to Auguste Chouteau in 1806.[8] The oldest Western specimen known to the writer was brought to light in the course of excavating the site of the Astorians' Fort Okanogan of 1811.[9] It is pictured in figure 54*b*. Some native artisans forged their own blades, and the sharply curved tip was not constant. An example of the native-made blade is shown in figure 54*e*. This more ambitious curved tool is No. 5026 in the Oregon Historical Society Collections, where it is recorded as "obtained from a Northwest Coast Indian." A long bone handle an-

[8] Auguste Chouteau Papers, Missouri Historical Society, St. Louis. Hunt and Hankinson, jobbers, billed Chouteau, August 29, 1806, for "crooked knives" at 25¢ each. Wilson Malcolmson: "Trade Goods—1941," *The Beaver* (December 1940), pp. 38–9, cites a Hudson's Bay Company list, 1748, in which *mocotaugans* appear—"the curved canoe knives as old as history."

[9] G. F Grabert: "Interim Report on the Wells Reservoir Salvage Archeology Project. Part 1, 1963," MSS, Univ. of Washington (1964), p. 13.

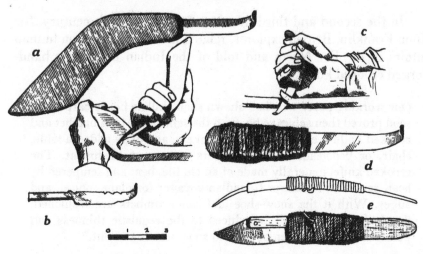

FIG. 54.   *The Crooked Knife.*

a, Mistassini knife from northern Quebec; the drawing is after Rousseau: *The Beaver* (September 1949). *b*, crooked knife recovered at the Astorian site, Okanogan; the drawing is after Grabert: "Interim Report." *c*, Southern Cree knife; the drawing is after L. L. Rue: *The Beaver* (Autumn 1961). *d*, Canadian crooked knife; the drawing is after *Rod and Gun in Canada* (February 1947). *e*, Northwest Coast-type crooked knife; Oregon Historical Society, Portland. Drawings by Glen Dines.

chors the butt portion of the blade, thereby enabling the user to obtain a two-handed grip when heavy carving was to be done. An extension of the bone along the back of the blade forward toward the tip gives further protection to gripping fingers. A wrapping of rawhide thong surrounds the central portion of the handle. This knife presumably found use in the carving of bold relief on totem poles. Its structure is such that it would stand up under the most vigorous use in strong, skilled hands.

With the crooked knife and the ax, the Indian or the Eskimo [1] can accomplish wonders in any woodworking. Canoes, paddles, ax and adz handles, wooden spoons, wooden bowls, drinking cups, snowshoe frames, etc., are produced with a skill that rivals the work of the white craftsmen equipped with the very best of modern tools.

---

[1] The Portland (Oregon) Art Museum owns a long-handled, hand-forged crooked knife somewhat similar to figure 54*e*, which was collected among the Eskimos.

In the second and third decades of the nineteenth century, Sir John Franklin, British explorer, related his observations on human affairs in the Far North and told of the Indian use of the hand-forged crooked knife:

> Our working party who had shown such skill as house carpenters soon proved themselves to be, with the same tools (the hatchet and crooked knife), excellent cabinet makers, and daily added a table, chair, or bedstead, to the comforts of our establishment. The crooked knife, generally made of an old file, bent and tempered by heat, serves an Indian or Canadian voyager for plane, chisel, and auger. With it the snow-shoe and canoe timbers are fashioned, the deals of their sledges reduced to the requisite thinness and polish and their wooden bowls and spoons hollowed out.[2]

The Beaver magazine of the Hudson's Bay Company has been generous through the years in featuring articles that give the crooked knife a place in America's cultural scheme. The drawings in figures 54a and 54c were prepared from photographs reproduced in *The Beaver*. Figure 54a represents a Mistassini knife (Cree affinity) from northern Quebec; the technique shown in figure 54c is an adaptation taken from L. L. Rue's photograph of a Barriere (Southern Cree) craftsman.[3] The knife shown in figure 54d is featured in *Rod and Gun in Canada*.[4]

The crooked knife continues in use among northern peoples, and blades like figure 54b are still to be had from the Hudson's Bay Company stores. Currently they are called "canoe knives," but the wider uses to which they are put are the same as in earlier days. The natives continue to make their own handles for the trade blades, and some ambitious workers still make both the blade and the handle. In other words, there persists here an artifact and a trait that has not changed one whit for two hundred years or more—probably much more.

---

[2] John Franklin: *Narrative, to the Shores of the Polar Sea, 1819–1822* (2 vols.; London, 1824), II, 3–4, quoted in Grace Lee Nute's *The Voyageur* (New York and London, 1931), p. 245.

[3] Jacques Rousseau: "Mistassini Calendar," *The Beaver* (September 1949), p. 36; Leonard L. Rue, "Barriere Indians," *The Beaver* (Autumn 1961), pp. 30–1. See also *The Beaver* (December 1940), pp. 38–9; (March 1941), p. 27; (December 1948), p. 6.

[4] *Rod and Gun in Canada* (February 1947), p. 27.

Pocketknives and the Russell "Barlow"

THE clasp knives that we discussed (pages 171–2) are to be classed with the knives which follow. Additional small clasp knives are included in our present section which has to do with pocketknives, generally.

Small folding or "shut" knives, as they are termed by some Sheffield manufacturers, appeared a couple of thousand years ago. The basic design of handle and pivoted blade, or blades, remained surprisingly constant through the centuries. To the uninitiated the structural features and the problems of assembly of jackknives are complicated; yet the manufacturer's wholesale price for the product was low. Even among the fur traders the middleman's price was ten to thirty cents per jackknife as shown by John Johnston's accounts for 1802–11.[5] During the years indicated, Johnston handled 17 dozen jackknives as against 27 dozen other knives, mostly "scalpers." Even this proportion reflects a greater interest in pocketknives than was manifested by Far West Indians. The Western Indian had no pocket.

Nevertheless jackknives turn up on Indian sites everywhere; military posts and trading centers also yield numerous specimens whenever the sites are investigated by archeologists. The pocketknife always has been important to men—and to boys—almost universally. During the later years of the mountain man, manufacturers began to add "gadgets" to the traditional one- or two-blade jackknife type. One of the specimens treated in the following survey shows some of the innovations. Generally, however, the specimens illustrated tell a story of resistance to change. The pocketknives of the Western fur traders were essentially the same knives that appealed to the Revolutionary soldiers and to the men who settled the international trade disputes in the Old Northwest.

An Indian burial at the onetime Shawnee Village, "Old Chillicothe," near Circleville, Ohio, yielded the jackknife shown in figure 55a. It was here that Logan, Chief of the Mingoes, resided in 1773. The heavy bolsters of this knife, its bone scales, and the

[5] Bert J. Griswold, ed.: *Fort Wayne, Gateway of the West, 1802–1813* (Indianapolis: Indiana Library and Historical Dept.; 1927), pp. 426–536 ("Col. John Johnston's Indian Agency Account Book, 1802–1811").

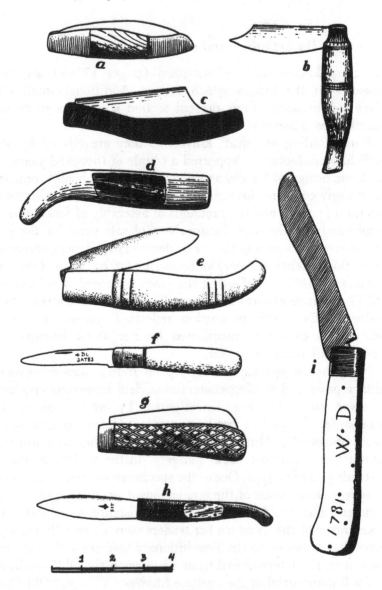

FIG. 55. *Pocketknives.*

a, jackknife from a Shawnee village, Western Reserve Historical Society, Cleveland. *b*, British soldier's Knife, No. 652, Lexington Museum, Lexington, Massachusetts. *c*, French soldier's bone-handled clasp knife, Fort Ticonderoga Museum, New York. *d*, English clasp knife, Fort Ticonderoga Museum, New York. *e*, English clasp knife, Trailside Museum, Bear Mountain State Park (formerly No. L 500 in the Museum of the City of New York). *f*, Barlow knife, No. 1323,

Oregon Historical Society, Portland. *g*, swell-end Jack, Villa Louis, Prairie du Chien, Wisconsin. *h*, English clasp knife, No. A 2680, Minnesota Historical Society, Minneapolis. *i*, jackknife carried during Revolutionary War, No. 197, Missouri Historical Society, St. Louis. Drawing by William Macy, Jefferson National Expansion Memorial, St. Louis.

single steel blade are typical of 18th century (and earlier) jack-knives; they are remarkably intact. The specimen is owned by the Western Reserve Historical Society, Cleveland.

The Lexington Museum, Lexington, Massachusetts, owns the knife pictured in figure 55*b*. The record states: "Knife No. 652 was taken from the first British prisoner captured at Lexington, April 19, 1775." The makeup of this wooden-handled piece is much the same as William Clark's knife (fig. 56*c*).

Excavations near Crown Point, Vermont, uncovered a human skeleton which was accompanied by objects that indicated that the remains were those of a French soldier. His musket is described as "Charleville 1750" (Model 1746 [?]). The bone-handled clasp knife illustrated in figure 55*c* was one of his pieces of equipment. It is now in the Fort Ticonderoga Museum.

The British-type clasp knife shown in figure 55*d* was found at Fort Ticonderoga and is exhibited there. It is similar to the mid-eighteenth-century English clasp knives found at Fort Michili-mackinac described on page 170. Another English clasp knife, which has an all-metal handle, is pictured in figure 55*e*. It was found between the walls of an old house in lower Manhattan. The Trailside Museum, Bear Mountain State Park, New York, exhibits it.

The bone-handled Barlow knife illustrated in figure 55*f* is No. 1323 in the Oregon Historical Society. A Barlow of this size and shape but with a wooden handle was found in the trapper haunts near Weiser, Idaho. It is catalogued as No. 694–19 in the Idaho Historical Society, Boise. A tremendous number of cheap Barlows were manufactured in the Stannington district, near Sheffield, by several firms; so many came from there that the name "Stanning-ton Barlow" was coined. A Barlow knife is a jackknife, of course, that dates back to the seventeenth century. The distinguishing feature is the extra long bolster. Legend has it that the brothers Barlow devised this feature in order to give strength to the cheapest jackknife they could make. Other manufacturers adopted the long bolster, and their knives also became known as Barlows. The type is still on the market and is still named Barlow. The specimen pictured bears the maker's name, "Gates."

The "swell-end jack" (fig. 55g) was recovered during the excavation of the military post Fort Crawford, and is exhibited at the historic house museum, Villa Louis, Prairie du Chien, Wisconsin. It has a checkered bone handle and a single blade with a sheepfoot point. A rusted mass of jackknives, apparently identical in style with this one, were taken from the decomposed cargo of an English (?) freight ship that went down near Manasquan Inlet, New Jersey. Expert antiquarians who studied the recovered cargo in 1957 estimated the date of sinking to be "about 1830." The historic remains were sold at auction by the State of New Jersey on January 18, 1958.[6]

The Minnesota Historical Society owns the small clasp knife shown in figure 55h. It was grubbed out from under the roots of a tree on Elk River north of Minneapolis in 1853. A small plate of bone is mounted in its iron handle, and the initials "F I T" appear on the blade. Both handle and blade are quite like those on the English clasp knives recovered at Michilimackinac, which Maxwell dates as 1760's to 1770's.[7]

The Missouri Historical Society has an extra large bone-handled jackknife, which is represented in figure 55i. It was carried by William Depew, a Revolutionary soldier who was killed by the British in 1781. Jackknives usually were carried by every soldier of the day, both British and American. New York and New Hampshire made them a requirement, but the knives were personal purchases. The Depew knife was lent to the Missouri Historical Society by H. G. Depew.

The swell-end jack illustrated in figure 56a was found under a building in the Forty-Niner town Columbia, California. Its spear-pointed master blade is rusted but intact; its second blade is broken. The checkered bone handle, well made though it be, is fairly typical of the very cheap jackknives distributed by the hundreds of thousands during the 1830's and 1840's. It was the middle of the

[6] Photographs and news release supplied by Public Information Office, State Department of Conservation and Economic Development, Trenton, New Jersey, 1958.
[7] Maxwell: *Excavations*, p. 106 and Pl. X b.

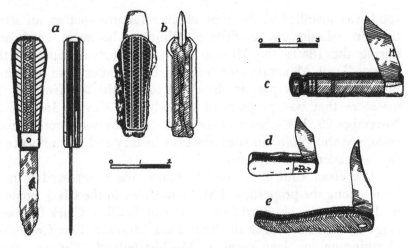

FIG. 56.   *More Pocketknives.*

a, typical swell-end jack, 1840's; State Park Museum, Columbia, California. *b*, swell-end jack with ivory spud for fleshing; Whitman Mission, Walla Walla, Washington. *c*, William Clark's clasp knife; State Park Museum, Fort Columbia, Washington. *d*, Russell Barlow knife; Los Angeles Museum. *e*, French clasp knife; History Museum, Tadoussac, Quebec. Drawing by Glen Dines.

nineteenth century or later before synthetic materials displaced bone as a cheap hafting material. The specimen is exhibited in the State Park Museum at Columbia.

Another swell-end jack with bone handle is shown in figure 56*b*. It is distinguished by an unusual chisel-like ivory spud mounted in the butt. Beginning in the middle of the nineteenth century, all manner of special attachments were added to jack-knives: spikes, awls, corkscrews, bottle openers, files, stone hooks, hoof files, fleams for bleeding, speying and castrating blades, fish scalers, pruners, budding and grafting blades, and still others. The spud here shown is unique in the writer's experience. Such a tool would have served nicely in fleshing the fine pelts taken from the smaller fur bearers. This specimen was recovered by National Park Service archeologists when excavating at the Whitman National Historic Site, near Walla Walla, Washington, and is now exhibited in the National Park Service Museum at that place. The chemical effects of ground water upon the brass lining of the knife produced heavy incrustation of the metal parts. Mechanical relationships are obscured, but there is some evidence that the ivory spud was installed at the time of manufacture—not as an after-thought. Missionary activities at Whitman began in 1836, and during the 1840's the Mission was an important depot on the Oregon Trail. Mountain men frequented the center from its founding and they took part in the effort to aid the survivors of the massacre that was perpetrated there by the Cayuse Indians on November 29, 1847. Some of the artifacts recovered through excavations at the Whitman site reflect the history and the influence of the fur traders and trappers.

The clasp knife illustrated in figure 56c is reported to have been among the properties of William Clark in the Clark home in St. Louis. It was obtained from a niece of William Clark Grecken-ridge and is exhibited in the State Park Museum, Fort Columbia, Washington, on loan from J. M. McClelland. The one piece wooden handle has no lining. The single big blade is mounted under a metal bolster, and a spring extends part way down the back of the handle. Stamped on the blade is the initial "M." There is no record regarding Clark's use of this knife while on the Lewis and Clark Expedition, but the piece may well be old enough to have seen such service. Its working principles are somewhat similar to the mechanism of the French clasp knives treated on page 170.

The wooden-handled John Russell Company Barlow knife from the Los Angeles Museum (fig. 56d) is later than the mountain-man period, but similar Barlows had been in use in America at least as early as the Revolution. In the early 1800's John Johnston, Indian trader at Fort Wayne, Indiana, ordered "1 doz. Barlow knives @ 10 shillings, 2 pence." Again, in 1810, Johnston ordered "2 doz. Barlow knives @ 9 shillings, 9 pence per doz." [8] The Barlow was in general use everywhere in the Western fur fields. Previous mention of its early-day use in Oregon and Idaho was made in connection with figure 55 (p. 221).

At the historic French traders' center, Tadoussac, at the mouth of the Saguenay, is a small museum of the fur trade. Here is exhibited the horn-handled clasp knife shown in figure 56e, which has not been subjected to the ravages of burial in the ground. The tip of the blade was broken off, and some previous owner reshaped the point; otherwise the specimen is in its original condition. It is a

[8] Griswold, ed.: *Fort Wayne*, pp. 426, 622.

"living example," so to speak, of the traditional French clasp knives discussed on pages 170–1.

Frontier Surgical Knives and Their Substitutes

THE bona fide doctors of medicine who entered the Far West during the mountain-man period were few indeed; nevertheless, medical kits and stocks of drugs accompanied the larger trapper-trader parties to the wilds. Even individual trappers sometimes carried a few medicines plus the appurtenances that might facilitate the dressing of wounds and the mending of broken bones. Lewis and Clark had led the way in this wilderness practice. Bloodletting was still a universal recourse in treating almost any indisposition during the early nineteenth century, and lancets for bleeding were in the possession of many individuals, including frontiersmen. Not many of the once-common little instruments are to be found in museums today. The Missouri Historical Society, St. Louis, owns the one shown in figure 57. The museum record states: "Obtained from a great-great grandson of Daniel Boone; reportedly, it found use in the hands of Boone during those days when most families had their own lancet, and nearly all ailments were treated by taking a quantity of blood from the patient." [9] The small steel blade folds into a handle of tortoise shell. The case is made of a composition resembling stiff papier-mâché and has un-

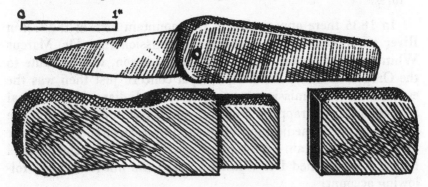

FIG. 57. *Lancet.*

This is recorded as the personal instrument of Daniel Boone. Missouri Historical Society, St. Louis. Glen Dines drawing.

[9] Personal letter, George R. Books, director, to C. P. Russell, February 23, 1965.

dergone so much handling that its exterior surface has a leather-like quality.

The surgery performed by the mountain men on occasion was resolute and usually grisly. Surgeons' knives were not standard equipment. Josiah Gregg provided a vivid eyewitness account of action taken by members of a wagon train of the 1830's on the Santa Fe Trail in saving the life of a man whose arm was gangrenous. The victim had pulled his gun from a wagon, muzzle end first, and the hammer was pulled back in the process. The resulting accidental discharge of the piece sent the shot into the owner's arm, shattering it. The injury was neglected until gangrene set in; then the victim begged for help. Gregg wrote:

> The only case of instruments available consisted of a handsaw, a butcher knife, and a large, iron bolt. The teeth of the saw being considered too coarse, they [the "surgeons"] went to work and soon had a set of fine teeth filed on the back. The knife, whetted keen, and the bolt laid on the fire, they commenced the operation, and in less time than it takes to tell it the arm was opened round to the bone, which was almost in an instant sawed off; and with the whizzing hot iron the whole stump was so effectually seared as to close the arteries completely. Bandages were now applied and the company proceeded on their way. The arm healed rapidly and in a few weeks the patient was sound and well. Perhaps he still lives to bear witness to the superiority of the hot iron over ligatures.[1]

In 1835 there appeared with the mountain men at the Green River rendezvous that paragon among missionaries, Dr. Marcus Whitman. The doctor, a physician and surgeon, was en route to the Oregon country, and his principal concern just then was the establishment of missions among western Indians, not medical service to beaver trappers. However, he had with him some of the equipment of his medical profession and he acceded to the pleas for help made by certain hard-bitten hunters. The Reverend Samuel Parker accompanied Dr. Whitman, and from him comes the following account:

> While we continued in this place [the environs of Fort Bonneville] Dr. Whitman was called to perform some very important surgical operations. He extracted an arrow point, three inches long, from

[1] Josiah Gregg: *Commerce of the Prairies* (2 vols.; New York: H. Langley; 1844), I, 59–60.

FIG. 58.   *Dr. Whitman Removing Arrow Point from Jim Bridger's Back.*

This drawing by William Macy is in the Jefferson National Expansion Memorial, St. Louis.

the back of Captain Bridger, which was received in a skirmish three years before with the Blackfeet Indians. It was a difficult operation because the arrow was hooked at the point by striking a large bone and a cartilaginous substance had grown around it. The doctor pursued the operation with great self-possession and perseverance; and his patient manifested equal firmness. The Indians looked on meanwhile, with countenances indicating wonder, and in their own peculiar manner expressed great surprise when it was extracted. The doctor also extracted another arrow from the shoulder of one of the hunters, which had been there two years and a half.[2]

William Macy's interpretation of the Whitman-Bridger episode is presented in the figure 58 drawing.

What may have become of Dr. Whitman's surgical knives can only be conjectured. The Whitman Mission, founded in 1836 six miles west of present-day Walla Walla, was destroyed by Indians in 1847. Thirteen of the inhabitants, including Dr. and Mrs. Whitman, were killed. Sets of surgical knives that were owned and used by pioneer military surgeons are now owned by the U. S. Army Medical Museum, Washington, D.C.; some are contemporary with Dr. Whitman's knives. *Ciba Symposia* presents a clear photograph of a field case containing such early-day surgical knives.[3]

THE SIGNIFICANCE OF KNIVES IN THE TRAPPER'S SCHEME

AS WAS TRUE OF GUNS, THERE WAS SOMETHING VERY PERSONAL and intimate about the mountain man's favorite knife. He was given to endowing it with a personality, and often there seemed to be a sentimental attachment as well as an appreciation of its practical worth. A good many instances of loss or theft of favorite knives are recorded, and usually a very determined effort was made by the owner to retrieve the valued arm. Sometimes this involved tedious backtracking on dimly marked trails—even mortal combat. The written record of such recoveries in the Far West begins with the Lewis and Clark *Journals*, 1803–6, and is repeated time and again in diaries and narratives written by mountain men. In short, the iron knife was essential to the white trapper and was hardly less valued by the Indian.

The slender, rather brittle dagger was brought to the New World by the very first European adventurers and continued to find some favor in the eyes of both whites and Indians through all the periods of American history. It was not unknown in the Far

[2] Samuel Parker: *Journal of an Exploring Tour Beyond the Rocky Mountains* (Ithaca, N.Y., 1838), p. 76, quoted in C. P. Russell: "Wilderness Rendezvous Period of the American Fur Trade," *Oregon Historical Quarterly* (March 1941), p. 32. This was the first item to give notoriety to Marcus Whitman in the West.

[3] "The Army Surgeon," *Ciba Symposia* (1940). Isobel Stevenson: "Beginnings of American Military Medicine," *Ciba Symposia* (February 1940), p. 352.

West of the mountain man, but neither was it very important there. Stout, broad daggers and short-blade dags, or "stabbers," were in much greater demand among Indians, especially in the northern parts of the mountain man's domain. They were in use in the Northwest long before the mountain man arrived. These knives were essentially English products, and generally they were distributed by the North West and the Hudson's Bay companies. Some of these early long, broad, spear-pointed daggers of English origin were of the bowie type, in that they had a guard. In truth, they represented a survival of a medieval knife form. They continued in limited use down through the bowie-knife heyday, and usually their Indian owners were entirely unacquainted with the white man's enthusiastic adoption of the type in the South and Southwest beginning in the 1830's to 1840's.

The ubiquitous "scalper" was the big knife item in the beaver trade. Ordinary cheap butcher knives, dubbed scalping knives, were shipped by the hundreds of thousands from England's cutlery works and, after 1830, from American knife factories to the Western trading posts and wilderness trade centers. Exhaustion of the supply of beaver pelts did not put an end to this knife trade. The period of buffalo-hide hunting witnessed an ever greater use of butcher knives, including the stout, curved skinning knives by whites and Indians alike. Inexpensive though they were, individually, butcher knives constituted the basis for a Western wilderness business that in its retail aspects ran into hundreds of thousands of dollars each year. The gross profit to the traders was about 1,000 per cent, an estimated gain that is hardly realistic. The cost of conducting the trade sometimes included heavy loss of human lives and damage to trading posts, even destruction of entire expeditions with fur returns, equipment, and specie "gone with the wind."

One brand of butcher knife deserves a special place in any study of the Western beaver business. It is the "Green River" knife, produced by J. Russell and Company of Massachusetts beginning in 1834. The mountain man seized upon it as his own during a decade, and the Green River Works became identified with the Western fur trade much more definitely than did any other single cutlery company.

In the published histories of knives in America, the bowie knife made the biggest "splash," the long-lasting ripples still lapping within today's knife picture. Bowie knives appeared among Santa

Fe traders during the time of the wagon trains, and the mountain man encountered them in Taos and elsewhere in the Southwest; therefore it is certain that they were known to the Western beaver trappers during the 1830's and 1840's. They did not become popular, however, on the northern plains and in the Rockies during the period of the mountain man. Out of the confusion of bowie-knife types and styles, which "evolved" so rapidly in Sheffield and in the eastern United States, one heavy, broad blade with clipped point—the kind popularized by Colonel James Bowie personally— is recognized as "classical." The modern U. S. Army knife, Mark 3, traces its ancestry to the bowie knives, as do some of the fine-quality hunting knives now on the market.

An interesting occurrence among the artifacts dug up at several fur-trade sites, historic military establishments, and long-gone Indian villages is the folding or clasp knife, which sometimes is recovered in numbers. They are European; those from France are quite readily distinguished from others. Many bear trademarks or the name of the manufacturer, thus providing a potential key to the periods of use by forgotten peoples—a dating that must of course depend upon the documentary chronology of the cutlery industry in France. As yet, no one has researched these commercial documents.

The peculiar "crooked knife" of the northern Indian tribes was a very small item in the trade so far as the volume of business was concerned, but from the standpoint of usefulness it was and is important to certain peoples. It entered the northern realm of the mountain man and appears on his invoices. Specimens also turn up at certain sites of his activities. Because it serves a special purpose, it differs from any other knife. It is still being used and is marketed as the "canoe knife," yet it is little known outside of anthropological circles and in primitive camps of the north country. The crooked knife constitutes one of the unique "living" artifacts representative of persisting ancient traits and techniques.

Innumerable unclassifiable big and small knives and a classified miscellany of pocketknives, fleshing knives, surgical knives—even table knives—went to the Far West with the beaver trappers. Relics of these historic objects are brought to light at practically every archeological dig conducted on Western fur-trade sites. Predecessors of the mountain men, pursuing the Indian trade in the South and in the old Northwest, had used and sometimes traded similar out-of-the-ordinary knife types; in effect, there was "nothing new under the sun" among the knives of the mountain men. The one notable earmark which gave distinction to some of the knives of the Far West was the "Green River" trade name and the connotation of grit and self-reliance with which it endowed the average owner of such weapons. Indians obtained Green River knives, but generally the owners who made them renowned were white Americans—traders, beaver trappers, and buffalo hunters. Together they shaped a chapter in knife history that has not yet been publicized in an adequate way.

CHAPTER V

The Ax on America's Frontiers

BEFORE LEWIS AND CLARK

THE STORY OF THE IRON AX IN AMERICA IS PARTLY THE AC-count of the introduction of iron to a Stone Age culture, partly the story of the white man's personal use of the implement in conquering the New World wilderness, and partly the record of the evolution of an ancient European heirloom in the hands of pioneer American smiths and woodsmen. Each of the three phases is important; together they constitute something of the saga of a nation in the making, for in America the ax and its attributes of progress constitute an institution.

With a flow of movement reminiscent of the caterpillar's tread, the Indian trade in less than two centuries moved inland from the Atlantic seaboard to the Great Lakes, the Ohio Valley, and the Mississippi. Another hundred years elapsed before it reached the eastern flanks of the Rocky Mountains, and except for Spanish activity in the extreme southwest, yet another fifty years passed before it extended to the Pacific. In the impact of this European commerce and international rivalry upon the primitive red man, the ax was out in front. In first contacts it aroused the most covetous desires on the part of the Indian and left a voluble record in the traders' journals. Only firearms and rum finally rivaled it in importance to the Indian, and these commodities were not immediately included in the trade.

Projected against the background of the history of competition between contending nations and the story of the ultimate ascendancy of the United States in the trade and in national stature is a complicated but discernible picture of the iron ax in the New World. That picture, if properly developed, can be made to have significance and value above its antiquarian interest, for within it is the key to some of the problems of the local historian. A part of the picture is to be seen in the pages that follow. However, many details of origins and trade relationships are not defined. Possibly some of the leads contained herein or perhaps the very incompleteness of the picture here presented will stir interest in historic sites having significance as yet unknown, or will encourage further systematic study of collections of iron objects already assembled in many convenient centers. The data to be derived from historic axes themselves are subject to organization and may be interpretable if studied in conjunction with the related documents. The related documentary and objective materials are being brought together by discerning workers now intent upon the union.

Currently constructive work along this line is being done on a number of historic fur-trade sites, and the axes and tomahawks recovered in these excavations sometimes prove their importance to the historian-archeologist responsible for deciphering the complicated evidences upon which he must base his dating and his conclusions regarding the interrelationships of the long-gone peoples involved.

Inferior trade axes were subject to breakage in use, but even as discarded, broken artifacts they have resisted further major deterioration; their assembled fragments tell a story to be added to the record. Good axes recovered in the digs usually are intact in body and form, even though they have suffered surface oxidation and turn up as coated and rust-pitted relics. The techniques of the investigator sometimes triumph over such superficial deterioration, and even small smith's marks come back into evidence, badly rusted though the iron may be.

Of the some one hundred axes treated in the present chapter, about one half were taken from sites in the Appalachian Range and eastward. Within this group, much of the early history of the development of the ax in America may be discerned. One fourth of the over-all selection here illustrated came from the Great Lakes–Mississippi River axis, and the remaining one fourth is Western and Far Western. In the latter group, of course, are the axes of the mountain men.

At this juncture, some readers particularly concerned with the tools and the trade goods of the Western trader-trapper may question: "How is the wheat to be told from the chaff?" Actually, there is little or no chaff. The axes of the mountain men get their definition only when viewed in the light thrown upon them by the broader exposition of the general ax-tomahawk story.

The remaining pages of this section give an abbreviated account of the ax in the early American West. Tremendous territories, half a dozen nations of white men, a score of major trading companies, and a hundred tribes of Indians enter the story. Even the abbreviation must be complicated, labyrinthine, and full of convolutions. Stripped to its bare bones the account may be outlined as follows.

The iron axes distributed in the early Far West came from:

1. The North. These were brought by the French and English beginning in mid-eighteenth century.
2. The Pacific Coast. British, American, and Russian ships introduced them in the 1790's.
3. The South and Southwest. Spanish and French interests distributed axes during the late eighteenth century, and later.
4. The East. The United States trade began with Lewis and Clark, 1804.

From the beginning of the white contact period Western Indians displayed some whims of preference in acquiring their axes. The spontoon-type tomahawk and the Missouri war hatchet had little to commend them from the standpoint of efficiency in use, but they were the special favorites of certain Western Indians. However, the staple in the Western trade was the conventional "French" ax. The pipe tomahawk, that standard adjunct in parleys and beloved weapon in combat, also was in evidence in the early 1800's.

The cost of axes procured by Western traders was fairly uniform in the wholesale houses of Canada and the United States, but the retail sale price varied. A trade ax delivered to the Far West during the 1790's cost the trader about sixteen times more than was the wholesale price in Montreal or Philadelphia. In the 1820's the differential became more favorable to the Western trader— about five times the wholesale price in the East. During the 1830's and throughout the remainder of the mountain-man period, this rate remained fairly constant; such changes as occurred tended to favor the trader.

The retail price exacted from the Western trapper—Indian and white alike—varied, but it was always as great as the traffic would bear. A thousand per cent markup was a usual potential (gross), but the net return was diminished drastically because of the deaths and defections of many debtors, heavy overhead met by the trader, and losses of beaver and other fur returns in transit.

In the long-range view of the fur trade in the West the ax was not a big item on the ledgers and business balance sheets, but it was of vital importance to the comfort, security, and general morale of every man and woman, white or red, on the frontier. It was indispensable. Until that day when the blacksmith arrived, both the Indian and the white man clung to his ax with desperate tenacity, repairing its breaks and cracks with sewed, wet rawhide, cherishing its remains, and fostering its further usefulness.

Recorded instances of pilferage of axes by Indians are numerous in the saga of the mountain man. One concludes that the thieves often were driven by something other than their ever-present spirit of deviltry and the desire to count coup; they coveted the ax because of its intrinsic worth to them.

This study approaches the subject as directly as possible—through the axes themselves. The Western specimens investigated found their historic use in the areas that now are Alaska, Colorado, the Dakotas, Missouri, Montana, Nebraska, New Mexico, Oregon, Texas, Washington, and Wyoming. Some are privately owned, but most are in public museums where, ideally, they receive study and professional handling by curators. Historical data, more or less dependable, accompany the accession records. Those axes recovered through archeological excavation often have been accorded chronological assessment and are in effect datum points of service to investigators engaged in studies of other related sites. Only recently has the historian-archeologist made a determined, large-scale effort to publish well-illustrated reports on his individual field projects, thus disseminating the information gained locally. These reports and the recovered artifacts to which they pertain, coupled with such historical information as may be obtained from documentary sources, represent interpretive accomplishments of an order quite superior to most of the published findings of twenty years ago. As a matter of fact, the American archeologists of

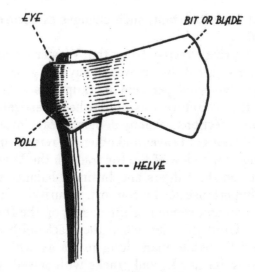

FIG. 59. *Ax Terminology.*

The specimen is an English colonial piece of the late seventeenth century, owned by the Bucks County Historical Society, Pennsylvania. It consists of HEAD and HELVE. The head has an *eye* into which the fore end of the helve is fitted. The metal above the eye is termed the *poll*, and the elongated *blade* has a sharpened *edge*. When reinforcing projections extend back from the eye, as in the present instance, they are referred to as *ears*. William Macy drawing, Jefferson National Expansion Memorial, St. Louis.

earlier years, with few exceptions, tended to avoid involvement in problems posed by historic objects. Papers on historic axes in America bearing dates of publication earlier than 1910 are few indeed.

The abundance of historic ax material in some museums has encouraged certain directors to analyze, interpret, and publicize portions of their holdings. For the most part, the recent presentations pertain to "tomahawks" particularly. Woodward's "The Metal Tomahawk," Courville's "Trade Tomahawks," and Peterson's *American Indian Tomahawks* are examples. In geographic scope, these studies are all-inclusive; understandably, the axes of the mountain men have not been separated from the general array.

As attested by the early records of the Indian trade, certain Eastern Indians were fairly inundated by enormous consignments of axes. Some axes and tomahawks were given freely to the tribesmen in connection with the Indian gift policies adopted by the competing Europeans who took over America; a greater number were exchanged by white traders for peltry. In contrast with the Eastern picture, it can be said with certainty that no great flood of axes ever reached Far Western tribesmen.

Of the axes treated and pictured in the present work, about one third were manufactured for the white man's personal use—not for trade. Generally these tools were readily recognized because of structural features that mark them. They were not spurned by the Indian, of course, but if the Indian got them, usually it was through theft or accident; they were not objects of regular trade, but a few turn up in Indian graves and at village sites.

By the time that the mountain man "entered the jousts," some of the Indians with whom he was to deal had been supplied earlier with limited numbers of axes and tomahawks. For the most part, these had come from French and British sources to the north and east, from Spanish and French distributors in the South and Southwest, and from British and American trading ships that had served the natives of the Pacific Coast for several decades. Occasionally an Indian of the Rocky Mountains owned an iron ax in 1800, although he may never have seen a white man. Intertribal trade, based upon an aboriginal system of long standing,[1] provided a vehicle for the distribution of a number of classes of the white man's goods into territory to which the white man had not penetrated. As far as axes are concerned, this resulted in a few fixations among the Far West savages; for examples see the "spontoon" type tomahawk (fig. 72) and the "Missouri war hatchet" (fig. 74). Some of the earliest white traders in the Far West bowed to the Indian whim and for a while supplied these special weapons as demanded. In the case of the Missouri war hatchet, the demand and the attempt to supply persisted for quite a while indeed; the peculiar weapon was still in demand even after the mountain man and his particular style of beaver trade had passed from the scene.

There were other whims and fancies displayed in the mountain man's trade in axes, but the substantial items in the trade were the ubiquitous "French" trade ax (fig. 67) and the pipe tomahawk in one or another of its "national" forms (figs. 72 and 73). The mountain man's personal tomahawk was ordinarily the typical

[1] See John C. Ewers: "The Indian Trade of the Upper Missouri before Lewis and Clark" quoted in Carl P. Russell: *Guns on the Early Frontier* (Berkeley: Univ. of California Press; 1957), pp. 34–7.

hunter's hatchet (figs. 64*f*, 64*h*, and 64*j*) that had been used by frontiersmen, both civilian and military, since pre-Revolutionary days. Some white trappers among the mountain men, especially the Cajuns and Canadian Frenchmen, never adopted the hunter's hatchet; they clung to the same small French ax that was traded to the Indians (fig. 60). However, the greater number of the Far West trappers used a weapon that in its basic particulars resembled the hatchet favored by trappers and sportsmen today (fig. 64*j*).

FIG. 60. *Hudson's Bay Company Employee with Belt Ax, 1847.*

Above is A. H. Murray's field sketch of his half-breed assistant, Manuel, in action. The sketch was made on the Bell River in the Porcupine-Yukon locality. In Murray's words it shows "a sash in which he [Manuel] carried a small Hudson's Bay axe" (from Clifford Wilson's "Founding Fort Yukon," *The Beaver* [June 1947], p. 39). Obviously, Manuel's belt ax is a French-type trade piece.

In the earliest terminology of the explorers and frontiersmen in the New World, the small ax intended to be used by whites was called a "hatchet." The tools are so named by Cartier on the St. Charles, 1535 ("hachotz"); by Captain John Smith in referring to equipment carried to the upper reaches of Chesapeake Bay in 1608; by Champlain on the St. Lawrence in 1608 ("hatchette"); by Strachey in connection with Virginia weapons of 1610; by Stuyvesant in New York, 1667; and by Catesby in the Carolinas of the early 1700's. The iron hatchets presented by Cartier and observed with some surprise by Captain John Smith and by Champlain in the hands of northern Indians were not the earliest European axes to reach the red man. Lucas Vásquez de Ayllón provided the savages of the lower Savannah River (South Carolina-Georgia) with Biscayan hatchets in 1525-6. These small axes were observed in use and were reported by some of the companions of de Soto in 1538.

All Algonquian and Iroquoian Indians, immediately upon acquiring the iron hatchet, seem to have named it "tomahawk" after the aboriginal weapon which it replaced. Captain John Smith prepared a brief Indian vocabulary in 1607 or shortly thereafter in which he listed "tomahacks" as synonymous with axes. Ultimately some white men borrowed the Indian word and used the term for their own hatchets. The word soon found general use throughout the northern parts of the continent. Meriwether Lewis in 1803 designated the armory-made hatchets and pipe axes of the Lewis and Clark Expedition as "tomahawks." He had among his personal effects at the time of his death in 1809 "one tomahawk— handsomely mounted."

THE IRON AX GOES UP THE MISSOURI

PROBABLY, THE LEWIS AND CLARK PIECES WERE THE FIRST American tomahawks to be introduced to the Indians of the Far West, but there is unmistakable evidence that some English specimens had preceded; at any rate, small axes and war clubs had been distributed upon parts of the Canadian Great Plains clear to the Rocky Mountains by Anthony Hendry of the Hudson's Bay Company in 1754-5. Cree and Assiniboin middlemen, already experienced in the trade, guided Hendry. In his *Journal*, Hendry testifies that "there are scarce a gun, kettle, hatchet, or knife

amongst us, having traded them with the Archithinue natives." [2]
One concludes, however, that there was no adequate, well-
sustained system of northern high plains trade during the half
century following the Hendry venture. Despite the fact that Canadian traders brought more iron axes to the Blackfoot country beginning in the last decade of the eighteenth century, Alexander
Henry the Younger, as late as 1811, wrote of the Piegan, a Blackfoot unit: "Many families are still destitute of either a kettle or an
axe." [3] Lewis and Clark, while with the Shoshone in August 1805,
reported: "We found no axes nor hatchets among them." On August 24 Lewis wrote: "I now produced some battle axes which I had
made at Fort Mandan with which they were much pleased." [4]

We pick up snatches of information regarding the English
axes in the early Far West from the *Journals* of Lewis and Clark,
and a very few precious specimens of the axes themselves are still
extant (see figs. 72, 73, and 74). As stated previously, a few
armory-made tomahawks were taken to the tribes of the Plains and
the Rockies by Lewis and Clark, but a greater number of axes and
war clubs were forged in the field by members of the exploring
expedition, especially by John Shields and Alex Willard. In their
writings, Lewis and Clark placed no monetary values on these
axes, but the weapons did bring something of prime importance to
the expedition—Indian corn. The Fort Mandan axes of 1804–5
went to the Grosventre and the Mandan principally, but they did
not "stay put"; Sergeant John Ordway found some of them in the
possession of the "Pahmap" Indians at the mouth of Potlatch
River, Idaho, when the returning explorers passed that way in
April, 1806. The mouth of the Potlatch is some 750 miles, airline,
from the Mandan villages. [5] It seems entirely proper to place the
Lewis and Clark tomahawks at the top of the chronological list of
mountain-man axes.

Even before Lewis and Clark returned to their St. Louis start-

[2] L. J. Burpee, ed.: *The Journal of Anthony Hendry, 1754–1755* (Ottawa:
Royal Society of Canada; 1907), p. 351.
[3] Alexander Henry and David Thompson: *New Light on the History of the
Greater North-West*, ed. Elliott Coues (New York: F. P. Harper; 1897), p. 724.
[4] Bernard De Voto, ed.: *The Journals of Lewis and Clark* (Boston: Houghton Mifflin; 1953), pp. 218, 222, 226.
[5] Milo M. Quaife, ed.: *The Journals of Captain Meriwether Lewis and
Sergeant John Ordway, 1803–1806* (Madison: Wisconsin Historical Soc.;
1916), p. 353.

ing point in 1806, American traders and trappers were en route to the upper Missouri beaver country that the explorers had tested. With these pioneer traders went the usual complement of trade goods, including axes. No inventories with price lists of the merchandise carried by the Lisa-Drouillard expedition of 1807–8 or the Lisa-Missouri Fur Company ventures of 1809–13 are at hand, but an idea of the costs of axes and tomahawks during this period is to be had; the United States Indian Trade Office in its Day Book E, opening with January 1, 1809, records:

Cost in Dollars and Cents, 50 pipe tomahawks like sample provided to James Maury, Liverpool, and to be imported on the ship, *William and John*, in Oct. 1810—

Cost of the axes in Liverpool	$100.56
Freight from England	1.63
Cartage in America	.53
Duties and permits	18.78
	$121.50

Thus, in this instance, the cost of each English tomahawk pipe delivered to a Baltimore warehouse in 1810 was $2.43. Cost-wise, American smiths were able to compete with the British manufacturers, but for a time the quality of the American product failed to satisfy the Indian. This is discussed further on page 281. At this point perhaps it is sufficient to note that the U. S. Indian Factory at Fort Wayne, Indiana, in 1802 and from 1806 to 1811 inventoried the American pipe tomahawks at $1.50 each.[6] Probably these were without ornament and of plain finish as is the specimen shown in figure 73h. In 1812 the Indian Trade Office, George Town, listed among annuity presents "18 pipe tomahawks @ $4.07, each, and 6 @ $4.50, each." [7] Within a few years the Trade Office was again distributing on a sales basis the more costly English products, including "brass pipe tomahawks @ $2.50, each." [8] (See Chapter v, pages 281–2.) It is not implied, however, that all American manufacturers limited their output to low-cost, mediocre pipe toma-

[6] Bert J. Griswold, ed.: *Fort Wayne, Gateway of the West, 1802–1813* (Indianapolis: Indiana Library and Historical Dept.; 1927), pp. 418, 472 *passim*.

[7] U. S. Indian Trade Office, Day Book E, beginning January 1, 1809.

[8] U. S. Indian Trade Office, Invoice Book (George Town, D.C., 822–3).

hawks. Some American craftsmen produced the finest specimens to be found; Joseph Jourdain, Green Bay, Wisconsin, was one of these. An example of his work is pictured in figure 73*e*.

The axes, half axes, and hatchets that constituted the major items in the ax trade are well represented in the business records, both in Canada and the United States. The Hudson's Bay Company records present many details of the ax business conducted by that company as early as 1671, and the North West Company records, 1783–1821, also are revealing. The affairs of both of these Canadian giants embraced parts of the Far West long before the mountain man arrived, and after he did come the English operators impinged upon him in numerous places south of the Canadian boundary. The story of the trade ax in the West, then, cannot be stripped down to something that is solely "United Statesiana."

During the opening years of the nineteenth century, blacksmiths in Philadelphia and in George Town, D.C., were receiving $1.00 apiece for 5-pound felling axes, 62½¢ for 2½-pound half axes, and 33⅓¢ for 1-pound hatchet-tomahawks.[9] These were wholesale prices paid by the United States government and by the head offices of trading companies. The cost of these axes to traders in the field varied, of course, with the distance from the base from which came the supply. In the case of the North West Company, the base was Montreal, and it may be assumed that the prices charged by Montreal blacksmiths was approximately the same as those quoted above for Philadelphia. As stated, the value of the axes increased as the merchandise reached distant trading centers. In 1795 the North West Company computed the advance over Montreal prices as follows:

In Detroit prices were three times more than "prime cost," or
Montreal price;
At Michilimackinac, 4 times;
At Grand Portage, 8 times; and
At Lake Winnipeg, 16 times.

In other words, a 1-pound hatchet-tomahawk that cost 33⅓¢ in Montreal was inventoried in a Lake Winnipeg trading post at approximately $5.33 (21 shillings, 1795 basis). The company

[9] U. S. Office of Indian Affairs, Account Book (Philadelphia, 1808).

agents in the outposts were free to advance the prices still further, if they saw fit to do so.[1]

Alexander Henry testified that the Indians of the Saskatchewan in 1775 paid three beaver pelts (which in Montreal were worth $6.00) for a 1-pound hatchet. In 1811 David Thompson, then west of the Rockies, reported "3 Half Axes" still in his possession as being worth four beaver pelts each. At this time the beaver would bring $2.50 each in the East. John Jacob Astor testified to the U. S. Congress that in October 1813 the North West Company took from his Astorians large felling axes valued at $3.33 each, half axes worth $2.00 each, and hatchets worth $1.00 each. The axes, 466 of them, were the products of the Astoria blacksmith shop, and the iron for them reached the Columbia via sailing ship from New York. The price paid to Astor by the Canadians was one third less than the quoted value. (See Mr. Astor's inventory, page 403.) The returns to the Nor'westers, when the axes were traded for beaver pelts, greatly exceeded the purchase price, of course. It is worthy of note that the North West Company, soon after taking Astoria, shipped a cargo of Columbia beaver to Canton, China, and there received the equivalent of $3.85 per pelt.[2] Alexander Ross, who traded some of the Astorian axes to Okanogan Indians, estimated that these beaver pelts which sold for $3.85 apiece cost his company "an average of but 5½ d. apiece, . . . a specimen of our trade among the Indians."[3] If Ross is to be relied upon, we learn here that 1 hatchet brought 10 beaver pelts at Okanogan. It seems certain, however, that in this instance Ross was a great optimist; his estimate of the profits on the axes traded at Okanogan may not have been based upon the long view of losses met elsewhere by his employers. For example, Columbia River Indians seized "33 large axes; 84 half axes, 66 small axes; and 2 square hand axes," and paid nothing whatever. This loss occurred on July 4, 1814, and, as reported by Alexander Henry, the stolen axes seem to have been a part of the same Astorian properties referred to above.[4]

[1] La Rochefaucauld-Liancour: *Travels in Canada, 1795* (Toronto, 1917), p. 115.

[2] Paul C. Phillips: *The Fur Trade* (2 vols.; Norman: Univ. of Oklahoma Press; 1961), II, 337.

[3] Alexander Ross: *Adventures of the First Settlers on the Oregon or Columbia River*, ed. Milo M. Quaife (Chicago: Lakeside Press; 1923), p. 163.

[4] B. C. Payette, comp.: *The Oregon Country under the Union Jack? Henry's Astoria Journal* (Montreal, 1961), p. 63.

In 1821 Nicholas Garry of the Hudson's Bay Company, writing about his trade in the Hudson Bay drainage basin, stated that "1 hatchet is worth 2 beaver." Garry's list of trade values for 1821 also indicate that a trade gun brought 11 beaver, and a 3-gallon kettle was worth 6 beaver.[5] At this time an average beaver pelt was worth about $6.00 in Michilimackinac; so, theoretically, Garry was getting around $12.00 for a small ax that cost 50¢ or less in Montreal.

When in 1826 William Ashley sold his beaver business to Smith, Jackson, and Sublette in Cache Valley near the site of present-day Hyrum, Utah, the remainders of the trade goods that were still in his possession were transferred to the new company. The bill of sale shows no trade axes, but four "square" felling axes are listed at $2.50 each.[6] Presumably, these were camp axes similar to the American ax pictured in figure 61*f*. On the occasion of this sale, Ashley entered into formal agreement with Smith, Jackson, and Sublette, contracting to deliver to them certain merchandise needed for the 1827 rendezvous planned for Bear Lake. Trade axes ("squaw axes") at $2.50 apiece find a place in the list of prescribed trade items.[7]

At Fort Union on the Missouri, the American Fur Company in July 1832 charged Johnson Gardner, mountain man, $3.00 for a small ax, presumably a hatchet, and $6.00 for a larger one, probably a "square" one. Gardner paid his bills at Fort Union in beaver pelts at the rate of $4.125 per pound, or about $5.50 per pelt delivered at Fort Union.[8] It appears, therefore, that by 1832 the mountain man on the Missouri could obtain two hatchets for one beaver. At about this time, the same two hatchets would have brought two beaver pelts if traded at Fort Hall, west of the Rockies, some 700 miles southwest from Fort Union.[9]

The statistics just quoted are compared more readily and comprehended better when reviewed in tabular form:

---

[5] Quoted in Harold A. Innis: *The Fur Trade in Canada* (New Haven: Yale Univ. Press; 1962), p. 319.

[6] Chittenden: *American Fur Trade* (1954 edn.), I, 4.

[7] John E. Sunder: *Bill Sublette, Mountain Man* (Norman: Univ. of Oklahoma Press; 1959), p. 245.

[8] Chittenden: *American Fur Trade* (1954 edn.), II, 943–5.

[9] W. Clement Eaton: "Nathaniel Wyeth's Oregon Expedition," *Pacific Historical Review*, IV: 2 (June 1935), pp. 111–12.

EASTERN PURCHASE PRICE VS. WESTERN SALE PRICE,
SMALL AXES OR HATCHETS

	I	II	III
Year	Prime Cost (in Dollars) of One Ax (Tomahawk Size)	Retail Price (in Beaver) of One Ax	Retail Price (in Dollars) of One Ax
1. 1775	.33 at Montreal	3 at Saskatchewan River	6.00
2. 1795	.33 at Philadelphia	3 at Lake Winnipeg	5.33
3. 1811	.62½ at Montreal	4, "west of the Rockies"	10.00
4. 1813	1.00 (Astoria-made)	10 at Okanogan	22.50
5. 1821	.50 at Montreal	2 at Hudson Bay	12.00
6. 1826–7	.45 at New York	½ at Bear Lake, Utah	2.75
	(The $2.75 was contract price to middleman)		
7. 1832	.45 at New York	½ at Fort Union	3.25
8. 1832	.45 at New York	1 at Fort Hall	6.00

The "prime cost" (column I) is derived from documents that are not subject to misinterpretation, and the return in beaver pelts (column II) is quoted from the writings of men who did the trading. The return in dollars and cents, as entered here (column III), is not realistic since most of the figures pertain to values that could be realized only after the furs arrived at such markets as Montreal and New York. Costs of processing and delivery are not reckoned; further, not all of the pelts collected and paid for in the field reached the markets. These expenses and losses in transit reduced the average monetary return to something less than that shown in column III. It is next to impossible to determine the over-all expense of the traders who supplied the axes to Indians. Nathaniel J. Wyeth estimated that his merchandise would be worth in the Rocky Mountains 400 per cent of its original cost, so that his $.45 ax (item number 8 in the table) exchanged for a beaver pelt worth $6.00 seemed to be a highly profitable piece of merchandise. But Wyeth failed in the fur trade. It is unreasonable to indicate a hard and fast percentage of profit. It seems correct to say, however, that the mountain man during the first two decades of his activities (1804–20) realized a greater gain in his ax business than was the case during the period from 1820 to 1840. Consistent with this premise, we note that such statistics as are available suggest a far greater number of axes in the Western trade during the latter period. Competition between traders meant an increase in the over-all volume of the trade but not necessarily a greater profit to individual traders. A goodly number of adventurers fared better than did Wyeth, but highly successful trading enterprises that yielded fortunes were few indeed. In all of the trading, the ax was a minor item in a pecuniary sense but was an essential piece of equipment to both the Indian and the white trader-trapper.

The field records of the trading companies contain a number of stories regarding the vital role of the ax in the everyday procedures of the mountain man. Indians, professing friendship, sometimes found temptation too great and purloined the trader's camp axes at the very moment when the white man was extending the hospitality of his larder. Lewis and Clark wrote the first of the stories regarding the ends to which indignant victims of the thieves might go in recovering their axes.[1] Probably the most tragic occurrence growing out of the theft of a camp ax was the massacre of Jedediah Smith's party on the Umpqua River in 1828.

Smith's party of eighteen men and many horses reached the Umpqua via the Central Valley of California, the Trinity River, and the coast of northern California and southern Oregon. Movement through the untracked mountains of the Trinity and along the narrow strip of beach closely bordered by the forested bluffs of the rocky coast necessitated much clearing of the way with axes. By the time the fatigued party and 300 horses reached the more favorable terrain along the Umpqua, everyone was exhausted and, no doubt, more than ordinarily conscious of the usefulness of the ax. The day preceding their arrival at the Smith River camp, a thieving Indian stole an ax. Harrison Rogers, Smith's lieutenant, wrote:

Saturday July 12 [1828], we commenced crossing the [Umpqua] River early and had our goods and horses over by 8 o'c. then packed up and started a N. E. course up the River and traveled 3 M. and encamped. Had several Indians along, one of the Inds stole an axe, and we were obliged to seize him for the purpose of tying him before we could scare him to make him give it up. Capt. Smith and one of them caught him and put a cord around his

---

[1] Paul Allen, ed.: *History of the Expedition under the Command of Captains Lewis and Clark* (2 vols.; Philadelphia, 1814), II, 305–6; Quaife, ed.: *Journals*, pp. 308, 338.

neck, and the rest of us stood with our guns ready in case they made any resistence [sic.], there was about 50 Inds present, but did not pretend to resist tying the other.

The episode of theft and chastisement seemed to pass as experiences of no great moment to these Kelawatset Indians. On July 13, the party of white men proceeded upriver to the Smith River camp, where trading was conducted quietly with another group of 50 or 60 Indians. On July 14, Jedediah Smith with two of his men set out in a canoe to scout out a route for continued travel toward the Willamette. In their absence, about a hundred Kelawatsets entered the camp ostensibly to trade. Suddenly they attacked the scattered and unsuspecting trappers with their axes, murdering all but Arthur Black, who, although wounded, managed to break away from his assailants and escape into the forest.

Smith and his two companions returned in their canoe to the vicinity of their camp shortly after the massacre. They, too, were fired upon by the Kelawatsets, but they quickly moved to the riverbank opposite the concealed savages. As had Black, Smith and his men fled to the coast and by dint of great effort and some good luck—in the form of Indian guidance—made their way to Fort Vancouver, where John McLoughlin, Hudson's Bay Company Factor, gave them every succor and ordered an expedition to recover Smith's properties stolen by the Kelawatsets.[2] In the course of the search for the widely distributed beaver pelts, horses, and other loot, Hudson's Bay Company officials recovered the precious journals of Harrison and Smith and obtained and recorded some significant testimony given by Indian participants in the massacre. In essence, they learned that by forcing the return of the stolen ax on July 12, "Jedediah had humbled a chief of the Kelawatsets, and this man now plotted vengeance. Fuming over his disgrace, back to the Kelawatset camp went this Indian. For a long time he harangued his fellows, urging them to fall on the white strangers and wipe out the memory of the shame that had been put upon him."[3] The "wiping out" was accomplished almost entirely through the murderous use of axes.

This particular horror story is not exactly duplicated in the

[2] Dale L. Morgan: *Jedediah Smith and the Opening of the West* (Indianapolis: Bobbs-Merrill; 1953), pp. 267-9, 274-9.
[3] Maurice S. Sullivan, ed.: *Jedediah Smith, Trader and Trail Breaker* (New York: Press of the Pioneers; 1936), p. 174.

mountain man's ax saga, but it finds numerous parallels beginning with the *Tonquin* disaster in 1811 and continuing with lesser consequences in most of the mountain man's territory throughout the years of his dominance, up until and including the Whitman massacre in 1847.

The American Ax and Its Antecedents

The "French" Ax and the Fur Trade

A century or two before the birth of Christ, men of Tenian culture exploited deposits of iron ore along the northern coast of Spain. Important among their iron products was the "La Tène" ax shown on the map (specimen no. 1). This implement, even at that early period, had been in use for a long time and had been distributed throughout practically all of the regions noted on the map. Through the centuries it continued to hold its important place in the cultural advance, and the Spanish iron mines, among others, continued to provide the raw material that made possible its manufacture.

From the simple La Tène or Celtic ax there sprang before A.D. 1200 a variety of implements and weapons—Roman, Burgundian, Frankish, Russian, Slavish, Viking, and Persian forms of garish character, many of them impractical exaggerations. These were followed by the amazing array of battle-axes produced during the Middle Ages. The museums of Europe literally overflow with flamboyant iron axes made before America was discovered. Few of the freakish forms persisted in use, but the original, basic La Tène iron ax (no. 1) lasted through all the centuries of experimentation and strife. By the time Europeans set foot in the New World, their workaday axes were of the type shown in specimen no. 2—a pattern that does not much differ in its essential parts from the ancient ax of the Celts (no. 1). Interestingly enough, the same iron ores of Biscay that provided raw materials for some of the La Tène axes yielded the stuff for many sixteenth-century axes, and the 1,000-year-old sites of Celtic forges afforded place for Spanish smithies.

Because French merchants encouraged mass production and because sixteenth-century French ships brought great numbers of these axes to the natives in America, the term "French ax" was quite generally applied by peoples other than French. Actually, the ax was not especially French; all of Europe made and used it. Willy-nilly, the name "French ax" has persisted in America.

For obvious reasons (see specimen no. 2), "Biscayan" also was a designating term for the same axes during the beginnings of the

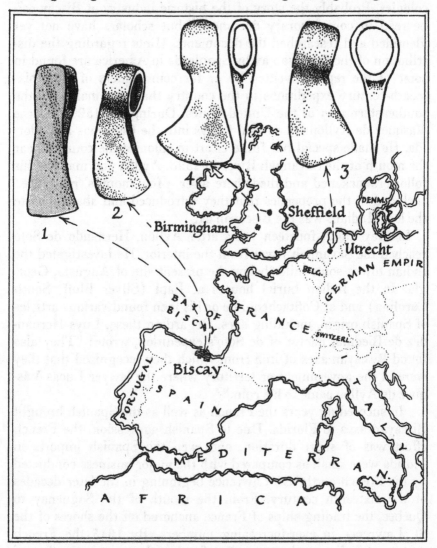

The "French" Ax and the Fur Trade.

Specimen no. 1 is a Celtic ax, ancient ancestor of the common European ax. No. 2 is a "Biscayan hatchet" of the early trade in America. No. 3 shows a Holland-made trade ax. Specimen no. 4 is an English hatchet.

American trade and continued in fairly common use for more than a hundred years. The smithies at Biscay supplied a notable part of the ax import-export business conducted by the French, and the Spaniards also shipped the same ax to some of their American colonies. Probably the story of the historic industry at Biscay can be read in contemporary documents, but scholars have not yet identified and researched the documents. Hints regarding the distribution of the Biscayan ax by Spaniards in America are found in some of the reports written by or for commanders of early sixteenth-century expeditions in the country that now makes up the southeastern part of the United States. During the 1520's, Lucas Vásquez de Ayllón led several forays into the Carolinas and Florida. He made special but futile effort to colonize the country near the mouth of the Savannah River in 1526. Ayllón and many of his followers sickened and died there after a few months' residence.[4] Included in the properties that they introduced and abandoned to the local Indians was the Biscayan ax.

In May 1540, fourteen years after Ayllón, Hernando de Soto reached the Savannah River from the interior. He investigated the Indian towns some miles below the present site of Augusta, Georgia. In the Indian burial houses at Ilapi (Silver Bluff, South Carolina) and at Cofitachequi he or his men found various articles of Spanish origin, including axes. Regarding these, Luys Hernández de Biedma, Factor of de Soto's expedition, wrote: "They also found Biscayan axes of iron from which they recognized that they were in the government or territory where the lawyer Lucas Vásquez de Ayllón came to his ruin."[5]

In succeeding years the French as well as the Spanish brought Biscayan axes to Florida. Due to Spanish aggression, the French effort was of short duration, and even the Spanish imports in Florida were small as compared with the major business conducted by the French on the St. Lawrence beginning in the later decades of the sixteenth century. From the mouth of the Saguenay to Quebec, the trading ships of France anchored off the shores of the St. Lawrence in ever-increasing numbers. By 1615 the French pattern of Indian trade was well defined, and presently the flow of

---

[4] John R. Swanton: *The Indians of the Southeastern United States*, Bureau of American Ethnology Bulletin 137 (Washington, D.C., 1946), pp. 36-7.

[5] E. G. Bourne, ed.: *Narrative of the Career of Hernando de Soto . . .* (2 vols.; New York: Allerton Book Co.; 1922), II, 100; Swanton: *Indians*, pp. 45-6.

Biscayan axes to New France was voluminous and constant. The Montagni–Algonquin–Huron Indian Confederation saw to it that the French trade goods moved westward into the hands of Great Lakes tribesmen who had not yet seen white men. Thus the French ax took root in the North and became traditional.

At this time, the English were establishing their tobacco colonies in tidewater Virginia and Maryland. Military procedures were very necessary in wresting the lands from the Indians, and, of course, English axes figured in the warfare and in clearing the farms. However, agriculture was a principal objective of the Englishmen, and no such flood of trade axes came to the tidewater frontier as was seen on the St. Lawrence. The same can be said about much of the New England frontier that the English created in the seventeenth century, although the fur trade did enter here and for a time there was demand for French axes along the Connecticut and in the Massachusetts backcountry. How specific the Englishmen were in selecting their trade ax is revealed in the early records of the Hudson's Bay Company:

> Committee meeting 8th February 1671/2. That Mr. Millington bee desired to take care for providing one thousand *biscay hatchets*, one half of three pounds and one half of two pounds a piece, to bee sure that they bee such as are for trade with indians and not such as are for the inhabitants of Canada.

And on the occasion of a meeting November 27, 1673:

> That Mr. Raddison attende Mr. Millington forthwith with a patterne of *biscay hatchets* to be provided for this country, such as are usually sent from thence for France to serve the Indians in and about Canada, and that Mr. Millington bee desired to give order for two thousand hatchetts to be brought from Biscay by the first opportunity.[6]

That these Hudson's Bay Company axes moved quickly into the West is shown by the testimony of French traders at Green Bay, who in 1683 talked with Indians from the "Assiniboie (sic) River," already in possession of some of the Biscay hatchets traded at Fort Nelson.[7] It is worthy of note that these early Biscay hatch-

[6] Hudson's Bay Company Minute Book, beginning October 24, 1671, pp. 28, 72, quoted by Innis: *The Fur Trade*, p. 123.
[7] Innis: *The Fur Trade*, p. 48.

ets were much heavier than are the later trade axes that came with the American trade.

During the early decades of the seventeenth century, the Dutch brought their system of Indian trade to the Hudson, the Connecticut, and the Delaware. The trade ax, as always, was of prime importance. The Dutch ax differed in no structural particular from the Biscayan hatchet, but it was made in the Netherlands by Dutchmen (specimen no. 3). The liaison with the Indians in what is now the State of New York resulted in the concentration of Utrecht hatchets in the territories of the Iroquois. In 1638 the New Sweden Company entered the fur trade in the Delaware Valley, but they did not trade Swedish axes; Dutchmen participated in this venture as partners, and the Swedes' trade axes were products of the shops at Utrecht. For seventeen years New Amsterdam put up with the competition offered by New Sweden, but in 1655 Peter Stuyvesant led a force of Dutchmen against the Swedish Fort Christina (Wilmington) and in a bloodless attack put an end to all of New Sweden. Thereafter for ten years the trade on the Delaware was entirely Dutch, but in 1664 the Delaware developments and all of New Netherland were seized by the English.

This seizure did not put an immediate end to the importation of Dutch merchandise. Many Dutch traders persisted in their business under British permits. In New York in 1667 some of the lingering Dutchmen petitioned the king of England for permission to bring from Holland three ships each year. Stuyvesant explained to British authorities that the New York beaver pelts had always been purchased from the Indians with commodities brought from Holland—"hatchets, and other iron work made in Utrecht, and much esteemed by the natives. It is to be feared that if these commodities fail, the very trade itself will fall, and the French of Canada will be in control." The king granted the request, ordering that the Dutch be allowed to trade for seven years.[8]

Some English trade axes were taken to America as early as 1590.[9] The record is not clear as to just when the first *heavy* demands for trade axes were placed upon Sheffield and Birmingham. Both had been celebrated for their ironworks since the early

[8] E. B. O'Callaghan, J. R. Brodhead, *et al.*, eds.: *Documents Relative to the Colonial History of the State of New York* (15 vols.; Albany: Weed, Parsons; 1853–87), III, 164–7.

[9] William H. Holmes: "The Tomahawk," *American Anthropologist*, No. 2 (1908), p. 268.

seventeenth century. Before the end of that century, Biscay and Utrecht fade from the record of the American trading companies, and the English axes (shown in specimen no. 4) appear more frequently in the documents of the fur trade. At first these products of the English forges weighed 2 to 5 pounds each, as did most of the Biscayan and Utrecht trade axes. Not all of the English axes were flattened laterally, as shown in specimen no. 4; the round eye of Biscay and Utrecht continued in the majority. As the trade advanced during the eighteenth century, the fieldmen of all nationalities had impressed upon them the need for lighter, more portable axes, and hatchets weighing as little as 1 pound came into favor for use on the trail. The establishment of forges in the more accessible, permanent posts and the employment of blacksmiths during the last half of the eighteenth century became regular practice within the Hudson's Bay and North West companies.[1] Gradually the service of the ax supply became more independent of the manufactories in England. During the Revolution and thereafter such cities as Boston, New York, Philadelphia, and Baltimore became centers for smithies, and simultaneously great numbers of country blacksmiths were busy throughout the Atlantic states. Immediately after the war, the production of American trade axes was widespread and voluminous. In pattern, they did not differ from the 300-year-old Biscayan axes. One of the startling things to be said about them is that they are still being manufactured in quantity by the Collins Company of Collinsville, Conn. For nearly a century they were made in the Collinsville factory, but in recent years the production has taken place in subsidiary plants in Mexico City; Cali, Columbia; and São Paulo, Brazil, where the demands of the Antilles, Mexico, and South America are met. Here the old-time patterns are still the great favorites. Some fifty-five models and sizes of the French ax are pictured in the Collins Company catalogue of 1919.[2] One of these patterns is still made in Collinsville.[3]

The Development of the American Ax

AN enlarged version (fig. 61a) of the ancient ax of the Celts was brought to America by the first colonists. With it they opened the

---

[1] Innis: *The Fur Trade*, p. 156.
[2] Collins Company, 1919, pp. 18–24.
[3] Personal letter, C. M. Elston to C. P. Russell, September 4, 1958.

forests and created farms and homes. Whether they were from the forges of the British, Dutch, or French most specimens closely followed the ancient pattern. Today this ax of our forefathers is referred to as the "French" ax, but it is no more French than Polish. It is the typical all-European ax that has continued in use in the "old country" since the dawn of Christendom and is still manufactured and used in its original form throughout much of Europe. In the hands of American woodsmen and blacksmiths it underwent gradual change (figs. 61c and 61d) until from it evolved a more efficient implement, the American ax (fig. 61f)—the first constructive change in the iron ax in two thousand years.

It is not implied that ax types other than the ancient Celtic pattern do not exist in the Old World, but the 2,000-year-old model is still basic and preferred throughout Central Europe. In the United States the old pattern is little used but, as previously stated, it is still manufactured by the Collins Company in its subsidiary factories in Mexico and South America for customers in the Latin American countries. In these localities it is not utilized for trade with aborigines; it is the all-purpose tool of the white man, just as was the ax (fig. 61a) in the hands of the earliest colonists in North America.

The French, Dutch, Swedish, and English settlers who carved the first farms and village sites from the New World forests placed unquestioned reliance in two principal auxiliaries afforded by their Old World legacy: the gun and the ax. The impact of the wilderness brought to the pioneers the shocking realization that not all of the heritage acquired in the European environment could be completely serviceable in the wild forest environment. The big European felling ax (fig. 61a) was good, but it was not good enough for the extraordinary demands put upon it by woodsmen in the tremendous forests of America. Seemingly endless tracts of great trees were to be felled in order that fields and pastures might be opened; log houses and barns were built in clearings; crude furniture and farm implements were manufactured; in short, the livelihood of the entire body of farmer-settlers depended in great part upon the cutting of trees. After a few generations of determined, ingenious newcomers had waged war against the American forests, it was obvious to the "choppers" that a heavy poll made for efficiency in chopping. In little more than a century of trial and experiment, the old "French" ax was largely replaced by the American ax as the workaday tool of the white man in the colonies.

Figure 61a represents the woodsman's ax, now specimen no. 25.0c at Colonial Williamsburg. This large felling ax was brought to light in the course of the excavations that preceded the restoration of Williamsburg, Virginia. It is typical of the European chopping ax ("French" ax) and identical in shape with axes used by early colonists in Maine, New York, or Georgia. The straight helve or haft in this figure was supplied by the artist. Counterparts of both ax and handle may be found today in Europe wherever trees are cut.

Figure 61b shows a specialized ax of the "French" type found on Jamestown Island, Virginia, 9 inches below the grass roots. A number of such axes have been found on Jamestown Island, but none were unearthed in nearby Williamsburg. This appears to be a mortising tool or, perhaps, a splitting implement, but it retains the very light poll and heavy bit of the European ax and, except for the lateral extension of the eye (ears), is similar to the "French" ax. Beauchamp[4] gives a drawing of an ax from New York which originally was like that shown in figure 61a but which was ground down to provide a tool similar in proportions to this Jamestown specimen.

An Anglo-American ax from the Essex Institute, Salem, Massachusetts, is presented in figure 61c. This ax figured by Mercer[5] is presumed to have been made about 1750. The poll has been considerably lengthened and weighted in order to partially counterbalance the bit, which is somewhat shorter than the bit of the typical European ax had been. This may be regarded as an intermediate stage in the development of the American ax. In the McCord Museum, Montreal, is an ax (No. 1678) attributed to the period of the French and Indian War that is similar to the specimen shown here. Another found in the wreck of the gunboat *Philadelphia*, sunk in 1776, displays the same characteristics.

Figure 61d shows a woodsman's ax found at the Raleigh Tav-

[4] William M. Beauchamp: *Metallic Implements of the New York Indians*, New York State Museum Bulletin 55 (1902), p. 65.

[5] Henry C. Mercer: "Ancient Carpenter's Tools, Part 1," *Old Time New England*, XV: 4 (April 1925), pp. 173–4. The same material appears in Henry C. Mercer's *Ancient Carpenter Tools* (Doylestown, Penn.: Bucks County Historical Society; 1929), pp. 1–328.

ern, Williamsburg, Virginia (No. 2.2.17 B1, Williamsburg Restoration, Inc.). Compare the weight of metal at the top of the eye of this ax with the same metal shown in figure 61b. Just as figure 61c, this specimen shows a lengthening of the poll as a step toward counterbalancing the bit.

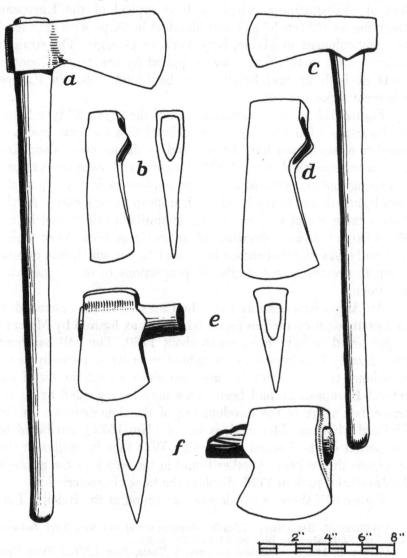

FIG. 61. *The Development of the American Ax.*

The drawing by William Macy is in the Jefferson National Expansion Memorial, St. Louis.

Illustrated in figure 61c is an American ax from the Great Smoky Mountains National Park (Mountaineer Museum, Gatlinburg, Tennessee). Here the bit is greatly shortened and the square poll is enlarged and weighted, thereby forming an ax type entirely unknown outside of America. In New England and the Middle Colonies it appeared about 1740 and was firmly established before the Revolution.[6] Originally the helve was straight, as shown in figures 61a and 61c. The type became popular as the "Kentucky pattern."

Figure 61f shows a relic of the Revolution from the gunboat *Philadelphia*. This is an early American ax that remained at the bottom of Lake Champlain in the wreck of the *Philadelphia* from 1776 to 1935. It is almost square, and the heavy poll outweighs the bit. With this implement there could be no "wobble" in the stroke; its bite was deep and its accuracy positive. It constituted a distinctly new tool quite equal to a great pioneering function. This particular specimen with known history is a treasure among the collections. Fittingly, it is preserved in the U. S. National Museum,[7] and our illustration is used with the permission of that institution.

The Ax in the Making

ONE method of making the American ax involved the welding together of two roughly shaped slabs of iron (fig. 62a) over a handle pattern (not shown in the figure) so as to provide the eye. The cutting edge of the ax was provided with a steel blade (fig. 62b), which was welded into the open end of the bit (fig. 62c). The illustration is after Mercer. This process of steeling an ax was not followed universally; see the Manhattan specimen (fig. 62d) and the Williamsburg example (fig. 62g).

Trade axes were commonly made from a single elongated flat plate of iron, one end of which was hammered out while hot and wrapped around a pattern to form the eye (fig. 62e). At Fort Vancouver numerous trade axes were found which display suc-

[6] Mercer: "Ancient Carpenter's Tools," p. 172.
[7] Lorenzo F. Hagglund: *A Page from the Past. The Story of the Continental Gondola, "Philadelphia"* (Whitehall, N.Y., 1936), pp. 1–24. See also *Daily News* [Burlington, Vt.] special historical tabloid (1935). Philip K. Lundeberg, curator, National Museum, informs that a monograph is in preparation which describes the recovery of the gondola. (Letter, Lundeberg to Russell, May 1, 1964, and MS [1964].)

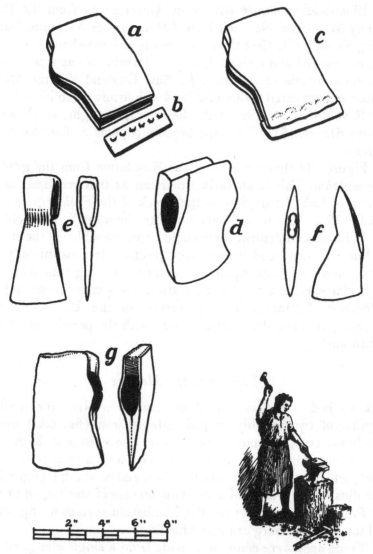

FIG. 62.   *The Ax in the Making.*

Drawing by William Macy, Jefferson National Expansion Memorial, St. Louis.

ceeding steps in the manufacture of the Hudson's Bay Company trade ax.[8] In some tomahawks (fig. 62*f*) the entire axhead was shaped in red-hot metal which, when cool, was perforated by drill-

[8] Louis R. Caywood: *Final Report Fort Vancouver Excavations* (Nat'l Park Service, Region Four, 1955), p. 34, Fig. 8.

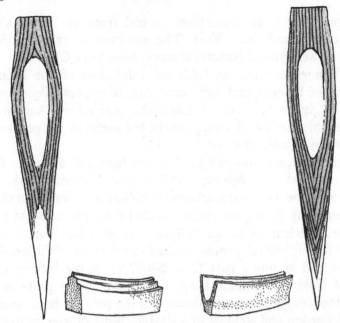

FIG. 63. *The Last of the "Inserted" and "Overcoat" Steeling.*

Since the 1930's improved methods of fabrication have done away with the "two-piece" ax; the modern ax is made from one solid chunk of high-carbon steel. Depicted here are methods that were intermediate between the old-time steeling and the modern one-piece ax. The ax at left weighs 3½ pounds; the steel-wedge insert weighs 12 ounces and is welded into the bit to become the cutting edge. The insert is sufficiently massive to permit of repeated grinding and sharpening. At right is another 3½-pound ax. The steel cap welded over the edge of the bit weighs 4 ounces. This method of steeling an ax was regarded to be inferior to the insert method. The drawing is after the Collins Company *Catalogo Illustrado*, p. 6.

ing to make the eye (fig. 62*f*). The process of tempering these axes varied in proportion to the conscientiousness of the makers and the circumstances under which they did their smithing. See figure 69*i* and Woodward.[9]

After the first rough weld, shown in figure 62*c* the ax was given final shaping, and the steel blade was ground to sharpness.[1]

[9] Arthur Woodward: "The Metal Tomahawk," *The Bulletin of the Fort Ticonderoga Museum*, VII (January 1946), pp. 2–42.

[1] Figures 62*a*, 62*b*, and 62*c* are from Mercer: "Ancient Carpenter's Tools"; see also Woodward: "The Metal Tomahawk," p. 8.

Figure 62*d* is an incomplete axhead from an Indian site on Manhattan Island, New York. The specimen is exhibited in the American Museum of Natural History, New York City.

A Tennessee trade ax from the collections of the Memphis Museum of Science and Industrial Art, Memphis, Tennessee, is shown in figure 62*e*. The blacksmith's welded eye has broken, revealing his method of wrapping the hot metal of the poll around a pattern so forming the eye.

Figure 62*f*, a tomahawk head of late fur-trade days was found near Mammoth Hot Springs, Yellowstone National Park. It is preserved in the Yellowstone Museum collections. Note that the eye was formed by three perforations drilled through the solid metal.

The American ax shown in figure 62*g* was dug from the back yard of the eighteenth-century Coke-Garret house, Williamsburg, Virginia and is now a part (No. 2-8-27A) of the history collections of Colonial Williamsburg. Oxidation of the parts has revealed the welded joints and shows that the poll has been weighted by the insertion and welding of a sizable chunk of iron between the two slabs of metal that make up the axhead.

The American Ax and Its Intermediaries

FOR nearly a century after the American ax was perfected, older ax types lacking niceties of balance continued to be manufactured in America as well as in Europe. These various forms, intermediate between the typical European ax and the distinctive American product, found use along with the better tool to which they had given origin, and it is not unusual for the archeologist and historian to uncover specimens in one site that are representative of all stages in the development of the American ax. A good example of this overlapping is seen in the axes from the recovered hull of the Continental gondola *Philadelphia*, which was sunk in 1776. The "French" ax (fig. 69*k*), an intermediate ax like figure 61*c*, and a full-fledged American ax (fig. 61*f*) all found use by the Continental fighters who manned the *Philadelphia*.

Figure 64*a* shows a relic of Fort St. Clair, Preble County, Ohio. The fort, a stockade for storage purposes, constituted a lesser link in the chain of establishments erected by American troops between Fort Washington (Cincinnati) and Lake Erie during the fateful expeditions against the Northwest Indians in 1791–2. Note that this ax has a short bit but a light poll. It is clearly intermediate between the European ax and the American tool. It may well be one of the axes used in the construction of the old fort. The Ohio State Museum owns the specimen.

Figure 64*b* is a heavy chopping ax of early American proportions. It found use in Oregon's forests in pioneer times, and now is specimen No. 74 in the Oregon Historical Society, Portland.

Figure 64*c* shows a hatchet captured from Indians near present-day Winneconne, Wisconsin, during the Blackhawk War of 1832; now in the Western Reserve Historical Society, Cleveland, Ohio.

A New England ax intermediate between the British felling ax and the American ax is shown in figure 64*d;* it is from the Vermont State Cabinet, Montpelier, Vermont.

Figure 64*c* is a heavy-polled ax from the scene of the massacre of Moravian Indians by American militiamen in 1783 at Gnadenhutten, Ohio. Ohio State Museum.

A hatchet of distinct American type from Fort Ticonderoga, New York, is illustrated in figure 64*f*. It is part of the Fort Ticonderoga collections.

Figure 64*g* shows a Hudson's Bay Company ax of general "French" characteristics that shows an American influence in its elongated poll. It is said to have been made and used at Fort Nisqually, Washington, in 1833. The specimen is no. 1282 in the Washington State Historical Society, Tacoma, Washington. A similar specimen was recovered at Fort Vancouver. The senior blacksmith at Fort Vancouver was an American, the Astorian William Cannon, or "Channing." [2]

Figure 64*h* is a pioneer hatchet, "Kentucky pattern," from the North Carolina side of the Great Smoky Mountains National Park, now part of the National Park Service Historical Collections, Great Smoky Mountains National Park.

A small broadax with weighted poll and grooved bit is shown in figure 64*i*. It is recorded as having been made in Salem, North Carolina, in 1810, and is now in the North Carolina State Historical Museum, Raleigh, North Carolina.

[2] Caywood: *Final Report, Fort Vancouver Excavations*, pp. 18, 34.

Figure 64*j* illustrates the type of "Yankee" hatchet carried in the belts of trappers and buffalo hunters during early days of the white man's activity on the plains and in the Rockies. This specimen is owned by the Historical Society of Carlsbad, New Mexico.

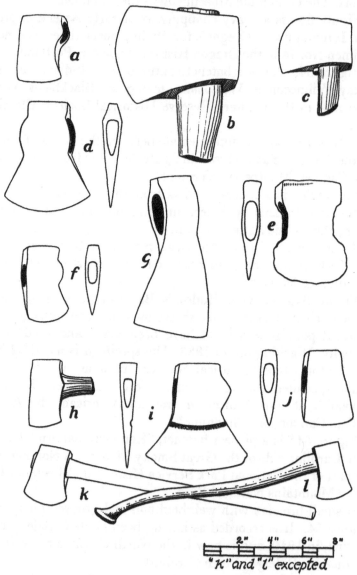

"*K*" and "*l*" excepted

FIG. 64. *The American Ax and Its Intermediaries.*

Drawing by William Macy, Jefferson National Expansion Memorial, St. Louis.

The Collins Company still features the model, "para cazadores" (for hunters).

Shown in figure 64k is a straight-hafted "Yankee" chopping ax of the early nineteenth century, now in the Oregon Historical Society. Some manufacturers still supply the straight-handled "Rectos." [3]

Figure 64l shows a modern "Yankee" ax and helve. The curved American ax helve came into general use about the middle of the nineteenth century. It makes for ease of handling and accuracy of stroke, a fitting adjunct to the efficient axhead which it carries.

U. S. Government Hatchets

FIGURE 65a shows a deeply rusted U. S. Army belt ax or tomahawk of the early period marked "U. S." It was found in the southern part of Rush County, Indiana, near town of Milroy in 1959. The specimen is owned by Wm. Fingerhuth, Tiffin, Ohio.

Regarding the early government tomahawk, Callender Irvine,

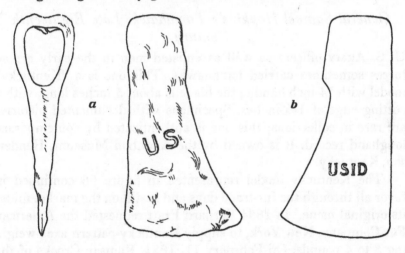

FIG. 65. *U. S. Government Hatchets.*

The U. S. Army belt ax shown in *a* was sketched from the specimen by John Barsotti, September 30, 1959. The Indian Department belt ax (*b*) was sketched from the specimen by John C. Ewers, October 1, 1946.

[3] Collins Company: *1919 Catalogo Illustrado*, p. 68.

Commissary General's Office, Philadelphia, wrote to Benjamine Moore at Hartford, Connecticut, January 3, 1815:

> Mr. B. Moore
> Sir:
>   Your letter of the 21st ultimo received. I want three or four thousand Tomahawks made soon. If you have any desire to undertake them you had better come to this city, when a pattern will be exhibited to you. . . .
>
> *Your obed. Servt.*
Callender Irvine [4]

For an eighteenth-century U.S. military tomahawk of slightly different form, see B. R. Lewis's *Small Arms*, Plate 22.

Figure 65*b* shows an Indian Department belt ax found in a grave near Old Ponca Agency. It is marked "U S I D"—a symbol still used by the Indian Service. The specimen was transferred from the Army Medical Museum to the U. S. National Museum on January 27, 1884; it bears catalogue No. 73064.

General Samuel Hopkins's Tomahawk, Late Eighteenth Century

U. S. ARMY officers as well as enlisted men in the early armed forces sometimes carried tomahawks. This one is a "Kentucky" model with 14-inch handle; the blade is about 5 inches long, with a cutting edge of 1⅞ inches. Specimens with documented histories are rare in collections; this one is authenticated by contemporary longhand record. It is owned by the Audubon Museum, Henderson, Kentucky.

The Kentucky model represented in figure 66 continued in favor all through the fur-trade days and is still on the market under its original name.[5] In 1834 Bernard Pratt requested the American Fur Company, New York, to supply Kentucky-pattern axes weighing 3 to 4 pounds. On February 11, 1834, Ramsay Crooks of the American Fur Company replied: "There is no such thing to be found here. They are all much heavier—say 5 to 6 lb. Some of the *Yankee pattern* of about the weight required can probably be had and I beg you immediately inform me whether these last will

---

[4] James E. Hicks: *Note on United States Ordnance* (2 vols.; Mount Vernon, N.Y., 1940), II, 61.

[5] Collins Company: *Catalogo Illustrado*, pp. 11, 12; *Catalogo M. Facoes*, p. 31.

FIG. 66. *General Samuel Hopkins's Tomahawk, Late Eighteenth Century.*

This Kentucky-pattern ax is owned by the Audubon Museum, Henderson, Kentucky, and is reproduced here by their permission. Drawing by William Macy, Jefferson National Expansion Memorial, St. Louis.

answer. This axe is every way as good as the other; the only difference being the shape." [6] The "Yankee pattern" is shown in figures 64*k* and 64*l*.[7]

Solomon Juneau, American Fur Company agent in Milwaukee, in a letter of March 7, 1845, ordered from his company in New York 3 dozen "hunters hatchett." Mr. Crooks asked Juneau to be specific. The reply came: "The hatchett are made just like the heavier American ["Yankee"] axe with short handle to it and they probably weigh one pound or thereabouts." [8] Figure 64*j* represents the type of ax wanted in Milwaukee.

[6] American Fur Company Papers, Letter Book 1, p. 156 (microfilm reel 1).
[7] See also Collins Company: *Catalogo Illustrado.*
[8] American Fur Company Papers, Letter Books, item no. 14828 (microfilm reel 36).

British Soldier of the 42nd, "Black Watch," Late Eighteenth Century

THE "Black Watch," even in 1758, was regarded to be a veteran regiment in America's backwoods warfare. It and a dozen regiments of "Rangers," enlisted men, noncommissioned officers, and officers alike, were equipped with hatchets during the 1760's and also during the Revolution. The tomahawks were usually of the type later called "Yankee pattern," but it is unlikely that they were so designated by the Englishmen.

FIG. 67. *British Soldier of the 42nd, "Black Watch," Late Eighteenth Century.*

The drawing is by William Macy, National Park Service. It is used with the permission of Fort Ticonderoga, New York.

French Grenadier's Hatchet, Early 1700's

FIGURE 68 shows Saint Remy's sketch of a French grenadier's hatchet published in 1702. He referred to the small ax as "hatchet with hammerhead." [9] Small axes of this shape, with hammerheads, were in use in France during the first century A.D. Spanish axes of much the same configuration but lacking hammerheads have been recovered in Florida (see figure 78d).

Marshal Ney, who was active with the French army during the late 1700's and early 1800's, wrote: "The Cavalry soldiers . . . shall each have a small hatchet in the left holster instead of a second pistol. This hatchet consists of a hammer and a blade in the shape of a half moon, formed of a single piece of metal. At the

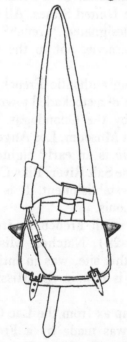

FIG. 68. *French Grenadier's Hatchet, Early 1700's.*

This sketch by Saint Remy was published in 1702, and reprinted by James R. Hicks in his *French Firearms*, 1939, p. 332.

[9] James E. Hicks: *French Firearms, 1702* (Mount Vernon, N.Y., 1939), p. 332, Pl. 100.

bottom of the handle there shall be a screw ring to enable the rider to fasten his horse to a tree, etc." [1]

A hatchet continues in regular use in the French army to this day. The 1914–18 issue is pictured in figure 70*h*.

EXAMPLES OF TRADE AXES

"French" Types

SOME of the specimens in figure 69 definitely came from France and were traded to the Indian by Frenchmen. Others came from England or were made in America by British smiths and reached the Indian via Great Britain's trade systems. Still others were made and traded by Americans after both French and British interests were removed from the United States. All of them, regardless of origin, are commonly designated "French" trade axes. The name pertains to the type or style, not to the national origin of the specimen.

Figure 69*a* shows an authentic French ax of the seventeenth century found at the site of a stockaded town in New York that was occupied about 1640 by the Onondagas. The specimen is No. 6416.1 in the Southwest Museum, Los Angeles, California.

Shown in figure 69*b* is an early eighteenth-century trade ax plowed up in 1850 on the Salt River, Pike County, Missouri, at the site of an early trade establishment. It is item No. 8, Missouri Historical Society, St. Louis.

In figure 69*c* is a small French ax from excavations at the Fatherland site (1700–29), Natchez, Mississippi. The Natchez tribe, which occupied this site, was in intimate contact with the French. The specimen is now in the Mississippi State Museum, Jackson.

Figure 69*d* is a camp ax from the Lac Courtes Oreilles Reservation, Wisconsin. It was made by a French blacksmith for a member of the Isham family of the Chippewa early in the nineteenth century. The haft is original. It is item No. E-704, Wisconsin Historical Society, Madison.

Shown in figure 69*e* is an Iroquois ax in the collections of the American Museum.

[1] Marshal Ney: *Military Studies Written for Use of Officers* (London: Bull and Churton; 1833), p. 73.

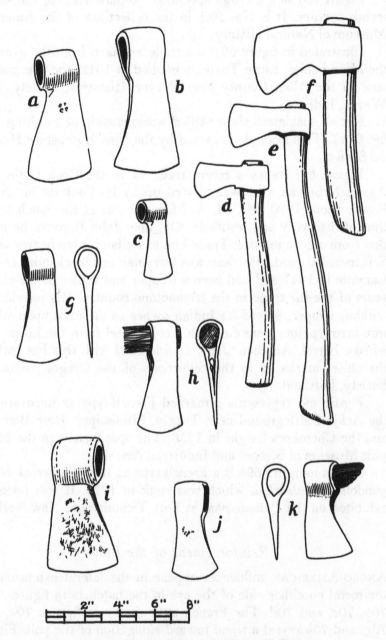

FIG. 69. *Trade Axes of the "French" Type.*

The drawing is by William Macy, Jefferson National Expansion
Memorial, St. Louis.

Figure 69*f* is a Cayuga specimen, "Squaw Ax," of the seventeenth century. It is No. 50.1 in the collections of the American Museum of Natural History.

Illustrated in figure 69*g* is a trade ax taken from the grave of the Miami chief, Little Turtle, who died in 1812; the specimen is now in the Allen County–Fort Wayne Historical Society, Fort Wayne, Indiana.

Not all specimens show skilled workmanship of smithing (see fig. 69*h*). This example is owned by the New Hampshire Historical Society.

Figure 69*i* shows a recent trade ax in the Cook Collection, Agate, Nebraska, that was plowed up by H. Cook on his Agate Ranch about 1890. Mr. M. A. Mooseau was at the ranch at the time of discovery and testified: "Old man John Bordeau he make that from old wagon tire. Trade him to Indian for ten beaver skins. Soft iron. No good." Bordeau was ferryman and blacksmith at Fort Laramie in 1847 and had been a trapper and trader in the earlier years of the fur trade in the tramontane country. His inferior ax, without temper, served its Indian owner as an anvil upon which iron arrow points were cut with a cold-chisel from the hoops of a whisky barrel. Another "J.B." ax, identical with this but lacking the chisel marks, is in the collections of the Oregon Historical Society, Portland.

Figure 69*j* represents a marked French-type ax uncovered at the Ackia Battleground near Tupelo, Mississippi. Here Bienville and the Cherokees fought in 1736. The specimen is in the Memphis Museum of Science and Industrial Art.

Shown in figure 69*k* is a French-type ax from the wreck of the gondola *Philadelphia*, which was sunk in 1776. It was formerly exhibited on the *Philadelphia* at Fort Ticonderoga, New York.

Reinforcement of the Poll

ANGLO-AMERICAN influences appear in the lateral extensions of the metal on either side of the eye in the hatchets in figures 70*a*, 70*b*, 70*c*, and 70*d*. The French axes shown in figures 70*e*, 70*f*, 70*g*, and 70*h* reveal a trend toward elongation of the poll. Figure 71 depicts the full development of this strengthening feature.

In figure 70*a* is a small hatchet found at the head of Lake

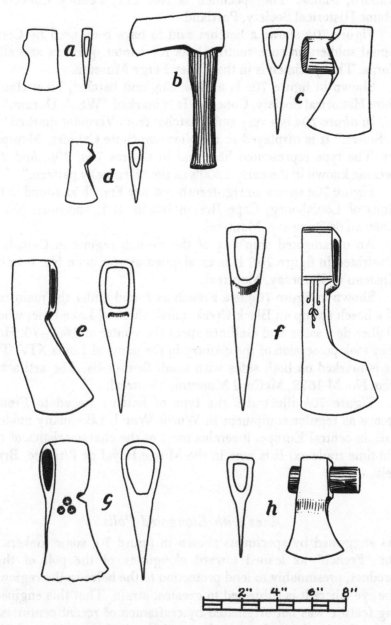

FIG. 70. *Reinforcement of the Poll.*

The drawing is by William Macy, Jefferson National Expansion Memorial, St. Louis.

Auburn, Maine. The specimen is No. 111, Penney Collection, Maine Historical Society, Portland.

Figure 70*b* shows a hatchet said to have been used by Continental soldiers in constructing huts for winter quarters at Valley Forge. The specimen is in the Valley Forge Museum.

Shown in figure 70*c* is a New England hatchet, New Hampshire Historical Society, Concord. It is marked "WS J. Durant."

In figure 70*d* is a very small hatchet from Vermont marked "A. J. Stowe." It is displayed in the Vermont State Cabinet, Montpelier. The type represented here and in figures 70*a*, 70*b*, and 70*c* became known in the early 1800's as the "Kentucky pattern."

Figure 70*e* shows an eighteenth-century French ax found in the ruins of Louisbourg, Cape Breton Island. It is specimen No. 7, Château de Ramezay, Montreal.

An ornamented ship's ax of the French regime in Canada is illustrated in figure 70*f*. It is catalogued as specimen No. 6 in the Château de Ramezay, Montreal.

Shown in figure 70*g* is a French ax found under the main root of a beech stump on Black Creek, north shore of Lake Erie, where Dollier de Casson and Gallinée spent the winter of 1669–70. Here they took possession of the country in the name of Louis XIV. The ax is marked on both sides with small fleur-de-lis. The artifact is item No. M-1672, McCord Museum, Montreal.

Figure 70*h* illustrates the type of hatchet issued to French troops as regular equipment in World War I. Like many modern axes in central Europe, it retains most of the characteristics of the old-time trade ax. It is now in the Musée Royal de l'Armée, Brussels.

Axes with Elongated Polls

As suggested by specimens shown in figure 70, some makers of the "French" ax leaned toward elongation of the poll of their product, presumably to lend protection to the helve in the region of the eye where it is subjected to greatest strain. That this engineering feature was not originated by craftsmen of recent centuries is attested to by the ancient specimens shown in figures 71*a* and 71*b*; that the design yielded practical advantages to the users of the ax is suggested by the fact that the elongated poll prevailed through the periods represented by the series shown here, and still is a characteristic of many of the modern axes in Europe. It is unlikely that these carefully made and comparatively costly implements were often made available to Indians. They were tools of the white man rather than objects of trade.

Figure 71a shows a prehistoric ax from mounds in County Antria, Ireland.[2] Similar axes of Roman, Frank, and Viking origin, dating back to the first several centuries A.D., are found throughout northern Europe. The advantages of strength and protection to the helve afforded by the elongated poll were discovered very early in the development of the ax.

A weapon of the Franks (A.D. 500–800) of Kerlich origin is illustrated in figure 71c. It is catalogued as No. FG 694, Germanisches Museum, Nuremberg.

Shown in figure 71c is an Austrian ax, probably a carpenter's tool, of the fifteenth century, which was found during excavations made near Salzburg. In 1936 the author examined carpenter's hatchets on the counters of Salzburg hardware stores that were quite like this old ax, lacking only the perforation in the blade. This specimen is No. 2296, Stadt Museum, Salzburg.

Figure 71d shows a Midwest pioneer's ax of the early nineteenth century. A buttress-like extension of the poll protects the helve. The artifact is No. 14 in the Allen County–Fort Wayne Historical Society, Fort Wayne, Indiana.

Shown in figure 71e is a small tool of broadax type found in the town of Kossuth, Manitowoc County, Wisconsin. Reinforcement of the poll and resultant strengthening of the helve was obtained by extending the metal above and below the eye. The specimen is catalogued as No. A-6085-2266, Wisconsin Historical Society, Madison.

A pioneer's tool, or perhaps a trade ax, from Manitowoc County, Wisconsin is illustrated in figure 71f. The full extension of the poll affords strength and also counterbalances the bit. It is No. A-6084, Wisconsin Historical Society.

The specimen in figure 71g is credited to an early blacksmith of St. Louis County, Missouri. It is now in the Missouri Historical Society, St. Louis.

Figure 71h "perhaps found use by an Indian ally of the British in the War of 1812"; it is from Geauga, Lake County, Ohio. The

[2] Mercer: "Ancient Carpenter's Tools," p. 167.

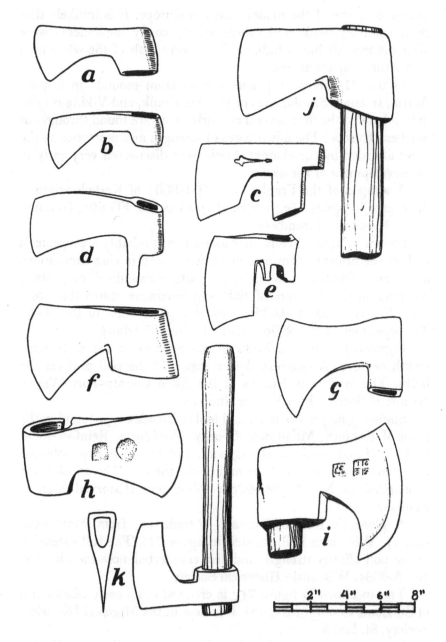

FIG. 71. *Axes with Elongated Polls.*

This drawing by William Macy is owned by the Jefferson National Expansion Memorial, St. Louis.

heart-shaped depression has stamped in it a date which appears to be 1808. The specimen is owned by the Western Reserve Historical Society, Cleveland, Ohio.

Figure 71*i* shows a small "broad" ax probably of Dutch origin. The New York State Museum's inquiries made in Holland and England failed to identify the specimen. The ax was found in an old stone wall at Amsterdam, New York, and is now No. 3547, New York State Museum.

Shown in figure 71*j* is a modern German felling ax that was used in Halberstadt, East Prussia, in 1880. It was brought to Pennsylvania by its owner in 1890. Note the slightly thickened, flattened poll which is elongated to give full protection to the heavy helve.[8]

The specimen presented in figure 71*k* is a broadax-type hatchet carried by Serbian troops as regular equipment during World War I; it is now in the Musée Royal de l'Armée, Brussels.

The "Spontoon"-Type Tomahawk

EAST and West and in the Deep South, there occasionally come to light dagger-like blades of iron bearing an eyed poll into which a haft once was fitted. Some of these are plain in outline; others are decorated at the upper end near the eye with curled processes shaped so as to suggest the fleur-de-lis. Some museum curators express the belief that these weapons were improvised from old French spontoons. It is probable that outmoded military spears were a glut on the European market during the early centuries of colonization in America. Winged lance heads, the Carolingian form of the sixth and seventh centuries, produced by the Franks in France and Italy, lead the elaborate procession of French, Swiss, and Italian spontoons of the fleur-de-lis pattern that found military use in Europe for a thousand years. No doubt they were available in some numbers to the makers of tomahawks for the American trade, but there is no good evidence that they found such renewed use. However, in the light of evidence provided by the Tunica cemeteries in Mississippi (fig. 72*b*), it is reasonable to claim a French relationship for the spontoon tomahawk. In all likelihood, it

[8] Ibid., pp. 167–8.

was also made by British smiths, and Meriwether Lewis has testified to the fact that his blacksmiths made it for the Mandans.

Meriwether Lewis, writing at the Mandan village in which his party spent the winter of 1804–5, described the awkward ax (shown in fig. 72a) that the local Indians demanded of his blacksmiths and added: "The older fassion [here figured] is still more inconvenient. It is somewhat in the form of the blade of an Espantoon, but is attached to a helve of the dementions before discribed [14 inches in length]. The blade is sometimes by way of ornament perforated with two, three, or more small circular holes. The following [fig. 72a] is the general figure."[4] This "older fashion," perhaps, is the progenitor of the so-called French style of pipe tomahawk (fig. 72e), and the "Minnewauken"-type pipe tomahawk (fig. 73c). McGuire[5] records that an old Indian on the Sioux reservation near Devils Lake, North Dakota, testified that his father's people obtained this style of ax from the French when his tribe lived in Wisconsin.

Figure 72b shows a spontoon- or halberd-type tomahawk from a grave in the historic Tunica cemetery opposite the mouth of the Red River in Mississippi. The tomahawk was near the abdominal region of a male skeleton. The French were with the Tunica during the first decades of the eighteenth century, and this specimen is reasonably attributed to the French.[6]

Figure 72c is described as a "tomahawk from an Indian village site on Lake Champlain. Probably made in France." The specimen is owned by the Fort Ticonderoga Museum, Fort Ticonderoga, New York.

The specimen shown in figure 72d is not a spontoon type. For a description of it, see page 283 (fig. 73).

Shown in figure 72e is the pipe tomahawk with which the Cayuse Indian To-ma-has killed Dr. Marcus Whitman in 1847 near present-day Walla Walla, Washington. Although it is attributed to the Hudson's Bay Company, its genesis from the French spontoon-type tomahawk (figs. 72a, 72b, 72c, and 72f) is obvious.

---

[4] Reuben G. Thwaites, ed.: *Original Journals of the Lewis and Clark Expedition, 1804–1806* (Cleveland, 1904), I, 255.

[5] George A. West: "The Aboriginal Pipes of Wisconsin," quoting McGuire, in *The Wisconsin Archeologist* (April 1905), pp. 62–3.

[6] James A. Ford: "Analysis of Indian Village Site Collections from Louisiana and Mississippi," Louisiana Geological Survey in *Anthropological Study No. 2* (November 1, 1936), p. 139.

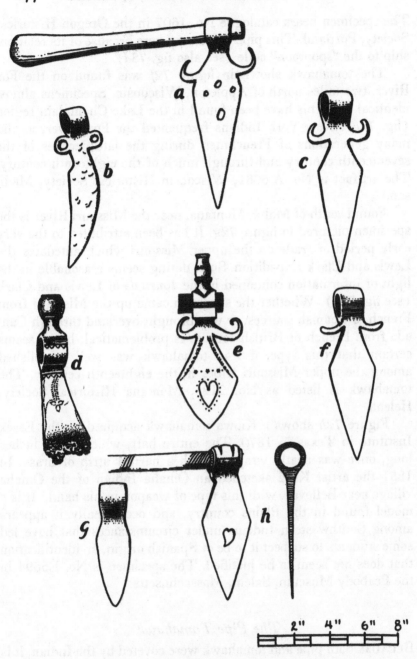

FIG. 72. *The "Spontoon"-Type Tomahawk.*

This drawing is by William Macy, Jefferson National Expansion
Memorial, St. Louis.

The specimen bears catalogue No. 1607 in the Oregon Historical Society, Portland. This pipe is pictured here because of its relationship to the "spontoon" style (see also fig. 73*a*).

The tomahawk shown in figure 72*f* was found on the Fox River, two miles north of Appleton, Wisconsin. Specimens almost identical with this have been found in the Lake Champlain region (fig. 72*c*). New York Indians frequented the Fox River, as did many generations of Frenchmen during the late decades of the seventeenth century and through much of the eighteenth century. The artifact is No. A-6081, Wisconsin Historical Society, Madison.

Found south of Malta, Montana, near the Missouri River is the specimen pictured in figure 72*g*. It has been attributed to the very early period of trade on the upper Missouri which antedates the Lewis and Clark Expedition. Such dating seems reasonable in the light of information contained in the *Journals* of Lewis and Clark (see fig. 72*a*). Whether the specimen came up the Missouri from French or Spanish sources, or was brought overland through Canada from French or British sources is problematical, but it seems certain that this type of iron tomahawk was well established among the upper Missouri tribes in the eighteenth century. The tomahawk is listed as No. 2125, Montana Historical Society, Helena.

Figure 72*h* shows a Kiowa tomahawk acquired by the Essex Institute in Texas in 1870. The entire haft, which is 22 inches long, once was neatly wrapped with a narrow strip of brass. In 1851 the artist Kurz sketched an Omaha Indian of the Omaha village near Bellevue, with this type of weapon in his hand.[7] It is a model found in the Plains country, and occasionally it appears among Southwestern Indians under circumstances that have led some students to suspect it to be of Spanish origin, an identification that does not seem to be justified. The specimen is No. E6694 in the Peabody Museum, Salem, Massachusetts.

The Pipe Tomahawk

BECAUSE both pipe and tomahawk were coveted by the Indian, it is not surprising that some canny trader of the distant past conceived of combining the two to make a particularly appreciated prize for

[7] *American Anthropologist*, X (1908), p. 10.

gift and trade. The date of this invention is not recorded, but specimens are known to have been in use early in the eighteenth century, and at the time of the Revolution the pipe tomahawk was widely distributed. The type shown in figure 73a is regarded to be of French design; figure 73e shows the standard British type; and figure 73i represents the so-called Spanish form. The pipe tomahawk has no known prototype; it is a distinct American specialty. That it was not purely a ceremonial adjunct or a mere fad in pipe fashions is attested to by many records of its terrible death-dealing qualities over much of the North American frontier.

Fig. 73a shows the pipe tomahawk with which To-ma-has killed Dr. Marcus Whitman, at Waiilatpu, the Whitman Mission (now a National Monument), six miles west of present-day Walla Walla, Washington [8] (see also fig. 72e). The weapon is said to have been traded to To-ma-has by the Hudson's Bay Company. It is a good example of the "French" type of tomahawk pipe. The Oregon Historical Society, owner of the tomahawk (No. 1607), also owns copy of a daguerreotype portrait of To-ma-has with this tomahawk in his hand (No. 2001).

Figure 73b shows an exaggerated form of the "French" tomahawk pipe attributed to the Blackfeet, in which tribe it was the property of "Growing Grass," a medicine man. Many things about it bespeak the workmanship of some frontier smith.[9] It is now No. 2104, Milwaukee Public Museum.

The specimen shown in figure 73c is referred to by some writers [1] as the "Minnewauken" type. Since this form can be likened to the spontoon-type battle ax that the Mandans demanded of Lewis and Clark in 1805,[2] and because many specimens have come from the Assiniboins and the Devils Lake country, there may be some reason for terming it the "Minnewauken" type (see figs. 72a and 72g). However Beauchamp [3] figures a pipe tomahawk similar in every way to this one that found early use among the Onondagas

[8] Frances Fuller Victor: *The River of the West* (Hartford, 1870), pp. 410–18.

[9] George A. West: "Tobacco, Pipes, and Smoking Customs of the American Indians," *Bulletin Public Museum, Milwaukee*, XVII (1934), pp. 323–4 and Pl. 244, Fig. 6. See also George A. West: "The Aboriginal Pipes of Wisconsin," *The Wisconsin Archeologist* (April 1905), p. 61.

[1] West: "Aboriginal Pipes," pp. 62–3; "Tobacco, Pipes and Smoking Customs," pp. 323–4 and Pl. 244, Fig. 6.

[2] Thwaites, ed.: *Journals*, I, 255.

[3] Beauchamp: *Metallic Implements*, p. 67.

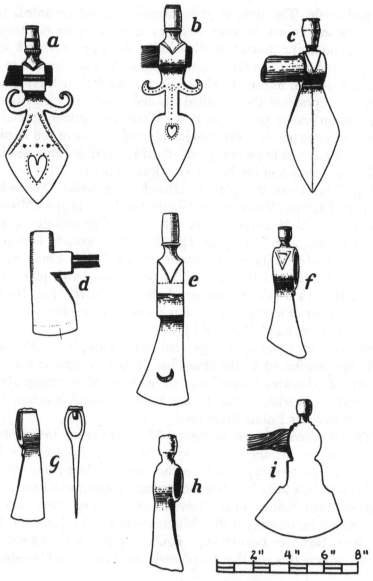

FIG. 73. *The Pipe Tomahawk.*

The drawing is by William Macy, Jefferson National Expansion Memorial, St. Louis.

in New York; the one here shown is a New York specimen in the New York State Museum, Albany.

Figure 73d is an unusual pipe tomahawk collected by Kontschnitt in New Orleans in 1887. It is owned by the Museum für Völkerkunde, Berlin, where it is specimen No. IV-B-1697.

Shown in figure 73e is a Wisconsin pipe tomahawk of standard British type made by the well-known artisan Joseph Jourdain, who established his business in Green Bay in 1798. It was obtained from an Indian chief at Watertown, Wisconsin, in 1883.[4] The specimen is No. 13160 in the Milwaukee Public Museum. A similar tomahawk pipe with an original handle or stem 24 inches long, once the property of Tecumseh, Shawnee chief, and used by him in his many negotiations with British and American representatives in the late eighteenth and early nineteenth centuries, is preserved in the Ohio State Museum, Columbus.

Figure 73f is a British-type pipe tomahawk from the Champlain Valley. The cutting edge has been broken. The specimen is owned by the Vermont State Cabinet, Montpelier, where it is catalogued as item No. 153.

Figure 73g represents a tomahawk pipe from which the bowl has been broken. It was found by J. Baptiste Picard at Lachine, near Montreal, in 1867. With it were parts of a human skeleton and a knife. It has been attributed to the Iroquois and is thought to be a relic of the Lachine massacre of 1689.[5] If this could be established as fact, the specimen would be listed as the oldest known pipe tomahawk. It is preserved in the McCord Museum, Montreal.

Regarding the early practice of fastening a separate pipe bowl to the ax proper, the Superintendent of the U. S. Indian Trade Office, George Town, D.C., had something to say. On April 4, 1809, he wrote to his representative in Philadelphia:

My neighbor, Mr. Charles Love, who is going to your city will deliver a sample tomahawk (pipe) which I have with some pains and expense procured. It is exactly such as the northern tribes require. It is made for use of edge as well as pipe. Those heretofore made in Philadelphia, I find from all quarters, are unfit for

[4] West: "Aboriginal Pipes," pp. 59–60. *Collections*, State Historical Soc. of Wisconsin, Vol. XX, p. 100 (portrait).

[5] Justin Winsor, ed.: *Narrative and Critical History of America* (Cambridge, Mass., 1884), IV, 350–1. See also Girovard: *History of Lake St. Louis*, p. 127.

use as to edge, and have served only to give away to the old men to smoke with and use in their dances. They are quite too tawdry. I beg you will see as early as possible some of your best white smiths and cutlers, and that you will let me know what they will want exactly for say one or two hundred immediately, and shall occasionally want many more. You will please remark that this model must in no way be deviated from. The same form precisely must be used for pipe, for eye, for blade, and the pipe must be made in the solid and not screwed, brazed, or welded. They will not stand the knocks which it is requisite they should often give. The blade must be well tempered and steeled so as to carry a good edge, the thickness and weight as nearly as possible similar to the model and the ornamental part exactly the same.[6]

The specimen illustrated in figure 73*h* was found on the site of Fort Winnebago, Columbia County, Wisconsin, and is now No. A-14300 in the Milwaukee Public Museum.

Figure 73*i* shows a "Spanish"-type pipe tomahawk found in an Indian grave in Umatilla County, Oregon. The specimen is now No. 258 in the museum of the Oregon Historical Society. In the National Museum, Washington, D.C., are similar pieces with the crescent-shaped blade; one is from West Virginia (catalogue No. 1351), and another is from Ohio (No. 7339). Probably the Nestor for the Spanish tomahawk pipe idea is J. D. McGuire, whose "Pipes and Smoking Customs"[7] first referred to the now much publicized "Spanish" specimen, No. 1351, in the National Museum. The Southwest Museum and Fort Ticonderoga have specimens of unknown origins, and West reports one in Coahuila, Mexico.[8] M. R. Harrington[9] and Courville[1] also tell of the Coahuila specimen, and in these published articles is found the thin documentation for a bona fide Spanish-made pipe tomahawk. Some researchers have concluded that the Spaniards never did produce a Spanish pipe tomahawk but drew upon French supplies for their presentation pieces and trade goods of this class.[2]

[6] U. S. Indian Trade Office, Letter Book, beginning October 31, 1807.

[7] J. D. McGuire: "Pipes and Smoking Customs of the American Aborigines," *Report, U. S. National Museum* (1897), Part I, pp. 464–7.

[8] George A. West: "Tobacco Pipes and Smoking Customs," p. 321.

[9] M. R. Harrington: "An Archaic Axe," *The Masterkey*, XXIII: 6 (1949), p. 176, and "Archaic Axes Still Used in Mexico," *The Masterkey*, XXIV: 3 (1950), p. 88.

[1] Cyril B. Courville: *Trade Tomahawks*, Southwest Museum Leaflets, No. 30 (1963), p. 8.

[2] Woodward: "The Metal Tomahawk."

Evidences of the Spanish practice of calling upon French and English mercantile firms for general supplies of Indian trade goods are readily cited; for eighteenth-century goods which Spanish interests distributed in the area which is now Kansas, see Carlyle S. Smith's "European Trade Material"; in 1783 Spanish authorities in Louisiana arranged for the distribution, under Spanish auspices, of English goods to the Creek Confederation, the Choctaw, and the Chickasaw; [3] and in the late decades of the eighteenth century, the French merchants Alesis Grappe, Dupin, and Morière of New Orleans supplied Spanish officers with French goods destined for the Caddo.[4] This is not to say that Spanish industry was incompetent, but the fact remains that through much of the period when the pipe tomahawk was in vogue, Spaniards in America were depending on other nations to supply a notable part of their Indian trade goods. This circumstance rather beclouds the question of the manufacture of pipe tomahawks in Spain or Mexico. On the basis of facts so far established, it is not sound to assert that there was a true Spanish pipe tomahawk. In truth, it has not been proven that any trade axes were manufactured by Spaniards later than the seventeenth-century Biscay hatchets, which were the standard during the early periods of the trade in the New World. In the present study the only authentic Spanish axes encountered were a few novelty pieces, presumably manufactured as gifts to Indians, and a number of bona fide Spanish battle axes and tools manufactured for the use of the white man.

All of the specimens pictured in figure 73 are of tempered steel and, obviously, were made for deadly business as well as for smoking and ceremony. When new or in use they were bright, handsome, and impressive pieces of equipment dear to the savages who possessed them. In addition to the pipe tomahawks made of iron, others made of brass and pewter appear in collections. Figure 72*d* shows a brass pipe tomahawk of unknown origin that prior to World War II was preserved in the Museum für Völkerkunde, Berlin. Once it had a cutting edge of steel dovetailed and brazed into the bit. The steel has not withstood the ravages of time and the elements and is badly oxidized. A Canadian specimen somewhat similar to this with all parts intact has been drawn by Beauchamp,[5]

[3] C. P. Russell: *Guns*, p. 39.
[4] Herbert E. Bolton, ed.: *Athanase de Mezières and the Louisiana-Texas Frontier, 1768–1780* (2 vols.; Cleveland: Arthur H. Clark Co.; 1914), I, 143–5.
[5] Beauchamp: *Metallic Implements*, Pl. 20, Fig. 88.

who reported that in 1902 pipe tomahawks of the kind were still to be seen in the possession of Indians on New York reservations. West [6] describes others from Indiana, Wisconsin, New York, and California. The U. S. National Museum has one, No. 5952, from Cattaraugus, New York, and one from Shawnee country is owned by the Ohio Historical Society.[7] Boyle refers to one of these brass specimens in the Provincial (Royal Ontario) Museum, Toronto, Canada, as "a piece of honest work, beautiful and useful." [8]

Pewter pipe tomahawks of little value in war but no doubt satisfactory for ceremonial purposes were used by New York tribes.[9] Stone pipe tomahawks shaped like the metal specimens were made by many tribes. They could not have withstood the strain of battle, but they served well as pipes, and their ceremonial significance was equal to their more fearsome progenitors. In recent years the crop of catlinite pipe tomahawks has degenerated into a line of curios.

Because the pipe tomahawk is so distinctly an American institution and one that bespeaks a great deal of artistry as well as mechanical ingenuity, it deserves renewed and deeper study. At this writing it is not possible even to conjecture about the circumstances surrounding its invention. When did it first appear? What native interests were first concerned, and who and where were the white men who developed it? Ample material in the shape of three-dimensional objects is available, but the documentary sources have not been sought out and explored. It would seem that the pipe tomahawk presents one of the more challenging problems open to the antiquarian and the anthropologist.

The Missouri War Hatchet

LEWIS and Clark found the ax shown in figure 74 in use on the Missouri in 1804–5. The Mandans withheld their corn from the

[6] George A. West: "Tobacco, Pipes and Smoking Customs," pp. 318–19.
[7] See R. G. Morgan: "An Engraved Tomahawk Pipe," *Museum Echoes* (1947).
[8] David Boyle: "Notes on Primitive Man in Ontario," Annual Archeological Report, Appendix, *Tenth Annual Report of the Minister of Education* (Ontario, 1895), p. 31. The "brass smoking tomahawk," valued at 4 to 10 shillings each, appeared frequently and in lots up to 100 in the inventories of the King's Stores in the British posts on the Northwestern frontier during the French and Indian War, 1755–63, and during and immediately following the Revolution. See *Illinois Historical Collections*, Vol. XI, and *Michigan Pioneer Historical Collections*, Vol. X, p. 497.
[9] Beauchamp: *Metallic Implements*, Pl. 22, Figs. 94 and 95.

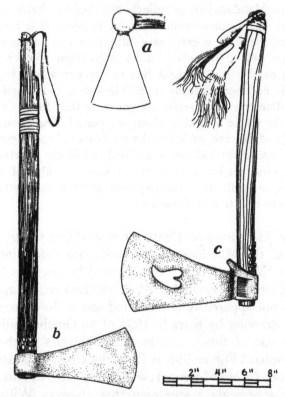

FIG. 74.   *The Missouri War Hatchet.*

This drawing is by William Macy, Jefferson National Expansion Memorial, St. Louis.

Lewis and Clark larder until the white blacksmiths had duplicated for them a number of these clumsy axes, following models already in the hands of the Mandans. The type seems to have been a favorite with most of the Indians below the great bend of the Missouri River, and it continued in vogue until the middle of the century. Figure 74*a* presents William Clark's drawing of the ax specified by the Mandans. Under date of January 28, 1805, Clark recorded that several Indians visited the Lewis and Clark encampment among the Mandans "wishing to get war hatchets made"; at that time Clark drew the figure shown. On January 29 he wrote that the axes were being made, "the only means by which we precure Corn." [1] Meriwether Lewis describing this ax on February 5, 1805, wrote:

[1] Thwaites, ed.: *Journals*, I, 251–2.

They [the Mandans] are peculiarly attached to a battle axe formed in a very inconvenient manner in my opinion. It is fabricated of iron only, the blade is extremely thin, from 7 to 9 inches in length and from 4¾ to 6 inches on its edge from whence the sides proceed nearly in a straight line to the eye where its width is generally not more than an inch. The eye is round and about an inch in diameter, the handle seldom more than fourteen inches in length, the whole weighing about one pound. The great length of the blade of this axe, added to the small size of the handle renders a stroke uncertain and easily avoided, while the shortness of the handle must render a blow much less forceable if even well directed, and still more inconvenient as they uniformly use this instrument in action on horseback.[2]

Figure 74*b* shows an Osage ax resembling the pre-Lewis and Clark ax of the Mandans. Woodward[3] has determined that this model, his "Missouri type," was favored by the Iowa, Sauk, Fox, Kansas, Pawnee, Comanche, Mandan, Dakota, Osage, and Oto tribesmen but apparently never found use in the eastern woodland region. A drawing by Kurz in 1851 of an Omaha Indian at Bellevue, with one of these axes in hand, appears in the *American Anthropologist*.[4] Figure 79*b* is from the Chicago Museum of Natural History (Field Museum), where it is listed as Nos. 59130 and 59131. It represents a specimen that answers William Clark's description fairly closely. The U. S. National Museum has one with its original handle, which is even more like Clark's sketch. It was in Comanche ownership when collected by V. J. Evans. The National Museum acquired it in 1931.[5]

Figure 74*c* is from the Ogallala of the Dakotas, No. 1-4605. The specimen is in the American Museum, New York.

Spiked Tomahawks

MODELED, perhaps, on the lines of the European battle ax of medieval times, many spiked tomahawks with both straight and curved protuberances at the top of the poll were produced by smiths of all the lands catering to the warlike Indian. Specimens are found

[2] Ibid., p. 255.
[3] Woodward; "The Metal Tomahawk," p. 33.
[4] *American Anthropologist*, Vol. X (1908), p. 11.
[5] Letter, John C. Ewers to C. P. Russell, October 1, 1946.

westward into the Rocky Mountains and, as inferred by the records accompanying those figured here, the spiked ax found use as long as the Indian made war upon the white man and upon his own red brother.

Figure 75a is from Onondaga, New York; it is specimen No. 582, American Museum. Beauchamp [6] illustrates an Onondaga specimen seemingly identical in size and design with this. On both sides of the bit appear the initials "J. G."

Shown in figure 75b is a tomahawk with its original haft found near Columbus, Montana. It is in the Yellowstone Museum, Mammoth Hot Springs, Yellowstone National Park, Wyoming.

Figure 75c is from the Fort Ticonderoga collections, Fort Ticonderoga Museum, New York.

A Penobscot tomahawk is shown in figure 75d. Axes mounted with a shank and ferrule in lieu of an eye are uncommon. The specimen is No. $\frac{50}{7389}$ in the American Museum, New York.

Figure 75e shows a spiked tomahawk credited to the Winnebagos and obtained from them in Nebraska. It was contained in a war bundle.[7] It is catalogued as No. 14-40-1b in the Museum für Völkerkunde, Munich.

The specimen in figure 75f is from Carlisle, Pennsylvania; it is now in the Pennsylvania State Museum, Harrisburg.

The specimen shown in figure 75g was found in a grave, presumably of an Indian, in Lakeside near Fort Wayne, Indiana. Perhaps it was an English carpenter's tool put to war use. It is preserved in the Allen County–Fort Wayne Historical Society, where it is item No. 12. A similar specimen from an Indian grave in Idaho is No. 541-C in the Idaho Historical Society. Sergeant Patrick Gass, carpenter, carried one of these on the Lewis and Clark Expedition. It is owned by Owen Buxton, a member of the Gass family.

Figure 75h shows a tomahawk taken from a Sac Indian killed at the battle of Pecatonica during the Black Hawk War. The haft is studded with brass tacks. It is now No. E-149, Wisconsin Historical Society, Madison.

The specimen in figure 75i is recorded as from Lake County,

[6] *Metallic Implements*, Pl. 23, Fig. 91.
[7] C. W. Lenders, in *Zeitschrift für Ethnologie* (Berlin, 1914), XLVI, 404–20.

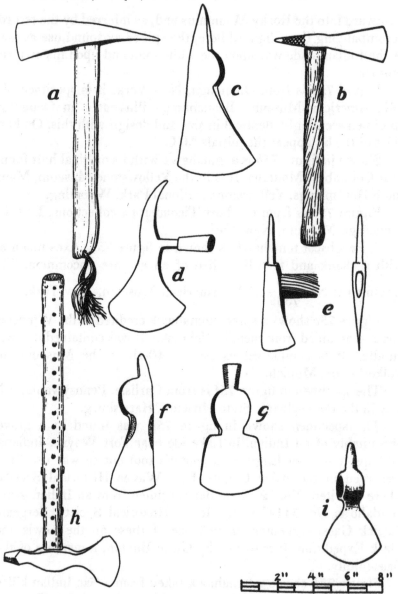

FIG. 75. *Spiked Tomahawks.*

The drawing by William Macy is in the Jefferson National Expansion Memorial, St. Louis.

Illinois. It is No. 109 in the collections of the Washington State Historical Society.

No doubt a few original European battle axes of medieval pedigree were brought to America by early adventurers, but the great bulk of the American tomahawks that resemble the battle ax were merely made in the pattern of the earlier dealers of death and destruction. Many of them show superior workmanship and true pride of accomplishment on the part of the artisans who made them. In the hands of the American savage they witnessed bloody combat and murder through four centuries of conflict. The record shows clearly that the white trader and frontiersman also took the tomahawk unto himself. Early American troops were armed with them (pages 262 and 263), and before the close of the Revolution British soldiery received regular issues of these weapons (page 266). Figure 76 illustrates nine characteristic tomahawks—and one freak.

Figure 76a shows a spiked tomahawk from St. Charles, Missouri, in the collections of the Arkansas History Commission.

The specimen in figure 76b was found on an Indian mound at Cahokia, Illinois. It is preserved in the Missouri Historical Society, St. Louis.

Shown in figure 76c is an exceptionally well formed tomahawk found during the excavation of a cellar adjacent to Bog Brook in Hebron, Maine. It is presumed to be of English manufacture. The specimen is No. 110 in the I. W. Penney Collection, Maine Historical Society. The last of the French wooden ships of war carried small boarding hatchets of this same style and workmanship. They were issued in accordance with regulations. On the handles were iron belt hooks.[8]

Figure 76d bears the impress "Seyfert, Philadelphia." The specimen is owned by the Cranbrook Institute, where it is item No. 938.

Shown in figure 76e is a "tomahawk" that is not a tomahawk, from a Caddo Indian site in Montgomery County, Arkansas. Comment regarding this specimen is given on page 294 (fig. 78a). The specimen is in the Dorris Dickinson Collection, Magnolia, Arkansas.

Figure 76f shows a New York specimen, now in the New York State Museum, Albany.

[8] Personal letter, Alfred F. Hopkins to C. P. Russell, August 20, 1946.

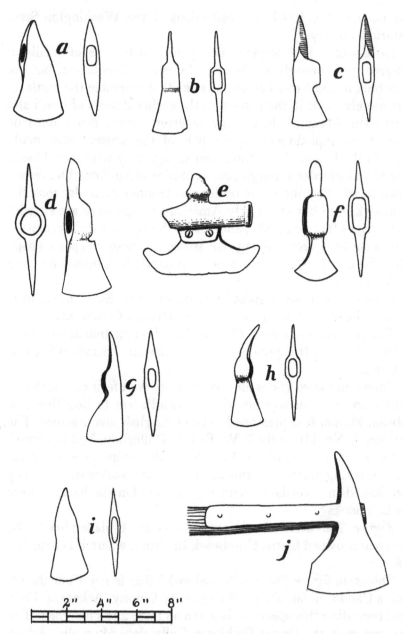

FIG. 76. *More Spiked Tomahawks.*

This drawing is by William Macy, Jefferson National Expansion Memorial, St. Louis.

From Green Island above Troy, New York, comes the specimen pictured in figure 76g. It is No. 29889 in the New York State Museum, Albany.

The tomahawk shown in figure 76h is similar to several additional specimens recovered at and near Crown Point, New York. It is preserved in the New York State Museum, Albany.

The specimen pictured in figure 76i was discovered four feet below the surface of the earth in the course of the demolition and removal of an ancient building at Canton Point, Maine. Canton Point was the site of a principal post among the Rockameko Indians as early as 1698–9.[9] The tribe was nearly destroyed supposedly by smallpox in 1755, and the village was abandoned. White settlers took possession in 1790.

The specimen shown in figure 76j is perhaps a medieval battle ax or a more recent naval boarding ax; recorded to have been in the hands of the Micmac Indians. The helve is original. Similar axes of known provenance made in the fifteenth, sixteenth, and seventeenth centuries are preserved in many European museums. This ax is preserved in the McCord Museum, Montreal, where it bears No. 1079.

Tomahawks with Curved Projections Above the Poll

In the land of the Iroquois, especially, exaggerated forms of the spiked tomahawk are quite common. The reverse curve of the spike on these models renders the appendage quite ineffective in warfare and a nuisance from the standpoint of maneuverability; yet they must have found some favor, for they were distributed throughout the northeastern sections of America. Perhaps the rakishness of their lines appealed to their red owners. Among these axes with curved spikes is found the comparatively rare form which lacks perforation or eye. The head of the ax and the elongated shank with which this type was attached to the helve were forged in one piece (figs. 77f and 77h). A metal ferrule fitted over the helve as the shank was inserted made for security of attachment (see figure 75d).

There is no adequate explanation for the Indians' choice of this poorly balanced ax (fig. 77a) with its incongruous curved spike

[9] *Maine Historical Society Collections*, Baxter MSS, V, 517.

and inefficient, light helve; yet the model turns up occasionally on early eighteenth-century sites in eastern Canada, New York, and New England. The specimen is No. 4236, Château de Ramezay, Montreal.

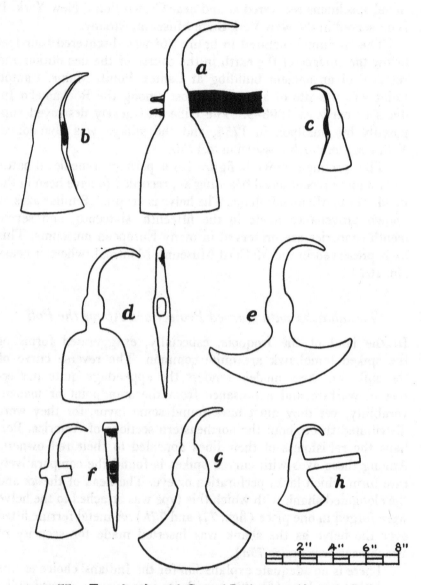

FIG. 77. *Tomahawks with Curved Projections Above the Poll.*

The drawing is by William Macy, Jefferson National Expansion Memorial, St. Louis.

Figure 77b shows an Iroquois tomahawk, now No. 4210 in the Château de Ramezay, Montreal.

A fairly common form of tomahawk found in many Iroquois sites is shown in figure 77c. It is in the Fort Ticonderoga Museum, Fort Ticonderoga, New York.[1]

The specimen presented in figure 77d was found at Franklin, Vermont. It is preserved as No. 154 in Vermont State Cabinet collection, Montpelier.

Figure 77e is from Fort Ticonderoga, New York. The Franks and the Vikings anticipated this model one thousand years before it appeared in New York.

Shown in figure 77f is a tomahawk with a metal shank (broken) continuous with the bit. Originally the iron shank was inserted in the end of a haft of wood and was held in place there by a metal ferrule driven back upon the wood. It was found at Swanton, Vermont, and now is item No. 152 in the Vermont State Cabinet. Similar specimens from Fort Bull near Rome, New York, are described by Beauchamp.[2]

Figure 77g was found near the Lake George battlefield, New York. It is now in the Fort Ticonderoga Museum, Fort Ticonderoga, New York. Howard D. Rodee, Columbus, Ohio, has one like this, which is 11½ inches, top to bottom, and weighs two pounds.[3]

Figure 77h is from Fort St. Frédéric (1731–59) or Fort Amherst (1759–81), both at Crown Point, New York. It is now in the Museum of the Crown Point State Reservation, New York. Beauchamp[4] describes an ax in the Johnstown Historical Society Museum that has a slender shank some 7 inches long for insertion in a haft of wood. It was found eight feet underground at Johnstown, New York.

Miscellaneous Axes from Spanish and Russian Sites

WOODWARD[5] expresses the belief that Spanish traders did not distribute Spanish axes but drew their supplies of trade axes and

[1] See Woodward: "The Metal Tomahawk," Fig. 6; also see a similar ax in Beauchamp: *Metallic Implements*, p. 66 and Pl. 24, Fig. 101.

[2] Beauchamp: *Metallic Implements*, p. 66 and Pl. 21, Fig. 89.

[3] Rodee to C. P. Russell, February 22, 1960 (7 sketches; 1-page MS).

[4] Beauchamp: *Metallic Implements*, p. 66 and Pl. 27, Fig. 116.

[5] Woodward: "The Metal Tomahawk," p. 33. See also H. E. Bolton: *Athanase de Mezières*, I, 143–5, 148. Regulations prohibited the importation and distribution of English goods in the lower Mississippi country in the eighteenth

other goods from French sources. Review of the findings of the present author substantiates this idea. The Spanish axes shown here are obviously the tools of Spanish workmen, not objects of trade. The axes from Russian localities (figs. 78*b* and 78*e*) show British affinities, and if they were used or traded by the Russians in Alaska it is quite probable that they came originally from England. John Jacob Astor, importer of British goods, once supplied the Russian trade in Alaska and later the Russian-American Fur Company obtained its goods from the Hudson's Bay Company.

Figure 78*a* shows an unusual iron "ax" with a removable steel blade found in a Caddo site near Collier Creek across from Buttermilk Springs, about two and a half miles northeast from Caddo Gap in Montgomery County, Arkansas. The site was excavated by Dorris Dickinson in 1927. The only additional object of purported trade origin brought to light was a pottery pipe bowl made in the form of a human turbaned head. Both the "ax" and the pipe bowl were examined by the author with the permission of Mr. Dickinson.

Reasonably, a question is raised regarding the authenticity of this "Spanish-type ax" and its screw-fastened steel blade. Charlie Steen of the National Park Service, in a letter to the author in 1956, called attention to another almost identical "ax" said to have been found in the 1920's at the Menard Mound, which is also in the Caddo Gap region. Officials of the American Tobacco Company, who examined photographs of the Menard Mound specimen, conjectured that it was once a part of a plug tobacco cutter manufactured in recent decades for the use of retailers who sold "Battleaxe" chewing tobacco. Regarding the same pieces, Harold L. Peterson wrote on April 5, 1965: "I have seen perhaps a dozen, including one still mounted with its frame and cutting board. I illustrate it as an example of something that is not a tomahawk." This circumstance points to one of the public relations hazards of *interpretation* sometimes met by the historian-archeologist. No doubt the American Tobacco Company representative is right, yet the Caddo country where the queer "axes" were found is De Soto's province of Tula, where he spent part of the winter of 1541–2, and

---

century. One ordinance of 1770 provided that "no English Merchandise shall be introduced among the Indians under the penalty inflicted upon contraband traders. . . ." "Pick-axes," "hatchets," and "tomahawks" are listed by Mezières as required in this period for trade with the Grand Cadaux and the Petit Cados.

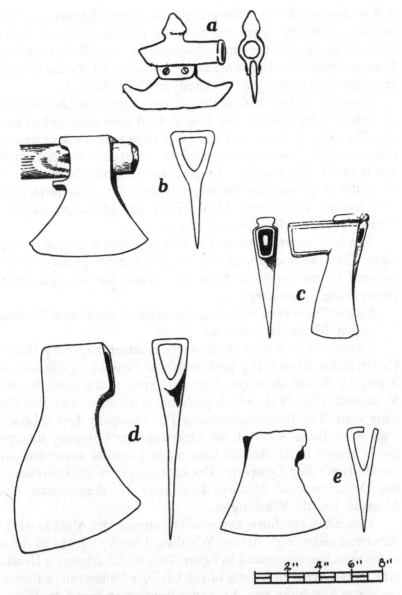

FIG. 78. *Miscellaneous Axes from Spanish and Russian Sites.*

This drawing is by William Macy, Jefferson National Expansion Memorial, St. Louis.

it is understandable that the private collectors who own the "axes" should cherish the hope that they are sixteenth-century Spanish relics or, at the latest, eighteenth-century pieces. Both French and Spanish trade establishments are recorded to have existed during the eighteenth century in the vicinity of Caddo Gap.

No other ax dealt with in the present chapter has threaded bolts or screws in its makeup, but long-sleeved eyes with spiked terminals like this one do occur. Figure 80*d* shows what might pass as a relative of the Caddo piece—until the materials are compared— and in the British Museum, London, are a number of Persian axes of similar shape and size, lacking only the bolts of the interchangeable feature of the steel blade. They are identified merely as "16th–19th centuries, Persian" (fig. 81).

The only cogent comment at this juncture still raises a question: The manufacturer of the tobacco cutters perhaps was influenced by the design of Near East relics, but who planted the pieces in the Caddo sites?

Figure 78*a* is used with the permission of the Dorris Dickinson Collection, Magnolia, Arkansas.

Figure 78*b* is a relic of the early nineteenth-century Baranov Castle, Sitka, Alaska. It is presumably of Russian significance, but it may be British in origin. Note similarity to the specimen from Wisconsin (fig. 71*e*), which probably is an American Fur Company item. The Russian-American Fur Company first contracted with John Jacob Astor of the American Fur Company to supply goods needed in Alaska and later made a similar agreement with the Hudson's Bay Company. The specimen is in the collections of the Department of History, University of Washington, State Museum, Seattle, Washington.

This Sitka specimen has relatives among the Alaskan axes in American collections. Arthur Woodward kindly agreed to the use of his sketches (presented in figure 79), which depict: a Russian-type ax recovered by a crew of the Civilian Conservation Corps at the site of Old Sitka (no. 1), and a Russian ax found by William Laughlin on Umnak Island in the Aleutians (no. 2). Ax no. 1 is preserved in the museum of the University of Alaska, Fairbanks; no. 2 is in the University of Oregon Museum, Eugene. Quite possibly, these specimens were tools of the white men—not trade pieces. In 1847 Alexander Hunter Murray of the Hudson's Bay Company, Fort Yukon, dealt with some of the same Indians served

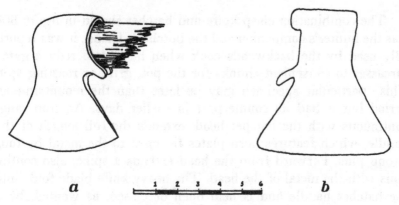

FIG. 79. *Two Axes from Russian Sites in Alaska.*

These sketches are presented courtesy of Arthur Woodward.

by the Russians on the lower Yukon. He wrote: "The Russians bring no regular axes [for trade], only a flat piece of steel which the Indians fasten to a crooked stick with battiche." [6]

Figure 78c shows an ax of fine design and finish that was recovered from a ruined building of the Spanish period (eighteenth century), Pensacola, Florida. The specimen is owned by the St. Augustine Historical Society, St. Augustine, Florida.

In figure 78d is a Spanish ax (sixteenth–nineteenth centuries) found during the excavation done by the St. Augustine Historical Restoration in St. Augustine. It is in the collections of the St. Augustine Historical Restoration, St. Augustine.

The specimen shown in figure 78e was found at Valdez, Alaska, buried in gravel sixteen feet below the surface. It was uncovered in the course of placer-mining activities. With it was the tooth of a sperm whale. It is believed by its discoverer, Jack Tansey, to have been traded by the Russians, but just as figure 78b, it may be of British manufacture. Both British and American ships brought English trade goods to the Alaskan coast in the eighteenth to nineteenth centuries. The ax figured is in the Roy Van Vleck Collection, Jackson, Wyoming. An ax (No. 62579, National Museum, Washington, D.C.) somewhat similar to this specimen was removed from a Chumash grave at La Patera, Santa Barbara County, California, by members of the Wheeler Survey party. It was accompanied by Russian trade beads and an English rum bottle.

[6] Clifford Wilson: "Founding Fort Yukon," *The Beaver* (June 1947), p. 42

The combination clasp knife and hatchet shown in figure 80*a* was the hunter's companion and the butcher's friend; it was reportedly used by the backwoods cook when he had to reduce game carcasses to convenient chunks for the pot, grill, or roasting spit. This particular specimen may be later than the mountain-man period but it had its counterpart in earlier days. An iron tang, continuous with the hatchet head, extends the full length of the handle, which features horn plates fastened to the metal by four strong pins. Forward from the head extends a spike, also continuous with the metal of the head. The heavy knife blade folds into the hatchet handle and is held open or closed, as wanted, by a spring mechanism similar to the device on French clasp knives described on page 170. The hatchet head with its spiked top and spiked terminal is suggestive of certain French and Spanish fighting axes of a thousand years ago and of some of the Alpine (Swiss) battle axes of the fifteenth century. More significant, probably, is its resemblance to the more recent halberds to be found in America as well as in Europe. Some students recognize a "halberd tomahawk" in the story of the ax in America.[7] In the present case, it seems most likely that the upper spike and forward prick found their principal use in turning and adjusting sizzling slabs of meat as they cooked on a wilderness grill. The specimen is No. 0540, Cabildo, New Orleans (lent by H. Gibbs Morgan).

Lull and Hefter, in their "Spanish Corps of Engineers in Florida, 1802," [8] present definite facts regarding certain tools brought to America by the military of Spain in the opening years of the nineteenth century. The Royal Sappers and Miners had with them the ax-adz shown in figure 80*b*. In side view, the tool looks like one of the spiked tomahawks so long and so widely used by American Indians everywhere, but the end view reveals that the "spike," in reality, is a well-proportioned small adz. The wooden handle is 21 inches long.

This long-handled tool, presented in figure 80*c*, which resembles a battle ax of the Middle Ages or a more recent naval boarding ax, was brought to America by the same Spanish regiment of engineers that used the hatchet-adz shown in figure 80*b*. It was a

[7] Harold L. Peterson: *American Indian Tomahawks*, p. 94.

[8] Francisco Ferrer Lull and J. Hefter: "The Spanish Corps of Engineers in Florida, 1802," *Military Collector and Historian*, XVI: 4 (Winter 1964), p. 112 and Pl. 250. The ax data is from *Elementos de Fortificación*, by General Ignacio Mora (2 vols.; Mexico, 1830), II, Pl. 42.

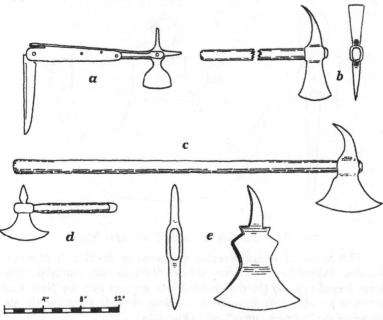

FIG. 80. *Spanish-Type Axes.*

Three of the axes (*b*, *c*, and *e*) have definite Spanish connections; specimens *a* and *d* may not have been made by Spaniards but they show Spanish characteristics. Spain did not "have a corner" on the Spanish-type ax.

wood-cutting and demolition tool intended solely for the white man's use, but had it been found in an Indian camp or an Indian grave, no doubt it would be classed as a war ax (see fig. 76*j*). The firsthand information regarding this piece was provided in 1830 by General Mora, who has been previously quoted by Lull and Hefter.

The tobacco cutter "ax" (fig. 78*a*) prompts one to scrutinize the general record of axes in America to discern possible sources for this imaginative piece. A similar short-handled, spiked tomahawk (fig. 78*d*) is shown in the hands of the Cherokee chief, "Man Killer," portrayed by an unnamed artist when three Cherokees visited the British Court at London in 1762. The portrait and the drawing of the ax are reproduced in Swanton's *The Indians of the Southeastern United States*, Plate 9. This purported Cherokee ax is strikingly similar, superficially, to the "Caddo ax" shown in figure 75, and is quite like a specimen in the British Museum

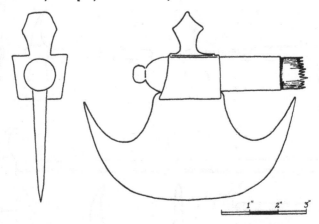

FIG. 81. *Persian Ax with Removable Blade.*

This is one of several Persian specimens in the British Museum, London, judged by the curators to be of "16th to 19th centuries." The long-sleeved eye and the detachable blade suggest that the Near East patterns possibly may have been a source of inspiration for the designer of the "tobacco cutter" relic (Fig. 78*a*).

recorded as "Persian, 16th–19th centuries." Like the "Caddo" piece (fig. 78), the Persian relic has a separate steel blade clamped between the open jaws of the sleeve-like member that constitutes the poll and eye. No screws or rivets are in evidence, however. See figure 81.

This Spanish battle ax (fig. 80*e*) is preserved in the Palace of the Governors, Sante Fe, New Mexico, where the museum record states: "Many of these weapons were parts of every early Spanish expedition sent to New Mexico, and they continued in use during the period of colonization." This general style of axhead was favored in Spain during the sixteenth and seventeenth centuries, but it was not limited to Spain; in the Tower of London, the Prussia Museum, Germanisches Museum, Schweizerisches Landesmuseum, etc., are axes of much the same form that were found in Denmark, Germany, East Prussia, and Switzerland—all sixteenth- or seventeenth-century recoveries. However, no evidence has come to light showing that Dutch, Swedish, French, or English interests brought the same ax type to America; only the Spaniards seem to have made it a part of their expeditionary equipment.

It is to be noted that among the great number of smaller tomahawks held in American collections are numerous specimens that display the spike and crescent-shaped cutting edge commonly regarded to be characteristic of the "Spanish-type" ax. Fourteen specimens of this kind are pictured in our figures 75, 76, and 77. Four of the fourteen may possibly have had a Spanish origin; the others quite definitely are English, French, or American. This circumstance, of course, does not render the term "Spanish type" inapplicable to certain axes that did not come from Spain or from Spaniards, but it suggests that more than a few blacksmiths manufactured "Spanish-type" axes with no thought whatever of Spain or of Spaniards. Also, it gives emphasis to the idea that the classification of any ax by nationality is suspect unless a combination of

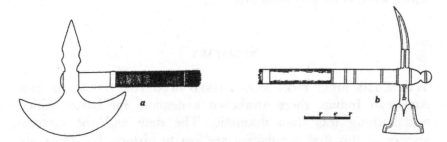

FIG. 82. *Extraordinary Axes in the Trade.*

The upper figure (*a*) shows a bona fide, silver-inlaid Persian battle ax with a 24-inch handle meticulously fitted. For 5 inches behind the eye, the handle is covered with snakeskin. This is followed by 8 inches of buckskin tightly applied, then there is another 5-inch cover of snakeskin. The terminal 3 inches of handle are naked. This ancient Indo-Persian relic was included in a lot of Indian artifacts acquired by Dr. Cyril B. Courville. The snakeskin-buckskin covering on the handle is "presumably of Indian application."

The presentation ax (*b*), also owned by Dr. Courville, is recorded to be of mid-eighteenth-century French origin. The long-sleeved eye, blade, and spike are richly inlaid with a yellow metal. The 26-inch wooden handle is encircled with two brass bands ½ inch wide. A decorative tuft of 10-inch hawk feathers tied with sinew dangles from the end of the handle, presumably a concession to aboriginal ornament added by the Indian who obtained the piece in the course of the Frenchman's giftmaking. It is worthy of note here that during the death throes of New France in the 1750's, the French government was lavish in doling out presents to Indians. Francois Bigot declared that four hundred million francs were expended by his service of supply at this time in an attempt to assure positive alliance with certain Indian tribes, old friends, and new (Jacobs: "Presents to Indians," pp. 245–56). The sketches by Dr. Courville are used by permission.

criteria—physical, archeological, or documentary—contribute to unmistakable identification. Sometimes the investigator will feel that the manufacturer of an ax under study has "done him wrong"; research may show the specimen to be a bona fide Spanish ax, yet it may display only those physical characteristics generally accepted as English.

All told, it is rash to categorize each and every ax by nationality. During the eighteenth and nineteenth centuries, the country forges in the United States were producing any or all forms of axes demanded by the trade—French patterns, English and Spanish types, "Kentucky" and "Yankee" patterns—and a variety of styles which were in no way standard.

SUMMARY

WHEN THE FIRST IRON AXES PASSED INTO THE HANDS OF THE American Indian, there awakened a demand for barter which was nothing less than dramatic. The date and the circumstances of this first acquisition are lost to history, but there are testimonials to the fact that it took place prior to the recorded landings of those Europeans who were intent upon regular settlement or trade.

Cabot, close in the wake of Columbus, brought the iron of Britain. He found that the Basques had already preceded him to Newfoundland. Gaspar Corterreal of Portugal opened the sixteenth-century intercourse by bringing the wares of his homeland. In return for the kindnesses bestowed upon him, he shipped native captives back to Europe. Norman, Breton, Portuguese, Spanish, and English fishermen early in the sixteenth century haunted the cod banks of Newfoundland and continued the desultory trade practices of the Basques. They fished but they also exchanged iron axes for American peltry.

The French Trade Ax

IN 1524, Verrazano, in behalf of King Francis I of France, skirted the entire coast from Florida to Maine and distributed at least a sample of the white man's line of goods designed to lift the savage out of the Stone Age. A few years later Jacques Cartier brought more French goods and gained his first knowledge of things American. When in 1534 he sailed into the Gulf of St. Lawrence, he was already acquainted with the Canadian shores. He came again in 1535 and spent the winter in the vicinity of present-day Quebec. His gifts of "hachotz" to the Micmacs and Saguenays are a matter of record.[9] The poorly recorded activities of French fishermen on the banks of Newfoundland throughout the remainder of the sixteenth century developed in the minds of French merchants the idea that a definite fur trade in America could be remunerative. A number of adventurers were attracted to the business, and the close of the century found the first officially recognized American trading post established at Tadoussac, at the mouth of the Saguenay River.

During the first years of the seventeenth century, Captain Samuel Champlain and Sieur de Monts entered earnestly upon trade and colonization at Tadoussac and elsewhere in the St. Lawrence and Bay of Fundy (Acadia) regions. Their enterprises were conducted under the auspices of Henry IV of France. Champlain's *Voyages* contains a number of accounts of the joyous acceptance of the iron ax by the Indian.[1]

By 1608 Captain John Smith found that the ax of the Frenchman had already come overland from Canada to the upper reaches of the Chesapeake Bay. The Tockwoghes, the tribe in possession of the axes, testified that they had obtained the implements from the Susquesahanocks. Smith visited this tribe also and was informed by them that their iron tools and weapons came from the Atquanahucke and the Massawomekes, of the Iroquois, who were in direct touch with the French traders on "the river of Cannida." [2]

At the Battle of Lake Champlain in 1609, it was disclosed to the French that the local Mohawks were armed with iron axes, yet white traders had not come up the Hudson River with trade goods

[9] H. P. Biggar, ed.: *The Voyages of Jacques Cartier* (Ottawa, 1924), pp. 53, 60, 121, 125, 233.
[1] W. L. Grant, ed.: *Voyages of Samuel de Champlain, 1604–1618* (New York, 1907). See also H. P. Biggar, ed.: *The Works of Samuel de Champlain* (Toronto, 1922–36), I–V. In a painting of the massacre of the Jesuits Brébeuf and Lalemant by the Iroquois in 1649, which is reproduced in *Historiae Canadensis sen Novae Franciae* by Francisco Creuxiux (Paris, 1664), typical French axes are shown being heated in an open fire. A necklace of the red-hot axheads hangs around the neck of one of the doomed Fathers. An interpretation of this scene appears in C. W. Jefferys: *The Picture Gallery of Canadian History* (3 vols.; Toronto, 1945), I, 106.
[2] Beauchamp: *Metallic Implements*, pp. 16–17, quoting Captain John Smith.

prior to that year. It seems probable that the early iron armament of the Mohawks came from the same French sources on the St. Lawrence which, indirectly, supplied the Indians of Virginia and Maryland, as observed by Captain John Smith.

During the middle decades of the seventeenth century, the Hurons, despite their enmity for the Iroquois on the St. Lawrence, came regularly to the French traders in the Iroquois zone for axes and other trade goods. When bands of the Hurons and Ottawas were driven westward after 1663, they went to Green Bay on Lake Michigan, thence via the Fox and Wisconsin rivers across the Mississippi. With them went the iron ax into the land of the Sioux. These Western Indians had not yet obtained iron tools. They entreated the strangers to share with them their iron. "When they got a few trifles they lifted eyes to the sky and blessed it for guiding to their country these people who brought iron." [3] At about this same time representatives of the Ottawa carried the goods of the French traders to the Crees north of Lake Superior. The Crees willingly gave up all of their beaver robes for iron axes and made handsome gifts as inducements to the Indian middlemen to return with trade goods each year.

In this first system of direct trade and distribution through middlemen, the iron ax of the Frenchmen was spread through the region of the Great Lakes along the St. Lawrence, in the present-day New England states and New York, south to the Chesapeake Bay, even west to the Mississippi—all prior to the advent of permanent British trade in the North. The early regime of the French traders was not free from strife with the Indians after Champlain's clash with the Iroquois on Lake Champlain in 1609, nor were conflicts with rival nations avoided. The Iroquois attacked the French repeatedly, and in 1628 a fleet of British war vessels invaded the New France. For three years thereafter an English garrison occupied Quebec. However, this war between England and France was brought to a close in 1632, and by terms of the peace New France and Acadia were restored to the French temporarily. The struggle against the Iroquois continued as long as the French were on the continent.

---

[3] Harold A. Innis: *The Fur Trade in Canada* (New Haven: Yale Univ. Press; 1930), pp. 41–2, quoting Perrot Nicholas: *Memoire sur les Moeurs . . . des Sauvages de l'Amerique Septentrionale* (Paris, 1864).

The Ax in the English Trade

IN 1668 the British Hudson's Bay Company began its phenomenal business and made its first contributions to the promotion of the iron-ax trade in America. One of the diarists whose writings are preserved in *Jesuit Relations* recorded in September, 1671: "On the 17th, five canoes bearing Attikamegues and Mistassirinins, came bringing word that 2 vessels had anchored in Hudson's Bay and conducted extensive trading with the savages. . . . They showed us a hatchet and some tobacco which they had obtained from a Papinachois who had been on a trading trip toward the north sea that very summer." [4] That the Hudson's Bay Company officials were swayed in their choice of trade goods by the wares of the French is evidenced by the company's Minute Book of 1671, which contains instructions for the procuring of Biscay hatchets. [5] The Biscay hatchets referred to were the products of the many small manufactories of ironware that were active in almost every village in the three Biscay provinces of northern Spain. [6] The French, including the Basques, had drawn upon this source for many years. The weight of the axes specified by the committee, "two and three pounds apiece," is clear indication that the trade implements of that day were the medium-weight felling axes, not the lighter tomahawk that came into vogue later. Figures 69*a* and 69*f* and figures 70*e* and 70*g* show fair examples of the type. The minutes of November 27, 1673, throw further light upon the Biscay ax in that they were to be "such as are usually sent from thence for France to serve the Indians in and about Canada." [7]

Thus it may be inferred that the so-called "French" ax found its place in the minds of English traders and in the terminology of

[4] Innis: *Fur Trade* (1930 edn.), pp. 44–5, quoting *Jesuit Relations*, LVI, pp. 157, 177.
[5] Ibid., p. 127, quoting Canadian Archives, Hudson's Bay Company Minute Book (1671), p. 15.
[6] Harry Scrivenor: *History of the Iron Trade* (London, 1854), pp. 142–5. On page 18, Scrivenor quotes from Pliny the Elder, *Natural History* (first century A.D.): "But to return again to our iron: Of all mines that be, the vein of this metal is largest, and spreadeth itself unto most length everyway, as we may see in that part of Biscay that coasteth along the sea, and upon the ocean beneath, where there is a craggy mountain, very steep and high, which standeth all upon a mine or vein of iron."
[7] Innis: *Fur Trade* (1930 edn.), p. 128, quoting Canadian Archives, Hudson's Bay Company Minute Book (1673), p. 72.

the trade. The Dutch, the Swedes, and the Spaniards also brought axes to eastern America, but there is little evidence that distinctive types were featured by those traders. Trade axes were made in a number of localities in Spain, France, Holland, the Scandinavian countries, the British Isles, and later in America, but while the contour of the products of the many different smiths might vary slightly, the general model remained quite constant. Few of the axes traded were cast; each specimen was an individual product of the anvil and forge. Many makers put upon their axes distinctive marks or "smith's stamps," thereby providing a possible key to the history of the industry and trade that has not been deciphered (see pages 409–11). A heavy volume of the imports is evident in existing inventories and is further attested by the great numbers of the early axes that have been brought to light on the seventeenth-century Iroquois sites in New York. In this connection Beauchamp writes: "Hundreds have been found on Cazenovia Creek in Erie County. Large numbers on Cattaraugus Creek, kept the early blacksmiths supplied with good material, and Mr. Obed Edson recorded large finds in Erie and Chatauqua counties. Several hundred pounds of these were found on M. B. Crooks farm, 2 miles from East Aurora. Miles Bristol paid for two years tillage of his orchard lot with the axes he found at the village of Lima." [8] Mr. Ralph Lewis, reporting on the ax collection in the Buffalo Museum, states: "Trade axes were so numerous at the Boughton Hill site, Victor, N.Y., that blacksmiths of the vicinity collected 'wagon loads' for making iron tools because the iron was of unusually good quality. The axes seem to have been plentiful enough to serve as a source of supply for some time." [9] In addition to the collections of early French axes referred to in the explanatory notes accompanying the illustrations in the present chapter, important collections are preserved in the Holland Land Office Museum, Batavia, New York, the Buffalo Museum, and the Landis Valley Museum near Lancaster, Pennsylvania.

It seems likely that even the felling axes that were first supplied to the Indian were mounted upon short helves. They were

[8] Beauchamp: *Metallic Implements*, pp. 60–5.
[9] Letter, Ralph Lewis to Carl P. Russell, October 22, 1937. See also James Sullivan, ed.: *The Papers of Sir William Johnson* (Albany, 1921–33), IV, 559. On a list of goods required for the Indian trade submitted by Sir William Johnson, October 8, 1764, it is estimated that 10,000 axes could be sold each year to Indian hunters and their women. The axes were listed at 3 shillings each.

almost always referred to in the writings of contemporary Britons and Frenchmen as *hatchets*, implying that they were wielded by one hand. Van der Donck, referring to Indians of New Netherlands about 1650, applies the term "tomahawk" to the iron ax then in the hands of the natives. Thirty-eight years earlier, Captain John Smith recorded in his *Map of Virginia*,[1] that the Indians of Virginia used the term "tomahacks" for both the native war club and the iron hatchet. Soon thereafter the English colonists applied the name freely to the aboriginal Celt hatchet, the grooved stone axe, the falchion club, the spiked club, the glove-headed club, and the iron trade ax. Holmes concluded that it is impossible to determine whether or not the Indians limited it to a single form of weapon, but there is no question regarding the source of the term; it came from the Indians of Virginia and was first recorded by Captain John Smith in his brief vocabulary of Indian terms prepared some time during the years 1607–9.[2] Thereafter the use of the term spread to all settlements in America and to the mother countries. For four hundred years the word was synonymous with bloody warfare and surprise attacks throughout North America.

Toward the end of the seventeenth century, the specialized types of spontoon and spiked tomahawks began to compete with the conservative hatchet throughout the trade conducted by various national interests. Woodward opines that these flamboyant weapons were "sired by the felling axe; the mother was the more ornate battle axe of medieval Europe and Asia," an apt metaphor. During the eighteenth century, the many styles suggested in figures 72, 75, 76, and 77 of the present chapter found wide distribution among all Indian tribes and enjoyed some popularity among the white frontiersmen, but the spiked ax or spontoon type never entirely supplanted the "French" ax in Indian camp or on frontier settlement. On the contrary, the trend toward a practical, lighter belt ax of the "French" style was persistent, and the oddities among the tomahawks seem to have declined in popularity after the eighteenth century.

The tomahawk was the weapon often employed by the Indian

---

[1] *A Map of Virginia with Description of the Country* (Oxford: Joseph Barnes, Ptr.; 1612), Part I, p. 23.

[2] William H. Holmes: "The Tomahawk," *American Anthropologist*, X: 2 (1908), pp. 264–76. See also William R. Gerard: "The Term Tomahawk," *American Anthropologist*, X: 2 (1908), pp. 277–80; and D. J. Bushnell: "The Tradescant Collection, 1656," *American Anthropologist*, X: 3 (1908), p. 494.

in executing members of the tribe sentenced by regular dictum to death. Its symbolism in tribal oratory and in treaty-making is known to schoolchildren everywhere. "Tomahawk speeches" and "burying the hatchet" are expressions growing out of the imaginative minds of the Indian allegorists with whom both French and English dealt in the early decades of conflict on the St. Lawrence and along the Ohio. The pipe tomahawk, exclusively American and without precedent or prototype anywhere in the world, enabled the Indian to combine his mystical rites of tobacco smoking with the symbolistic uses of the tomahawk. It was indeed a smart trader who first conceived of this combination of coveted objects and introduced it to the trade.

The British military adopted the tomahawk as standard equipment during the French and Indian War. French soldiers previously had carried it in their American campaigns. In 1759 Wolfe, with Amherst's approval, prescribed the tomahawk as a part of the accouterment of the Light Infantry under his command,[3] and during the Revolution certain Regiments of Foot carried it. In the military stores surrendered by Cornwallis at Yorktown were hatchets and tomahawks. American Army units serving in frontier situations after the Revolution were supplied with tomahawks, and various U. S. arsenal records for 1793 show tomahawks on hand. The Lewis and Clark Expedition was issued tomahawks from the Harpers Ferry Arsenal in 1803.[4] An array of evidence could be assembled showing that white trappers and traders carried them and used them against both man and beast throughout the fur-trade period. They were no less important to the frontiersman in his contest with the wilderness than they were to the native savage.[5] Even during the period of the Santa Fe trade in the 1840's, leaders of the wagon trains advised each man in the companies to supply himself with a tomahawk,[6] and the later professional buffalo hunters clung to them as they did to their knives and rifles.

[3] John Knox: *Historical Journal of the Campaigns in North America, 1757–60,* I, 352–3.

[4] Woodward: "The Metal Tomahawk," p. 32.

[5] A significant instance of warfare between white traders and Indians growing out of the theft of an ax is found in the massacre of Jedediah Smith's party on the Umpqua in Oregon in 1828, see pages 246–7. See also S. A. Clark: *Pioneer Days of Oregon History* (Portland, 1905), I, 216–17.

[6] Rufus B. Sage: *Wild Scenes in Kansas and Nebraska, the Rocky Mountains, Oregon, California, New Mexico, Texas, and the Grand Prairies* (Philadelphia, 1855), p. 227.

In short, the tomahawk in its various forms prevailed as the most prominent object of utility, trade, and symbolism throughout the entire epoch of conquest and settlement in America. If it looms big in American legend and tradition, it is but taking its proper place in the history of the frontier. A new and exhaustive treatment of the subject is Peterson's *American Indian Tomahawks*.

The American Ax and the Western Trade

ABOUT the same time that pipe tomahawks appeared on the American scene, blacksmiths in the American forests began to experiment with the felling ax. The ax in Europe had experienced no significant change or improvement since the Celts invented their iron ax five hundred years before Christ was born (see map, page 249). To all intents and purposes, the "biscay hatchet," which in 1671 Mr. Millington was importuned to provide for "the Gentlemen Adventurers of England Trading into Hudson's Bay," was the same weapon made in the La Tène period. As a matter of fact, the Biscay hatchets were produced at the same place and from the same iron ores as were some of the Celtic axes of the La Tène. It may be stated further that the ax of present-day central Europe continues nearly everywhere in the image of the La Tène product. Only in America has a better chopping tool evolved. Here, since the close of the eighteenth century, a balanced, efficient woodsman's ax gradually has replaced the clumsy tool of ancient design. In America only the Indian trade adhered to the "French" ax through the nineteenth century. The story of the American ax is outlined in connection with the accompanying figures 61, 62, and 64.

The iron ax preceded the white man in his expansion westward. As has been stated, Ottawa middlemen in the early seventeenth century carried the French ax from the St. Lawrence and Michilimackinac into the land of the Sioux west of the Mississippi. French and Spanish traders took it from the Gulf of Mexico up the Missouri in the early decades of the eighteenth century, and before the close of that century British interests pushed it westward through Canada to the upper Missouri and the Rocky Mountains. In 1804–5 Lewis and Clark found it in the hands of most of the tribes that they came into contact with throughout their trip to the Pacific. Its presence on the Pacific slope is attributable to the coastal trade activities of Spanish, British, Russian, and Yankee merchantmen who had frequented the coasts of the old Oregon country for decades prior to the explorations of Lewis and Clark.

St. Louis traders, both Spanish and French, had exploited the lower Missouri basin since 1764, and some of the original trading companies persisted after the Louisiana Purchase in 1803 transferred land titles to the United States. The Missouri Fur Company, with headquarters at St. Louis, followed closely on the heels of Lewis and Clark in going to its headwaters. The John Jacob Astor expeditions to the mouth of the Columbia overlapped upon the earliest efforts of the Missouri Fur Company in the Rocky Mountains, and the English North West Company impinged upon both of them from the north. Before the first problems of commercial competition and international claims could be resolved in the West, actual war (the War of 1812) between Great Britain and the United States plunged Indian and trader alike into combat that affected the entire trade from the Great Lakes to the Pacific. Cessation of hostilities did not put an end to the competition between American and British traders in the tramontane country; on the contrary, the hottest rivalry and most extensive competition raged long after the Treaty of Ghent was signed on Christmas Eve, 1814. Thereafter a veritable army of trappers and traders pushed north, west, and southwest from St. Louis, carrying to established posts or to great seasonal marts in the wilderness an ever-growing volume of trade goods. From the British emporium on the Columbia other heavy stocks poured eastward and to the south into American territory. Yet another source of supply were the old Spanish towns in New Mexico, of which Santa Fe and Taos were the most important. Only the French interests were lacking in this Western trade, and even they were represented by ghostly reminders in the form of merchandise from Montreal and New Orleans bearing the traditional marks of the Bourbons.

The ax of course constituted a heavy item among the objects of trade and, as always, the "French" ax predominated. In the vast realm of mountains and plains so different in faunal, floral, and topographic characters from the lands of the Algonquin, Iroquois, and Muskhogean tribes in the East, one might reasonably expect to find a differentiation of the iron ax. However, such actual differences as exist are hardly important enough to mention. The "spontoon"-type tomahawk (fig. 72) and the "Minnewauken"-type pipe tomahawk (fig. 73) have been regarded by some students to be special Western forms but, as explained previously, both have their antecedents in the East. Only the "Missouri war hatchet" (fig. 74) seems to be a distinct Western form, and further study may reveal that it also originated in the Mississippi Valley or in the Southeast.

Smiths were as important to the Western trade as they were in the East. Their craftsmanship was a vital part of the function of established posts, and more than a few blacksmiths were practiced in the business of moving forge, anvil, and their stock-in-trade along with the camps of the nomadic people for whom they worked. Some record of their industry appears in the invoices of raw materials transported to the Western wilds, and in a few instances they are identified in the reports of the partners and clerks of the British companies, in the journals of the factors and commanders of the American posts, and in the writings of the few men of letters among the mountain men who scoured the stream courses of the entire West. The enduring products of their trade continue to turn up on the sites of their industry and throughout the expanse of wild land over which both Indian and white trapper hunted the beaver. Generally there is no concentration of relics such as were found on Iroquois sites, for example, but a goodly representation of their works occurs, and some valuable collections of axes and other iron objects of fur-trade significance have accumulated in the museums of the Western states.[7] These materials, as a rule, bespeak the transplanting of the seventeenth- and eighteenth-century trade-object types from the East. Even the axes produced by Spanish and Indian blacksmiths in the California Missions show no distinctive characteristics. Mission axes in the Los Angeles Museum find their counterparts in collections from seventeenth-century sites in New York or the maritime provinces of Canada.

[7] The tremendous accumulation of historic ironware and remnants of raw, strap, and bar iron from onetime stockpiles at Fort Vancouver constitutes an exception to the generality "no concentration of relics." During four years of archeological work at this Hudson's Bay Company headquarters site on the Columbia, 95,846 iron objects were recovered and catalogued. An excellent survey of these artifacts and scraps is found in Caywood: *Final Report*, pp. 32–45.

CHAPTER VI

Miscellaneous Iron Tools
and Weapons That Went
into the West

Mr. Astor's Inventory—The Basic Tools

HE VOLUME OF EXISTING MATERIAL PERTAINING TO THE frontiersman's implements and tools is actually large enough to embarrass the student who undertakes their identification, classification, interpretation, and publication. The three-dimensional objects are accumulating in numerous collections, and the documentary sources are abundant and replete with evidences of the origin, sale price, and distribution of these pieces; less is recorded regarding their practical use in the hands of frontier craftsmen. Meriwether Lewis provides us with a good starting point for our study; his 1803 requisitions for equipment and supplies to be used by the Lewis and Clark Expedition are preserved in the National Archives, and the Lewis and Clark *Journals* contain a number of testimonials regarding the use of tools in the field.[1] Enough of this extraordinary information is available to make a book on the his-

---

[1] The original requisitions are preserved in the National Archives, and they appear in R. G. Thwaites, ed.: *Original Journals of the Lewis and Clark Expedition* (8 vols.; New York: Dodd, Mead & Co.; 1904–5), VII, 231–46. Donald Jackson, ed.: *Letters of the Lewis and Clark Expedition* (Urbana: Univ. of Illinois Press; 1962), pp. 69–99, reprints them with related documents and adds his own valuable interpretive notes. An illustrated account of the three-dimensional properties of Lewis and Clark is given in the manuscript report by C. P. Russell: "Preliminary Exhibit Plan for Lewis and Clark Memorial" (Nat'l Park Serv., Fort Clatsop, Ore., 1959), pp. 67–127.

toric objects of Lewis and Clark provenance; a few of the pieces are treated in the pages that follow.

A second highly important source of information regarding early iron tools in the Far West is John Jacob Astor's inventory of his properties seized by the British North West Company at Astoria on the Columbia River in October 1813. Surprisingly, this great body of information has not been republished by scholars who have in recent years concerned themselves with the history of trade and merchandising in the early West. The inventory is much too extensive (forty-three pages printed in eight-point type) to be presented here in its entirety, but sections of it that pertain most directly to the subject matter of the present chapter are given in Appendix D (pages 402–7). The prices indicated in the inventory represent the values as appraised by the North West Company buyers. In a very few categories of goods, 100 per cent was added to the total cost of an item; in more instances, however, 75 per cent was deducted from the appraised worth. The total Astoria inventory, exclusive of furs on hand, amounted to $13,256.00. Mr. Astor testified to the United States Congress that this was one fifth of the true worth (see appendix for the partial Astor inventory).

Entirely similar but smaller lots of merchandise were turned over to the North West Company at Mr. Astor's outposts eastward from Astoria. The inventory for Okunaakan [Okanogan] was $2,333.5825; at Spokane House, $1,715.1725; and John Reed's party and the "Freemen" with him on the Snake were allowed $1,907.57, from which amount 50 per cent was deducted immediately. A final scraping of the bottom of the barrel swelled the merchandise accounted for to the extent of $853.805, and the final inventory at Astoria proper totaled $13,256.0075. Furs sold to the North West Company at Astoria amounted to $39,173.665, thus making the gross purchase price for the establishments and the furs $58,291.0175.

Alleged indebtedness assumed by some of Mr. Astor's representatives then at Astoria reduced the net proceeds of the sale to $42,281.50. The bill of sale but not the inventories has been published in B. C. Payette's *Oregon Country*.[2] The shipping of cargoes from New York to the Pacific shore was costly and fraught

[2] Payette, comp.: *The Oregon Country under the Union Jack: [Alexander] Henry's Astoria Journal* (Montreal, 1961), pp. xiv–xix.

with catastrophe, as witness the *Tonquin* disaster. Mr. Astor's allegation that he was robbed by the North West Company of 80 per cent of the true worth of his properties on the Columbia (he declared the total value to be $200,000) seems to be fairly substantiated by the Columbia inventories and the bill of sale.

Extant records of early merchandising in the Western fur trade are rich in detail. Contemporary with the above-described Astoria business are the accounts of Colonel John Johnston's United States Indian Agency at Fort Wayne.[3] These accounts are representative of the government's Indian factory system of trade. The invoices, inventories, and memoranda included in the account books present an excellent picture of the variety and quantity of merchandise handled, and they reveal the prevailing prices of the day. Generally these government prices are lower than those charged by the commercial companies of the same period. Rather complete information on the Indian trade goods distributed by the government from 1801 to 1822 is found in the account books—Day Books, Stock Books, Memoranda Books, and Letter Books—representative of the business conducted at the Indian Trade headquarters offices in Philadelphia and George Town, D.C. The westernmost Indian factory was Fort Osage on the Missouri. A summary report on these significant fur-trade papers was prepared by Dr. Alfred F. Hopkins in 1941–2.[4] It is in the library of the director's office of the National Park Service, Washington, D.C.

Data regarding merchandise for distribution as gifts to Western Indians by William Clark's St. Louis Indian Office, 1823, are found in the Forsyth Papers[5] owned by the Wisconsin Historical Society. Prices here compare favorably with prices charged by the commercial companies.

Mr. Astor's agents engaged in a phenomenally successful fur

[3] Bert J. Griswold, ed.: *Fort Wayne, Gateway of the West, 1802–1813* (Indianapolis: Indian Library and Historical Dept.; 1927).
[4] Dr. Alfred F. Hopkins, comp.: "Report on Indian Trade Objects Purchased by the U. S. Government through its several Superintendents of Indian Trade at Philadelphia, Penn., and George Town, D.C., from 1801–22, inclusive" (MSS), 56 typed pages.
[5] "Invoice of merchandise purchased and received as presents for Indians, 1823. . . . Apr. 28, 1823. Sundries received of Genl. William Clark for presents for Indians," in Forsyth Papers, Vol. 2, Draper Collection, Item 2, Wisconsin Historical Society. See also 17th Cong., 1st sess., Sen. Doc. 60, February 11, 1822, pp. 1–62, for detailed statements regarding trade goods and the firms that supplied the U. S. Indian Office.

trade after the fiasco on the Columbia. Until 1818 the Astor men concentrated on the Great Lakes trade with extensions into the Ohio-Mississippi region. In 1818, however, Russell Farnham of the Astor company was sent into the Missouri country to trade, and by the fall of 1821 Samuel Abbott, Astor's trusted agent, had established an American Fur Company Western Department with headquarters in St. Louis. Thereafter, the company linked with the Prattes and the Chouteaus proceeded slowly but surely on its march to monopoly in the West. Many of the letters and business records of the American Fur Company are available for study. The company's account books for the early business in Missouri have not been searched, but the manuscript "Invoice Book No. 1," owned by the Chicago Historical Society, provides some 300 pages of descriptive accounts, with prices, of all manner of merchandise shipped by the company from Michilimackinac to twenty or more outposts in Michigan, Wisconsin, Illinois, and Indiana in 1821 and 1822. A survey of the tools and ironworks in these inventories reveals that the items are much the same as those which Mr. Astor shipped to the Columbia, but generally the Michilimackinac prices of 1821–2 were 100 to 500 per cent more than the prices paid to the Astorians by the North West Company on the Columbia in 1813.

There are several additional important collections of American Fur Company manuscripts in the Public Archives of Canada, Detroit Public Library, Missouri Historical Society, State Historical Society of Wisconsin, Minnesota Historical Society, Chicago Historical Society, and The New-York Historical Society.[6] All shed light on the tools of the fur traders, but the "Orders Outward," "Orders Inward," "Ledgers," "Invoices," and "Inventories" contained in the massive assembly of American Fur Company Papers, 1831–49, owned by The New-York Historical Society are especially pertinent to our present account of tools in the West. Furthermore, the Papers are most workable because of the two-volume *Calendar*[7] and the remarkable national distribution of the 37-reel microfilm copy of practically all the manuscripts. Ramsay Crooks, Astorian, was made president of the company when Astor with-

[6] See the American Fur Company sources in the bibliography.
[7] Calendar of the American Fur Company Papers *1831–49* Grace Lee Nute, ed.: (Annual Report of the American Historical Association, 1944). (Washington, D.C.: U. S. Govt. Printing Office; 1945).

drew in 1834. Therefore the great body of the Papers are the expression of Crooks and his agents and portray very fully their way of life. West of the Mississippi, Pratte, Chouteau and Company (after 1838 Pierre Chouteau, Jr., and Company) constituted an affiliated firm. Its outposts and agencies were distributed from the Canadian border to Texas and westward across the Rockies. The Pratte-Chouteau business records are preserved in St. Louis and New York, where they served the present writer as one of the keys to the Western "tools" story. The tools themselves, as pictured in the illustrations that follow, are preserved in some forty museums and private collections, as indicated.

Needles and Awls

FIGURE 83a shows the rush matting needle that quickly replaced the aboriginal bone and wood versions of this simple tool so necessary to the primitive weaver. This flat "needle," or shuttle, served to interlace the horizontal strip of flattened rush (weft) with the vertical strips of the same material (warp) to make a fairly pliable, hard fabric—matting. The weaving was entirely a hand operation. No loom was required. The Indians of the Columbia River and parts of the Pacific Coast regions were especially noted for mats used as floor covering in their rectangular lodges, for side walls, doors, sun shades, windbreaks, coverings for piles of foodstuffs, for beds and bedding, for seats, and even for platters upon which to serve their food. The weaving of rush matting was not limited to Indians of the Far West; it was quite commonly practiced wherever the raw materials were abundant. For aboriginal matting needles recovered at a Fox Indian site, 1680–1730, see Wittry's paper.[8] The matting needle represented in figure 83a is No. A-80 in the Minnesota Historical Society collections and is attributed to H. M. Rice, a trader of the 1840's and 1850's at Sauk Rapids, Lake Prairie, middle-upper Mississippi River section.

Figure 83b shows an iron "moccasin" awl with a handle. This specimen is No. D48 in the American Museum, and is attributed to the Iroquois. Because rawhide, dressed skins, gut, bark—even thin panels of wood—entered into so many of the Indian's everyday

[8] W. L. Wittry: "The Bell Site; Early Historic Fox Village," *Wisconsin Archeologist*, XLIV: 1 (March 1963), p. 15.

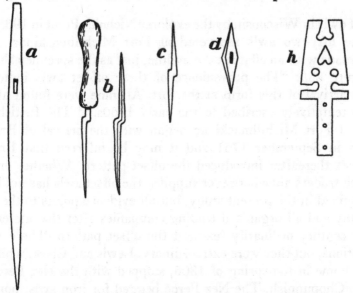

FIG. 83. *Some Small Implements Much Appreciated by Indians.*

Certain small iron tools were inexpensive but of prime importance in the Indian's daily work. Such were the various needles and awls supplied by the white man. Often the trader carried a generous supply of these easily transported items in order that he might win favor through the presentation of simple valued gifts that had cost him little more than the trouble of packing them. Drawing by William Macy, Jefferson National Expansion Memorial, St. Louis.

procedures of manufacture and repair, he found it necessary to incessantly sew, lace, and bind with sinew or rawhide thongs. To facilitate pushing the needle through exceedingly resistant materials, awls were used to break the way. Originally awls were polished, sharpened splinters of bone, antler, or wood. The white man brought to America the same iron awls that served Europe since the dawn of the Iron Age. The Indian seized upon the better implement. Seemingly, iron awls appear upon any and all invoices and inventories representative of the Indian trade, east or west, and through all the years. Maxwell publishes evidences that the earliest awls at Michilimackinac were tapered, cylindrical spikes of iron, pointed at both ends.[9] Charles E. Brown illustrates somewhat similar awls from Carcajou site, Wisconsin, and tells of the distribu-

[9] Moreau S. Maxwell: *Excavations at Fort Michilimackinac, 1959 Season* (East Lansing: Michigan State Univ.; 1961), pp. 88, 124.

tion of awls in Wisconsin by the explorer Nicholas Perot in 1965–6.[1] Of the fifty-two awls recovered at Fort Michilimackinac, nine were made with an offset at the middle, just as the specimen shown in figure 83*b*. "The provenience of these off-set awls indicates a late arrival of this form at the fort. All nine were found above levels tentatively ascribed to the early 1760s."[2] The British regime at Fort Michilimackinac began with the arrival of British troops in September 1761 and it may be inferred that British interests thereafter introduced the offset pattern. Whether or not French traders anywhere ever supplied the offset awls has not been determined in the present study, but all evidence points to the fact that any and all organized trading companies after the late eighteenth century ordinarily featured the offset pattern. There were exceptions, but they were extraordinary. Lewis and Clark, while en route home in the spring of 1806, stopped with the Nez Percé at Camp Chopunnish. The Nez Percé begged for iron awls, none of which remained in the skimpy stock of merchandise carried by the explorers at this juncture. Lewis wrote: "4 of our party pased the river and visited the lodge of the *broken Arm* for the purpose of traiding some awls which they had made of the links of a small chain belonging to one of their steel traps, for some roots. They returned in the evening having been very successful, they had obtained a good supply of roots and bread of cows."[3] It is unlikely that awls with an offset were improvised on this occasion. No forge was carried by the returning explorers. Such bending, straightening, and sharpening of the cold iron links as could be effected on a makeshift anvil with a hammer, pincers, and a file probably yielded nothing more than a fairly straight, sharp spike.

Figure 83*c* shows a "moccasin" awl, No. E-193 in the Minnesota Historical Society. The specimen is from the Sauk Rapids locality, Minnesota. Awls were shipped by the manufacturer and distributed by the trader without handles. A shaped and smooth section of deer antler usually was affixed by the Indian owner. British supply houses furnished many awls to the American trade. The American Fur Company Papers contain copies of many orders addressed to Hiram Cutler, Sheffield. "Our Indian awls are to be

[1] C. E. Brown: "Indian Trade Implements and Ornaments," *Wisconsin Archeologist*, XVII: 3 (1918), p. 62.

[2] Maxwell: *Excavations*, pp. 88 and 124, Pl. VIII.

[3] *Journals*, Lewis's entry for May 24, 1806; Allen, ed.: *History of the Expedition*, II, 299.

put up in papers of 50 each. They can be packed with fire steels and needles." Fifty gross was a usual complement, and, consistently, year after year the price paid to Cutler was about forty cents per gross. In the United States the book value was a dollar and a half per gross, or one cent each; in the field, "Indian" awls brought two to five cents each, if sold, but often they were handed out freely as good-will offerings. This was generally true of all companies all through the mountain-man period. Larger awls, termed "canoe awls," were inventoried at twenty-five cents each [4] and sold in the field at a mark-up as big as circumstances might dictate.

Figure 83*d* is described as a "snowshoe needle"; it is No. E-191 in the Minnesota Historical Society. Most northern tribes of Indians were adept in the ancient art of stringing strips of rawhide, usually deerskin, upon their own particular form of ashwood frame to produce the very necessary *raquette*. Usually, the stringing and spacing of the thongs was facilitated by the use of a short length of antler, deer, or caribou. The white man adopted the snowshoe enthusiastically and introduced the iron snowshoe needle as an "improvement" to be used by the native manufacturers, but the Indian craftsman did not always see it as such. The craft of snowshoe making persists in some localities as an Indian village enterprise,[5] and the minutiae of practices remain as of old, including dependence upon the primitive antler "needle." The iron specimen shown in figure 83*d* was obtained from a trader who had been active in the Sauk Rapids region, Minnesota, during the 1840's.

Spears, Harpoons, and Arrow Points

AMONG the specimens shown in figure 84 are a half-dozen lance heads favored by buffalo-hunting Indians, four barbed harpoons used by whites and Indians alike in spearing fish and muskrats, and a representative assortment of iron arrow points, large and small. The seven arrow points were recovered in northern and northeastern localities, but so far as their sizes and shapes are concerned, they might have been collected anywhere north of the Mexican boundary. The pattern exemplified by figures 84*n*, 84*o*, 84*p*, and 84*s* was the usual point produced in factories supplying

[4] American Fur Company Papers, 1821–2, (Invoice Book) "Illinois 1821."
[5] Adelaide Leitch: "Land of the Wendats," *The Beaver* (Autumn 1963), pp. 14–19 [good photos].

the trade. Others, like figures 84q, 84r, 84t are representative products of backcountry forges where, on occasion, red men as well as whites operated smithies.

Figure 84a shows a Sioux lance point with its original shaft, which is now owned by the Missouri Historical Society. The specimen was presented to R. Faribault by Chief Red Leg of the Sioux, who described it as "a warrior's lance, very old. It was used by my people in fights with the Chippewa." The shaft is 3½ feet long.

Figure 84b illustrates an iron spear point or knife blade from the Yellowstone Valley. This specimen is No. 7266 in the Yellowstone National Park museums. See page 333 for the use of similar blades in "dags" of the north land. These artifacts turn up occasionally on northern Indian sites anywhere and everywhere from New York to the Pacific.

Figure 84c is an extra-large blade, which is now item No. 2064 in the State Historical Society, Pierre, South Dakota. The eccentric tang suggests that this specimen may have served as a machete-type knife blade, but it would do equally well as a spear point.

The country-made spear point shown in figure 84d, No. 116 in the Washington State Historical Society, Tacoma, is recorded as found in an Indian grave in Wisconsin. Similar leaf-shaped iron points with short tang have been found throughout Iroquoia.

Figure 84e is a 10-inch iron spear point, cataloged as No. 117, Washington State Historical Society, Tacoma. W. P. Bonney of the society reported that this specimen was from Cairo, Illinois. Its unusual serrated base facilitated binding the head into the split end of a shaft.

Shown in figure 84f is a long-tang spear point in the Marvin Livingston Collection, Carlsbad, New Mexico. It was found in Dark Canyon in the northeast section of the Guadalupe Mountains. Note the smith's mark "A B 85." A point quite similar and of most excellent workmanship was found in a Caddo site, Arkansas, and is preserved in the Dorris Dickinson Collection, Magnolia, Arkansas.

Figure 84g is a Hatchilla Mountains spear point, No. M-232 in the Laboratory of Anthropology, Santa Fe, New Mexico. Like figure 84f, the blade is a diamond shape in cross section, and the tang is square in cross section. Some anthropologists have regarded these slender points to be of Spanish derivation, and it is likely that these particular specimens are Spanish; however, entirely similar bayonet points were excavated at Fort Washington,

183rd Street and Pinehurst Avenue, New York City. These Revolutionary War relics of Anglo-American origin now in The New-York Historical Society rather belie the idea that the model is characteristically Spanish.

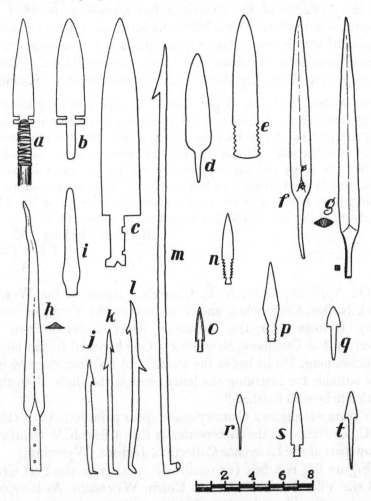

FIG. 84. *Iron Projectile Points.*

Arrowheads and spear points, both stone and metal, are present almost universally in collections of Indian artifacts. The iron points present a bewildering variety of sizes and forms. The Indian and probably the white trader were unaware of the fact, but not one of the styles of iron points in America was unique; each had had its counterpart during earlier periods in the Old World. Drawing by William Macy, Jefferson National Expansion Memorial, St. Louis.

Figure 84*h* shows a triple-edged lance head from Butte des Morts; it is catalogued as No. 396 in the Wisconsin Historical Society. This twisted specimen was once the personal property of Augustin Grignon, historical figure in the Wisconsin Indian trade and early affiliate of the American Fur Company. In 1835 the company ordered lances from Miles Standish, the celebrated manufacturer of beaver traps. These spear heads were requisitioned by Pierre Chouteau and Company, St. Louis, through Ramsay Crooks, American Fur Company, New York. Crooks wrote to Standish:

> 120 Assinboine lances as per sample. The tang to be 2 inches long and to have 3 holes in it for rivets at equal distance on the square part say 1 hole near the round, 1 hole near the extremity and the other hole half way between. The price to be $1.00, each. They are to be of your very best work, packed carefully and securely in good strong pine boxes—one or two boxes as you may deem best. Payment in six months after delivery to store No. 45 Liberty St., or in cash less 3½% discount at option of Co.
>
> Marginal Marking   35
P C & Co.
A.[6]

On April 26, 1836, A. P. Chouteau, trader to the Western Creek Nation, Comanches, and Wichitas, on the Verdigris and at Camp Holmes near the Canadian River, ordered from the American Fur Company, New York: "One hundred Indian lances, 18 inches long, 1½ inches at the shank, and 100 iron rings ½ inch wide suitable for fastening the lance head in the shaft. Both these articles to be well finished." [7]

Figure 84*i* shows a Country-made spear point found in 1910 by W. C. Lawrence on the Sweetwater at Burnt Ranch, Wyoming. It is now part of the Lawrence Collection, Jackson, Wyoming.

Figure 84*j* is a fish (or muskrat) spear from the Fort Crawford site Villa Louis, Prairie du Chien, Wisconsin. As is typical, there is a "heel" at the end of this small harpoon that made it possible to achieve a secure mounting on a shaft of wood. Any spearing of muskrats with this short shank would have been done in the open or through thin transparent ice. Only a long shank could reach a muskrat through the walls of a muskrat house.

[6] American Fur Company Papers, Memos, 1834–40, Vol. 1 (microfilm reel 20).

[7] American Fur Company Papers, Orders Inward, Vol. 1, p. 251.

Figure 84*k* shows a double-barbed fish or muskrat spear from the vicinity of the Jacques Vieau trading post. The specimen is preserved as No. 28012 in the Milwaukee Public Museum. There were three modes of mounting these spearheads on handles: 1. The outer surface at the end of the shaft might be grooved longitudinally and a depression made for the "heel" of the iron spear. The spear point was laid into the groove, the heel driven home, and the iron held rigidly against the wood by a tight wrapping of wet rawhide or wire. Or 2. the heel might be made small enough to permit of inserting the iron into a hole drilled in the end of the wooden shaft. In this method an iron ring, band, or ferrule was driven down upon the end of the shaft to make the wood take a tight grip upon the iron. 3. Some eighteenth-century specimens were made with a socket into which the handle entered. In this form there was no heel.

Iron "harpoons" find a place in fur-trade documents as early as 1643, in which year it is recorded that the Montagnais used them in killing beaver.[8] Nicholas Denys's *Description* for the 1670's says of the Micmac: "They practice still all the old methods of hunting, with this difference, in place of arming their arrows and spears with the bones of animals, pointed and sharpened, they arm them today with iron, which is made expressly for sale to them. . . . With respect to hunting of the beaver in winter, they do the same as they did formerly, though they have now a greater advantage with their arrows and harpoons armed with iron."[9] Wittry unearthed intact examples of the aboriginal bone harpoons in a Fox site of 1680–1730,[1] and recently Caywood recovered early iron specimens at Fort Meductic, New Brunswick.[2] The independent trader William Burnett at the St. Joseph River, Michigan, in 1799 ordered from his supplier in Montreal muskrat spears "made with a socket which the French call endouille."[3] In 1803 Meriwether

[8] Thwaites, ed.: *Jesuit Relations*, V, 143, and VI, 309–11.

[9] W. F. Ganong, ed. and trans.: *The Description and Natural History of the Coasts of North America by Nicholas Denys* (Toronto): Champlain Society; 1908), pp. 442–3.

[1] Wittry: "The Bell Site," p. 15, Fig. 7G.

[2] Personal letter, Louis R. Caywood to C. P. Russell, June 24, 1965.

[3] Burnett to Parker, Gerard and Ogilvy, Montreal, quoted in H. H. Hurlbut: *Chicago Antiquities* (Chicago: Eastman Bartlett; 1881), p. 68. Charles E. Brown: "Indian Trade Implements and Ornaments," *Wisconsin Archeologist*, XVII: 3(1918), pp. 74–5, reports the recovery of a socketed fish-muskrat-beaver harpoon in Wisconsin: "Recovered from the Lake Mendota bottom near Fox Bluff at Madison. It is 18⅛ inches long, square in section, with a conical socket

Lewis procured forty of these single-pointed "giggs" with barbs at Harpers Ferry. They were made to his order and by him added to the stock of merchandise carried by the Lewis and Clark Expedition for presentation to Indians. A Memorandum Book (1808) of the U. S. Indian Office, George Town, D.C., lists iron spears for muskrats and fish; the American Fur Company Invoice Book, "Illinois 1821," lists "25 rat spears @ .62½¢ . . . $15.62" in a shipment of trade goods sent from Michilimackinac; the Hudson's Bay Company's Chief Factor at Cumberland House, Saskatchewan River, in 1839 ordered from the York Factory: "60 long rat spears 3½ feet long . . . the old short ones I have on hand shall be repaired, and they with the 60 now asked for will be enough for next winter;⁴ and Francis X. Des Nover's Wisconsin Account Book of 1844 records the sale of two "rat" spears for $1.00.⁵ Thus, we observe there is a two-hundred-year documented record for the fish-muskrat spear, most of it pertaining to the northern country.

Figure 84*l* shows a double-barbed harpoon for fish or muskrats from site of the Hudson's Bay Company post at Trout Lake, Wisconsin. It is preserved as specimen No. H-3814–19 in the Wisconsin Historical Society. Several of these were found at Trout Lake, and others have been collected at the Grignon-Parlier trading post site at Rush Lake; the Jacques Vieau post at Milwaukee; Green Bay; Prairie du Chien; Crawfish River, Fall River; and the Carcajou site at Lake Koshkonong—all in Wisconsin.

Shown in figure 84*m* is a single-barbed harpoon with long shank especially for muskrats. It is recorded as having been used by Winnebago Indians. The specimen is No. E-198–199, Wisconsin Historical Society. In the 1840's Henry Thacker, a member of the Oneida Community but then a resident of Chicago, wrote an account of firsthand experiences in muskrat spearing. He turned in his manuscript to the Community, and it appears in the Newhouse *Trapper's Guide*.⁶ On a cold, snappy winter's day Mr. Thacker

---

in which is a rivet hole. The shaft where it joins the socket is about one inch square [and tapers]. The first of its two barbs is 4½ inches below the tip."

⁴ Chief Factor John Lee Lewis to James Hargrave, York Factory, February 5, 1839, quoted in Stanley P. Young: "The Evolution of the Steel Wolf Trap in North America," *Western Sportsman* (February 1941), p. 11.

⁵ C. E. Brown: "Indian Trade Implements," pp. 74–5.

⁶ *The Trapper's Guide* by S. Newhouse (Wallingford, Conn., 1867). An 1887 edition published in New York also contains the Thacker article, p. 146.

skated twelve miles up the North Fork of the Chicago River to marshes in the vicinity of present-day Skokie. There, among innumerable muskrat houses protruding above the ice of the marsh, he identified occupied houses by the deposit of white frost to be seen around the small air holes in the domes. Successively he approached occupied houses, drove his spear through the softest part of the walls as betrayed by the air hole, and impaled his victims on the long shank of his spear. Occasionally two rats were impaled by a single thrust. When a rat was hit, the spear was not withdrawn until a hole was chopped in the wall of the house, exposing the victim, which was then killed and removed, and the broken wall repaired. Mr. Thacker states that he took fifteen or twenty rats in a few hours, all that he could skin before the carcasses froze. He adds that a few rats were speared through 2 inches of clear ice as they swam under him. His spear was a rod ⅜ inch in diameter, 3 feet long, mounted in a ferruled wooden handle that also was 3 feet long.

W. Hamilton Gibson's *Tricks of Trapping* also describes the spearing of muskrats:

> Uncertain and unreliable, because the walls of the hut are often so firmly frozen as to defy the thrust. The spear is a single shaft of steel about eighteen inches in length and half an inch in diameter, barbed at the point and feruled to a solid handle five feet long. In spearing through the hut the south side is generally selected as being more exposed to the heat of the sun. Great caution in approaching the house is necessary as the slightest noise will drive out the inmates. The spear should be thrust in a slanting direction a few inches above the ice. When it has penetrated it must be left until a hole is cut in the wall with a hatchet through which to remove the game.[7]

Needless to say, the spearing of muskrats or beaver is passé as a mode of taking fur. This was true in the days of the author's boyhood, the early 1900's, but his Wisconsin homeland at that time still claimed numerous living citizens who had taken the bounty from the local fur fields, and their muskrat spears were to be found, with shafts intact, in granaries, tool sheds, and barns throughout the rural districts. The one in the author's tool shop did not get there because of any anthropological interests; it was a

[7] W. Hamilton Gibson: *Camp Life and the Tricks of Trapping* (New York: Harper & Bros.; 1881), pp. 183–4.

family property—a relic of practical "spearing" by a pre-Civil War generation that farmed the country around Lost Lake in Dodge County. These Yankee farmers were only a scant decade behind the Winnebago Indians and the French-Canadians who for two hundred years had harvested pelts on the same marshes.

Trade Iron into Arrow and Lance Points

FIGURE 84*n* shows a large "buffalo" arrowhead with a serrated tang. The specimen is No. 157 in the Missouri Historical Society, where it is recorded as being from the Sioux of South Dakota; it was collected in 1905. Stamped into the iron is ". . . J & Co.," which mark probably is the incomplete "P. C. J. & Co.," the trade mark of Pierre Chouteau, Jr. and Company, a big trading firm of the West operating out of St. Louis during the days of the mountain man. A number of identical points with the "P. C. J. & Co." intact are in existing collections.[8]

Figure 84*o* is an iron arrow point with a beveled edge. The specimen is preserved as No. H-391, Wisconsin Historical Society. The serrated tang was inserted into the split end of the arrow shaft, which was sufficiently slender to allow some of the iron teeth to project slightly beyond the rounded wood. A tight wrapping of fine sinew enclosed both teeth and wood. A thin glue prepared from hoofs was applied upon the wrapping. This hardened to make a firm and lasting binding.

Shown in figure 84*p* is a "buffalo" iron arrow point now in the State Historical Society, South Dakota. This specimen was taken from a bleached buffalo skeleton found years ago on the Dakota prairies. It was embedded in a vertebra. Long after the acceptance of the gun by the red man, he often clung to the bow and arrow as his best weapon in "running" buffalo. Osborne Russell, dependable observer and literate member of the trapper fraternity, provided an eyewitness account of buffalo slaughter with lance and bow and arrow. The place was Snake River country some forty miles west of the present Yellowstone National Park; the Indians were friendly Bannocks, and the date, October 1835. Russell wrote:

> I arose at sunrise and looking southwestward I saw dust arising in a defile which led through mountains about five miles

[8] C. E. Brown: "Indian Trade Implements," p. 67.

distant. Buffaloes were feeding all over the plain [before the defile]. I watched the motion of the dust for a few minutes, when I saw a body of men on horseback pouring out of the defile among the buffalo. The dust rose to the heavens. The whole mass of buffalo became agitated, producing a sound resembling distant thunder. At length an Indian pursued a cow close to me. Running along side of her he let slip an arrow and she fell. I immediately recognized him to be a Bannock with whom I was acquainted. He came to me and saluted in Snake, which I answered in the same tongue. . . . He said he had killed 3 fat cows and would kill one more and stop. So saying he wheeled his foaming charger and the next moment disappeared in the cloud of dust. In about half an hour he returned with a whole village and invited me to stop with him. While the squaws were putting up and stretching their lodges, I walked out with him to a small hillock to view the field of slaughter, the cloud of dust having passed away. The prairie was covered with slain. Upward of 1000 cows were killed without burning one single grain of powder.[9]

Figure 84*q* presents a small country-made iron arrow point. It is No. 1482 in the Bucks County Historical Society, Pennsylvania. This specimen was exposed by a woodcutter in 1882. It was embedded in a tree that had grown around it until it was enclosed within the center of the trunk. East and west, the tribesmen sought iron with which to tip their arrows. The Indian was adept at making his own iron points, using sheet iron, barrel hoops, and broken pieces of the white man's machinery. In some localities there were numerous Indian blacksmiths, but almost any Indian could fashion an iron arrow point without the benefit of a forge if he had access to a file, cold chisel, or hacksaw. Probably the most publicized instance of converting a machine to Indian armament was the demolition of the Lewis and Clark corn mill by the Mandans in 1805. The steel mill, which is accounted for in Captain Lewis's requisitions of 1803, was seen in action by the Mandans when a party visited Captain Clark on the expedition's keelboat on October 26, 1804. It was "the object which seemed to surprise them most. . . . It delighted them by the ease with which it reduced the grain to powder." On October 29, 1804, the explorers held a council with the Mandans. "A variety of presents were distributed, but none seemed to give them more satisfaction than

[9] Osborne Russell: *Journal of a Trapper* . . . (Boise, Idaho: Syms Fork Co.; 1921), pp. 40–1.

the iron corn mill which we gave to the Mandans."[1] Captain Clark's estimate of the Mandan "satisfaction" seems to have been mistakenly bestowed. In 1806 the Canadian Alexander Henry visited the Mandans and wrote:

> I saw the remains of an excellent large corn mill, which the foolish fellows had demolished on purpose to barb their arrows, and other similar uses, the largest piece of it which they could not break nor work up into any weapon, they have now fixed to a wooden handle and make use of it to pound marrow bones to make grease.[2]

Figure 84*r* shows a small Indian-made iron point. It is in the collection of The American Museum in New York City. The Indian was practical in making his arrow serviceable and proud in making its individual style or pattern conform to tribal tradition. However, the iron point, if made in the field, varied with the different circumstances under which the raw material and suitable tools became available to the tribesmen. Iron-tipped arrows were made in large numbers, because even under optimum conditions loss and breakage were to be expected. It was not unusual for big game animals to carry away the arrows that were supposed to kill them. One bit of testimony in this regard appears in a journal kept by a trooper of the Dodge Dragoon expedition in the territory of present-day Oklahoma:

> July 10, 1834. When we closed in upon this besieged buffalo as near as our horses would approach and at one well-aimed fire laid him prostrate, we immediately began butchering him. In his left shoulder, overgrown with flesh, we found the steel point of an Indian arrow which had no doubt been long there as the flesh around it had become completely calloused.[3]

Shown in figure 84*s* is a lethal point used by the Nebraska Sioux; it is now in the Union Pacific Historical Museum, Omaha. The tragic story of the murderous use of this specimen postdates the mountain man, but it is representative of many earlier attacks made upon trappers. This specimen was removed from the dead body of T. Tobin, foreman of a section gang at Overton, Nebraska.

[1] Allen, ed.: *History of the Expedition*, I, 117, 120.
[2] Elliott Coues, ed.: *The Manuscript Journals of Alexander Henry and of David Thompson . . .* (3 vols.; New York: F. P. Harper; 1895), I, 329.
[3] Company I Journal, Pawnee Pict Expedition, quoted by G. H. Shirk, ed.: "Peace on the Plains," *The Chronicle of Oklahoma*, XXVIII: 1 (1950), p. 16.

FIG. 85.   *Bannock Buffalo Hunt, 1835.*

"Upward of 1000 cows were killed [with lance and arrow] without burning one single grain of powder." (From an eyewitness account by the mountain man Osborne Russell.) James Mulcahy drawing, Jefferson National Expansion Memorial, St. Louis.

Sioux Indians in an attack on May 12, 1867, killed Tobin and all but one of the men who were with him. Richard Costin is named as the individual who removed the arrow point and attended the remains of the victims. To view Sioux war arrows and bows one should visit the Custer Battlefield Museum. Photos and a brief account of these weapons appear in Harry B. Robinson's *Guide to the Custer Battlefield Museum.*

Figure 84*t* is an iron point with a long tang. No. E-194 in the Minnesota Historical Society, it is recorded as having been obtained from a North Dakota donor. Sixteenth-century records tell that some southeastern Indians make arrows having "nocks and feathers . . . whereby they shoot very stedy; the heads of some are vipers teeth, bones of fishes, flint stones, *points of* [iron] *knives,* which they having gotten from the Frenchmen, broke the same and put the points of them in their arrows heads." [4]

As early as 1671 the Hudson's Bay Company ordered two gross of factory-made iron arrowheads. [5] It seems quite obvious that

[4] John Spark, quoted in J. R. Swanton: *The Indians of Southeastern United States,* Bureau of American Ethnology, Bulletin 137 (1946), p. 572.
[5] Canadian Archives, Hudson's Bay Company Minute Book of 1671, p. 72, quoted in Innis: *The Fur Trade,* p. 27.

the American aborigine generally craved and got by one means or another iron points almost immediately upon contact with the white man. Yet there was not always enough iron to meet the demand. A number of testimonials left by the mountain men show that more than a few Far Western Indians still depended upon flint and obsidian for arrowheads in the 1830's and 1840's.[6] This was seldom true, however, of the country from which the specimen shown in figure 84*t* came. From the days of Lewis and Clark, the Plains tribes had been catered to by white traders and blacksmiths of both the United States and Canada. Even in the early decades of the nineteenth century, the several trading posts along the Missouri maintained smithies, and a few Indians themselves knew the rudiments of blacksmithing and engaged in the craft—after a fashion.

Figure 86*a* shows an American pike found at Fort Washington, 183rd Street and Pinehurst Avenue, New York City, and now owned by The New-York Historical Society. The strap-socketed spearhead, such as this one, was one of several patterns adopted by Washington's troops in accordance with the general's orders issued at Valley Forge in 1777. Each officer serving on foot was directed to provide himself with a pole arm of this kind. Similar military specimens are owned by Fort Ticonderoga Museum. All appear to have been made by local blacksmiths. The strap socket makes for a strong and efficient mounting, but it is comparatively costly to manufacture. These military pieces may have inspired some Indian agents; at any rate, a few points of this design were procured for the tribesmen by the U. S. Indian Department early in the nineteenth century. No positive evidence has been found of the strap-socket pattern having been distributed to Indians by the trading companies.

This hollow-ground spear head (fig. 86*b*) was obtained by Captain George E. Albee of the U. S. Army from the Lipan Apache, and is now No. E-85 in the Wisconsin Historical Society. In lieu of a metal ferrule, a wrapping of rawhide thongs, applied wet to the end of the shaft, gives firm mounting of the point. This type of spearhead was favored by the Navajo and the Comanche as well as the Apache. Its hollow-ground feature differs from the

[6] Josiah Gregg: *Commerce of the Prairies*, ed. R. G. Thwaites (2 vols.; Cleveland, 1905), II, 324.

usual points distributed among most tribes. Presumably these hollow-ground points were of Mexican or Spanish origin and may date back to sixteenth- or seventeenth-century manufacture. Some, apparently, are made from Spanish swords, bear Toledo armorers' marks, and have engraved upon them maxims or salutations in Spanish script. One such, No. 111.333 in the Laboratory of Anthropology, Santa Fe, is classed as a "buffalo lance." Its blade, 14 inches with tang, is marked "Viva el Rey." It is still mounted on its 62-inch wooden shaft.

Figure 86c is a "buffalo lance" with its original shaft. It was collected in an unnamed Rio Grande pueblo and is now preserved in the American Museum, New York City. The slight curve in the 5-foot wooden handle is true to the style of many Indian lances in the Southwest. There is nothing distinctive about the ferrule-mounted tanged blade, which is of a style found almost everywhere among American Indians. Specimens nearly identical in pattern have been found at Eau Claire and Prairie du Chien, Wisconsin (Wisconsin Historical Society); in the Menomini country, Michigan (American Museum); Big Bend, Texas (Memorial Museum, Alpine); Shoshone country, Wyoming (Teton Hotel Collection, Riverton); Bannock country, Idaho (Idaho Historical Society); in Union County, Ohio (Barsotti Collection); and in California (Los Angeles Museum).

In California the spear of this type persisted in the hands of white men until the American period. In order that Mexican troops mustered for the repulse of invading United States forces in 1846 might be armed with lances, many "homemade" points were hammered out in numerous rancho and Mission blacksmith shops. Shafts were prepared from mountain ash or laurel, and often an improvised pennant was tied to them just below the spearhead. Micheltoreña's troops were so armed. In the Los Angeles Museum are specimens of these lances from the battlefield of Paso de Bartolo, near Los Angeles. Official reports of Kearny's attack upon Pico at San Pasqual, a hand-to-hand fight, record that only two of the sixteen or eighteen Americans killed were felled by bullets; Mexican spears accounted for the others. In Mexico at this time, United States troops also encountered bodies of men who placed great reliance on the lance. Major H. K. Craig reported on May 24, 1846, that eighteen lances were captured from the Mexi-

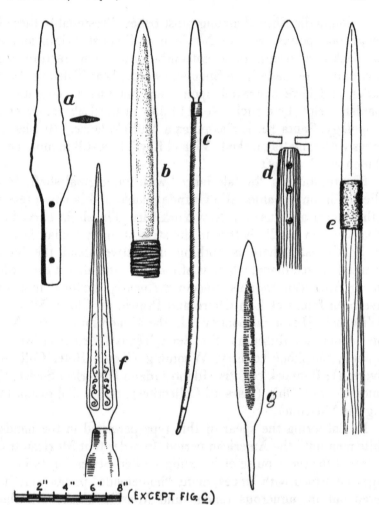

FIG. 86. *Pikes, Spears, and Lances.*

The lance of the Spaniards became a mark of their American occupation and persisted as such through three centuries. Even in the Mexican War the Spanish-type lance found effective use against United States troops. Indians adopted the spears of any and all national patterns, and the iron points became important articles of trade. William Macy drawing, Jefferson National Expansion Memorial, St. Louis.

cans at Palo Alto and Resaca; at Monterey on September 24, 1846, 43 lances were taken.[7]

Figure 86d is classed as an "American spontoon." The specimen was recovered at Fort Ticonderoga and is now exhibited there. In the terminology of the Quartermaster General of Revolutionary times, "Spontoon," "Pike," "Half Pike," and "Spear" were used synonymously. Such standardization as was attempted by the high command pertained to the length of staff, which for regular troops was specified as "six feet." The point figured here is much like the dag blades treated on page 320, and except for the greater length of tang, it closely resembles the blades used for spikes in war clubs described on page 175. As shown in figures 84a and 84b, this type of spear point was not limited to use by the military. Indian tribes of the Plains and the Rockies particularly are known to have used it. No clear evidence has been found showing an American source of supply; as in the case of the dag blades, an English source seems likely.

Figure 86e is a Navajo lance with its original shaft, which is preserved as specimen No. M-222, Laboratory of Anthropology, Santa Fe. It was obtained from the Navajos in Canyon de Chelly by Earl Morris in 1927. In lieu of a metal ferrule, a band of wet rawhide was sewed around the end of the shaft where the blade is mounted in the wood. Just as the specimen in figure 86c, the shaft, 17.75 feet long, is slightly curved at the small end. An 1882 photograph in Morris's possession shows this long lance in the hands of a Navajo, together with a bear that had been killed with the weapon.

Shown in figure 86f is a Spanish lance head marked (engraved on ferrule) "Santa Fe an. 1783." The specimen is preserved as No. B-96/55 in the Palace of the Governors, Santa Fe. The lance head is steel, ornamented with silver scrollwork. The metal ferrule, incomplete in the figure, extends 6 inches below the lance head. "Believed to have been carried by one of the soldiers stationed at the Palace of the Governors during the 18th Century." Both Coronado and Oñate [8] brought the same type of spear into the Ameri-

[7] S. V. Benet: *A Collection of Annual Reports and Other Important Papers Relating to the Ordnance Department* (Washington, D.C.: Gov't Printing Office; 1880), pp. 260–1.

[8] Harold L. Peterson: *Arms and Armor in Colonial America, 1526–1783* (Harrisburg, Pa.: Stackpole; 1956), pp. 318, 319. H. Charles McBarron's drawing of a Spanish lancer of the Oñate Expedition armed with the long spear is on p. 130.

can Southwest in the sixteenth century; the Indians of that section had, through three hundred years of contact, ample opportunity to become familiar with it. When the mountain man went among these peoples in the early decades of the nineteenth century, he found it to be the principal lance type used by the red warriors. The Indian pieces lacked the silver decorations.

Figure 86g shows a hollow-ground spear point found in Santa Fe Canyon. It is now in the Palace of the Governors, Santa Fe, New Mexico. Like the specimen shown in figure 86b, this point bears the marks of special crafting; it is not a run-of-the-mill trade piece. In the present survey of lance heads, pieces of this style were of Southwest provenance only.

Broadax, Adz, and Miscellaneous Tools

THE tradesman's tools appear quite commonly among the artifacts dug from historic ground at trading posts and Indian sites. Iron chisels and hoes were valid among the red man's implements where they replaced earlier stone and bone tools; the recovered broadax and carpenter's hatchet may be less persuasive in the eyes of the investigator excavating an Indian site. Actually, both the white trapper and the Indian commonly put these tools to uses not planned by the toolmakers. The carpenter's hatchet especially was prized by the Indian because it functioned perfectly as a tomahawk, and the big broadax sometimes was chocked into a stump at the Indian camp and made to function as an improvised anvil. Upon the flat of its poll strips of brass plate or sheeting were cut with a cold chisel to make arrow points, or to fashion the bangles and "jinglers" needed for the dancers' garb.

Figure 87a shows a country-made broadax that is preserved as item No. 223 in the Holland Land Office Museum, Batavia, New York.[9] The light poll and the round eye place this specimen in the European class. Often the broadax has a chisel edge that permits of a perfectly flat face on one side of the blade. The flat face contributes to the shaping of flat, fairly smooth surfaces on logs or beams, because, like a chisel, this chisel-edged, flat-faced ax blade "hews to the line." To assure good control in hewing, the broadax maker always provides a short handle, and in order that the chopper's

[9] I have the data on this broadax through the cooperation of Ralph Lewis. Lewis: 6-page MSS (February 6, 1938).

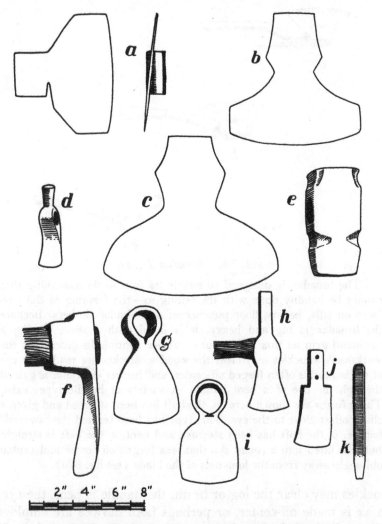

FIG. 87. *Broadax, Adz, and Miscellaneous Tools.*

Trapper-trader parties often went into the wilds well supplied with tools. Probably the most impressive evidence of this fact is the Astoria inventory (see appendix), but additional authentic lists exist that reveal a surprising variety of equipment used in camps and trading posts. Understandably the larger inventories pertained to centers served by water transportation, as were the posts along the Missouri River. William Macy drawing, Jefferson National Expansion Memorial, St. Louis.

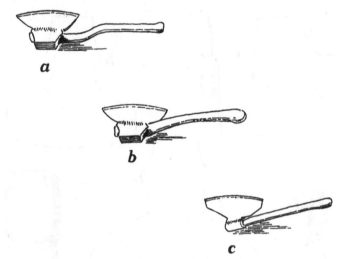

a

b

c

FIG. 88. *Broadax Types.*

The broadax is designed to enable its user to do something that cannot be handily done with the felling ax—the forming of flat surfaces on sills, beams, floor puncheons, and similar timbers. Because the broadax is big and heavy, it is fitted with a short handle; a two-hand grip on this haft assures precise control. In order that the workman's knuckles may clear the wood as strokes are made, the eye of the axhead is often forged off-center, and further clearance is gained through the use of a bent handle. A variety of handle types exist. Three forms are shown here: *a*, the haft has been steamed and given a sharp offset close to the eye. This type has been termed the "swayed" handle. *b*, the haft has been steamed and bent. *c*, the haft is straight but it is fitted into a round eye that was forged off-center and canted obliquely away from the long axis of the blade (see fig. 87*a*).

knuckles may clear the log or beam, the handle is bent, the eye of the ax is made off-center, or perhaps both devices are employed. Indians obtained the broadax occasionally by theft. One of the first recorded instances of such stealing appears in *Zebulon Pike's Arkansas Journal;* Pawnees on the Arkansas stole a broadax in 1806.[1]

A fur trader's broadax from the site of Fort Union, North Dakota, owned by the Montana Historical Society, Helena, is shown in figure 87*b*. This is one of two broadaxes found by M. B. Milligan in 1919 in the ruins of the blacksmith shop at this onetime largest and most important trading post in the western United States.

[1] S. H. Hart and A. B. Hulbert, eds.: *Zebulon Pike's Arkansas Journal* (Denver: Denver Public Library; 1932), p. 123.

FIG. 89.   *Fort Union, 1828–67.*

This emporium of the Western fur trade (near present-day Buford, North Dakota) occupied strategic place at the confluence of the Yellowstone and Missouri rivers. It was constructed under the supervision of the hard bitten Kenneth McKenzie, "King" of the Upper Missouri Outfit, American Fur Company, who may be credited with the traders' most ambitious construction project on the Missouri. Into his employ came tradesmen or mountain men who functioned in the building arts—carpenters, stonemasons, blacksmiths, coopers, boatbuilders, harnessmakers, saddlers, and, ultimately, wagonmakers. With the workmen came their tools. Since this post in the wilderness was well served from St. Louis by river transportation, it received tools in abundance, together with all manner of raw materials and heavy equipment needed in the shops of the establishment. The state now owns the site. See Ray H. Mattison's "The Upper Missouri Fur Trade" for a concise history of Fort Union. Drawing by William Macy, Jefferson National Expansion Memorial, St. Louis.

Figure 87c is the second broadax recovered at the site of Fort Union in 1919 and now is preserved in the Montana Historical Society collections. Probably no other trading post displayed more examples of the house carpenter's craft or more evidences of the use of the broadax than did the elaborate Fort Union complex. Nevertheless, the smaller Western posts also developed and maintained numerous cabins, warehouses, shops, blockhouses, palisades, and other wooden structures, all requiring the attention of men equipped with the broadax.

Figure 87d shows a small hammer-hatchet from the Cumber-

FIG. 90. *Fort Hall on the Snake, Interior View, 1834–55.*

The Bostonian Nathaniel J. Wyeth received shabby treatment at the hands of the Rocky Mountain Fur Company and declared to Fitzpatrick and William Sublette of that firm: "I shall roll a stone into your garden which you will never be able to remove." With his party of 41 men and 126 pack animals loaded with the rejected trade goods that he had brought from the East under contract with Milton Sublette, the outraged Wyeth left the Green River rendezvous and proceeded to the Snake River bottom. On July 16, 1834, he started the construction of a trading post at a site some miles north of present-day Pocatello, Idaho. Three weeks later the establishment, Fort Hall, was walled in with close-set cottonwood timbers which stood 15 feet high; bastions, a log storehouse, and cabins were under construction within the enclosure. John Townsend, the Philadelphia scientist and member of Wyeth's party, observed at this juncture that "the work is singularly good, considering the scarcity of proper building tools."

Fort Hall may be accepted as a fair example of the mountain man's small forts built in remote localities with a minimum of tools. Wyeth's equipment was assembled in the East ostensibly to transport a consignment of merchandise overland to a field party of the Rocky Mountain Fur Company. Building a fort did not figure in Wyeth's plan for this pack train, and construction tools were few or lacking in the packs. Even after three years of operation at Fort Hall, when Wyeth sold out to the Hudson's Bay Company, the carpenter tools and agricultural implements that changed hands were valued at no more than $45.00. It is of more than passing interest to note that under the aegis of the Hudson's Bay Company, agriculture became an important pursuit at Fort Hall. The British company continued to operate there for nine years after the settlement of boundary arguments in 1846. The agricultural produce grown at Fort Hall and the blacksmiths' service rendered there became of prime importance to emigrants making their way to Oregon; it is a foregone conclusion that the place was then fully equipped with appropriate tools.

A comprehensive account of Fort Hall history of Nat Wyeth's period, 1834–7, is available in Beidlemen's "Nathaniel Wyeth's Fort Hall." This paper contains an inventory of Wyeth's trade goods and other properties as of 1837. The illustration is based on a contemporary picture in 31st Cong., 2nd sess., Sen. Exec. Doc. No. 1. Drawing by William Macy, Jefferson National Expansion Memorial, St. Louis.

FIG. 91. *Trapper's Winter Cabin in the Friendly Flathead Country, 1833–4.*

Customarily the mountain men "holed up" during the coldest winter months. Certain timbered localities sheltered from storm and removed from the established paths of the hostiles became traditional with the trappers as wintering grounds. Among these favorite places were the Thompson's River, Montana; the vicinity of present-day Ogden, Utah; the mouth of the Muscle Shell; Brown's Hole on the Green River; the Yellowstone, now Livingston, Montana; White River, Utah; Cache Valley, Utah; the Snake, near present-day Menan, Idaho; the Taos and San Luis valleys in New Mexico, and scores of similar places where feed for horses and meat for men could be depended upon. Usually the Indian's leather lodge constituted the trapper's "house" in winter, but some log cabins were also built. The cabin here pictured is described by its builder, W. A. Ferris, a literary mountain man who left a most revealing account of trapper-trader affairs of the 1830's. On January 1, 1834, he wrote: "Our house was now advanced to putting on the roof, for which we had cut a sufficient number of poles, intending when properly placed to cover them with grass, and finally with a coat of earth sufficient to exclude rain or melting snow in the spring." A few days later: "Moved into our house, which was rendered extremely warm and comfortable by having the seams filled with clay, a chimney [and fireplace] composed of sticks and mud, windows covered with thin, transparent, undressed skins which admitted sufficient light, and yet excluded the rain and snow, and a floor constructed of hewn slabs." (Ferris: "Life in the Rocky Mountains," Vol. III, pp. 156, 164.)

Ideally the cabin builder would have equipped himself with spade or shovel, sickle, saw, broadax, mortise ax, adz, chisels, gimlets, augers, hammer and nails, a calking tool, and a trowel. Lacking these, Mr. Ferris and his half-breed assistants may well have accomplished everything with a felling ax, hatchet, knives, and a punch. Wooden pins and rawhide thongs might serve in lieu of spikes and nails, and a wooden paddle could take the place of shovel or spade. Hardwood wedges, driven by a wooden maul or the ax did very well in splitting out puncheons needed for the floor.

Eric Sloane (in *A Museum of Early American Tools*, pp. 24–5) gives an illustrated resume of five systems of notching and fitting logs for cabin walls. William Macy drawing, Jefferson National Expansion Memorial, St. Louis.

land Valley Forge Museum (now the Washington Memorial Museum). Probably this is an early lathing hatchet, a tool which because of its small size, light weight, and all-purpose features often was included in trapper-trader equipment, where it *did not* function in lathing.

Figure 87*e* is a heavy sledge hammer from the Hudson's Bay Company's Fort Nisqually, which was founded in 1833. It is pre-served in the Washington State Historical Society, Tacoma. As early as 1619, the English colonists in Virginia imported this type of sledge,[2] and thereafter the big blacksmith's hammers went to those English settlements and posts, east and west, wherever smith-ies were established. They weigh from 6 to 16 pounds and are relatively imperishable, but, seemingly, few with known histories have been preserved in museums. This is probably due to the fact that sledges were seldom abandoned, broken, or lost; they were usually transferred from declining establishments to new scenes of action and there continued in use.

Figure 87*f* shows a carpenter's adz recorded as having been made by D. F. Barton, New York, in 1832. It is now in the Washington State Historical Society, Tacoma. This specimen was used in Indiana by D. J. Settle in 1834 and was brought by him to

[2] J. Hudson: "Iron at Jamestown, Virginia," *The Iron Worker* XX: 3 (1956), p. 9.

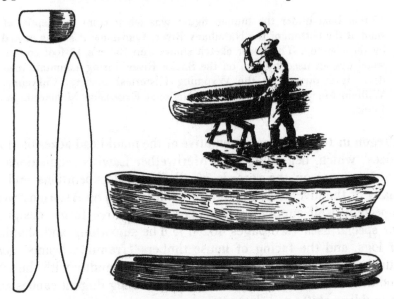

FIG. 92. *The Hand Adz and the Dugout Canoe.*

The trapper's life in the American wilds involved much activity in and on the inland waters. One of the great reliances of the beaver hunter was the log canoe; veritably it was an institution, east and west. Because cottonwood logs were to be had throughout much of the Western beaver country, many of the dugouts made by the mountain men were cottonwood. Pine trees served even better, and on the Pacific slope the acme of dugout perfection could be had in the Indian-made cedar canoes. If the adz appeared in backcountry trapper outfits, it was usually there because of its special usefulness in building dugouts. With felling ax and hand adz the selected tree could be cut, shaped, and hollowed with no great investment of time. Prior to his contact with the white man, the Indian combined fire and his stone or heavy shell scrapers in slowly hollowing out his log canoe. The hollow shell often was further shaped by filling it with water into which hot rocks were placed. The resulting hot water softened the wood, and it was possible then for the Indian to spread and shape the walls of the vessel by forcing transverse timbers between the gunwales. The white man dispensed with this shaping. Usually he attained a satisfactory result by chopping with the felling ax and broadax, when available, and with the steel adz. Thomas James tells of four men at the Three Forks of the Missouri, 1810, making two dugouts in three days. The west-bound Lewis and Clark party on the Sweetwater in October 1805 made four large dugouts and one smaller one from pine trees in nine days. Existing specimens of the trapper-trader dugouts are quite numerous. In this illustration the outline drawings at left represent a 15-foot cypress dugout preserved in the Cabildo, New Orleans. The

17-foot boat under the human figure was taken from the depths of mud at the bottom of the Natalbany River, Louisiana; it also is owned by the Cabildo. The lower sketch shows Jim Baker's 17-foot cotton-wood dugout used by him on the Snake River during mountain-man days. It is owned by the Wyoming Historical Society, Cheyenne. William Macy drawing, Jefferson National Expansion Memorial, St. Louis.

Oregon in 1849. It is representative of the maul-head adzes or "foot adzes" which, beginning with Meriwether Lewis's requisitions of 1803, appear on the records of all Western expeditions and in many of the inventories of the fur companies. The Astorians were especially well supplied with adzes of the three forms designed for special uses (see pages 402–7). The smoothing and shaping of logs, and the facing of house timbers (framing, beams, floor puncheons, sills, doors, etc.) were done most handily with the adz, and the tool was especially necessary in making dugout canoes and in building skiffs and flatboats.

In the southwestern United States, a rather distinct form of adz is found occasionally on historic sites of Spanish provenance (fig. 95). The uses to which this type of adz was put were the same as previously described. The Indians of the northwest coast, always superior in their wood-carving techniques, met the shortage of conventional adzes by devising their own adz, as pictured in figure 96.

Figure 87*g* is a heavy hoe of the early trade style. Now No. 28657 in the Milwaukee Public Museum, the specimen was recovered from a Menomini Indian site. Somewhat similar specimens, probably of French origin, were recovered by Quimby [3] at the Fort St. Joseph site, Michigan, and at the Fatherland plantation near Natchez, Mississippi, both of which were occupied by Indians and whites, 1700–60. In the statement of expenses met by the French in waging war against the Fox Indians in 1716, hoes are listed at "10 livres and 10 sols, each"—approximately $2.60.[4] In 1808 the United States Office of Indian Affairs paid 70¢ each for the largest (9-inch) hoes, Philadelphia-made; the American Fur Company in 1821 paid $1.25 each for "Canadian hoes." It is interesting to note that the Collins Company [5] still produces for the Latin Americas

[3] G. I. Quimby: "Indian Trade Objects in Michigan and Louisiana," Michigan Academy of Science, Arts, and Letters *Papers*, Vol. XXVII (1941), p. 548.
[4] Quoted by C. E. Brown: "Indian Trade Implements," pp. 73–4.
[5] Collins & Company: *Catalogo Illustrado*, p. 69.

FIG. 93. *Making the Expendable Flatboat.*

At numerous establishments on the Missouri, the Platte, the Yellowstone, and some other important tributaries, the fur companies commonly built large scows, or flatboats, in each of which two or three tons of furs and skins could be floated to St. Louis. Packs of buffalo robes were particularly regarded to be appropriate cargo. Upon reaching its destination, the flatboat usually was dismantled, and its rough planks and timbers were sold for lumber. Since the making of flatboats was premeditated, the "boatyards" were always supplied with appropriate tools needed for the projects. Felling axes, broadaxes, adzes, chisels, slicks, augers, hammers, nails, spikes, bolts, angle irons, calking irons and, of special importance, pit saws, crosscut saws, and handsaws were used. On the Missouri drainage, the lumber for flatboats ordinarily came from cottonwoods and hardwoods. West of the Rockies, flatboats were made by the Hudson's Bay Company for freighting on the Columbia system. Here the lumber was cut from pine trees, and the boats moved upstream as well as down; there was no intentional demolition of flatboats on the upper reaches of the Columbia. Ferris (in "Life in the Rocky Mountains," pp. 156, 180) tells of the delivery in December 1833 of fresh vegetables from Fort Colville to the Hudson's Bay Company employees deep in the Flathead country, "7 or 8 days journey" from the Columbia. The two flatboats that brought the vegetables made the return trip laden with furs. In April 1834 Ferris left Flathead Post on Clark's Fork of the Columbia in a flatboat "loaded with about a ton of merchandise for the Horse Plain, and manned by four stout Canadians who propelled it with poles where the water was shallow, but when its depth would not admit of this, recourse was had to paddles." There is here implied the circumstance of ambitious navigation, a picture that helps one understand the accumulations of artifacts unearthed at such remote trading post sites as Walla Walla, Okanagan, Spokane, and Flathead. Drawing by William Macy, Jefferson National Expansion Memorial, St. Louis.

"Hoes for Brush" that are heavy and of the same pattern as this Menomini piece.

Figure 87*h* is probably a shingling hatchet. It is preserved as No. B-130/51 in the Wyoming Historical Society, Cheyenne. Perhaps the most notable existing Western specimen of this class is the hatchet carried to the Columbia by Sergeant Pat Gass, carpenter with the Lewis and Clark Expedition. The specimen accompanied by documents is owned by members of the Gass family. Trappers' shingling hatchets were not limited to use in shingling, of course. Most of the "permanent" Western trading posts did have shake roofs, and interior walls sometimes were finished with shakes; shingling hatchets thus found a limited conventional use, but their real purpose in the hands of the trapper was to function as extra-good tomahawks. Indians everywhere looked upon them as all-purpose tools and were happy to get them. A number of Indian burials, east and west, have yielded specimens now preserved in museums.

Figure 87*i* shows an old-time hoe found at the Riggs-Williamson Mission site, near Montevideo, Minnesota. No. 507.

FIG. 94. *Making the "Mackinaw" Boat.*

The documents and the printed literature of the fur trade are quite replete with accounts of the Mackinaw boat since it found wide use for one hundred years or more on the Great Lakes, the Ohio, and the Mississippi as well as on the Missouri system. It was pointed at both ends, keel-less and flat-bottomed, 10 or 12 feet in the beam, about 40 feet long, 3 or 4 feet deep (hold), and with a cargo of some twelve tons, drew 18 or 20 inches of water. Like the flatboat, it was made in the vicinity of numerous trading posts along the Missouri; but unlike the flatboat, it sometimes made the tedious upstream journey back to the place of its origin. On the Great Lakes it navigated anywhere and everywhere under the propulsion of oars and the wind, but on the Missouri it was valued primarily for its capacity to transport sizable cargoes downstream quite rapidly and safely. At Mackinac Island during the early decades of the 1800's, the American Fur Company imported numerous "Mackina" boats and their sails and other accouterments from Montreal. One hundred thirty dollars for one complete outfit was the maximum price paid. On the Missouri, the American Fur Company, like all other interests there, made its own Mackinaw boats. An interesting running account of the production of the boats in 1832 at Fort Pierre is found in the daily log of that post (Chittenden: *The American Fur Trade* [1954 edn.] II, 975–83). The boat yard, named "Navy Yard" by the company, was the site of logging, sawing, and construction. The raw materials and the tools were the same as described for the flatboat shown in Figure 93—with emphasis on the pit saws. William Macy drawing, Jefferson National Expansion Memorial, St. Louis.

It is in the Minnesota Historical Society's collections. The Mission mentioned was active 1840–50, but the grounds thereabouts had been occupied earlier by a trading post. In the eighteenth century the shops at Fort Pitt were a source of supply for English-type hoes. In September 1761 the Huron Indians at Detroit asked Sir William Johnson to "procure us some hoes for our corn of which we stand in as much need as of anything else." Johnson instructed Croghan, his deputy: "I have promised the nations living in the neighborhood

FIG. 95. *Early Spanish Adz (Handle Supplied).*

This adz was found in the ruins of the Spanish Mission buildings at Galesteo, New Mexico. No. 99, Colorado Historical Society, Denver. This poll-less, round-eye form dates back to the 1600's (Sloane: *Early American Tools,* p. 27). It is still made by the Collins Company, Connecticut, for the Latin American trade as the "Modelo Español" (Collins Company: *Catalogo Illustrado,* pp. 25, 26, "Modelo No. 447" and "Modelo No. 520").

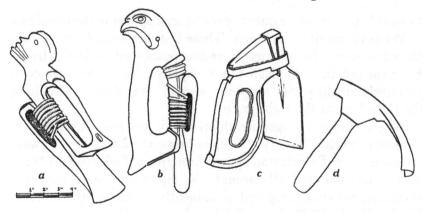

FIG. 96. *Northwest Coast Indian Adz.*

Pacific Coast Indian tribes produced some of the world's most interesting wood carvings, such as ornamentation of the plank walls of their houses, symbols on gravemarkers and "posts," and figurines and other decorations on their canoes. Even the canoes themselves are masterpieces of hand carving. These large carved objects find exquisite smaller counterparts in the form of bowls, platters, plates, tubs, buckets, spoons, and tool handles. Much of the finer carving was done with the crooked knife previously described (page 216), but the ax and the adz usually prepared the way. A small hand adz was particularly well suited for much of this work. In primitive times the coastal Indians mounted a Celt-like blade of chert or obsidian on a short wooden handle. After the white man brought the iron ax, these Indians did not long delay in adapting the trade-ax head to this special use. True to form, the Indian often made the wooden handle fancy as well as practical. This type of hand adz with removable iron blade may have been original with the Indians, but it was "nothing new under the sun." A similar tool (*c*) had long been in use by white men and is still to be had. Specimen *a* is from Nootka Sound; it is now in the Portland Art Museum. The adz shown in *b* was drawn after a photograph in Portland Art Museum. Specimen *c* is a hand adz made by the Collins Company. In *d* is a cooper's adz now in the Bucks County Historical Society, Doylestown, Pennsylvania.

of Detroit a parcel of hoes for weeding their corn fields. You will order a couple of hundred of the middling sort to be made immediately [at Fort Pitt] and sent by the first conveyance." [6] In the West, hoes in moderate numbers appear in the lists of merchandise procured by the Office of Indian Affairs and distributed as gifts to

[6] Sir William Johnson: *The Papers of Sir William Johnson* (13 vols.; Albany, 1921–62), III, 501.

Indians.[7] Hoes in lesser quantity sometimes appear in the manifests of Western trading companies. These last, presumably, were consigned to traders for local use at trading posts—not for Indian trade. Even though the American Fur Company's purchases were comparatively small, some "shopping around" was done in obtaining the right hoes at the right price.[8]

Figure 87*j* is a tanged ice chisel now in the Allen County-Fort Wayne Historical Society. "Picks to break the ice in winter" were included in the French trade goods brought to Tadoussac in 1626. From that time and all through the eighteenth and nineteenth centuries, ice chisels figured prominently in the northern trade. Umfreville, in 1790, listed the ice chisel as third in importance among the items necessary to the sustenance of the Indian and his family.[9] An example of the use of the ice chisel is pictured in figure 16, "The Old-time Indians' Winter Hunt" (page 98). Beauchamp illustrates and describes a tanged specimen found in Fleming, New York, in 1887, which is like the Fort Wayne piece.[1] The Astorians, who took sixty of these to the Columbia, designated them "Broad Ice Chisels" to distinguish them from the twenty-five "Narrow Ice Chisels" also in their possession (page 404). Rectangular ice chisels of this "broad" character are still on the market, but they are socketed.[2] During recent years a number of interesting slender, rodlike ice chisels, 10 to 16 inches long, have been recovered from riverbeds along the historic canoe routes between the Ottawa River and the Upper Great Lakes in the course of the "underwater search" conducted by the Minnesota Historical Society and the Province of Ontario.[3] Presumably these chisels were contained in kegs or bales of miscellaneous trade goods that were being transported into the interior of the country. The canoes in

[7] An order for 1,000 hoes to be supplied by N. Lloyd, Philadelphia, 1808, is detailed in "Letter Book, Pa., 198," U. S. Office of Indian Affairs, Philadelphia (MS), National Archives. See also invoice, merchandise received from Gen. William Clark for presents to Indians, 1823, in Forsyth Papers, Vol. 2, Item 2 (MSS), Wisconsin Historical Society.

[8] Edward H. Jacot, New York, was one of the jobbers who negotiated with Ramsay Crooks for a hoe contract. American Fur Company Papers, letter of December 21, 1841, Item no. 11915.

[9] *The Present State of Hudson's Bay*, quoted by Innis: *The Fur Trade*, p. 134.

[1] Beauchamp: *Metallic Implements*, p. 75, Fig. 76.

[2] Collins Company: *Catalogo Illustrado*, p. 58, No. 523.

[3] John Macfie in *Beaver* (Winter 1962), pp. 48–57; Sigurd F. Olson in *National Geographic* (September 1963), pp. 412–35; *Diving into the Past*, eds. Holmquist and Wheeler (1964), pp. 72–7.

which they traveled were overturned or otherwise wrecked in rough water, and the merchandise has reposed in the depths for a couple of hundred years or more.

Figure 87k shows a cold chisel from the site of the 1832 trappers' rendezvous, Pierre's Hole, Idaho. The specimen is preserved in the National Park Service Fur Trade Museum, Grand Teton National Park. The chisel was found in 1900 by Judge S. W. Swanner while digging post holes along the banks of Leigh Creek, Tetonia, Idaho. The artifact was 18 inches below the surface of the ground in a locality known to have been occupied by some of the trapper camps in 1832. Cold chisels, albeit few in number, have never been absent, beginning with the Lewis and Clark requisitions, from the Western fur traders' inventories and invoices.

Fire Steels and Tinder Boxes

INEXPENSIVE though it was, the fire-making flint and steel of the trader was of prime importance in his intercourse with the tribesmen. This was true in the earliest years of the trade and continued almost to its end. During the late eighteenth and early nineteenth centuries the popular lightweight steel retailed for a cent or two, and quite commonly it was presented without charge to the Indian whose good will was sought. The more sophisticated tinderboxes and strike-a-lights found only occasional use among Indians, but they were better known in the trading posts and in the wilderness camps of the white trappers. Probably the important thing to be said about any of these fire makers is that in their day they were almost indispensable, and even for the white man, they rested at the heart of his concept of and appreciation for fire. To the Indian, they became a part of the mysterious force that made fire sacred.

Figure 97a shows an oval fire steel from the site of Fort St. Joseph, Michigan; the specimen is now in the Fort St. Joseph Museum. This type appears among French artifacts of the late seventeenth and early eighteenth centuries, which have been recovered in a number of places in the Old Northwest,[4] and it continued to feature in the trade conducted by other nationals at least until

[4] Wittry: "The Bell Site"; Petersen: Gentlemen on the Frontier (Mackinac Island, Mich., 1964); Maxwell: Excavations at Fort Michilimackinac; and Brown: "Fire Steels," The Wisconsin Archeologist (January 1931).

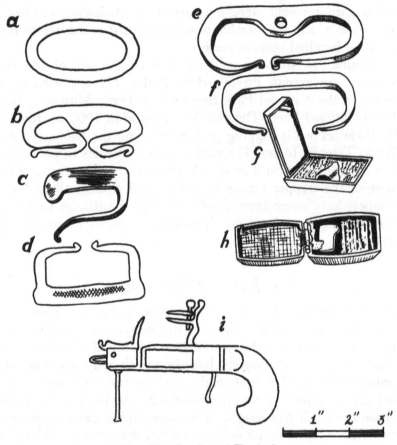

FIG. 97. *Fire Steels and Tinderboxes.*

White trapper and Indian alike made fire with flint and steel carried in the "possibles" bag. A slicing blow with the conveniently shaped steel struck against a small piece of flint caused sparks to fly. The downward directed shower of sparks was caught in a small bed of "punk" prepared for the purpose, and some of the fine fibers of inflammable tinder smoldered under the heat of the sparks. Dried, decayed maple wood was a favorite source of punk, but other decayed wood and also tow served. The tiny fire in the punk was coaxed into flame by the carefully controlled blowing of breath upon it. More substantial materials—dry wood shavings, fine splinters of wood, dry leaves and grass, and small sticks—were then used to kindle a bigger fire. The method was crude and troublesome, but it was an improvement upon the fire-plow and fire drill used by Indians through the millennia. James Mulcahy drawing, Jefferson National Expansion Memorial, St. Louis.

the 1840's. In the underwater search conducted at Double Rapids on the French River out of Lake Nipissing in 1961, oval steels were found in their original packs with appropriate flints inserted in the space in the center of the steels.[5] In the journals of some North West Company agents are several bits of testimony which reveal that Canadian fire steels were sometimes presented to Indians. On the Red River in 1800 Alexander Henry gave a single fire steel to an Indian servant. In 1806, when he was with the Mandans on the Missouri, Henry presented his Mandan host "one steel and five flints."[6] In 1805, on the Missouri above the Mandans, François Larocque gave to a party of Crow and Shoshone Indians "8 fire steels and flints."[7] The requisition for "Presents to be given to Indians" prepared by Meriwether Lewis in 1803 includes "288 steels for striking fire." It was planned that these should be handed out freely all the way across the country. Under "Camp Equipage" Lewis on the same occasion asked for "30 steels for striking or making fire, and 100 flints do do do." These were intended for the personal use of members of the Lewis and Clark Expedition.[8] The U. S. Office of Indian Affairs, Philadelphia, on February 29, 1808, ordered from William Gobright "6 gross fire steels to be imported by Teackle, and 2 dozen tin tinder boxes at 3.75 per dozen, complete with extinguisher, fire steel, and 2 flints, each."[9] In 1805–6 John Johnston at the Fort Wayne Indian Factory included in his account of disbursements "2 gross Fire Steels . . . $7.20."[1] One of the more interesting Indian Office transactions was conducted by an unnamed "Chief's Lady" who at the Detroit Indian Factory in 1822 paid "16 prime beaver pelts" (worth approximately $80.00) for an unspecified number of fire steels. If the price charged for these steels were at all in line with the then-prevailing Great Lakes value, the "Chief's Lady" needed two pack horses just to transport her steels.[2]

[5] John Macfie: "Short River Reveals Evidence of Long History," *Beaver* (Winter 1962), p. 52 (photo).
[6] Coues, ed.: *Manuscript Journals,* I, 97, 330.
[7] L. J. Burpee, ed.: *Journal of Larocque from the Assiniboine to the Yellowstone, 1805* (Ottawa: Publications Canadian Archives; 1910), p. 23.
[8] Jackson, ed.: *Letters,* pp. 72–3.
[9] Original order (MS copy) in National Archives, Washington, D.C.
[1] Griswold: *Fort Wayne,* p. 479.
[2] U. S. Indian Department, Day Book, April–August 1822 (MS in National Archives).

American Fur Company correspondence in 1838, 1839, and 1840 reveals that the oval steel commonly was sent into mountain-man country by Pierre Chouteau, Jr., and Company. These steels, "Warranted Bright Oval," were supplied by Hiram Cutler of Sheffield at 30¢ per dozen, and they came from the jobber put up in papers of one dozen to a package.[3] When Smith, Jackson and Sublette purchased the William Ashley merchandise in the field (Cache Valley, Utah) in 1826, fire steels were paid for at the rate of $2.00 per pound.[4] The oval steels are about 3 inches long, and the opening is big enough to allow the insertion of three fingers when the object is gripped for striking. The metal is flat and $3\frac{3}{16}$ inches thick; the weight, four or five steels to the pound.

Figure 97*b* shows a European fire steel A.D. 700–900; the specimen is preserved in the Naturhistorisches Museum, Vienna. It was found in a grave in southern Austria. The same form occurs in the graves of the Franks throughout much of modern France, and it persisted in most of south central Europe as long as fire steels were needed. For a specimen that came to America see figure 97*e*.

Shown in figure 97*c* is a more sophisticated fire steel used by a city dweller. It is part of the Morton Collection, Jefferson National Expansion Memorial, St. Louis.

Figure 97*d* is an Onondaga fire steel that was still in the hands of an Indian when collected in the late nineteenth century.[5] Brown describes and illustrates a similar piece found in a colonial tinderbox at Lexington, Massachusetts, which has the name "Harris" stamped on one face.[6] Approximately the same form is found at Fort St. Joseph, Michigan. These were individually forged—not mass-produced as were the "bright ovals" (fig. 97*a*).

Figure 97*e* shows a large example of the ancient Frankish form (fig. 97*b*) contained in a Menominee Indian medicine bag. The artifact is No. A-7051, Neville Public Museum, Green Bay, Wisconsin. During the very early years of contact with the whites, it was common practice among some tribes to make the town chief responsible for the care of the recognized sacred fire-making equip-

[3] American Fur Company Papers, items no. 5106, 5232, 7745 (microfilm reel 5); Orders Outward, I, 334, 383, in reel 12.

[4] Dale L. Morgan, ed.: *The West of William H. Ashley* (Denver: Old West Publishing Company; 1964), pp. 158–9.

[5] Beauchamp: *Metallic Implements*, p. 76.

[6] Brown: "Fire Steels," *The Wisconsin Archeologist*, Jan., 1931, pp. 65–68.

ment used in starting annual ceremonial fires. In some tribes, the custom was retained until well into the twentieth century. Speck says of the Yuchi in Oklahoma, originally a southern tribe: "A fire steel is more often used as a sparker, as it is more effective [than are the two pieces of flint of the ancient ceremony].[7]

The fire steel shown in figure 97*f* is a style favored by whites and Indians alike. The specimen is catalogued as No. 1986 in the Chamberlain Memorial Museum, Three Oaks, Michigan. A "Hudson Bay" fire steel is like this but with the curved ends extended until they touch.[8]

Figure 97*g* shows a tinderbox with flint and linen tow that is now part of the Chamberlain Memorial Museum collection, Three Oaks, Michigan. This small brass box has a hinged steel cover with a latch. When the cover is open, as shown, the edge provides the steel against which the small flint can be struck. Resulting sparks fall upon the tinder in the box, causing a tiny smoldering fire that can be coaxed into flames when placed under appropriate kindling materials.

Shown in figure 97*h* is an all-steel tinderbox with tinder and flint. It is specimen No. 169 in the Neville Public Museum, Green Bay, Wisconsin. Fibers of unspun flax and scrapings from linen cloth often constituted tinder for fire makers in the "settlements." In the wilds, a fairly suitable punk could always be obtained from dead pine trees or from dry, decayed portions of hickory, maple, or oak trees. Swanton quotes from a dozen accounts of Indian fire making written by observers in the 17th and 18th centuries.[9] The principle of ignition through the striking of sparks from steel was always the same, but the efficiency in arrangements of paraphernalia improved through the years. Ultimately, slivers of sulfur-tipped wood made it easier for the fire makers to transfer a flame from the glowing coal in the punk to the kindling of the fire proper. Handy little pocket-sized tinderboxes of the kind illustrated in figures 97*g* and 97*h* must have been popular; specimens are to be seen in many collections. There are also numerous specimens of larger types for

[7] Frank G. Speck: "Ethnology of the Yuchi Indians," *Anthropology Publications*, Univ. of Pennsylvania, I:1 (1909), p. 42.

[8] Charles E. Hanson has one in his Fur Trade Museum, Loomis, Nebraska, which was obtained from the Northern Plains Indian Arts and Crafts Association.

[9] John R. Swanton: *The Indians of the Southeastern United States*, Bureau of American Ethnology, Bulletin 137 (1946), pp. 422–7.

the home, in which the conventional steels, flints, and tinder are contained loosely in covered metal boxes—round, rectangular, and cylindrical.

Seldom did the trapper-trader write about his fire making, but George Ruxton, always to be depended upon for descriptions of the minutiae of the doings of the mountain men, has this to say about LeBonte's preparation for cooking the evening meal:

> Fire making is a simple process with the mountaineers. Their bullet pouches always contain a flint and steel, and sundry pieces of "punk"—a pithy substance found in dead pine trees—or tinder; and pulling a handful of dry grass, which they screw into a nest, they place the lighted punk in this, and, closing the grass over it, wave it in the air, when it soon ignites, and readily kindles the dry sticks forming the foundation of the fire.[1]

The occasion referred to was Ruxton's meeting with the trappers, LeBonte and Killbuck, in South Park, Colorado—Ute country—in the spring of 1847.

Figure 97*i* is a flintlock "strike-a-light" or fire lighter. The specimen is preserved as No. N-4937 in the Milwaukee Public Museum. Pistol-like strike-a-lights worked on the principle of the flint gun, but the pan ordinarily did not contain gunpowder. Tow, or "lint," was contained in the box under the frizzen. The cock, armed with a pistol flint, was pulled back and, when released by the trigger pull, descended upon the frizzen, which lifted under the impact, thus exposing the tinder to a shower of sparks. Under adverse conditions in wet or stormy weather, a few grains of gunpowder sometimes were added to the tinder, thus improving the chances of attaining a glowing coal in the box. Sometimes a rectangular, covered receptacle was built into the side of the strike-a-light as storage space for a reserve supply of tinder. The specimen illustrated has this receptacle. Strike-a-lights have been found in Iroquois graves that date back to the nineteenth century.[2] Evidence of their distribution in the early Far West has not come to the attention of the present writer, but, no doubt, they did find some

---

[1] Ruxton: *Life in the Far West* (Hafen edition) (Norman, Okla.: Univ. of Oklahoma Press; 1951), p. 44.

[2] T. M. Hamilton, comp.: "Indian Trade Guns," *The Missouri Archeologist* (December 1960), pp. 100, 112.

use by Western Indians and by traders and trappers. The use of the flintlock pistol and long arm in starting fires must have been fairly common practice among the mountain men, as it was among earlier eastern frontiersmen.[3] To make a flintlock gun function as a strike-a-light, it was only necessary to put a temporary plug in the touchhole—if the piece were loaded—bring the cock to full cock, lift the frizzen and place tinder in the pan in lieu of gunpowder, return the frizzen to its closed position, then pull the trigger. Sparks showered into the pan ignited the tinder, thus producing the glowing coal needed to fire the awaiting kindling materials.

In sunny weather, the "burning glass" afforded means of starting fires. The glasses quite commonly appear in the fur-company invoices, and Captain Meriwether Lewis wrote "100 Burning Glasses" into his requisition of 1803. Following through on the Lewis request, the supply officer, Israel Wheelen, ordered from C. and Th. Denkla of Philadelphia "8 [doz.] burning glasses 1½ Drs . . . $12.00." These lenses show up in the summary of Lewis and Clark purchases as weighing 11.25 pounds.[4] From the beginning of their westward trek, the explorers made it a point to present a "sunglass" or two to each group of Indians with whom they held council. The *Journals* record numerous instances of such giftmaking, and it appears that they still had some of the glasses on hand when they started the return journey in the spring of 1806. On April 2, 1806, Captain Lewis, then en route eastward on the Columbia, wrote: "Capt. Clark hired one of the Cashhooks [Indian] for a birning glass, to pilot him to the entrance of the Multnomah [Willamette] river and took him on board with him." [5] The United States Army at this time, and later, took cognizance of the usefulness of the burning glass as it offered instruction and guidance to troops: "If without other means of making fire, a spark may be obtained by taking out the object glass of a telescope, if there be one, and using it as a burning glass. The inside of a highly polished watch case also might answer." [6]

[3] John Dillin: *The Kentucky Rifle* (Washington, D.C.: Nat'l Rifle Ass'n; 1924), pp. 57–8.

[4] Jackson, ed.: *Letters*, pp. 72, 86, 93.

[5] Bernard De Voto, ed.: *The Journals of Lewis and Clark* (Boston: Houghton Mifflin; 1953), p. 339.

[6] Edward S. Farrow: *Mountain Scouting, A Hand-book for Officers and Soldiers on the Frontier* (New York, 1881), p. 75.

SUMMARY

THERE ARE CONCLUSIONS TO BE DRAWN FROM THE EVIDENCES afforded by the foregoing accounts. One seems especially worthy of a final note. There can be no doubt that the westering American frequently entered the wilds well prepared to establish many of the symbols of his civilization. Almost at once his trading posts became small islands of a culture largely new to the aborigines. The savage welcomed the conveniences to be acquired in the form of certain tools and he grabbed at the better weapons, but generally he could not have cared less about the niceties in the white man's ways. His women bowed to the trappers' needs, however, and the trappers adopted some Indian traits. A new breed of half-Indian presently made it easier for the white man to hold place as "top dog" in the wild West, and there came about a remarkable blending of Iron and Stone Age practices. The artifacts resulting from this acculturation constitute some striking evidences of the fallacy of the notion that wilderness "conquers" the invader; the invader's iron brought about a conquest all its own. Here the invading white man "rolled with the punches." Some of the punishment taken by him was devastating locally and temporarily, but on the broad front he overcame both the forces of nature and the hostilities of man. Iron tools in the hands of the white man contributed to this triumph, directly and insidiously, in that it lessened the Indian's old-time self-sufficiency. In a surprisingly brief moment the Indian became a dependent; he looked upon the trader's merchandise as necessary and, to a degree, he modified his traditional techniques so as to take advantage of iron tools. He craved the help of white blacksmiths and ultimately he himself attempted rudimentary work in iron. A few of his kind became expert and, with the exception of the most isolated groups, practically all embraced iron as a boon. The Stone Age ended in the American West very soon indeed after tool shipments of the kind itemized on pages 402–7 reached the wilds.

CHAPTER VII

Irons in the Fire

SHIELDS, WILLARD, AND OTHER EARLY SMITHS

IN A DAY OF INTERNAL COMBUSTION ENGINES, RUBBER TIRES, the ubiquitous hardware store, novelty shop, and five-and-ten, it is difficult to sense the smithy's onetime all-pervading importance in town and country. In 1796 Philadelphia counted a population of 55,000; the city directory for that year listed 133 blacksmith shops. This was not extraordinary; all cities needed and obtained a somewhat similar proportion of service from the ironworkers. Throughout the countryside also the traditional village smithy flourished and, as might be expected, the venturing pioneers who pushed the frontiers westward placed the blacksmith in the vanguard of their moving forces. The Hudson's Bay Company sent blacksmiths to the Bay posts very early in the development of wilderness business—even before the close of the seventeenth century. Blacksmiths of that day were paid from fifteen to twenty-five pounds per year. Those adept at repairing guns were in special demand. Bookkeepers at the posts received one half to two thirds the pay given to smiths. Bookkeepers were important also, but there was something immediately crucial about the services of the blacksmith. The French at Mackinac employed two blacksmiths there by 1742 or earlier and aspired to increase this number because of the demands made by the local Indians. British military forces stationed at Green Bay in 1761–2 were entreated by the

Indians there to bring a blacksmith or gunsmith to the post. Lieutenant James Gorrell complied with the request. By the second half of the eighteenth century, major establishments around Hudson Bay (York Factory, for example) engaged in a veritable manufacturing business turning out axes and other ironworks in volume. There is implied here that heavy equipment, such as forges and anvils, were brought to the posts and that raw materials—bar iron, round iron, sheet iron, etc.—were available to the smiths in the wilderness. No insurmountable problem of transportation was involved in setting up these shops; all of the posts mentioned were served by big boats navigating in deep waters. In the periods indicated, the greater part of the iron used was imported from Europe.

When Lewis and Clark organized their corps of discovery (1803–4), they made certain that some capable mechanics already in the Regular Army were transferred to their command. Ultimately several categories of handicrafts were represented in the enlisted personnel of the Lewis and Clark Expedition and, as was demonstrated in the course of the phenomenal trek, more than two of the men could do blacksmithing. However, two were especially identified as blacksmiths: John Shields, an enlistee from Kentucky, and Alexander Willard, who transferred from the U. S. Corps of Artillerists. Shields gave a great account of himself in serving the expedition, since he possessed exceptional skill in repairing guns (page 41). When in January 1807 Captain Lewis transmitted to the Secretary of War the roll of the men of the expedition, "with some remarks on their respective merits and services," he said of Shields: "John Shields. Private. Has received the pay only of a private. Nothing was more peculiarly useful to us, in various situations, than the skill and ingenuity of this man as an artist in repairing our guns, accouterments, etc; and should it be thought proper to allow him something as an artificer, he has well deserved it."

Willard was a youthful Yankee who served so well in his specified craft during the great march that Meriwether Lewis, as governor of the Louisiana Territory in 1808, made him a government employee responsible for the blacksmithing for the Sauks and Foxes at the villages near the site of the later Fort Madison. In 1809 under the aegis of William Clark, Willard was moved to the blacksmith's job at the Shawnee-Delaware agency.[1] More will be said later about blacksmiths at Indian agencies.

The forge, "bellowses," anvil, heavy blacksmith's tools, and iron stock taken by Lewis and Clark to Fort Mandan do not appear on Lewis's requisitions of 1803, and there are no known invoices pertaining to such items. However, the *Journals* contain numerous entries which show clearly that the fort boasted an equipped blacksmith shop and that the blacksmiths were kept well employed. Perhaps this equipment was obtained at the United States military establishments at Kaskaskia or from government stores at St. Louis. At any rate, blacksmith's equipment and supplies were on the Lewis and Clark keelboat when the expedition left Wood River in May 1804. John Shields and Alexander Willard "set up shop," at least in a temporary way, very soon after the "barge" was tied up before the site of the future Fort Mandan on November 3, 1804. Two weeks later the keelboat was unloaded, and on November 20 the fort was occupied. Thereupon Shields and Willard were really in business. All winter "the Indians brought corn, beans, and squashes, which they very readily gave for getting their axes and kettles mended. . . . The Indians come in great numbers for the purpose of having their utensils repaired. . . . The Indians continue to purchase repairs with grain of different kinds. . . ."

The fuel for the blacksmith's fire was "coalwood" (charcoal). Clark wrote: "We are now burning a large coal pit to mend the Indians hatchets and to make their war axes [text page 276], the only means by which we procure corn from them. . . ."

In the spring of 1805, Clark expressed his gratification: "The blacksmiths have proved a happy resorce in our present situation as I believe it would have been difficult to have devised any other method to have procured corn from the natives."

No one has determined the exact nature of the Fort Mandan forge. Quite certainly it was small but it was no miniature set. Its hearth (fig. 98a) received an air tube from the bellows and was supported at convenient level upon a pedestal of fieldstones. Presumably, the bellows was operated in conventional manner by a pivoted overhead pole, which under power applied by the smith's hand, lifted the hinged, flat bottom (fig. 98b) of the accordion-like

[1] Donald Jackson, ed.: *Letters of the Lewis and Clark Expedition, 1783–1854* (Urbana, Ill.: Univ. of Illinois Press; 1962), pp. 367, 372.

FIG. 98. *Lewis and Clark Blacksmith's Forge,*
Fort Mandan, 1804–5.

air pump. The lifting of the bottom, or floor, folded the leather walls (fig. 98c) of a lower air chamber. This folding compressed the air of the lower chamber, forcing it against the stationary middle member (fig. 98d) of the bellows in which is a release valve. Under pressure, the air from the lower chamber poured through this valve into an upper chamber that is also enclosed within leather walls (fig. 98e). Under compression, the air lifted the top member (fig. 98f) of the bellows, thereby enlarging the upper air chamber, as shown in the figure. When the pressure was sufficient, a valve leading to the air pipe opened and allowed the air to rush into the lower part of the charged firebox. This, of course, resulted in something of a blast of fire. Under its own weight the floor of the bellows would drop to "open" position as soon as the smith released the overhead pole. An intake valve allowed a new supply of air to enter the lower chamber, and the pumping and superheating could be repeated until the iron in the fire attained the desired bright-red color judged by the smith to be the sign of "readiness."

Clark reported: "The Indians here much surprised at the Bellos and our method of makeing sundry articles of Iron. They consider [the work] a very great medicine." The Mandans and Minnetarees made continuous demands upon the small smithy for repairs and replacements, but Shields and Willard managed to manufacture a few new axes to be carried westward by the expedition. When the Lewis and Clark party moved up the Missouri in the spring of 1805, the blacksmith's equipment was taken along;

however, Private Joseph Whitehouse records in his journal, June 11, 1805, that the cache made by the explorers at the Marias River received "the bellowses and tools." Captain Lewis elucidates in his journal entry at Marias River, June 9: "We had determined to leave our blacksmith's bellows and tools here and [just before caching] used them in making necessary repare of some of our arms, particularly my Airgun the mainspring of which was broken." There are numerous later records in the *Journals* which show that Shields continued to repair guns all along the way. Some of the work involved major jobs of replacing stocks, cutting gun barrels, shaping new springs, and making new lock parts. Obviously some tools, such as handsaws, a hacksaw, files, rasps, hand vise, light hammers, drawknives, chisels, and screwdrivers, were not left behind. The context of the diaries also confirms the idea that spare gun parts and some small supply of raw materials in the form of sheet brass, iron and brass wire, block tin, rod iron, and sheet iron continued to find place in the loads.

The Marias cache was visited on the return journey in 1806. Lewis records that the cache was lifted on July 28, and with the recovered properties the party proceeded down river to the Mandans. Sergeant Patrick Gass tells that on August 17, 1806, "Lewis and Clark presented our blacksmiths tools to Charbonneau supposing they might be useful to the [Mandans] nation." Capt. Clark recorded that Charbonneau was discharged and paid off on August 17. This interpreter, husband of Sacajawea, "was offered conveyance to the Illinois if he chose to go. He declined . . . observing that he had no acquaintance or prospects of making a liveing below, and must continue to live in the way he had done." So, Charbonneau and his "blacksmith shop" remained with the Mandans, thus establishing the earliest known "permanent" smithy on the upper Missouri.

The Smithy on the Fur Frontier

As told elsewhere (page 7), American traders and trappers entered the upper Missouri country hard on the heels of Lewis and Clark. Manuel Lisa, principal figure in the early trading ventures, was responsible for the next extension of blacksmithing on the Missouri. His lieutenant, Joshua Pilcher, testified: "The company of which I am a member has always kept several blacksmiths shops

FIG. 99. *Manuel Lisa (1772–1820)*.

"My blacksmiths work incessantly for them charging nothing"
(from the portrait in the Missouri Historical Society, St. Louis). Drawing by James Mulcahy, Jefferson National Expansion Memorial, St.
Louis.

in operation on the Missouri for the manufacture of some of the
above [knives, hatchets, axes, hoes, lances, battle axes, and beaver
traps]. At the time of the commencement of the late hostilities
[War of 1812] we had one at the Mandans, one at the Big Bend of
the Missouri [Fort Lisa or "Lisa's Fort"], and two forges at the
neighborhood of the Council Bluffs." [2] John C. Luttig, Lisa's clerk,
1812–13, at Fort Lisa and on Lisa's boats, quotes Lisa: "My
blacksmiths work incessantly for them [Minnetarees, Mandans,
and Assiniboins] charging nothing." [3] These were the old ac-
quaintances of Lewis and Clark from 1804 to 1806.

[2] U. S. Congress, *American State Papers* (1908), Senate Documents, "1824
Investigation of Indian Hostilities, West of Missouri River," pp. 451–7. (Reprinted in *Annals of Wyoming*, XV:3 (1943), pp. 198–220.
[3] Stella M. Drumm, ed.: *Journal of a Fur Trading Expedition on the Upper
Missouri, 1812–1813* (St. Louis: Missouri Historical Soc.; 1920), p. 22.

FIG. 100. *Jedediah Smith's Blacksmiths Made a Bear Trap for Father Sánchez.*

The blacksmith shop at Mission San Gabriel, California, in 1826. William Macy drawing, Jefferson National Expansion Memorial, St. Louis.

After the War of 1812 there came a wave of Indian trade that in the course of thirty years of beaver business brought more than a hundred trading establishments to the Far West. Some of these flourished for a season, then succumbed. Many others persisted, and their sites today hold flourishing cities or are recognized as historic places worthy of state or national ownership and protection. All of the more important posts offered blacksmithing services. Among the several Hudson's Bay Company posts south of the Canadian boundary were some that were especially distinguished because of their blacksmithing. Most important of these was Fort Vancouver, the site that has yielded the most extensive, if not the most important, mass of fur-trade blacksmith relics thus far recovered in the West. More specific references to the Fort Vancouver artifacts will be made on the pages that follow.

Sometimes the American trapping expeditions that struck out into the Western wilderness with no plans for a fixed fort and no conventional blacksmith shop in prospect did nevertheless employ blacksmiths. This was true of Jedediah Smith's California expedition of 1826. Two blacksmiths, James Reed and Silas Gobel, were members of Smith's party. When the Americans reached California's Mission San Gabriel in November 1826, they found a variety of neophyte industries in full swing, including blacksmithing. The blacksmith shop was quite fully equipped. Father Sánchez needed a heavy bear trap "for his orchard," but he and his local black-smiths were unacquainted with the mechanism of steel traps—it was said. No doubt, the sight of Jedediah's beaver traps inspired the priest's request, and the Americans' desire to return kindnesses prompted the proffering of the services. At any rate, under Smith's orders the blacksmiths Reed and Gobel collaborated in forging a big bear trap with heavy chain (fig. 100), and it was presented to Father Sánchez.[4] This, no doubt, was the first steel trap to be made by Americans in California.

Government-Employed Blacksmiths Among the Indians

BEGINNING in 1790 and continuing at intervals for about half a century, the United States enacted legislation designed to regulate trade and preserve peace on the frontiers.[5] Just as William Clark and Manuel Lisa had found in the early 1800's, many other government officials discovered that blacksmiths generally held the key to the Indian's heart. In treaties, blacksmiths, their tools, and the raw materials of their trade were often specified as parts of the concessions to be extended to the tribes. The blacksmiths were generally honest servants, complacent in the belief that the system of which they were a part would accomplish the ends described by their superiors. The superintendents and local Indian agents, on the other hand, displayed some skepticism regarding the endurance of the "permanent" Indian frontier defined by the Congress, and most of them must have read in the handwriting on the wall a warning that no lasting peace could persist in the face of explosive movements of white citizens, wholesale seizure of designated Indian lands, and the repeated Judas kiss of the Congress.

In the early 1830's General William Clark, the "Red-Haired Chief," was still the Indian superintendent in charge of the tribes

[4] Harrison C. Dale: *The Ashley-Smith Explorations* . . . (Cleveland: Arthur H. Clarke Co.; 1941), pp. 196, 200, 206, quoting firsthand account written by Harrison Rogers, Smith's clerk.

[5] Legislation was enacted in 1796, 1802, 1804, 1822, 1832, and 1834. The Act of 1832 set up a broad program of Indian affairs in the West. See H. P. Beers: *Western Military Frontiers, 1815–1846* (Philadelphia, 1935), p. 107; F. W. Seymour: *Indian Agents of the Old Frontier* (New York: D. Appleton-Century Co.; 1941), pp. 9–11.

of upper Louisiana, with headquarters at St. Louis. When Clark died in 1838, Ethan Allen Hitchcock took his place. F. W. Armstrong was superintendent of the "Western Territory," which embraced the country southward from St. Louis. "Wisconsin Territory" and "Iowa Territory" were two additional contemporary neighboring superintendencies. Under these superintendencies were "Indian agencies" and "subagencies" within which organizations the blacksmiths were employed. Before the close of the 1830's, some 40,000 Indians had been removed from their home territories east of the Mississippi to the Western frontier. By 1842 the removal process had taken more than 80,000 Indians into the West. In some cases, designated blacksmiths already on the job went with the tribes, but more frequently they gave up their government jobs and new appointees were hired in the West. One looks in vain for some published identification of these men; it seems worthwhile to present such meager information regarding blacksmiths of the above-mentioned superintendencies as has been preserved for the 1830's.

GUNSMITHS AND BLACKSMITHS EMPLOYED FOR INDIAN SERVICE
as Reported to Lewis Cass, Secretary of War,
by W. B. Lewis, 2nd Auditors Office, Treasury Department.
March 5, 1832.[6]

Name	Job	Where Employed	Salary Per Annum
Creamer, Phil.	Gunsmith	St. Louis	$600.00
Martin, Jacq.	Blacksmith	St. Louis	500.00
Floyd, Henry	Striker	St. Louis	250.00
Pool, James	Blacksmith-striker	Delaware Agency	740.00
Lawhead, B.	Blacksmith-striker	Delaware Agency	650.00
Dunlop, Robert	Gunsmith	Osage Agency	500.00
Carlisle, Wm.	Blacksmith	Osage Agency	400.00
Crate, Oliver	Gunsmith	St. Peters Agency	528.00
Casner, George	Blacksmith	Rock Island (Sacs)	400.00
Lebeau, J. B.	Gunsmith	Rock Island (Foxes)	400.00
Philbert, G.	Blacksmith-striker	Kanzas Sub-Agency	550.00

Name	Job	Where Employed	Salary Per Annum
Van Bibber, J.	Blacksmith	Ioway Agency	400.00
Holland, Wm.	Blacksmith	Peoria	400.00
Cherrier, Oliver	Blacksmith	Prairie du Chien	365.00
Lewis, John	Blacksmith	Upper Sandusky	469.00
Elliott, John	Blacksmith	Wapaghonetta	469.00
Smith, Jos.	Blacksmith	Eel River	400.00
Wilson, Robt.	Blacksmith	Eel River (Miamis)	400.00
Lindsey, John	Blacksmith	Eel River (Potawatomi)	400.00
Jourdain, Joseph	Blacksmith	Green Bay	360.00
Allard, Simon	Blacksmith	Mackinac	400.00
Smith, Wm. C.	Striker	Eel River	180.00
Keller, E. T.	Striker	Eel River (Miamis)	180.00
Lindsey, Wm.	Striker	Eel River (Potawatomi)	180.00
LaFarriere, L.	Striker	Mackinac	250.00
Irwin, J.	Gunsmith	Red River Agency	800.00
Spring, C.	Blacksmith-striker	Choctaw Agency	960.00
Terry, R. J.	Striker	Chickasaw Agency	840.00
Dodge, Israel	Blacksmith	Choctaw, West	800.00
Shaw, Wm. D.	Blacksmith	Creeks, West	350.00

It is interesting to note that Joseph Jourdain,[7] the only one of these mechanics to attain some fame later as an artist in his chosen field, was not in the higher salary bracket in the early 1830's. Jourdain, a Canadian, came to Green Bay, Wisconsin, as a boy. The trader Jacob Franks employed him just at the turn of the century, and soon thereafter Jourdain established his own smithy. He created a trademark, which appears on many of his beautifully

[6] 22nd Cong., 1st Sess., S. Doc. 101 (1832), I, 13–15.

[7] See p. 281 in this volume; Brown: "Indian Trade Implements," pp. 63–4; West: "Tobacco Pipes," pp. 59–60; H. L. Peterson: *American Indian Tomahawks*, p. 49. Peterson lists 66 manufacturers of axes and tomahawks (ibid., pp. 46–52). Two of the above Indian Service blacksmiths, John Lewis and Joseph Jourdain, are recognized in that list.

made pipe tomahawks—a crescent inlaid with copper. The Neville Public Museum, Green Bay, owns a collection of Jourdain pieces; each one shows meticulous workmanship in every particular. As an Indian Agency blacksmith, Jourdain could not specialize on pipe tomahawks, of course. He did general blacksmithing in Green Bay until a year or two after the above-mentioned report was written and then moved to Winnebago Rapids, where he died in 1866.

After William Clark died, the St. Louis superintendency retained the agencies at Fort Leavenworth, Council Bluffs, and the upper Missouri, with subagencies at the Great Nemaha and Osage rivers.[8] In St. Louis, Captain Hitchcock's tenure was brief; Joshua Pilcher, the mountain man, was in charge during 1839–41. He was followed by D. D. Mitchell, who served until 1843. Thomas H. Harvey took over in 1844. Thomas Fitzpatrick, renowned mountain man, was Indian agent for the upper Platte and the Arkansas during the Harvey regime.

After 1838 the superintendency for the "Western Territory" administered the agencies for the transplanted Choctaws, Creeks, and Cherokees. Subagencies were set up for the Osages and Senecas. At this time the total Indian population west of the Mississippi, including the recent immigrant tribes, was estimated to be 250,000. White settlers in the Indian country and along its fringes numbered more than 900,000 by 1840. The stage was already set for border enmities, intertribal fights, and outright Indian war against the whites. Both the Office of Indian Affairs and the Military[9] launched programs designed to postpone the fateful day of conflagration. Included in the preparations made by the U. S. government were expanded ventures in agriculture, exploitation of

[8] Important testimony by Indian agents is contained in "Report of Commissioner of Indian Affairs, 1838." 25th Cong., 3rd sess., S. Doc. 1 (1839), pp. 480–527.

[9] Beers's *Western Military Frontiers* provides a valuable outline of the Army's efforts to be prepared. The U. S. military arms and the Indian guns of the period are covered in C. P. Russell: *Guns on the Early Frontiers* (Berkeley: Univ. of California Press; 1957), pp. 142–218. The Office of Indian Affairs adopted a policy of arming the "removed" Indians in order that they might be more nearly self-sufficient in hunting and in meeting hostile Plains tribes. In the southern Plains the Comanche, Kiowas, Pawnees, and some of the Osages occasionally forayed in search of immigrant victims. North of the Arkansas other Pawnee bands, the Araphoes, units of the Sioux, and the Cheyennes often kept war parties in the field. The "hostiles" sometimes clashed with parties of traders-trappers as well as with immigrant Indians, and these fights influenced the plans for military posts and the movements of American troops, who by this time served the frontier. Generally the "hostiles" had little access to blacksmith shops.

the buffalo herds and the fur bearers, the building of wagon roads, and the development of better river transportation. All of these peaceful pursuits involved increased artificer personnel and the establishment of new and bigger shops. Some of this industrial advance focused upon the Indian agencies. Since the Western agencies and subagencies were quite numerous and their areas populous, the Indian Office in Washington found it necessary to authorize recruitment of additional blacksmiths and to procure appropriate tools and heavy equipment needed to "set up shop." At the same time, the necessary iron stock was purchased and transported to the West. Not all of the procurement was handled in Washington, and not all ironworks for Indians were manufactured by government blacksmiths. William Clark's accounts reveal that he obtained at least a part of his Indian goods from dealers and manufacturers in St. Louis. Leber Papin and his brother, Sylvestre, engaged in a private hardware business in St. Louis and conducted their own manufacturing enterprise. For many years Papin tools went to the local Superintendent of Indian Affairs as well as to the fur trading companies.[1] The tools and the iron stock used by an Indian Service blacksmith did not differ from other tools and raw materials of the time.

Iron Stock Tools and Raw Materials
of the Mountain Men

SEVERAL DECADES PRIOR TO THE AMERICAN REVOLUTION, GREAT Britain proposed to prohibit "the erection of any mill or other engine for slitting or rolling of Iron; or any plateing forge to work with a tilt hammer; or any furnace for making steel"—in America.[2] In 1785 a strict ban was published by the Crown prohibiting the exportation of machinery for the making of iron and steel, and "the exportation of the artificers themselves is more strictly prohibited. . . . Enticement of any one who has wrought in iron or steel manufactures to go to a foreign country is liable to one years imprisonment and a penalty of £500 for every person enticed."[3]

[1] Drumm: *Journal of a Fur-Trading Expedition*, p. 53.
[2] The original imprint of the bill is in the John Carter Brown Library, Brown University. Rejected in Parliament, the debate spread interest in American iron.
[3] David MacPherson: *Annals of Commerce* (4 vols.; Edinburgh, 1805), IV, 75.

Yet there were iron mines, smelters, and mills in many places in eastern America. Some smelters existed even in the early years of English colonization, such as Saugus, Massachusetts, and Falling Creek (Richmond), Virginia,[4] and all through the colonial period new iron mines were exploited and processes of production improved. The manufacture of *cast-iron* objects principally involved furnace work and molding. The iron kettles of the trader-trapper were cast, but most of the iron in the fur trade required processes other than casting. *Wrought iron* was obtained by purifying melted pig iron in a "puddling furnace" until it retained but little carbon and was tough and malleable. *Steel* was first made by heating two bars of wrought iron with charcoal or charred bone in a closed furnace for a long enough time to permit the surface of the iron to acquire a high carbon content, then the bars were fused or welded into shapes and sizes desired for handling in shops. The product was called *blister steel* because of the obvious impurities and imperfections of the weld. The improved or "crucible" method invented in Sheffield in 1742[5] continued as the principal method for more than a hundred years, and still constitutes the basis for modern procedures. The open-hearth methods of making steel were not perfected until after the mountain-man period.

By 1811 the iron industry at Pittsburgh had developed rolling mills where red-hot ingots of crucible steel were passed successively between rolls of various shapes. Quite rapidly other forges (lacking rolling mills) came into existence in Pennsylvania, Connecticut, Massachusetts, and in some of the cities around the Great Lakes. The Great Lakes industry imported its pig iron from the East. Iron stores were numerous in the Great Lakes centers, and in the 1830's Western blacksmiths usually had little trouble in procuring the materials of their trade.[6]

Among the available earlier records of purchases of iron stock for the use of an Indian Agency blacksmith are John Johnston's

[4] J. P. Hudson: "Iron at Jamestown, Virginia," *The Iron Worker*, XX:3 (1956), pp. 2–14.

[5] J. B. Himsworth: *The Story of Cutlery* (London: Ernest Benn; 1953), p. 72.

[6] This was not true in the 1820's. On April 3, 1822, Thomas Hempstead, St. Louis, wrote to Joseph Pilcher (both of the Missouri Fur Co.): "Carson had 150 traps made with the exception of the springs which could not be made as there has not been any steel in this place during the whole winter." (D. L. Morgan, ed.: *The West of William H. Ashley* [Denver: Old West Publishing Co.; 1964], p. 3.)

Fort Wayne, Indiana, orders placed in 1810 with the Office of Indian Affairs: [7]

> Accounts for 1810 . . .
>
> | | |
> |---|---:|
> | 5 bars German steel, 121 lbs. | $22.69 |
> | 2 Faggots Crowley steel | 60.00 |
> | 1 Faggot Blistered steel @ .12½ per lb. | 14.00 |

Fragmentary records of the North West Company's iron business for 1793 show that 210 pieces of bar iron and one anvil were shipped that year from Fort Erie to Detroit. Before shipping closed that fall, a part of the bar iron was moved from Detroit to Mackinac, a depot that soon, under John Jacob Astor, was destined to become important as an American blacksmithing center and distributing point.[8] The American Fur Company Papers afford numerous glimpses of the iron stock distributed to its outposts, with prices paid by the field agents. Quite revealing are the records pertaining to the shipment of some ten tons of iron stores from Mackinac to several company smithies in Michigan, Wisconsin, Indiana, and Illinois in 1821–2.[9]

The following is the compendium of orders filled by the American Fur Company, Mackinac in 1821–2. Shipments were made to various places and at various times during the two years.

Iron	200 lbs.	.10, for half axes	$ 20.00
Iron	1,704 lbs.	.10	170.40
Iron, round	115 lbs.	.12, for rat spears	13.00
Bolt iron	112 lbs.	.10	11.20
Nail rods	300 lbs.	5.50 per cwt.	16.50
Bar iron	1,205 lbs.	.18, for 37 bars	216.90
Bar iron, English	5.57 tons	82.50 per ton	459.61
Bar iron, Swedes	1.7 tons	97.50 per ton	165.50
Bar iron, Russian	200 lbs.	5.00 per cwt.	10.00
Swedes iron	51 lbs.	.18, for traps [1]	9.18
English iron	245 lbs.	.18, for axes	44.10
Steel	150 lbs.	.24	36.00
Steel	105 lbs.	.37½	39.38
Steel, Millington Crowley	100 lbs.	.37½	37.50

[7] Bert J. Griswold, ed.: *Fort Wayne, Gateway of the West, 1802–1813* (Indianapolis: Indiana Library and Historical Dept.; 1927), pp. 599, 624.

[8] Harold A. Innis: *The Fur Trade in Canada* (New Haven: Yale Univ. Press; 1962), pp. 224–5.

[9] American Fur Company Papers, 1821–2 (MS) Invoice Book No. 1—"Illinois, 1821."

[1] In 1840 the American Fur Co. was still procuring Swedish iron. The

The American Fur Company correspondence for the 1830's and 1840's contains a number of significant letters, orders, and inventories that have a bearing upon iron stock and blacksmithing. A few examples follow.

On January 11, 1836, L. M. Warren, company agent at La Pointe, Wisconsin, addressed Ramsay Crooks: "Mr. Newton [blacksmith] has always complained about Blistered Steel. He says it is impossible for him to warrant the halfaxes and tomahawks on account of the steel being so bad. Mr. Aitkens [company agent at the neighboring post, Fond du Lac] writes me that all his halfaxes and tomahawks are broke. Would it therefore not be best to use cast steel instead of the blistered steel? . . . Send us 100 lbs cast steel ¾ inch square [in cross section] and 100 lbs ½ inch square and also 10 lbs more of the double refined borax." [2]

As told previously, blister steel displays imperfections because of inclusion of carbon and other impurities; yet it is much harder than the iron from which it is prepared. Even in its homeland, some English blacksmiths objected to it for a time until they became accustomed to it and modified their old techniques to handle it. There may be some question regarding Mr. Newton's condemnation of the "blistered" steel supplied by the American Fur Company. The "cast steel," preferred at La Pointe, had been on the market at least as far back as the 1770's, first as a material for razor blades, then for general cutlery and tools. Actually, it is closely related to blister steel, but it is a product of the crucible and is even harder and of finer texture than is the blister steel. It was cast in ingots that were then rolled into the shapes and sizes wanted by the trade. This was the steel best adapted for most purposes. Occasionally certain axes, knives, and other tools recovered on fur-trade sites are found to be marked "Warrented Cast Steel." Most of these are products of tool factories, a few of which came into existence in America before the close of the mountain-man period. From evidences presented by the documents of the fur trade, we know that individual blacksmiths at the trading posts also used cast steel, but usually the artifacts themselves do not disclose this history readily.

specified dimensions, 1¾ inches by ⅜ inch and 1½ inches by ⅜ inch in section. These sizes found common use in hand-forged beaver traps. American Fur Company Papers, Crooks, Orders Outward, June 29, 1840, Vol. I, p. 369 (microfilm reel 12).

[2] American Fur Company Papers, 1831–49, Correspondence (1836).

Throughout the documentary record of iron purchases made
by any and all trading companies and the Office of Indian Affairs,
"shear steel" occasionally is specified. The nature of this material is
made clear by Mordecai,[3] who was writing at the same time that
Crooks prepared his orders in 1840. That it was regarded by
Crooks to be more valuable than other iron stock included in this
particular order is suggested by his memorandum of June 29,
1840. (No addressee.)

Memorandum of Iron and Steel for the American Fur Company

. . .

6 bars double refined Shear Steel 1 × 1½ inch
   Note—The Shear Steel to be packed in a box.

. . .

Ramsay Crooks [4]

On July 22, 1839, Samuel Abbott, in charge at Mackinac,
wrote to Crooks in New York ordering "pitch iron for tomahawks."
The term "pitch iron" does not appear on the usual lists and
inventories of the trade, but since Abbott was a seasoned old-timer
in the business around the Great Lakes, it is a foregone conclusion
that his use of the name grew out of established terminology that
was traditional, at least locally. Wrought iron of the day took on a
"pitch"-like stickiness when brought to the red heat necessary for
welding. This was the iron regularly used for all parts of the trade
ax, except the cutting edge which was an insert of steel (p. 257);
probably Mr. Abbott's "pitch iron" was the ordinary wrought iron.

A letter from James McKay at La Pointe to Crooks in New
York, April 5, 1841, asks for "hoop iron," another class that does
not appear on the usual earlier invoices and manifests of the fur
trade. In the West, Indians had long sought hoop iron for arrow
points, but the hoops they obtained usually came from damaged,
discarded, or pilfered kegs and barrels at Indian agencies, military
establishments, trading posts, or wagon trains. At La Pointe, as at

[3] "Shear steel is made from blistered or natural steel refined by piling thin
bars into faggots, which are brought to a welding heat in a reverberatory
furnace, and hammered or rolled again into bars; this operation is repeated
several times to produce the finest kinds of shear steel which are distinguished by
the names *half shear*, *single shear*, and *double shear* . . . according to the
number of times it has been piled." (A. Mordecai: *Ordnance Manual* . . .
[Charleston, S.C., 1861] p. 388 [1st edn. pub. in 1841].)
[4] American Fur Company Papers, 1831–49, Orders Outward, Vol. I, p. 369
(microfilm reel 12).

FIG. 101.   *Astoria, 1811.*

This was the seat of the first forge on the Columbia; William
Cannon was the blacksmith. Built by the party of Astor's men who
reached the mouth of the Columbia in Astor's ship *Tonquin* in the
spring of 1811. Under stress of war conditions (War of 1812) the
post and all of Mr. Astor's properties therein were sold by the Astorians to the North West Company in the fall of 1813—thus began the
British regime on the Columbia. Drawing by William Macy, after an
illustration in the Jefferson National Expansion Memorial, St. Louis.

other Lake Superior posts of the American Fur Company, the hoop
iron was needed in connection with the fisheries enterprise conducted by the company during the 1830's and 1840's.[5] Thousands
of barrels for salted fish were made locally, and the complexion of
the over-all tools picture for the Lake Superior fur-trading posts
was affected notably by the operation of fishing fleets, the processing (salting) of tremendous catches of lake trout and whitefish,
and the extensive cooperage business engaged in by the company.

Beginning with the 1813 Astoria inventory (page 407), iron
wire appears quite frequently on the fur trader's lists. No doubt
research would show that this class of material (in real sense, "iron
stock") was carried on trader's inventories at least a century earlier
than the Astoria records. Little or no work at a forge was involved
in making trade bracelets from heavy iron wire. Iron bracelets
were recovered in the "digs" at the Fatherland site, Natchez (occu-

[5] Grace Nute: "The American Fur Company's Fishing Enterprises . . . ,"
Mississippi Valley Historical Review, Vol. XII (1945), pp. 483–503.

FIG. 102. *Interior of a Blacksmith Shop at a Trading Post.*

Such a shop was built at Astoria in 1811. Some of the equipment and iron stock used by the Astorian smith is listed in Mr. Astor's inventory (see pp. 402–7). Beginning in the first decade of the nineteenth century (p. 362) and continuing through the Western fur-trade period, similar shops were provided at most of the trading posts throughout the Missouri and tramontane regions—the entire range of the mountain man. Glen Dines drawing.

pied 1700–29); at Angola Farm (occupied 1700–60); and at Fort St. Joseph, Michigan. Lawson among the Tuscarora from 1701 to 1709 saw bracelets of iron wire being worn.[6] As traded, these simple ornaments were bright and shiny and continued to be popular with Indians everywhere all through the fur-trade period. They were wanted in the West in the days of the mountain man, and William Ashley agreed to deliver to Smith, Jackson and Sublette at the Little Lake (Bear Lake) rendezvous, 1827, "Steel bracelets @ $1.50 per pair."[7]

[6] George I. Quimby: "Indian Trade Objects in Michigan and Louisiana," *Papers*, Michigan Academy of Science, Arts, and Letters, Vol. XXVII (1941), p. 548; John R. Swanton: *The Indians of the Southeastern United States*, Bureau of American Ethnology, Bulletin 137 (1946), p. 521.

[7] D. L. Morgan, ed.: *William H. Ashley*, p. 152.

In and around every active blacksmith shop, piles of refuse iron accumulate. In the old days, the discards included broken tools, horse and mule shoes, wagon parts, house hardware, harness parts, and fragments of implements of any and all kinds. Also, the cut ends of rods and bars rejected as waste as the blacksmith worked usually made up a significant part of the piles of scrap. Ordinarily some of the scrap was drawn upon in making certain repairs—even in producing new objects such as axes. The greatest collections of scrap iron studied at a fur-trading post were recovered in 1947–52 at the sites of the several forges that once flourished at Fort Vancouver, the Hudson's Bay Company headquarters on the Columbia. Here where shipping facilities were good, it would appear that a continuous supply of fresh stock iron imported from England made it quite unnecessary for the smiths to resort to scrap in turning out new work. A total of 95,846 pieces of iron were collected during the four years of excavating.[8]

Blacksmith Tools and Related Equipment

THE Astoria inventory of 1813 (page 407) reports a reasonable supply of iron stock, two blacksmith's forges are accounted for, but few blacksmith's tools are listed. Just why they are not listed is not apparent; for two years Mr. Astor's blacksmith and his helpers had engaged in producing "Columbia-made" ironworks. In addition to the unrecorded objects that had been traded to Indians, there were still on hand, when the North West Company took over, some 366 axes, 80 dozen knives, 11 gross of awls, 8 dozen iron hoops, 300 iron dogs, and dozens of miscellaneous iron tools—all recorded as products of the Astoria blacksmith shop. The tools used in doing so much work did not vanish, of course, but the record of their disposal disappeared.

A convenient source of information regarding a portable forge

[8] Louis R. Caywood: *Exploratory Excavations at Fort Vancouver* (San Francisco: Nat'l Park Serv.; 1947), pp. 14–16, and *Final Report, Fort Vancouver Excavations* (Nat'l Park Serv., Region Four, 1955), pp. 32–44. "It appears that iron was shipped from England in standard sizes in strap (flat), rod (round), bar (squared), sheet and plate. The processing [at the English mills] seems to have been well developed as the sizes drawn in sixteenths and eighths are accurate. . . . There were at least 49 different sizes of strap iron and 7 sizes of bar iron. There were also 7 thicknesses of sheet or plate ranging from $\frac{1}{32}$ inch to $\frac{1}{2}$ inch. Rods were found to have come in ten different diameters ranging from $\frac{1}{4}$ inch to $1\frac{1}{2}$ inch." (*Final Report*, p. 33.)

and its complement of smith's tools in 1840 is found in the U. S. Ordnance Department's specifications for equipping a field forge: [9]

Contents of Limber Chest of Forge A, Boxes A2, A4, and A5; and of the Forge body. (Two vehicles)

Hardie	1	.75 lb.
Files, assorted	12	10 lb.
Hand punches	2	2 lb.
Hand vice	1	1 lb.
Pair Smith's callipers	1	.40 lb.
Taps and dies	8	3.33 lb.
Die stock	1	6.25 lb.
Fire shovel	1	3.05 lb.
Poker	1	1.90 lb.
Shoeing Knife	1	.33 lb.
Hand hammer	1	3.50 lb.
Shoeing hammer	1	.82 lb.
Riveting hammer	1	1.80 lb.
Sledge hammer	1	10.50 lb.
Chisels for hot iron	2	3.00 lb.
Hand cold chisels	2	2.00 lb.
Chisels for cold iron	2	3.00 lb.
Smiths tongs	3	15.00 lb.
Nail punch	1	.80 lb.
Fore punch	1	1.00 lb.
Round punch	1	2.10 lb.
Creaser	1	1.00 lb.
Fuller	1	2.40 lb.
Pritchel	1	.85 lb.
Clinching iron	1	1.00 lb.
Oil stone	1	1.50 lb.
Leather aprons	2	3.00 lb.
Quart can sperm oil	1	2.70 lb.

Forge body. The bellows is a part of forge body. 250 lbs. of bituminous coal and the coal shovel are in the coal box. 120 lbs. of iron stock in the "iron room." The anvil, fixed on fireplace, weighs 100.00 lbs.; the vice, fixed on the carriage, weighs 29.00 lbs.[1]

A very informative series of articles regarding old-time blacksmith's tools and the mechanics of their use appear in *The Chronicle* of the Early American Industries Association.[2] More than a hundred drawings contribute to this interpretation, and contempo-

[9] Mordecai: *Ordnance Manual*, pp. 309–10.
[1] Ibid.
[2] Vols. XVII (1964) and XVIII (1965).

rary sources of information are cited. M. G. Chandler's "The Blacksmith Shop" gives a thorough account of the old-timer's techniques in making pipe tomahawks. Fifty explanatory diagrams and drawings make for reader interest and clear understanding.[3] Eric Sloane's *Museum of Early American Tools* presents numerous pen-and-ink drawings of many of the blacksmith's tools on our foregoing list.[4] The tools themselves, almost always in fragments, have been dug up in the course of archeological work at a number of western sites. Probably the biggest collection was made at Fort Vancouver. Caywood[5] tells of these finds and illustrates some of them in two photographs.[6] Swages, fullers, drifts, punches, chisels, tongs of several types, and pincers are represented in the Fort Vancouver recoveries. Sledges and lighter blacksmith's hammers are lacking, as seems to be the case at most of the fur-trade sites so far investigated.

Anvils, like inferior cannon, were left behind sometimes when trading posts were abandoned, but usually they were appropriated by passers-by long before archeologist-historians came along. Country-wide, anvils range in size from the big ones which received the blows of the gigantic trip hammers of such establishments as the early works on the Saugus[7] to the diminutive "Stake" anvils for the blacksmith's light work.[8] The present whereabouts of a bona fide fur trader's anvil is not reported in references currently available. Occasionally, anvils of the mountain-man period do appear in the documentary record. We learn from the *Ordnance Manual* that portable anvils carried with early nineteenth century Army field forges weighed a hundred pounds. It is safe to assume that many of the anvils taken to Western fur-trading posts were of this size. In 1822 the value of "1 large anvil" in the Great Lakes area was $27.00. Understandably, the same anvil delivered to a trading post on the Missouri was $90.00, or more. At Mackinac in 1822, a heavy bench vise was worth $5.00; the big post vise so important to voluminous, advanced blacksmithing was priced at $25.00. Only the big shops seem to have installed the post vise.

[3] Quoted in Peterson: *American Indian Tomahawks* (New York: Museum of the American Indian; 1965).
[4] (New York: Wilfrid Funk, Inc.; 1964).
[5] *Exploratory Excavations* and *Final Report*.
[6] *Exploratory Excavations*, Pl. 17, and *Final Report*, Pl. 16 B.
[7] Robert W. Howard: "Cradle of Industry: U.S.A," *American Heritage*, II:4 (1951), p. 27.
[8] Sloane: *Museum of Early American Tools*, p. 90.

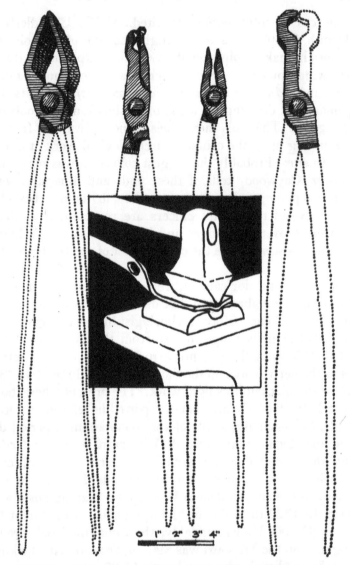

FIG. 103. *Fragments of Blacksmiths' Tongs Recovered at Fort Vancouver.*

During the excavation of the Hudson's Bay Company's Fort Vancouver, numerous parts of tongs were found; the four specimens shown here are representative. No complete tongs were recovered at this site. Blacksmiths generally made their own tongs. The central figure represents a jaw of a round-nosed tong in the making. The red-hot jaw rests upon a bottom swage held in the hardy hole of the anvil. A top fuller held against the jaw and, when struck with a hammer, quickly depressed the flat metal to make one half of the desired round-nosed tongs. The tongs specimens are from Caywood's *Final Report*, Pl. 16 B; the fuller and swage are after Early American Industries Association's *The Chronicle* (June 1965), p. 28. Drawing by Glen Dines.

Another piece of heavy equipment regularly present in blacksmith shops was the grindstone, which weighed 200 pounds or more. In 1822 the price charged by the American Fur Company at its Mackinac distributing center was 2¢ per pound. Ordinarily, the mounting of the revolving stone was done at the field station where the grinding was to be done.

Bellows get but small mention in the fur trader's property lists, and since the thin boards and the pliable leather of their makeup were fragile and perishable, few specimens have withstood the ravages of time. In the remote small smithies, the bellows might be the small hand-operated devices, foot bellows placed on the floor, or the conventional forge bellows of the type illustrated on page 360. Any hand bellows present in the larger Western posts were there primarily to serve fireplaces in living rooms, cabins, and shops; their use at the blacksmith's hearth (forge) was makeshift and temporary. The foot bellows was an inheritance from colonial times, and, again, this device would have been no more than a temporary expedient in a nineteenth-century blacksmith shop. The dependable method of obtaining a blast of air for the "permanent" forge was the installation of the conventional blacksmith's bellows to be pumped by an overhead pole mounted on a fulcrum.

Fuel for the forge was charcoal prepared locally. Beginning with the testimony of Lewis and Clark (page 359) and continuing through the records of the entire mountain-man period, there are numerous accounts of preparing charcoal for the forges on the frontier. Trees of hardwood species were sought for "burning" when they could be obtained, but softwoods also served. The collier's "pits," which were earth-covered piles—not holes in the ground—received fifty or sixty cords of wood, cut in four-foot lengths. Sod four inches thick was applied over the surface of the mound-shaped pile, except for openings near the ground. A small "chimney" in the center allowed air to circulate through the stack. Fine combustible material placed within the pile at the time of its building was then ignited at the openings, and a slow-burning fire spread through the pit. When flames came out of the chimney, that hole was closed to reduce the draft. The enclosed wood "sweated," and smoke emerged from all parts of the stack through small gaps in the sod cover. At this juncture, a heavier coating of earth was applied and the fire was moderated. In order that combustion might be equal throughout, holes were opened successively in various parts of the earth cover, and when the emerging black smoke became gray-blue smoke, the charring was regarded to be nearly complete, the holes were stopped, and the pile received another covering of earth. A few days later the pile was opened on one side to determine how successful the charring may have been. On the average, wood so burned yielded 16 or 17 per cent of its weight in charcoal. Obviously, these several steps in the burning required constant attention. The colliers lived in nearby temporary huts while the work was in progress.[9]

Blacksmiths in city shops and on the frontier, as well, generally adhered to charcoal for fuel. One of the exceptions was recorded by Samuel Collins, who kept a diary from 1826 to 1871. One of his 1830 memos: "Forged some *Yankee* axes this year in Lehigh [anthracite coal] fires and putting a mark on them, packed a few in each case. Did not discover that any greater proportion of them failed than of axes made exclusively with charcoal."[1]

The blacksmith's shopwork involved a great deal of hand forging of iron and steel. At his hand, as he stood by his forge, were the anvil and hammers and tongs. On the steel top of the anvil, the smith worked his wonders. Much of his performance depended upon his practiced eye; only experience could prepare him to "strike while the iron is hot." The piece of work in the white-hot coals changed its hue as it heated, and its color constituted the guide. If steel was made too hot, it lost its desired initial temper. If the job involved the welding of a piece of steel to an iron object, both metals had to be in the fire simultaneously, both had to reach the right stage at just the moment of welding, and both had to be

[9] Jackson Kemper: "American Charcoal Making in the Era of the Cold-Blast Furnace," *The Regional Review*, V:1 (1940), pp. 1–14, provides a highly satisfying description of experiences in making charcoal at Hopewell Furnace. This work was done for interpretive purposes under the guidance of the last of the oldtime colliers, and photos were made of all steps in the process. A series of ten revealing drawings and diagrams, "How Charcoal was Made," at the historic Elizabeth Furnace, George Washington National Forest, appear in *Grist*, X:4 (1966), p. 26. Mordecai: *Ordnance Manual*, pp. 395–6, gives a succinct account of charcoal making for the guidance of U. S. Army technicians.

[1] Quote from the Samuel Collins' manuscript diary was supplied by E. M. Elston, president of the Collins Company, Collinsville, Connecticut, September 4, 1958.

brought from the fire, placed together in proper relationship upon the anvil, and struck quickly at the right places with the right hammer. There could be no wasting of moments or movements; the smith had to know his materials and had to be precise in grasping his tools and in using them.[2] The novice could not become competent in this on a weekend of practice.

All through the fur-trade documents—orders, invoices, and inventories—are entries pertaining to borax and "double-refined borax." Borax was one of the materials used by the blacksmith to clean the surfaces of metals to be welded and to protect the metal in the fire from excessive oxidation. The quartz and fluorspar in sand served much the same purpose; if borax was not available, the blacksmith sometimes resorted to sand for the needed flux. Judging from the persistence of fieldmen in ordering, one concludes that borax was preferred by the backcountry blacksmiths.

Hand forging was a fairly universal first process in making knives, axes, traps, tools—in fact, in making almost all of the iron artifacts with which this book is concerned.[3] The move away from the ancient hand forging was effected slowly even in the great industrial centers. A number of blacksmiths of fur-trade days distinguished themselves, in one way or another, during the period of transition between old-time smithies and machine-shop industries. Three luminaries deserve special mention in this connection. The first is William Cannon,[4] the Astorian who remained with the British and held forth first at Fort George and after 1825 at Fort Vancouver, where for some thirty-five years he was the senior artisan. His fame rests in part upon his record of voluminous production of iron works and on his reputation as the pioneer in Columbia River industry. Five forges were operated at Fort Van-

[2] H. L. Peterson provides excellent analysis of the smith's problems in forging, welding, tempering, and grinding steel blades (*American Knives* [New York: Scribner's; 1958], pp. 144–6).

[3] Power-operated trip hammers had been used in the manufacture of stock iron for many decades before 1800, but power hammers for detailed shopwork were almost nonexistent until the 1830's or 1840's. German shops aroused worldwide interest in their procedures in forging blades. A Board of U. S. Ordnance Officers visited Solingen, Prussia, in 1840 to observe the forging of swords and sabers (U. S. Cong. [1841], pp. 84–91). In the United States, the John Russell Manufacturing Co., Massachusetts, installed water-powered trip hammers for forging knife blades, the first in America (see p. 199).

[4] John A. Hussey: *The History of Fort Vancouver* (Tacoma: Washington State Historical Soc.; 1957), pp. 48–9, 187, 196, 199, 200, 203; Caywood: *Exploratory Excavations*, p. 14, and *Final Report*, p. 18.

FIG. 104. *Fort Vancouver.*

Fort Vancouver was the British headquarters on the Columbia; it stood opposite present-day Portland, Oregon. After merging with the North West Company, the Hudson's Bay Company gave up Fort George (Astoria) and in 1825 moved to this locality, where agriculture could be practiced. Here and in the near vicinity five forges were operated. Drawing by William Macy after an illustration in the Jefferson National Expansion Memorial, St. Louis.

couver. They continued active well into the machine-shop era, and some of the Fort Vancouver techniques and many imports were of the new fashion, but, generally, the basic work of Mr. Cannon followed the pattern established by him at Astoria in 1811–13.

The second, Mr. Sewell Newhouse, began making steel traps in 1823 in Oneida County, New York. His hand-forged products were superior; during a quarter of a century of Newhouse blacksmithing, they built a good reputation for their maker and stirred widespread demand. In the 1840's Mr. Newhouse joined the Oneida Community, where he and a few assistants continued in the manufacture of hand-forged traps. Within a few years ingenious machines were invented at Oneida, which took over some of the work that heretofore had always been done by hand. Within a decade after the arrival of Newhouse most of the trap manufacture at Oneida was handled by machines, and production was enormous. The best grade of traps made by the Oneida Community retained the trade name "Newhouse." For more than a hundred years the name has stood for the best in steel traps—something of an institutional monument to one country blacksmith.

The third luminary, Jim Bridger, "Old Gabe" of the mountain

FIG. 105. *James Bridger, Mountain Man (1804–81)*.

The drawing by William Macy is after the portrait in the Jefferson National Expansion Memorial, St. Louis.

men, was a blacksmith before he was a trapper.[5] "He took the hair off'n beaver and Blackfoot with equal relish and consummate skill" and in the process built for himself a flamboyant reputation scarcely paralleled by any of his fellows. For forty years Bridger managed to go everywhere and do everything in the Western beaver country. He was one of the organizers of the Rocky Mountain Fur Company in 1830 and later became an employee of Pratte, Chouteau and Company. As the beaver business declined to the low ebb of the 1840's, Bridger anticipated the rush of emigrants. In 1843 he built Fort Bridger [6] on Black's Fork of the Green, where his blacksmithing,[7] general services of supply and, ultimately, his hospitality to travelers and his guidance of government expeditions added to his reputation. Probably some of the wonderful exploits attributed to "Old Gabe" cannot be substantiated, but enough of his doings were genuine, and enough of his "lucky breaks" have been documented to justify the word that he was mostly rawhide, cunning as a fox, and withal wise in his own generation.

Jim Bridger was sufficiently representative of the superior element in "This Reckless Breed" to place him here in our concluding lines. His life story [8] speaks eloquently of a significant period in our history that blazed briefly in the literature of the day and in the minds of contemporary men. "Old Gabe" and his fort yet march across the pages of many a book and magazine. As the years stretch farther and farther, leaving the doings of the mountain man away back in time, tradition and folklore sometimes snatch the torch from history; worse, theatricals sometimes tend to distort and misrepresent. Not often is the iron worker recognized in the popular accounts of frontier affairs to be the key man that he was. His white contemporaries acclaimed him as important, and the Indian accepted him as "Mr. Big." It should be affirmed here at this late date that the blacksmith and the gunsmith on the frontier performed unique and important service to the nation. Partly because

[5] As a stripling he was apprenticed to Phil Creamer, St. Louis blacksmith (see p. 365).

[6] Robert S. Ellison: *Fort Bridger, Wyoming* (Casper, Wyo.: Historic Landmark Commission; 1931, pp. 1–58).

[7] The Bridger steel trap reported on p. 118 is of this period.

[8] Bridger was accorded book-length treatment by General G. M. Dodge in 1905, by J. Cecil Alter in 1925 (renewed in 1963), by Louis O. Honig in 1951, and by Gene Caesar in 1961.

FIG. 106. *Fort Bridger.*

Here the mountain men helped materially in converting the wilderness traffic from pack-train methods to wagon transport. Drawing by William Macy after an illustration in the Jefferson National Expansion Memorial, St. Louis.

of their works, westward expansion was unalterable and on time. There will yet be an appropriate memorialization of frontier workers in iron.

Discerning governments, federal, state, and local, have taken timely action in preserving and interpreting historic sites,[9] and in collecting, studying, and interpreting historic objects. The sites, the museums, and the publication programs which relate to them now hold the promise of better public appreciation of a precious heritage. May the present account of iron and iron men on the beaver front be accepted as a contribution to the effort.

[9] Some thirty parks and memorials, state and national, in the Far West now protect fur-trade sites. A greater number of preserves in the East feature fur-trade remains.

Historic Objects as Sources of History

ADVENT AND GROWTH OF THE HISTORIAN–ARCHEOLOGIST PROGRAM

FOR CONVENIENCE, I SHALL BE ARBITRARY IN RECOGNIZing three stages in the development of the historian-archeologist program in America:

1. The day of the Wisconsin School, early 1900's.
2. The period of Arthur C. Parker, Clark Wissler, and the concurrent "New Deal" activities, 1930's and 1940's.
3. The postwar period, which I choose to regard as continuing, currently.

I am confident there are workers who feel that the above chronology is poorly conceived, but perhaps it will suffice for present purposes.

In my view, Carl Russell Fish (not a relative of the writer) was among the first to urge historians to embrace three-dimensional objects as "documents" among historical records. His essay "Relation of Archaeology and History" was first read before the Wisconsin Archeological Society at Madison on July 29, 1910. In referring to then-neglected historic objects, Dr. Fish said:

> The first duty of the archaeologist is to discover such material and to verify it; the next is to secure its preservation. . . . Then comes the task of studying it; classifying it and arranging it, and making it ready for use. At this point the function of the archaeologist ceases and the duty of the historian begins; i.e., to interpret it, and

to bring it into harmony with the recognized body of information regarding the past. It is not necessary that different individuals in every case do these different things . . . nearly every historian should be something of an archaeologist and every archaeologist should be something of an historian. . . . When the archaeologist ceases from the preparation of his material, and begins the reconstruction of the past, he commences to act as an historian and has to call up *a new range of equipment, and a new set of qualifications* [italics mine].

Thus it seems apparent that the astute Dr. Fish anticipated the disciplines of the historian-archeologist more than half a century ago, but most of his colleagues remained passive. Nothing effective was done by either the universities or the museums of this country to set up the "new range of equipment," nor did they recognize any need for the "new set of qualifications." Such research and identification as was done in the field of historic objects was undertaken by men and women having an antiquarian turn of mind. Seldom were their findings taken seriously by the profession. I think there is fair evidence of the truth of this assertion in various papers published by competent investigators who focused upon the prehistoric or aboriginal artifacts from their digs but tossed aside or evaded the "contact junk" encountered.[1] Sometimes these archeologists included a few historic objects in the plates accompanying their published papers but made no comment in their texts regarding the significance of the historic objects. One gets the impression that generally the anthropologist shunned historic objects. Some of the trade objects recovered by unsympathetic archeologists found their way into museum collections, where they are still to be seen, but often the meager data that accompanies them lend but little to any definitive understanding. Yet it must be said that these orphan artifacts are valued by certain present-day workers who have the initiative to study and the resourcefulness to "put two and two together." Shining examples of constructive work done with long

[1] Arthur Woodward: "Archeology—The Scrap Book of History," *Regional Review*, Nat'l Park Serv., Richmond, Va., I:2 (August 1938), pp. 8–10. Mr. Woodward is a senior member within the current generation of archeologist-historians. Inasmuch as he worked with Reginald P. Bolton during the 1920's, he constitutes something of a link with the earlier generation. In that pioneer group, besides Bolton and Fish, were such workers as William M. Beauchamp, W. L. Calver, Charles E. Brown, Henry C. Mercer, David L. Bushnell, W. Holmes, and George A. West. Each of these men is to be credited with publications that are milestones in historic-site archeology.

neglected Western collections appear in T. M. Hamilton's "Indian Trade Guns." [2] Here is a work that really challenges the historian-archeologist to begin studying the accumulated artifacts piled up but never identified by our predecessors.

But, getting back to the chronology for the movement to recognize historic objects as sources of history, in 1938 our well-loved American Indian, Dr. Arthur C. Parker, made a plea for better use of three-dimensional "documents" in presenting history through museum exhibits. He wrote:

> History *can* be written by piecing together the evidences of man's thought as revealed by his handiwork. But this history cannot be reconstructed by haphazard methods. Visible storage in museum cases of miscellaneous articles is not history. It is confusion. Order and sequence are necessary . . . and to attain this order the student must be able to classify and assign his material culture objects to their proper places. [Dioramas and life-size groups are good] but if we are unable to have such presentations, we may still show the horizontal stratification of our culture by exhibiting representative utensils, implements, etc., of each stage of our historical development, so "writing" a record of cultural progress comparable to the better types of ethnological exhibits. . . . *When our workers are able to understand the ethnology of the whiteman* . . . museums of history will take on a new and more significant meaning.

I do not know whether Parker was at all conscious of the admonitions voiced by Dr. Fish thirty years earlier, but his thinking had entered the same channels. Fish had said: "Where have our carpenters, our stonemasons, our iron workers, our woodsmen, our miners, our boatmakers, our millers, and our gun manufacturers come from, and what tricks of the trade have each contributed? Studies of these things reveal something of the soul of the people."

At the time that Dr. Parker was perfecting his history exhibits at Rochester, New York, the National Park Service obtained funds with which to develop museums in a number of the nation's most important historic places. Without much prior notice the bureau found it necessary to locate and employ a staff of curators, museum planners, and preparators who could begin work immediately, without the benefits of special training for the special jobs in hand. Of the thirteen curators on that early staff, most were trained

[2] In *The Missouri Archeologist* (December 1960), pp. vii–226.

anthropologists recently out of college. They went to work in such field areas as Colonial National Historic Park, Virginia; Morristown, New Jersey; Fort McHenry National Monument, Maryland; Ocmulgee, Georgia; Chickamauga and Chattanooga National Military Park, Georgia and Tennessee; Guilford Courthouse, North Carolina; Shiloh, Tennessee; and Vicksburg, Mississippi. Extensive collections of historic objects already were on hand in all of the areas, and in some instances notable additions to the collections were acquired through excavations after the museum program was started. The curators did their best as they shaped exhibit plans to utilize the rich cultural materials at their command but, with four exceptions, they confessed to their overwhelming difficulties in discerning the significance of the "relics" to which they had had no previous introduction. The park historians, fellow workers with the curators on the field jobs, in most cases were unable to give much assistance in handling the three-dimensional objects.

I mention these circumstances without any intention of disparaging the individuals. I have been in touch with these same pioneer curators during the thirty or more years that have elapsed. With the exception of two who have died, these men are enjoying successful careers in the National Park Service or in leading universities and museums, and a couple of them are now expert in the field of historic objects. But the point I would make is that in 1935–6 neither the history nor the anthropology departments in colleges and universities provided training in the handling of history materials having three-dimensional characteristics.

With a thought to publicizing the unfavorable situation, the American Association of Museums scheduled a paper, "The Use of Historic Objects as Sources of History," for the History Museums Section at its annual meeting in Detroit in 1940. This paper [3] advocated that the association take steps to establish trial courses at the university level for the purpose of training historians, archeologists, and curators to use artifacts as research and interpretive materials in history. Consistent with the views of the day regarding student preparation for museum work, the speaker urged that the educational phase of training be offered in the

[3] By C. P. Russell. MS in National Park Service Museums Library, Washington, D.C.

university and that the training phase be given in selected museums.

There was no direct response to the paper from the organization, but among the officers were men active in the American Council of Learned Societies, a group then headed by Dr. Waldo Leland with headquarters in Washington. Presently Dr. Leland asked the National Park Service to delegate someone to discuss the history-archeology problem with his council at a regular meeting. The Service complied, and the story was presented to this panel of philosophers and educators very much as it had been given to the museum people. The subject was accorded rather full discussion, but the consensus was that historic objects belonged in the museum realm not in the university curriculum; "anyhow, where could a professor be found who is prepared to teach this subject?"

Apparently only Dr. Leland of the Learned Societies visualized the practicability of adding historic objects to the teaching materials in a university history department. He suggested that a foundation might be induced to provide funds with which to establish a chair at William and Mary as a start in launching the desired courses of training. He expressed intention of carrying the matter to other congresses but advised that it might be politic to "sell" the idea of such curricular expansion first to some of the regularly employed historians and archeologists already in the National Park Service. Since the leaders in the National Park Service Branch of Historic Sites were already "sold," there was no problem in arranging pertinent staff meetings.

The fact that a specialized job was to be done in so many different parks and monuments with few or no employees available who might be equal to the task engendered a certain determination. In March 1940 several interbranch conferences were held in the National Park Service Director's Office, Washington, in order that staff historians, archeologists, and museum workers might air their views regarding the impasse. Four two-hour meetings were held. Detailed minutes of the sessions are still available for reference.[4] The conferees were experienced in various aspects of interpretive work in the field; at this late date it is interesting to note, in the record of the discussions, the maturity and directness of their

[4] R. F. Lee and C. P. Russell, eds.: *Historic Objects; Their Place in Research and Interpretation* (Washington, D.C.: Nat'l. Park Serv.; 1940), 56 pp. (mimeographed).

approach to a discipline that at the time did not even have a name.

In effect, these men confessed to inadequacy in meeting obligations in handling cultural objects, but they recognized clearly enough that because of the basic values—"historic objects have a statement to make just as do written sources"—someone would have to master these three-dimensional materials. In their own words:

> The historic objects now in possession, or destined to come into the ownership of the National Park Service henceforth shall receive the best care, study, and interpretive use possible under existing limitations imposed by lack of knowledge and experience. . . . Every effort is to be made to bring about establishment of courses of training in colleges and universities designed to prepare historians, anthropologists, and museum curators to work with historic objects. Pending the day when especially prepared employees may be recruited from the universities, the National Park Service must utilize its existing staff leadership in conducting in-service training designed to increase the capacity of presently employed field men to work more effectively in the realm of historic objects.

World War II brought disruption and near disaster to many plans projected by the National Park Service; the anticipated plans of the interpreters for in-service training collapsed because of the drastic cuts in personnel and appropriations. One notable triumph was gained before the blow fell; Ned J. Burns's *Field Manual for Museums* was published by the Government Printing Office in 1941. This book became an important instrument in advancing the parks museum program. The National Park Service outlook upon its responsibilities in the field of historic objects is given on pages 22–3 and 105–7 of that volume.

The five-year interruption of normal progress in National Park Service programs brought about by war caused serious setbacks, but fortunately most of the Service personnel concerned with historic sites and historic objects returned to their jobs. Dr. Leland, as a member of the Advisory Board, remembered his earlier explorations in the matter of training specialists in history-archeology. In May 1946 an important conclave of Service officials and numerous educators, historians, and anthropologists from universities and museums of the eastern United States was called in Colonial National Historical Park, Virginia. Dr. Leland's American Council met the travel expenses of those not employed by the government.

Dr. J. C. Harrington of the National Park Service managed the meeting; R. F. Lee, Chief of the History Branch, National Park Service, sounded the keynote: "How can the existing body of physical sources of history within NPS areas best be utilized in writing American history? How are students to be trained to approach physical sources as part of their schooling?"

Potentially it was a high-powered conference. Participating in the discussions were well-known anthropologists, historians, and educators from Johns Hopkins, Harvard, Duke, William and Mary, the University of Virginia, the University of North Carolina, Louisiana State University, Williamsburg Restoration, Inc., the Philadelphia Museum of Art, and the United States National Museum. The idea of training students to become proficient in using historical objects seemed to set some of the university professors back on their heels. A number of them spoke with some regrets about the "yawning gap between historians and the sites and artifacts of history," but a general doubt was expressed regarding the practicability of detaching students from their campuses for long-enough assignments on archeological digs.

> Universities have done little or nothing about such student training because they cannot afford to spend money and time on it, at the same time that presently-prescribed programs of teaching are in progress. In any event, average graduate students would have great difficulty in mastering the intricacies of identification of cultural materials even in the laboratory, not to mention the added difficulties of identifying artifacts as they come from the ground. In other words, students who have signed up for history have not planned to be archeologists. Today graduate students in history seldom are given enough training in handling manuscripts. The proposed additional training in handling three-dimensional objects would strain a university history department and its average student beyond established limits.

No one professor uttered all of these comments, but the connotation of several short speeches added up to the above pessimistic outlook.

J. O. Brew of Harvard sounded a more optimistic note as he made a plea for recognition by the panel of the pressing need for historian-archeologists. He quoted Dr. Harrington's assertion that the National Park Service had immediate need for one hundred specialists in this field. He remarked that in his own fieldwork at Concord he found much pottery in the form of sherds that could not be dated. "The hardware encountered offered a similar problem. Digs in Arizona recovered 17th century Spanish objects about which full information could not be obtained." He urged that a clearing house for the identification of historic objects be established even though definitive descriptions might be impossible in some instances. He also urged that publication of finds be a regular procedure, although interpretation may of necessity be imperfect.

Dr. Frank Setzler of the National Museum asked for the establishment of standards in identifying historic objects.

> In museums, workers are constantly confronted with problems of identifying objects. This panel should not limit its thinking to the Colonial period; we face the broad field of historic objects and we should recognize the need to improve the knowledge imparted to any and all students of history. The National Museum needs able men at this moment to enter the field of cultural objects. The museum staff cannot take time to teach, and, presently, universities do not have professors who are equal to the task. There is occasion for this conference to perform a broad public service, as well as a service to the National Park Service.

Fiske Kimball, Philadelphia Museum of Art, observed:

> Probably universities are not as well prepared to meet the problems described as are the great museums which own large collections. Men prepared to teach any part of the subject, cultural materials, are snatched up by museums. Even the museums do not have trained personnel capable of handling all problems of identification. I subscribe to J. O. Brew's plea for publication. Field reports should not be held secret; the National Park Service should publish its reports; Williamsburg should make known its finds, even though interpretation may not be perfect. Workers in the museums of the country will find it possible to contribute to understanding of three-dimensional objects if they can study published reports. Everybody can benefit if the reports get distribution.

Kendrow of Williamsburg expressed intention of making better progress in publishing, but he explained that major efforts were still directed upon the study of the physical remains requiring exposition, and that the editors in his organization were hesitant.

To this Dr. Kimball said: "The mistake in the past grows out of striving for perfection. Publish in the raw, but publish without delay. Even pictures of the physical materials will serve an important purpose if they are distributed."

Here Harrington spoke of the example of Lambeth Delft found at Jamestown: "The American Wing was about to publish a definitive paper on delftware without knowing of the major collection at Jamestown." R. F. Lee of the National Park Service outlined the scope of the historic sites under the administration of the Service and advocated that a practicable scheme for shaping and maintaining a cumulative record of cultural materials be set up, "starting now." Dr. Charles Porter, also of the National Park Service, proposed the "organization of a society of antiquarians, not in the old sense of antiquarianism, for the exchange of knowledge and for joint study of objects." Marshall gave a warm second to this proposal. "In Great Britain it is dignified to be an antiquarian. The United States should breed some." (It is of more than slight significance that Williamsburg ultimately imported one of the English antiquarians as Chief Archeologist.)

Dr. Leland concluded the discussions with an admonition to the National Park Service to establish and publicize a practical guide to the physical remains (cultural objects) in its possession.

During the twenty years that have elapsed since Dr. Leland's Jamestown meeting, the ranks of the historian-archeologists have grown considerably. The reasons are not far to seek.

1. Many of the states of the Union and numerous historical societies, museums, universities, and other organized groups have established state parks, memorials, and similar reservations upon sites where historic events transpired. In order that these sites may be protected, managed, and interpreted it is necessary often to practice the best possible historic-site archeology. Historian-archeologists (or potential historian-archeologists) are searched out, cultivated, and hired by the state and private agencies concerned. Currently they continue in this employment.

2. The responsibilities of the National Park Service have not diminished since 1946; on the contrary, additional historic sites have been acquired, and investigative work has been intensified at some of the earlier reserves. Under the authority of the Historic Sites Act of 1935, the Park, Parkway and Recreation Area Study Act of 1936, and the Flood Control Act of 1944, the National Park

Service cooperates with and obtains assistance from federal (the Smithsonian Institution, especially) and state agencies in conducting archeological surveys and salvage on numerous sites, some of which are threatened by the widespread program of dams and reservoirs now in progress throughout much of the country. In this extensive salvage work, historic sites as well as the prehistoric centers are precisely located and excavated in order that historical data and historic objects may be saved. Here, at the moment, is the larger realm of the historian-archeologist.[5]

3. Among the miscellaneous programs that demand the attention of the historian-archeologist is the relatively new underwater archeology. In this field lies the opportunity to link certain historic sites in such a way as to clarify the history of some international relationships; also, through the recovery and comparison of artifacts to contribute importantly to the long-wanted standardization of identification. Obviously a great new realm is opened by this expansion of the frontiers of exploration and discovery. In truth, underwater archeology may well constitute a new dimension of the historian-archeologist's discipline needed to round out the profession and to perfect the organizational scheme visualized in 1946.

It would be satisfying to say that the objectives set forth at the Leland-Harrington forum in Colonial National Historical Park twenty years ago are close to attainment, but no such good report is given. In the words of one of the leaders who has busied himself continuously in historic-site archeology:

> Thinking back on the Jamestown conference [1946], I regret to say that nearly every one of the problems and concerns we talked about then are still with us—acceptance by historians, training for this kind of archeology, access to specialized data, publishing results, etc. There has been progress in each, but it is slow. . . . One of the more encouraging advances is the contributions forthcoming from continued conferences such as those organized by Stanley South. A host of people are now in or on the fringes of this new field. Some are making real contributions, but our basic problem is the same as it was 25 years ago—we still have to turn to "Indian" archeologists to dig historic sites.[6] . . . In regard to

[5] Archeological work on pipelines and highways adds two significant salvage activities to the National Park Service archeology program.

[6] Regarding this matter, Ivor Noël Hume observes: "Even today fine archeologists trained to excavate and study the cultures of the Southwestern Indians are sent to work on colonial sites in Virginia" (*Here Lies Virginia. An Archeological*

examples of published reports in this field the list is becoming extensive, but we still have the same old problem of finding publication outlets; the reports get into weird places.

A significant move was made in 1949 when the military-minded element among the historian-archeologists established their own society, The Company of Military Collectors and Historians, in Washington, D.C. They created the journal *Military Collector and Historian*, thus providing the quarterly outlet for a wealth of original material on one class of historic objects. This classified literature so created, assembled, and integrated through a quarter of a century exceeds in interest and value anything created and released by other antiquarians in America. The Company hews to its line, never boasting of its unique accomplishment, but in its success, I think, is encouragement for the establishment of the much-needed all-inclusive society of historian-archeologists.

A variety of reasons have been advanced for the failure of the academic historians to give hearty support to "antiquarianism." To me the reasons do not seem valid, but the fact remains that no real union has been attained. Perhaps it is worthwhile to review the steps taken during the past decade looking toward the all-important coalition.

In the 1950 *American Heritage* William S. Powell adopted Dr. J. C. Harrington's appellation "Historic Site Archeology" and summarized the projects then in work. Included was a Florida underwater job, but no reference was made to it as "underwater archeology." Generally the release constituted applause for the successful birth of a new discipline and a new national interest in history. Understandably Mr. Powell conceived of the main objective as being principally "rebuilding" and he therefore advanced the descriptive term "restoration archeology." Also in 1950, The New-York Historical Society published Calver and Bolton's important *History Written with Pick and Shovel*, designed to encourage and guide the growing fraternity of military specialists and other fieldworkers. Heizer's *Manual of Field Methods* also appeared in 1950.

During the 1950's fieldwork in Virginia continued, and numerous historic sites in Arizona, California, Canada, Florida, Michi-

---

View of Colonial Life and History. [New York: Alfred A. Knopf, 1963], p. 97). Mr. Noël Hume fails to point to a source of trained historian-archeologists who might be recruited for the colonial digs.

gan, Pennsylvania, Rhode Island, and Washington were excavated. At least one of the resulting reports, Harrington's *New
Light on Washington's Fort Necessity*, published in 1957, stands
as a classic. By 1957 the professional concern with historic-site
archeology was such as to prompt the American Association for
State and Local History to schedule a panel discussion, "The Artifact in History," at its annual meeting in Columbus, Ohio. Here for
the first time the usefulness of the historic object was discussed pro
and con in the light of a considerable body of data derived through
practical experience. Probably the most constructive offering was
made by Harrington, who at the close of his recounting of examples persuaded his listeners:

> Artifacts *can* be employed as nondocumentary sources by histo-
> rians; they not only fill in missing details, but may even furnish
> extremely critical information. . . . Their value to the historian is
> in proportion to how much is known of their cultural context in a
> given historical situation. A rusty fragment of a matchlock firing
> mechanism found at Jamestown, with pertinent archeological
> data available to the scholar, constitutes a unique and valuable bit
> of historical source material. Depending upon the particular his-
> torical problem under consideration, this artifact might well be
> more valuable than a complete gun of the period, bought from a
> collector [for exhibit purposes].

Patent though this reasoning be, the number of professional
historians who hear it (or read it) is infinitesimal. The historians'
doubts expressed in 1946 still prevail—"Universities cannot afford
to spend money and time on historic objects, and yet conduct their
presently prescribed programs." A greater and more deplorable
circumstance is seen in the academic historian's seeming adherence
to the Hogarthian belief voiced so long ago, "the artifact stops
short of any possibility of truly reconstituting the picture of the
human past; to that end the literary documents are all-essential,
now and in future." The works of two historians, Bloch (1953)
and Hockett (1955), offer hope that the profession ultimately will
take a more searching look at the three-dimensional source materials.

It seems pertinent to refer here to the *Bulletin* and to the new
"Technical Leaflet" series published by the American Association
for State and Local History. The editorial outlook is sympathetic to
the cause of the historian-archeologist, and sometimes the printed

subject matter constitutes argument for a wedding of the laboratory and the historians' classroom. Potentially the American Association for State and Local History offers liaison.

At the annual meeting of the American Anthropological Society in Washington in 1958, there was featured an important "Symposium on the Role of Archeology in Historical Research." Techniques at the dig, collaboration between specialists, "intellectualization" of the results of the dig, and cultural reconstruction and publicizing finds were narrated by five "kingpins" of the profession, and their papers were discussed by five equally distinguished members. The record of this meeting provides the most sophisticated expressions extant of the philosophy of the historian-archeologist. I like the words of the speaker who closed the meeting: "The historian-archeologist must be competent in historical research as well as in archeology. He must have a basic knowledge of architecture. Finally, he must be an anthropologist, for *it is the study of cultures and the physical entity of man himself that gives to him insight in human perspective.*"

Among the speakers at this 1958 meeting, only J. O. Brew referred to training: "The universities are still not providing their students with concepts, much less training in this growing field."

Since 1958 Harvard has shaped a course of training, and Professor Anthony Garvan of the University of Pennsylvania initiated one on material culture. At Pennsylvania also, Dr. John L. Cotter conducted a field school in historic-site archeology during the summer of 1963.

At the University of Arizona in February 1964, Arthur Woodward launched a prescribed college course, "Historical Archeology," under the joint aegis of the departments of anthropology and history. His course has lapsed, however.

Instruction not of college level, but deserving of mention, is given at Cooperstown, New York, where the New York State Historical Association has conducted sessions on "Managing Small Museum Collections," including historic objects. This is a part of the Annual Seminars on American Culture offered to amateurs and professionals. Since 1947 twenty of the seminars have been held.

The Museum Division of the National Park Service, Washington, conducts an annual museum methods training course. "Historical objects receive attention in this training, and the responsibility for care of historic objects is written into the job description of

Regional Curators. We stress the need for research on our historical collections and try to pave the way for such research."

By way of recapitulation I would say that two or three of the goals defined by the conferees at Jamestown in 1946 have not been attained:

1. There is no central clearing house for the identification of historic objects; no established standards useful in identifying and comparing historic objects; and no step has been taken toward the creation and maintenance of a cumulative record of America's cultural materials.[7]

2. The desired "Society of Antiquarians" has been advocated by one or more speakers whenever historian-archeologists gather, but until recently nothing practical had been done toward the founding of a society. Just as this book was to go to press we received the welcome news that the Society for Historical Archaeology has been established under the presidency of John L. Cotter. It is proposed that the society shall publish an annual journal, *Historical Archaeology*, and *Current Year*, a report on field activities.

To be somewhat less negative in ending this work, I say that very constructive steps have been taken under the pioneering efforts of Harrington and the later contributions of South, Noël Hume, Goggin, Cotter, and others to give definition to the discipline of the historian-archeologist. At least a beginning has been made in establishing university courses designed to prepare future historian-archeologists. One course is in a department of history, one in archeology, and a third receives the blessings of both a department of anthropology and a department of history. It is too early to say whether or not the future development of the special curriculum will reside generally in American history (as I think it should), but it is not too early to predict that presently the training will be available in one or another department in numerous institutions and, eventually, there will come the full-fledged "school" of historic-site archeology.

The dramatic qualities of recovered weapons and of certain

---

[7] In 1963 Harper & Row published *Soldier and Brave*, "a record of Indian-connected sites without parallel in our historical literature." This is the first major publication of the National Survey of Historic Sites and Buildings, National Park Service. In 1964 *Colonials and Patriots*, in the same series, was produced by the Government Printing Office. These books do for two classes of historic sites the service that should be done for historic objects.

Indian trade pieces appeal to the curiosity of almost every citizen; public interest is good. So far as dedicated collectors are concerned, interest is lively, and the educated concern they show usually is helpful to the historian-archeologist and to his broad program of research. This book is directed to the average reader and to the collector as well as to the professional curator of history. May it testify to the fact that even now a certain continuity and an all-important partnership prevail in the efforts exerted by the dirt-encrusted digger and the researcher among the documents.

A P P E N D I X B

John Jacob Astor's Inventory of Tools and Blacksmithing Equipment on the Columbia River, 1812–1813

SURPRISINGLY ENOUGH, THE EARLIEST LARGE LOT OF IRON tools used in the Far West by American trader-trappers is also the one of which we are best informed. The unique information is available because John Jacob Astor desired to make it a matter of record on the books of the United States Congress. A detailed inventory of Astor properties on the Columbia was prepared by Mr. Astor's clerks in connection with the "sale" of Astoria to the North West Company in October 1813. This analysis of equipment and trade goods found no published outlet during the troubled years of war and recovery from war, but in 1823 Mr. Astor testified to the Congress regarding his losses resulting from the fiasco at Astoria. Some eighty printed pages carry his story. Following are the items of ironworks in the Astoria inventory.

> From "Message of the President of the United States [James Monroe] Communicating . . . documents relating to an establishment at the mouth of the Columbia River." House Document 45, 17th Congress, 2nd Session. Jan. 27, 1823, pp. 1–80. Read and tabled.
> Inventory of Sundries delivered to the North West Company, Astoria, October, 1813.

AXES, ADZES, HOES, SAWS, ETC.

(A few of the items were new; as indicated, most were in use by "house carpenters" and other Astorian field crews.)

8	Large Abertsins English axes	@ 1.72¼ each	13.78
8	Large English axes, used	1.72¼	13.78
1	Large carpenters broad axe	3.00	3.00
2	Carpenters broad axe, used	3.00	6.00
1	Coopers' broad axe	3.00	3.00
2	Small square-head axes, Columbia-made	1.50	3.00
25	Large Canadian axes, Columbia-made	2.50	62.50
17	Large Canadian axes, used, Columbia-made	2.50	42.50
282	Half axes, Columbia-made	1.50	423.00
2	Half axes, used, Columbia-made	1.50	3.00
157	Small axes, Columbia-made	.75	117.75
4	Small axes, used, Columbia-made	.75	3.00
1	Iron wedge, used	.50	.50
4	Carpenters' adzes	2.50	10.00
1	Ship carpenters' adze	2.50	2.50
3	Canoe adzes, used	2.00	6.00
2	Grooving adzes	2.00	4.00
1	Grooving adze, used		1.75
103	Large iron dogs	1.50	154.50
2	Pair dogs, used		1.00
194	Small steel dogs	.75	145.50
3	Cross cut saws	3.50	10.50
3	Whip saws, used	6.50	19.50
3	Fret saws, used		.37½
1	Compass saw	1.50	1.50
2	Compass saws, used		1.25
1	Hand saw, used	2.00	2.00
1	Sash saw, used		1.81
3	Saw sets	.25	.75
2	Saw sets, used	.25	.50
2	Large garden hoes	.22	.44
2	Small garden hoes, used	.22	.44
9	Small garden hoes, used	.22	1.98
1	Iron trying square	4.00	4.00
1	Claw hammer		.25
1	Claw hammer, used		.75

4	Masons' hammers, 19 lbs., used		4.75
2	Trowels, used	.25	.50
4	Spades, used	1.12½	4.50
1	Iron rake, used		1.00
3	Pick axes, used	1.75	5.25
2	Crow bars, 38 lbs., used		5.70
2	Brace and 16 bits		9.39
1	T-Bevil, used		.68½
1	Scythe, used		1.00
2	Grind stones, used		9.28

BOAT BUILDERS' TOOLS IN USE, BOAT YARD, ASTORIA

2	Broad axes	3.50	7.00
1	Small English axe	1.72½	1.72½
1	Augur, 1 inch		.50
1	Ships carpenters' adze	1.75	1.75
1	Square head half axe	2.00	2.00
1	Bevil		.68½
4	Firmers chisels		.80
4	Socket chisels		1.24
6	Iron clamps, 26 lbs.	.25	6.50
1	Spike gimlet		.27
1	Gauge		.56¼
4	Gouges	.25	1.00
1	Hatchet		1.72¼
1	Clinch hammer		.43¾
1	Claw hammer		.75
6	Caulking irons	.36	2.16
1	Drawing knife		1.12½
1	Top mall		.40
1	Mallet		.40
1	Double iron fore plane		2.31
1	Jack plane		1.18½
1	Smoothing plane		.93¾
1	Bead plane		1.06
1	Hand saw		2.00
1	Hand saw, broken		1.50
1	Oil Stone		3.12½

SMALL TOOLS AND MISCELLANEOUS IRON IMPLEMENTS, ASTORIA

1¹⁄₁₂	Gro. canoe awls	@ .12 each	18.72
14⁸⁄₁₂ dz.	shoe makers awls		.76
9⅝	Gro. Indian awls	3.00 gro.	28.87½
4	Screw augers, 9½ qrs.		1.18¾

7	Screw augers 35 qrs.		13.12½
2	Pod augers 7½ qrs.		.75
2	Chandlers' augers, 8 qrs.		1.00
2	Tap borers	.21	.42
1	Bung borer	1.00	1.00
6½ dz.	socket chisels, 2″ to ½″		17.71
8	Chisels for Indians	.12	.96
60	Broad ice chisels		15.90
25	Narrow ice chisels		6.62½
13	Morticing chisels, used	.33⅓	4.33
23	Firmers chisels, used	.20	4.60
3	Cold chisels	.25	.75
17½	Pairs fish darts	.25	4.37
1	Rasp, used		.34¼
68	Files. Round, flat, half-round, triangular, square		11.27½
11	Hand saw files, used		3.62½
1	Spike gimlet		.27
1	Spike gimlet, used		.27
4¾ dz.	Nail gimlets		1.59¼
½ dz.	Gimlets, used		.37½
5	Marking irons		.90
1	Small grapnell	.25	.25
2	Grapnells, 124 lbs.		18.60
1 dz.	Crooked knives	.20	2.40
22	Iron knives handled	1.00 dz.	1.83¼
104	Steel knives not tempered	1.75	13.70¾
29	Large steel blades	.20	5.80
61⁵⁄₁₂ dz.	iron blades	.75 dz.	46.06½
64	Steel blades	.80 dz.	4.26
1	Crow bar, 19 lbs.		1.52
1	Harpoon		.50
23	Boarding pikes	1.50	34.50
1	Plumb bob, used		.12
3	Screw drivers, used		.93
1	Mortice gauge, used		1.12
1	Set scribing gouge (10), used		1.50
6	Gouges, used		1.50
2	Cone gouges, used		.50
1	Drawing knife, used		1.12½
1	Spoke shave, used		.62½
1	Pair pincers, used		.31
1	Pair pincers		1.75
1	Pair pliers, used		.25
3	Punches, used		.28

CARPENTERS' PLANES

1	Carpenter's long jointer	1.94
1	Drawing knife	1.12½
1	Double iron smoothing plane, used	1.13
1	Carpenter's fore plane	1.69
2	Single iron fore planes, used	2.87
1	Carpenter's smooth plane	.75
2	Double fore jack planes, used	2.31
1	Pair match planes @ 3.87½	7.75
1	Pair small match planes, used	1.94
1	Plough and stop plane, used	3.88
2	Rabbit plane 2 inch, used	2.05
1	Rabbitt plane, 1¼ inch, used	1.06
1	Rabbit plane, ¾ inch, used	.68½
1	Bead plane, ½ inch, used	1.06
1	Bead plane, ¾ inch, used	1.12½
1	Bead plane, ¼ inch, used	1.06
8	Plane irons, used	2.64

FISH HOOKS

234	Large salmon Kirby hooks, per C 1.50	3.51
645	Fish hooks, assorted	3.35¼
170	Cod hooks	1.80¼
1	Shark hook	.75

COOPERS' TOOLS IN USE IN BARREL SHOP, ASTORIA

1	Broad axe	3.00	3.00
1	Brace and bits	1.14	1.14
1	Bung borer	1.00	1.00
1	Tap do.	.21	.21
1	Pair compasses	2.00	2.00
1	Cold chisel	.08	.08
1	Iron driver	.50	.50
3	Setts iron tress hoops	1.00	3.00
1	do. wood do. do.	.80	.80
1	Rivetting hammer	.43¾	.43¾
1	Beckiron	12.00	12.00
2	Jointers, with double and single irons	4.00	8.00
1	do. do. single do.	2.00	2.00
1	Marking iron	.16	.16
1	Inshare	.33¼	.33¼
1	Flagging iron	.50	.50

2	Drawing knives, (Alberson's)	1.12½	2.25
1	Hollowing do.	.75	.75
1	Rounding do.	.75	.75
1	Punch	.08	.08
1	Rule, of twelve inches	.25	.25
2	Crow stocks	1.25	2.50
1	Handsaw	2.00	2.00
1	Vice	.25	.25
1	Frow	1.00	1.00

IRON STOCK, ETC., ASTORIA

4	lbs. iron for setting poles	.25	1.00
7⁵⁄₁₂	dz. iron hoop, doz.	.30	2.22½
1014	lbs. blistered steel	.07¼	73.51½
14	cwt 15 lbs. square iron	5.62½	82.31
6	cwt 7 lbs. flat iron	5.62½	38.32
6	cwt 25 lbs. iron for spikes	5.75	37.22
4	cwt 23 lbs. round iron	6.50	27.33¼
2	qrs. 4 lbs. hoop iron	8.25	4.42
23	lbs. iron wire	.33	7.59
2	Blacksmiths' forges	50.00	100.00

APPENDIX C

Markings on Axes and Tomahawks

NOT ALL HISTORIC AXES WERE MARKED, BUT MORE than a few bear names, symbols, and signs, as well as a variety of decorations. Sometimes it is difficult to identify the smith's "touch marks" or trade symbols among the miscellany of decorative filed lines, cusps, and notches; the mixtures of scratchwork, scrollwork, and floral engravings; the stamped diamonds, hearts, crescents, crosses, stars, and chevrons; and the variety of inlays—silver, brass, pewter, and copper—featuring round or oval discs, crescents, bands, circles, triangles, diamonds, and hearts. In a very few instances the inlays are gold. Occasionally the workmanship on these decorations bespeak the skill of master craftsmen; more often they are crude and tell of the enthusiasm of smiths who were capable in forging but unpracticed in engraving. The dies and punches used by many blacksmiths gave fairly uniform results, however, and some axmakers attained pleasing results through simple stamping of designs on their products. A few of these artificers adopted a given pattern of ornamentation and repeated it on ax after ax, thereby establishing something of a trademark; the greater number, however, seem to have regarded each ax to be an entity in itself, and there is little rhyme or reason to their ornamentation. "Touch marks," on the other hand, were punched into the ax with steel dies adopted by the smiths somewhat as personal signatures. No one has devised a key for the identification of the smiths who made the marks. The assortment of unidentified

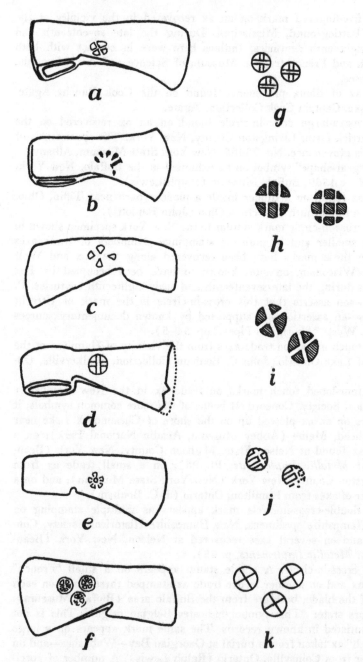

FIG. 107. *Some Smith's Marks on Trade Axes.*

a, four-lobed, single punch mark on an ax collected at Grand
Marais, Minnesota. No. 6768, Minnesota Historical Society, St. Paul.

b, five-fingered mark on an ax recovered in the vicinity of the Ackia Battleground, Mississippi. During the late seventeenth and early eighteenth centuries, Indians here were in contact with both English and French traders. Museum of Science and Art, Memphis, Tennessee.

c, ax of Sioux provenance found on the Cook Ranch, Agate, Nebraska. Captain Cook Collection, Agate.

d, extra-large cross-in-circle found on an ax recovered on the Kirkpatrick farm, Livingston County, New York. The specimen is of Iroquois provenance. No. 23885, New York State Museum, Albany.

e, "gear-shape" symbol on ax exhumed in the Buffalo, New York, area. No. c 4569, Buffalo Museum (Ralph Lewis).

f, ax found on a timber inside a pioneer barn near Tiffin, Ohio. William Fingerhuth Collection, Ohio (John Barsotti).

g, cross-in-circle mark similar to the New York specimen shown in *d*, but smaller and in multiple stampings. Numbers of trade axes bearing these marks have been recovered along the Fox and Wolf rivers, Wisconsin, on sites known to have been occupied by Fox Indians during the late seventeenth and early eighteenth centuries. P. V. Lawson asserts that this cross-in-circle is the mark of Utrecht exports—an assertion not supported by known documentary sources (G. A. West: "Aboriginal Pipes," pp. 54–5).

h, touch marks on trade axes from the vicinity of Hamilton at the head of Lake Ontario. John C. Bonham Collection, Walkerville, Ontario.

i, four-lobed touch marks on trade ax in the New Hampshire Historical Society, Concord. It is one of the more common symbols; it appears on an ax plowed up on the shore of Chesuncook Lake near Moosehead, Maine (Abbey Museum, Acadia National Park); on a large ax found at Nelson Flats, Madison County, New York (Beauchamp: *Metallic Implements*, Pl. 23); on a small trade ax from Livingston County, New York (New York State Museum); and on a number of axes from Hamilton, Ontario (J. C. Bonham).

j, double-cross-in-circle mark appears as multiple stamping on New Hampshire specimens, New Hampshire Historical Society, Concord, and on several axes recovered at Nelson, New York (Beauchamp: *Metallic Implements*, p. 65).

k, cross-in-circle. A single stamp appears on a small "French" trade ax and on another larger trade ax stamped three times on each side of the blade; both are from the Buffalo area (Buffalo Museum). Curators state: "This symbol indicates Belgian origin." This is not substantiated in known records. The same mark appears on a large "French" ax taken from a burial at Georgian Bay—Wabashee—and on another from Coinsville, Ontario (Ralph Lewis). A number of specimens from several New York sites have it.

l, a typical "French" trade ax marked with circles enclosing eight radial lines. It is one of a number of specimens so marked that were

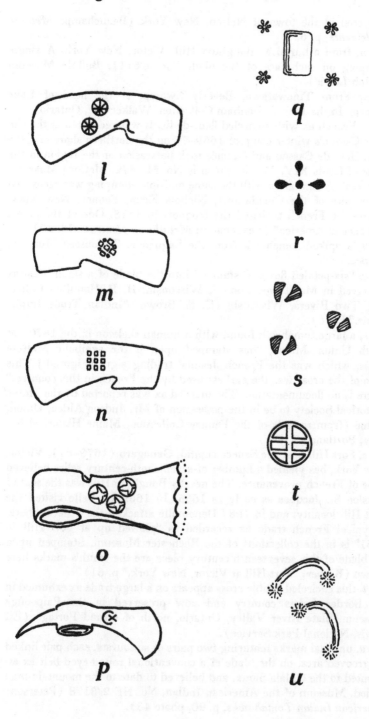

recovered in the town of Nelson, New York (Beauchamp: *Metallic Implements*, p. 65).

m, from a burial at Boughton Hill, Victor, New York. A single stamping on each face of the blade. No. c 6111, Buffalo Museum (Ralph Lewis).

n, From Tinawatawa, Beverly Swamp, at the head of Lake Ontario. In the John C. Bonham Collection, Walkerville, Ontario.

o, French ax with encircled fleur-de-lis. It was recovered at the site of de Casson's winter camp of 1669–70 on the northern shore of Lake Erie. Here de Casson and Galinée took possession of the region in the name of Louis XIV. The specimen is No. M-1672, McCord Museum, Montreal. A similar ax with the same multiple stamping was recovered at the site of the Oneida fort, Nichols Farm, Fenner, New York, "where the French besieged the Iroquois in 1615. One of the oldest iron axes in America" (Beauchamp: *Metallic Implements*, Pl. 20).

p, a spiked tomahawk from the Saguenay. Tadoussac Museum, Quebec.

q, "six-petaled flowers" stamped into the blade of a small broadax recovered in Manitowoc County, Wisconsin. H. P. Hamilton Collection, Two Rivers, Wisconsin (C. E. Brown: "Indian Trade Implements," Pl. 5).

r, a large tomahawk found with a human skeleton in the 1870's at South Union, Maine, "has stamped upon it the symbolic Maltese Cross, which was the French Jesuits' trading sign. [Figured.] This form of the cross was the earliest used by the French in this country." There is no documentation. The marked ax was reported by the Maine Historical Society to be in the possession of Mr. Judson Alden, Union, Maine (from records of the Penney Collection, Maine Historical Society, Portland).

s, Fort Hill near the Seneca capital, Ganagaro (1670–87), Victor, New York, has yielded a number of seventeenth-century relics believed to be of French provenance. The nearby Boughton Hill was the seat of Mission St. Jacques as early as 1655. In 1669 La Salle visited the Fort Hill locality, and in 1687 Denonville attacked the Senecas there. A typical French trade ax recorded as "plowed up at Fort Hill in 1861" is in the collections of the Rochester Museum. Stamped upon the blade of this seventeenth-century piece are the smith's marks here shown (Barber: "Fort Hill at Victor, New York," p. 61).

t, this encircled double cross appears on a large trade ax exhumed in the Border Lakes country and now preserved in the Paipoonge Museum, Slate River Valley, Ontario, north of Grand Portage (Elt Davis, National Park Service).

u, unusual marks featuring two pairs of sunbursts, each pair linked by grooved arcs, on the blade of a conventional round-eyed belt ax attributed to the Oglala Sioux, and believed to date to the mountain-man period. Museum of the American Indian, No. HF 2/3178 (Peterson: *American Indian Tomahawks*, p. 90, photo 43).

symbols presented here may serve as an inducement to some
worker with a detective turn of mind. It is to be noted that marked
or decorated axes are in the minority; the greater number of old
axes now in collections are devoid of discernible marks or decorations of any kind.

The Names and Initials of Makers of Axes

A veritable multitude of blacksmiths made axes; some
catered to white men who needed tools for their own use, but
many smiths were in the business of supplying the needs of the
Indian. The great majority of these artificers get but little recognition in the literature, and comparatively few "signed" their products. It seems worthwhile to take some note here of those workers
who did "make their mark" in the form of conventional stamped
names or initials on their axes, or who were accorded place in the
contemporary documentary record of the trade.

A few lists of makers of axes are available to the researcher.
The Hudson's Bay Company's London and Canadian offices have
been cooperative in compiling the names and dates of manufacturers who supplied all manner of trade goods to the company up to
and including 1821.[1] Woodward gives good attention to numerous
smiths of all periods,[2] and Peterson lists 106 blacksmiths and
dealers who made or distributed axes in America during the eighteenth and nineteenth centuries.[3] Our list below is original and does
not duplicate the others, but certain individual blacksmiths encountered in our independent study were also recognized and listed
by Peterson and by Woodward. Also, our list does not repeat the
listing of U. S. Indian Office blacksmiths of the 1830's, as given on
pages 365–6, except as some individual smiths on the 1830's list
were found to be active prior to the 1830's or are recognizable in
some status other than employees of the United States government.

---

[1] "Names of Firms Supplying Trading Goods to the Hudson's Bay Company
Prior to 1821" (MS), 8 pp. Copies of the manuscript list are to be found in many
American libraries, including the Western Museum Laboratory, National Park
Service, San Francisco.

[2] "The Metal Tomahawk," *Bulletin of the Fort Ticonderoga Museum*, Vol.
VII (January 1946).

[3] *American Indian Tomahawks* (New York: Museum of the American
Indian; 1965), pp. 46–52.

Blacksmiths Who "Signed" Their Axes, or Are Recognized in the Fur Trade Documents of Their Day

"A. A. & T. Co. / Glassport / Pat Apl——." Stamped on a camp hatchet of recent vintage in the Cook Collection, Agate, Nebraska. The specimen was presented to Captain Cook by Dull Knife of the Northern Cheyenne, who in the early twentieth century regularly came with a band of followers to the Indians' ancestral village site near the Cook ranch house.

François Albert, Montreal blacksmith, moved to Mackinac, 1818–19, where the American Fur Company paid him $300 per year (Wisconsin Historical *Collections*, XII, 122).

Joseph Albot, British government blacksmith in New York, 1755–63 (Sir William Johnson Papers, II, 636).

J. B. Allere, U. S. Indian Department, part-time blacksmith, Chicago, 1820. His rate of pay was $40 per month (American State Papers, Indian Affairs, II, 403–4).

Jean-Baptiste Amyot-Vincelot, French government blacksmith at Michilimackinac, 1742. Records show that he had served there since 1727—the earliest indentifiable individual in the present list (Wisconsin Historical *Collections*, XVII, 372).

John Andrus "signed" the much-publicized tomahawk presented to the Seneca chief, Cornplanter. The specimen is preserved in the New York State Museum, Albany. A portrait shows a similar tomahawk (McKenney and Hall: *History of the Indian Tribes of North America*, I, 85, and in La Farge: *American Indian*, p. 57).

Étienne Ballard, British government blacksmith at Detroit, 1778 ([Michigan] *Pioneer Collections*, IX, 470–71).

J. B., for John Bordeau, mountain man turned blacksmith. He had a forge at Fort Laramie in the 1840's and perhaps earlier. A marked specimen was found at Cook Ranch, Agate, Nebraska, in 1890 (Fig. 69i, page 270).

P. E. B. & Co. appears on one side of the blade of a brass pipe tomahawk of the "Missouri war hatchet" style. It was collected from the Chippewa at White Earth, Minnesota, in 1879, and even then it was regarded by tribesmen as a tribal heirloom. Dr. W. Thornton Parker, Northampton, Massachusetts, collected and retained the piece; descriptive matter and photographs are in the U. S. National Museum (letter, Ewers to Russell, October 1, 1946).

Ryer Bowen, British Indian Department blacksmith, New York, 1755–63 (Sir William Johnson Papers, III, 163).

Jim Bridger, celebrated mountain man who was a blacksmith as well as fur trader from 1820 to the 1840's (pp. 382–4 of the text).

R. Broderick, U. S. Indian Department blacksmith, Piqua, Ohio, during 1820's. He was paid $470 per year (American State Papers, Indian Affairs, II, 366, 403–4).

J. M. Brown, U. S. Indian Department, part-time blacksmith, Green Bay, Wisconsin, 1820 (American State Papers, Indian Affairs, II, 403–4).

William Burnett, U. S. Indian Department, part-time blacksmith, Green Bay, Wisconsin, 1820 (American State Papers, Indian Affairs, II, 403–4).

John Cambell, U. S. Indian Department blacksmith, Michilimackinac, 1822. He was paid $671 per year (American State Papers, Indian Affairs, II, 366).

William Cannon, Astorian blacksmith; later he was an important Hudson's Bay Company personage at Fort Vancouver (Hussey: *Preliminary Survey . . . Fort Vancouver*, pp. 48–9, 187, 196, 199, 200, 203; Caywood: *Exploratory Excavations*, p. 14, *Final Report*, p. 18, and pp. 140–381 of this volume).

Lefèvre Chaparo, British government blacksmith-at-large, 1778 ([Michigan] *Pioneer Collections*, IX, 470–1).

—— Chauvin, British government blacksmith, Detroit, 1796 ([Michigan] *Historical Collections*, XII, 191).

Collins & Co., Hartford (Collinsville), Connecticut, established in 1826; blacksmiths—Samuel W. Collins, Daniel C. Collins, William Wells. The marked specimen here listed is a conventional cast-steel "Yankee"-type square-poll belt ax, No. 179 in the Collins line. It was obtained from a Sioux source and is now No. 154021 in the U. S. National Museum. Its Indian-made haft is 28 inches, as compared with the original Collins handle of 14 inches. In 1919 this hatchet, as well as some fifty additional models of axes of the old-time fur-trade designs, was still offered by the Collins Company. Today the big selection of "French" axes are not manufactured in Collinsville, but some models are still made in the Collins Company factories in Mexico City, Cali, Colombia, and São Paulo, Brazil—living American relics, so to speak, of the onetime predominant fur traders' stock-in-trade. The current demand is not from fur traders, of course, but from Latin American peoples who live close to the soil. (Collins & Co.: *Catalogo Illustrado*, p. 14; letter, C. M. Elston to C. P. Russell, June 24, 1965).

Piter Conin, British government blacksmith at New York, 1755–63 (Sir William Johnson Papers, II, 578).

Philip Creamer, U. S. Indian Department blacksmith, St. Louis, 1822. He was paid $780 per year (American State Papers, Indian Affairs, II, 366).

Peter Cremar, British Indian Service blacksmith at New York, 1755–63 (Sir William Johnson Papers, II, 639).

Henry Deringer, the famous maker of guns, Philadelphia. Despite hot dissension regarding Deringer's default in connection with a contract for U. S. rifles in 1814, he obtained numerous sizable government contracts during subsequent years. In 1816 Deringer contracted to make brass pipe tomahawks for the Office of Indian Trade. Fifty-one of these were delivered to the government, for which he received $2.50 each (National Archives, U. S. Indian Office Manuscripts, 1816).

H. E. Dimick, St. Louis gunsmith, 1840's and later. In the heyday of his business, Horace Dimick employed a score or more artisans. It is quite possible that some of his employees were skilled in making pipe tomahawks. It is a fact also that Dimick made wholesale purchases of percussion revolvers and other ironworks manufactured in factories other than his own, upon which the Dimick name was stamped. Pipe tomahawks may have been included in this business. At any rate, the Museum of the American Indian owns a pipe tomahawk of Nez Percé provenance upon the blade of which appears "H. E. Dimick / St. Louis." Peterson pictures the specimen in photograph No. 153 of his *American Indian Tomahawks*.

Benjamin Doyle, British Indian Service blacksmith at Grand River, 1796. He was paid 63 pounds, 17 shillings, 6 pence per year ([Michigan] *Pioneer Collections*, V. 25, 108).

—— Dufrene, British gunsmith at Montreal, 1796 ([Michigan] *Historical Collections*, XVII, 218).

Louis Duplesis, British Indian Service blacksmith, Ouiatanon, Indiana, 1778. Here the forges of the French dated back to the early decades of the eighteenth century ([Michigan] *Pioneer Collections*, IX, 470–1).

W. S. / J. Durant appears on an English-type square-poll camp ax with ears (best known to the fur trade of the early 1800's as the "Kentucky" pattern); the specimen was collected in New Hampshire. On the reverse side are initials "A. E." It is preserved in the New Hampshire Historical Society, Concord (fig. 70c, p. 272).

François Dyelle, British Indian Service blacksmith, Miami on the Maumee River, 1778 ([Michigan] *Pioneer Collections*, IX, 470–1).

Augustine Feltcan, British government blacksmith at Michilimackinac, 1779 (Wisconsin Historical Collections, XII).

G. is the initial stamped on the blade of a brass pipe tomahawk collected in the Shawnee country between Old Chillicothe and Old Piqua, Ohio. This is one of the brass specimens with the steel edge "dovetailed" (Richard G. Morgan: "An Engraved Tomahawk Pipe," pp. 15–16).

J. G. were the initials on both sides of the slender blade of a spiked tomahawk which, at the time of reporting (close of the nineteenth century), was owned by Wilson Johnson, Onondaga Reservation (Beauchamp: *Metallic Implements*, p. 66, Pl. 23).

M. G. were the initials incised on both sides of the poll of a 10-by-10-inch broad ax that is recorded to have "hewed the timbers for the blockhouse at Sacketts Harbor (Naval base, Lake Ontario, War of 1812)." The specimen is in the Holland Land Office Museum, Batavia, New York (Ralph Lewis MS [1938]).

— Gallarno, blacksmith at the Grignon trading post, Green Bay, Wisconsin, 1790's. Later he worked at Prairie du Chien (C. E. Brown: "Indian Trade Implements," pp. 63–4).

Silas Gobel was one of two blacksmiths with Jedediah Smith's California expedition, 1826 (Dale: *Ashley-Smith Explorations*, pp. 196, 200, 206; pp. 363 and 364 of this volume).

C. Gove. Two Potawatomi pipe tomahawks in the Museum of the American Indian bear this mark by Carlos Gove. Gove, a U. S. Cavalryman, entered the Indian Service after the Seminole War and in the 1840's was gunsmith at the agency on the St. Joseph, Michigan. Later he made rifles in St. Louis, Council Bluffs, Cheyenne, and Denver. In *American Indian Tomahawks* Peterson finds that the pipe tomahawks mentioned date to Gove's period at St. Joseph (Gluckman and Satterlee: *American Gun Makers*, p. 79).

H. Hackman, British blacksmith at Toronto in the 1790's. He

was paid 85 pounds, 5 shillings, 4 pence per year ([Michigan] *Historical Collections*, XXIV).

William A. Hall, part-time U. S. Indian Office blacksmith at Chicago in 1820 (American State Papers, Indian Affairs, II, 403–4).

F. Hoff, Lancaster, Pennsylvania, maker of silver-and-gold-inlaid pipe tomahawk now in the Clem Caldwell Collection. It is a presentation piece of the early nineteenth century. Peterson says: "The finest encountered" (*American Indian Tomahawks*, p. 139, photo No. 303).

—— *Holtzappfel:* see the section on the British "broad arrow" (pp. 422–3).

Jacob Irvin, U. S. Indian Office blacksmith, Natchitoches, Louisiana, 1822. He was paid $800 per year (American State Papers, Indian Affairs, II, 366).

Ronaldo Johnson, Aquasco, Maryland. As a step in filling an order for 600 axes placed by the U. S. Indian Trade Office, George Town, D.C., on August 12, 1808, Mr. Johnson delivered 176 axes in October 1808. The acknowledgment: "On weighing the axes which should have gone to five pounds each, I was astonished to find they are ½ pound to a pound-and-a-half too light. I did not return them, but, certainly, no more will be received of those weights" (Account Book, Office of Indian Affairs, Philadelphia, contains copy of the order of August 12, 1808; Letter Book, George Town, D.C., commencing October 1808 contains copy of the criticism of the Johnson axes. MSS now [1965] in National Archives).

Samuel Johnson, U. S. Indian Office blacksmith, Chicago, 1822. His salary was $540 per year (American State Papers, Indian Affairs, II, 366).

Joseph Jourdain, U. S. Indian Office blacksmith, Green Bay, Wisconsin, 1820's and 1830's. His most excellent pipe tomahawks, often marked with an inlaid crescent in copper, won for him wide recognition (see text pp. 281, 366; G. A. West: "Tobacco, Pipes," pp. 59–60; *Wisconsin Archeologist*, IV:3 and 4 [1905]; Wisconsin Historical Collections XX, 100, 339).

G. K. are the initials on an 8-inch square-poll felling ax with a flaring blade. The specimen was recovered in a 15-foot gravel drift when laborers made a road cut at Ouray, Colorado. It is No. OH-185, Colorado Historical Society.

Rudolph Koch, independent blacksmith at Michilimackinac, 1768 (Sir William Johnson Papers, VII, 341).

Augustin Lefoi, British Indian Department blacksmith at Detroit, 1778 ([Michigan] *Pioneer Collections*, IX, 470–1). In 1820 Lefoi—or Lafoy—was still at Detroit as an employee of the U. S. Indian Office.

John Lewis, U. S. Indian Office blacksmith at Detroit and at the Upper Sandusky Indian Agency, 1820's and 1830's. He was paid $470 per year (American State Papers, Indian Affairs, II, 366).

F. Lusignant, part-time blacksmith for the U. S. Indian Office, Fort Wayne, 1820 (American State Papers, Indian Affairs, II, 403–4).

George Meldrum made tomahawks for the British Indian Department, Michilimackinac, during the 1780's ([Michigan] *Pioneer Collections*, VIII, 473–4).

S. Miguel. A square-poll 7-inch tomahawk with flaring blade in the collections of the Missouri Historical Society bears the name "- - - - Norte S. Miguel" stamped vertically on the blade.

Benjamine Moore, Sutton, Massachusetts, was an employee of the U. S. War Department who inspected military arms at Springfield and at Hartford in 1810–15. He has been listed as a manufacturer of military tomahawks of the same period (Hicks: *Notes on United States Ordnance*, II, 61).

—— Newton, American Fur Company blacksmith at La Pointe, Wisconsin, in the 1830's (text p. 371).

J. O. were the initials within a cartouche on the flaring blade of a tomahawk found in a swamp in the immediate vicinity of Jackson, Wyoming. The poll of this small ax is unusually long and the eye is big. The specimen is preserved in the Museum of the Frontier, Jackson, Wyoming (W. C. Lawrence, March 25, 1965).

William Opy, British Indian Department blacksmith at New York, 1755–63 (Sir William Johnson Papers, II, 617).

Leber and Sylvestre Papin manufactured axes in St. Louis during the 1830's (see text p. 368).

Parke: see the section on the British "broad arrow" (p. 421).

George Platt, British Indian Department blacksmith at St. Joseph (Canada), 1797 ([Michigan] *Historical Collections*, XX, 638).

William Printup, British Indian Department blacksmith, New York, 1755–63 (Sir William Johnson Papers, II, 611).

Pierre Provinsalle, part-time U. S. Indian Office blacksmith at Saginaw, Michigan, in 1820 (American State Papers, Indian Affairs, II, 403–4).

C. R. are the initials on a 5-inch broadax found at Manitowoc Rapids, Wisconsin. Accompanying the initials is an outlined cross made with circular punch marks (C. E. Brown: "Indian Trade Implements," p. 68).

T. R. are the initials within a cartouche on trade axes, both large and small, found at Seboomook Lake on the West Branch of Penobscot River, Maine. A specimen is in the Sisco Collection, Rockwood, Maine (John S. Sisco).

James Reed was one of two blacksmiths with Jedediah Smith's California expedition in 1826 (text pp. 363–4).

Seyfert / Philad. was stamped horizontally on the blade of a round-eyed spiked tomahawk, now No. 938 in the collections of the Cranbrook Institute (our fig. 76*d*, p. 290).

William Shaw, George Town, D.C., made axes for the U. S. Indian Office in 1811 (Account Book, U. S. Indian Office, Philadelphia [MSS], National Archives).

John Shields was the Lewis and Clark blacksmith, 1803–6 (text p. 358).

O. B. Sprague is the name stamped vertically on the blade of a Chippewa pipe tomahawk of the first half of the nineteenth century. It is now No. 18/4928 in the Museum of the American Indian, New York City (Peterson: *American Indian Tomahawks*, p. 116).

A. J. Stowe appears on the blades of two small Vermont tomahawks having pronounced ears. They are Nos. 615 and 616, Vermont State Cabinet, Montpelier.

W. Swain, U. S. Indian Office blacksmith, 1822. His salary was $780 per year (American State Papers, Indian Affairs, II, 366).

James Terry, U. S. Indian Office blacksmith, Chickasaw, 1822. He was paid $504 per year (American State Papers, Indian Affairs, II, 366).

I. V. are the initials within a cartouche on the blade of a "French"-type ax that was found embedded in a stump at Pays Plat, a small Indian settlement on the Ontario shore of Lake

Superior, site of a onetime Hudson's Bay Company post. The specimen is preserved in the Paipoonge Museum in the Slate River Valley just north of Grand Portage, Minnesota (Elt Davis, May 3, 1962).

—— Vassueur, British Indian Department blacksmith at Mackinac in 1796, when the British establishment was relinquished to the Americans. He did not accompany his old employers when they moved to St. Joseph Island, Ontario ([Michigan] *Historical Collections*, XII, 191, 239, 249).

J. Walker, U. S. Indian Office blacksmith. He received $780 per year (American State Papers, Indian Affairs, II, 366).

Richard Whitehouse, U. S. Indian Office blacksmith at Fort Wayne, Indiana, 1822. His salary was $684 per year (American State Papers, Indian Affairs, II, 366).

Alexander Willard, Lewis and Clark blacksmith, 1803–06. He was employed later as blacksmith for the Sauks and Foxes, and still later at the Shawnee-Delaware Agency (text p. 358).

W. A. Woodruff is the maker's name on a much-decorated silver presentation pipe tomahawk inscribed to the Delaware Tom Hill of Frémont-California fame. The specimen is No. 362064 in the U. S. National Museum.

Of the 73 individuals and firms in the foregoing list, the greater number were independent smiths (22), employees of the U. S. Indian Office (22), or British government employees (19). Nothing conclusive is offered by these statistics, since the sources of information drawn upon are not representative of the entire field. The American fur-trading companies, for example, employed blacksmiths at almost all "permanent" posts, but the records of such employment are scattered, fragmentary, or nonexistent. Something more satisfactory than the existing lists may be attained, however, when a comprehensive research project is set up among collaborating workers both in Europe and America. As yet no one has studied and reported upon the hundreds of European manufacturers and exporters who supplied the American fur trade with Indian goods during the 300 years and more of wilderness merchandising. Ironmongery lends itself nicely to such investigation because of the volume and variety of remains already preserved in collections or to be found in the ground at historic sites. Reasonably, we conjecture that marked axes are more numerous than presently reported; small collections repose unnoticed in numerous small museums and in the hands of private collectors everywhere; all should be publicized. The unraveling of the story of the American blacksmith in the Indian trade may be facilitated by the better identification and interpretation of all old axes, including the European imports.

THE BRITISH "BROAD ARROW"

THE "BROAD ARROW" MARK OF HIS BRITANNIC MAJESTY'S GIFT merchandise appears on at least a few axes now in collections. Since there are a tremendous number of British axes that in the course of a hundred years were presented to the Indian tribes of New York and the Old Northwest, it is surprising that existing relics of the gift system are so rare. Among the United States Indians who enjoyed the British largess were the Chippewa, Delaware, Huron, Iroquois, Munsee, Ottawa, Potawatomi, Sauk and Fox, Shawnee, and Winnebago. The War of 1812 did not end the gift making to United States tribes. Even in 1828, thousands of United States Indians journeyed to Amherstburg, Ontario, across from the Detroit area, and to St. Joseph Island near the Mackinac Straits, to receive their annual bounty. It was estimated by the British officials responsible for the distribution of the presents that some $100,000 was expended annually in making these gifts.[4] Estimates of needs for gift goods and inventories of merchandise in store, especially at Detroit, St. Joseph Island, and Drummond Island, were prepared annually and are a matter of record.[5] Axes and tomahawks made up a notable part of the consignments. It is questionable that all gift axes were marked with the broad arrow, but an eyewitness writing about the Indian pilgrimages to Malden (Amherstburg) testified "that the British continued after the War [1812] to make annual gifts in June. . . . All of the guns, tomahawks, knives, and a specially made hoe bore the mark of the British Crown." [6]

When the broad arrow was stamped in the wood of a haft or the stock of a gift gun, it was a half inch or more in length, large

[4] [Michigan] *Historical Collections*, XXIII, 159–60, 171, 174.

[5] [Michigan] *Pioneer Collections*, IX, X; *Historical Collections*, XVI, XIX, XX. The cited records pertain to the period 1778–1815. The gift merchandise was shipped from central stores at LaChine and Montreal to the Western posts indicated.

[6] [Michigan] *Historical Collections*, XXXVIII, 665.

enough to be conspicuous. On the grip of an early nineteenth-century trade gun from the Shawnee Indian town on the Mad River, the mark is "I ↑ D" (British Indian Department).[7] Sometimes only the "I D" appears on the gift pieces.[8] Another version of the mark as stamped in wood is "B ↑ O" (British Ordnance).[9] Peterson found the small but sharply incised broad arrow, "↓," unaccompanied by initials on the blade of a Mohawk pipe tomahawk by Parke, and another from the Sisseton Sioux by Holtzapfel has on its blade the British Ordnance sign, "B ↑ O." Both of these specimens are in the Museum of the American Indian.[1]

The United States government, although engaged in the non-profit factory system of trade, carried on to a degree in the tradition of gift making as set by the French and the British. In connection with the many treaties made with practically all of the tribes, merchandise was often included in the terms of settlements. No prescribed mark specifically related to gift making was placed upon these payment pieces. However the government did mark some of its axes, and some of the marked pieces passed to Indians by one means or another.

"U. S." TOMAHAWKS

WHEN IN 1792 "MAD ANTHONY" WAYNE ORGANIZED HIS forces preparatory to his campaign against the British-supported Indians of the Old Northwest, he equipped his rifle companies with tomahawks and scalping knives. One of his orders drawn upon the Quartermaster General in this connection is published in the Michigan Pioneer and Historical Society's *Historical Collections*,[2] and what may well be one of the Wayne tomahawks is pictured on page 263 of this volume. Another similarly marked specimen, also found in Ohio and believed to be of the same period as the first

---

[7] C. P. Russell: *Guns on the Early Frontiers* (Berkeley: Univ. of California Press; 1957), pp. 119–20.
[8] C. E. Hanson, Jr.: *The Northwest Gun* (Lincoln: Nebraska State Historical Society; 1955), p. 84.
[9] Woodward: "The Metal Tomahawk," p. 23. See also S. J. Gooding's "The Top Hat Cap," *The Canadian Journal of Arms Collecting*, IV:1, pp. 26–27.
[1] Peterson: *American Indian Tomahawks*, pp. 103, 106, photos No. 113 and 126.
[2] XXXIV, 349–50.

mentioned, is reported by Peterson.[3] Yet another "U. S." toma-hawk, but of unknown provenance, is shown in Peterson.[4] Both of the last-named pieces have hammer polls and both have a car-touche in which maker's names, now illegible, were stamped. The U. S. Indian Office distributed axes marked "U. S. I. D." An example of these from the Plains country is owned by the U. S. National Museum and is pictured on page 263. The over-all story of tomahawks in the hands of American soldiers and among the properties of the U. S. Indian Department is eminently worth the telling; some concerted study will be necessary, however, if the obscure facts are to be assembled.

[3] *American Indian Tomahawks*, p. 100, photo No. 98.
[4] Ibid., photo No. 302.

APPENDIX D

Representative Fur Returns, American Fur Company, Indiana, 1839–1841

THE 892 BEAVER SKINS IN THIS COLLECTION, VALUED AT $4,558.13, represent about 10 per cent of the entire returns. The big item is 254,994 raccoon skins valued at $246,069.21. Second in importance are the deerskins weighing 430,620 pounds and valued at $122,807.96.

With the exceptions of William Brewster's Michigan collection and parts of B. F. Hollister's Ohio collection, these furs and skins constitute a one-year catch principally in Indiana. There were other fur companies and a number of independent buyers competing in Indiana with the agents of the American Fur Company; therefore, the grand total here shown does not represent all of the furs taken in Indiana in 1839–40.

This document is of interest because it provides sharp contrast with the returns of the mountain men west of the Rockies, where shipments were almost always exclusively beaver. At the trading posts on the Missouri and in the establishments of the Hudson's Bay Company in the Pacific Northwest, the lesser species of fur bearers appear on the returns much as in the present Indiana example—but with varying proportions. Raccoon and deerskins, for example, were never the leading items on the Missouri or in the Pacific Northwest. This table is item No. 16551 in the American Fur Company Papers and is reproduced here through the courtesy of The New-York Historical Society.

General Recapitulation of Furs & Skins Shipped by Detroit Department in 1840 with average cost of the same including Expences. — Viz

In Amount of disbursements made for the purchase of Furs & Skins, viz	254.994 Racoon Skins — 0 96 206.064 21
by William Brewster 63.034.88	36.596 Mink — Do — 20 10.638 40
" James M. Spafford 120.957.89	167 Swiss do — 0 20 33 40
" B I Hollister 92.793.24	3.762 Marten — Do — 14 5.643 -
" I. E. Phelps 11.668.98	643 Fisher — Do — 24 1.607 50
" N D Gnoss 76.107.93	581 Bear — Do — 44 3.195 50
" John Irey 39.772.27	290 Bear & Cub — Do — 1.450 -
" Wm I Starling 15.382.76 419.631.95	333 Cub Bear — Do — 24 632 50
	11.734 Grey Fox — Do — 28 5.397 64
For this Amount of disbursements made on account of Fur Expenses by the following persons viz	2.914 Red — Do — 14 4.006 75
William Brewster 175.87	99 Cross — Do — 14 198 -
James M Spafford 6.338.78	3 Silver — Do — 14 20 -
B I Hollister 8.240.98	4.041 House Cat — Do — 48 1.931 83
I. E. Phelps 3.333.77	96 Lynx — Do — 14 192 -
N I Gnoss 3.860.79	133 House — Do — 18 23 14
John Irey 5.221.78	2 Pole — Do — 14 25
N I Sterling 1.146.61 32.818.62	854 Wolf — Do — 14 140 50
	33 Badger — Do — 14 2 88
	22 Ground Hog — Do — 14 2 75
	6 Muskrat — Do — 8 37
	2 Panther — Do — 14 1 08
	422 Rabbit — Do — 1 4 22
	1 Dog — Do — 4 28
	213 Squirrel — Do — 1 2 13
	107.862 No 1 Musk Rats — of 18403.75
	79.312 " 2 " — 4.957.00
	10.334 Kitten " — 206.68
	22.899 Assorted " — 4.983.60
	259.145 25.550.03 25.550 03
	893 Beaver Skins 1215¾ — 50 4.558 13
	Castoreum 1696 — 24 67 -
	2.731 Otter Skins — 24 13.655 -
	36 Elk " 418 " fine Skin 24 90 -
	125.096 L Deer Skin 358.266 @ 13 96 702.60
	13.671 Red " 36.088 " 4 9.783 -
	3.340 Blue " 9.808 " 38 3.065 -
	7.283 Short " 17.442 " 20 7.487.16
	2.169 Fawn " 1.758 " 4 438.62
	3.298 Ribbed " 7.695 " 35 2.693.25
	Grey " 5.610 " 27 1.514.70
	Red " 795 " 4 298.31
	Blue " 73 " 38 22.81
	Short " 151 " 20 bags
	Fawn " 33 " 4 5.50
	143 Deer " — 4 143.00
	9.944 " ¾ damaged 2.098 " 20 419.60
	180 Ribbed ¾ " 367 " 4 91.76
	Minor ¾ " 477 " 10 47.70 172.807 96
	430.610 Rents.
$ 452.450 57	$ 452.450 57

     E&OE   Detroit, 28 August 1840

            William Brewster
            Agent Am Fur Co

Bibliography

Acker, Robert: "Traps and How to Make Them." Reprinted in *Strand Magazine* (n.d.). 4 pp.

Adair, Douglass: "The Axe in America" vs. Turner's Frontier Theory. Personal letter to C. P. Russell, September 25, 1946. 3 typed pages.

Alexander, Tony: *Practical Hunters & Trappers Guide*. New York: H. L. Perce; 1889. 121 pp.

Allan, Iris: "Colin Fraser Lives On." *The Beaver* (Winter 1959), pp. 38–43.

Allen, Paul, ed.: *History of the Expedition under the Command of Captains Lewis and Clark*. 2 vols. Philadelphia, 1814.

Alter, J. Cecil: *James Bridger, Trapper, Frontiersman, Scout, and Guide*. Salt Lake City: Shepard Book Co.; 1925. Rev. edn. publ. by University of Oklahoma Press in 1963.

American Anthropologist, Vol. X (1908), p. 10.

American Fur Company: Letter Books, 1816–30, Vols. 1, 2, and 3 (MSS), photostats, State Historical Society of Wisconsin, Madison. (The Chicago Historical Society has one lot, December 18, 1816, through May 30, 1817. Copies were made in 1918 from original MSS then at Michilimackinac.)

———: Account Books and Ledgers, Montreal and Michilimackinac, 1817–34 (MSS), Public Archives of Canada, Ottawa.

   Book 1—April 1817–November 1822, introductory pages, Montreal; remainder, Michilimackinac. Contains fragments extending into 1834.

   Book 2—April 1, 1817–August 11, 1819; April 1–May 13, 1817 at Montreal; remainder at Michilimackinac.

   Book 3—April 19, 1827–September 15, 1832; at Michilimackinac.

———: Blotters, Ledgers, and Invoices Outward, Michilimackinac, 1819–34 (MSS), Public Archives of Canada, Ottawa.

   1. Blotter, August 12, 1819–October 6, 1819.

2. Ledger to September 1834.

3. Ledger, June 1827–October 1834.

4. Invoices Outward, August 1830–May 1834.

American Fur Company: American Fur Company Papers, 1831–49 (MSS), The New-York Historical Society. More than 18,000 pieces, correspondence, order books, ledgers, etc. These have been copied on 37 reels of microfilm; sets are available in many large libraries. *See also* Nute: *Calendar of the American Fur Company Papers.*

Andersch Brothers: *Hunters and Trappers Guide.* Minneapolis, 1903. 431 pp., illus.

Annals of Wyoming: "Investigation, 1824, of Indian Hostilities West of Missouri River," XV:3 (July 1943), pp. 198–220.
Contemporary documents and letters.

Baillie-Grohman, William A.: *Camps in the Rockies.* New York, 1910, pp. 1–438. Orig. edn. 1882.

Baird, P. D.: "Expeditions to the Arctic." *The Beaver* (June 1949), pp. 41–7.

Ballantyne, Robert Michael: *Hudson Bay, or Every-day Life in the Wilds of North America.* London, 1859. (Earlier edn. 1848; another edn. 1857.)

Barber, Daniel M.: "Fort Hill at Victor, New York." [Seventeenth-century trade axe.] Rochester Museum Arts and Science *Museum Service* (April 1964), pp. 58–61.

Barsotti, John: "Mountain Men and Mountain Rifles," Part I, in *The Gun Digest*, 8th edn. (Chicago, 1954), pp. 153–6.

———: Detailed report on six pipe tomahawks, one spike tomahawk, one U. S. belt ax (early) and one 7-inch, but heavy, "squaw" ax, from Fort Clark Indian burial. Manuscript letter and nine measured drawings.

Batty, Joseph H.: *How to Hunt and Trap.* New York: A. Cogswell; 1878. 220 pp.

Beauchamp, William M.: *Metallic Implements of the New York Indians.* New York State Museum, Bulletin 55, Albany, 1902, pp. 1–86. 38 Pls.

———: *Metallic Ornaments of the New York Indians.* New York State Museum, Bulletin, Albany, 1903.

Beers, Henry Putney: *Western Military Frontiers, 1815–1846.* Philadelphia, 1935, pp. vi–227.

Beidleman, Richard G.: "Nathaniel Wyeth's Fort Hall." *Oregon Historical Quarterly.* (September 1957), pp. 196–250.

Benet, Brig. Gen. Stephen V.: *A Collection of Annual Reports and other Important Papers Relating to the Ordnance Department.* Washington, D.C.: Gov't Printing Office; 1880, Vol. II (1845–60), pp. 1–725.

Benton, Brev. Col. J. G.: *A Course in Ordnance and Gunnery.* New York: Van Nostrand; 1883, pp. 1–585.

Berry, Don: *A Majority of Scoundrels.* New York: Harper & Row; 1961. 432 pp.

Biggar, H. P., ed.: *The Works of Samuel de Champlain.* Toronto: Champlain Society; 1922–36, Vols. I–VI.

Biggar, H. P., ed.: *The Voyages of Jacques Cartier*. Ottawa, 1924, pp. xiv–330.

Bloch, Marc: *The Historian's Craft*. New York: Alfred A. Knopf; 1953.

Blumenthal, Walter Hart: "George Washington and Border Warfare. Condoned Scalping." New York Westerners *Brand Book*, XII:1 (1965), pp. 5–6, 16–20.

Bolton, Herbert E., ed.: *Athanase de Mézières and the Louisiana–Texas Frontier, 1768–1780*. 2 vols. Cleveland: Arthur H. Clark Co.; 1914.

Bosworth, N.: *A Treatise on the Rifle, Musket, Pistol and Fowling Piece*. New York: J. S. Redfield; 1946. Facsim. edn. by Standard Publications, Huntington, W. Va.

Bourne, Edward Gaylord, ed.: *Narratives of the Career of Hernando De Soto . . . as Told by a Knight of Elvas and in a Relation by Luys Hernández de Biedma, Factor of the Expedition*. 2 vols. Trail Makers Series. New York, 1904; and 2 vols. American Explorers Series. New York: Allerton Book Co.; 1922 (II, 100, for Biscay hatchets).

Boyle, David: "Notes on Primitive Man in Ontario," in Annual Archeological Report, Appendix, *Tenth Annual Report of the Minister of Education* (Ontario, 1895).

Brew, J. O.: "Research Collaboration of the Archeologist, Architect, Engineer, and Historian." Report, Symposium of the American Anthropological Association, Washington, D.C. 6 pp. Mimeographed.

Brown, Charles E.: "Indian Trade Implements and Ornaments." *The Wisconsin Archeologist*, XVII:3 (1918), pp. 61–97.

"Fire Steels." *The Wisconsin Archeologist* (January 1931), pp. 65–8.

Brown, Dick: Personel letter to C. P. Russell, November 1, 1965, re chain saw *vs.* double-bitted ax.

Brown, Mark H., and Felton, W. R.: *The Frontier Years*. New York, 1955, pp. 1–272, photos by L. A. Huffman.

Buck, Al: *Knife Know-How*. San Diego, Cal., 1964, pp. 1–12 and suppl.

Buehler, Maynard P.: "10 of the World's Most Powerful Rifles." Orinda, Cal., n.d., pp. 1–20.

Buffinton, A. H.: "New England and the Western Fur Trade, 1629–1675." *Publications*, Colonial Society of Massachusetts, Vol. XVIII (1917), p. 165.

Bulliard, Pierre (C. Kresz): *Aviceptologie française*. [Nets, snares, blinds, live-traps.] Paris: Corbet; 1830. 372 pp., illus.

Burns, Ned J.: *Field Manual for Museums*. Washington, D.C.: Gov't Printing Office, 1941, pp. xii–426.

Burpee, L. J., ed.: *Journal of Larocque from the Assiniboine to the Yellowstone, 1805*. Publications Canadian Archives, No. 3, Ottawa, 1910, pp. 1–82.

Bushnell, D. J.: "The Tradescant Collection, 1656." *American Anthropologist*, No. 3 (1908), p. 494.

Byrne, Oliver: *Practical Metalworker's Assistant*. Philadelphia, 1851.

Camp, Charles L., ed.: *James Clyman, 1792–1881*. Portland, Ore.: Champoeg Press; 1960. Orig. edn. publ. San Francisco, 1928, pp. 1–247.

Caesar, Gene: *King of the Mountain Men.* [Jim Bridger.] New York: E. P. Dutton; 1961. 317 pp.

Campion, J. S.: *On the Frontier.* London, 1878, pp. xiv–372. Illus.

Carnegie, William: *How to Trap and Snare.* London: Shooting Times; 1910. 227 pp.

Caywood, Louis R.: *Exploratory Excavations at Fort Vancouver, 1947.* San Francisco: National Park Service; 1947, pp. 1–21. 30 pls. Mimeographed.

————: "Excavating Fort Vancouver." *The Beaver* (March 1948), pp. 4–7.

————: *Exploratory Excavations at Fort Spokane.* Vancouver, Wash.: National Park Service; 1950 (distributed 1951). Mimeographed.

————: *Archeological Excavations at Fort Spokane, 1951, 1952, and 1953.* National Park Service, Region Four, 1954, pp. xii–85. 6 figs., 11 pls., 2 maps. Mimeographed.

————: *Excavations at Two Okanogan Sites, 1952.* National Park Service, Region Four, 1954, pp. ix–44. 7 pls., 3 maps. Mimeographed.

————: *Final Report, Fort Vancouver Excavations.* National Park Service, Region Four, 1955, pp. xv–75. 16 figs., 24 pls., 3 maps. Mimeographed.

Chittenden, Hiram M.: *The American Fur Trade of the Far West.* 3 vols. New York: Harper Bros.; 1902.

————: *The American Fur Trade of the Far West*, ed. Stallo Vinton. 2 vols. New York: Press of the Pioneers; 1935.

————: *The American Fur Trade of the Far West*, ed. G. L. Nute. 2 vols. Stanford, Cal.: Stanford Univ. Press; 1954.

Clark, S. A.: *Pioneer Days of Oregon History.* 2 vols. Portland, Ore., 1905.

Cleland, Robert Glass: *Early Sentiment for the Annexation of California.* Austin, Tex., 1915.

————: *A History of California: American Period.* New York: The Macmillan Co.; 1923, pp. xvi–512.

————: *This Reckless Breed of Men.* New York: Alfred A. Knopf; 1950, pp. xv–361.

Cline, Walter M.: *The Muzzle-Loading Rifle—Then and Now.* Huntington, W. Va.: Standard Printing and Publishing Co.; 1942, pp. 1–162. 95 photos.

Clyman, James: *see* Charles L. Camp, ed.: *James Clyman, 1792–1881.*

Coghlan, H. H.: "The Evolution of the Axe from Prehistoric to Roman Times." *Journal of the Royal Anthropological Institute, Great Britain and Ireland*, Vol. LXXIII (1943), pp. 27–56.

Cole, Fay Cooper: *The Long Road from Savagery to Civilization.* Baltimore, 1933, pp. xi–100. Illus.

Collier, Donald; Hudson, Alfred E.; and Ford, Arlo: "Archeology of the Upper Columbia Region." *University of Washington Publications in Anthropology*, in cooperation with the Eastern Washington State Historical Society and the State College of Washington, Seattle, IX:1 (1942), pp. 1–178. 22 pls., 16 figs, map.

Collins Company: *Catalogo Illustrado de Herramientas* . . . Hartford, Conn., 1919, pp. 1–76.

Collins Company: *Catalogo M. Facoes* . . . Collinsville, Conn., 1958, pp. 1–40. Illus.

Cooper, John M.: *Snares, Deadfalls, and Other Traps of the Northern Algonquins and Northern Athapaskans.* Washington, D.C.: Catholic Univ. of America; 1938, pp. 1–150. 82 figs., 14 photos.

Copeland, Peter F., and Zlatich, Marke: "Hero Galley. Virginia State Navy, 1776–1778." *Military Collector and Historian,* XVI:4 (1964), pp. 114–16.

Cotter, John L.: summary of discussions on "Role of Archeology in Historical Research." Symposium of the American Anthropological Association, Washington, D.C. 3 pp. Mimeographed.

Coues, Elliott, ed.: *The Expeditions of Zebulon Montgomery Pike.* 3 vols. New York: F. P. Harper; 1895.

———: *New Light on the Early History of the Greater Northwest: The Manuscript Journals of Alexander Henry . . . and of David Thompson, 1799–1814.* 3 vols. New York: F. P. Harper; 1897, I, xxviii–446.

Courville, Cyril B.: *Trade Tomahawks.* Southwest Museum Leaflets, No. 30, Los Angeles, 1963, pp. 1–14.

Cowie, Isaac: *The Company of Adventurers.* Toronto: W. Briggs; 1913.

Cox, Ross: *The Columbia River,* ed. E. I. and Jane R. Stewart. Norman, Okla.: Univ. of Oklahoma Press; 1957. 398 pp., illus. Orig. publ. in London, 1831.

Craighead, Frank, and Craighead, John: *How to Survive on Land and Sea.* Annapolis: U. S. Naval Institute; n.d., pp. xiii–264. Illus.

Cran, J.: *Blacksmith Shop Practice.* 2nd edn. Machinerys Reference Series, No. 61. New York: The Industrial Press; 1910. 40 pp., illus.

Creuxiux, Francisco: *Historiae Canadensis sen Novae Franciae,* Paris, 1664.

Dale, Harrison Clifford: *The Ashley-Smith Explorations . . . 1822–29.* Cleveland: Arthur H. Clark Co.; 1918, pp. xii–352. Illus., maps. Also a 1941 edn., Cleveland: A. H. Clark Co. 360 pp.

Davis, Theodore: "The Buffalo Range." *Harper's Monthly Magazine* (January 1869).

Dee, Henry, ed.: *The Journal of John Work, 1835.* Memoir 10, Archives of British Columbia, 1945. Appeared orig. in *British Columbia Historical Quarterly* (April and July 1944).

DeLesse, Andre: *Chasse Elevage et Piegeage.* Paris: J. B. Baillière & Fils; 1905, pp. xii–535.
Illustrates a number of traps, both French and English.

Denys, Nicolas: *see* Ganong, ed.: *The Description and Natural History* . . .

De Voto, Bernard: *Across the Wide Missouri.* Boston: Houghton Mifflin; 1947, pp. xxvii–483.

———, ed.: *The Journals of Lewis and Clark.* Boston: Houghton Mifflin; 1953, pp. lii–504.

Diderot, Denis, and d'Alembert, Jean: *Encyclopédie au Dictionnaire Rai-*

sonné des Sciences. 3rd edn. 45 vols. Geneva, 1778–81. Pls. in Vol. XXXIX.

Digby, Lt. William: *The British Invasion from the North,* ed. J. P. Baxter. Albany: Joel Munsell's Sons, 1887.

Dillin, John G. W.: *The Kentucky Rifle.* Washington, D.C.: National Rifle Association; 1924, pp. viii–133. 126 pls. Later edns. 1944, 1946.

Dobie, J. Frank: *Tales of Old-Time Texas.* Boston: Little, Brown; 1955, chap. on Bowie knife. 336 pp., illus.

———: "Jim Bowie's Knife." *Saga Magazine* (May 1956), pp. 12–15, 85–8.

Dodge, Gen. Grenville M.: *Biographical Sketch of James Bridger . . .* New York, 1905, pp. 1–27. Portrait; folding view, Fort Bridger.

Douglas, Walter B., ed.: *Thomas James, Three Years among the Indians and Mexicans.* St. Louis: Missouri Historical Society; 1916, pp. 1–316. Illus.

Downey, Fairfax: *Indian Wars of the U. S. Army, 1776–1865.* New York: Doubleday; 1963, pp. xii–248.

Drahos, Nick: "Evolution of Steel Traps." *The National Humane Review* (December 1951), pp. 18–19, 21.

Drumm, Stella M., ed.: *John C. Luttig's Journal of a Fur-Trading Expedition on the Upper Missouri, 1812–1813.* St. Louis: Missouri Historical Society; 1920, pp. 1–192.

Eaton, W. Clement: "Nathaniel Wyeth's Oregon Expedition." *Pacific Historical Review,* IV:2 (June 1935), pp. 101–13.

Ellison, Robert S.: *Fort Bridger, Wyoming. Brief History.* Casper, Wyo.: Historical Landmark Commission; 1931, pp. 1–58.

Elston, C. M. (Collins Company): Personal letter to C. P. Russell, September 4, 1958, re early-day Collins axes.

Everhart, William C.: "The Fur Trade, Theme XV, Westward Expansion. National Survey of Historic Sites and Buildings." Washington, D.C.: National Park Service; 1960, pp. iv–143. Multilithed.

Ewers, John C.: *The Role of the Indian in National Expansion,* Part II. Washington, D.C.: National Park Service; 1938, pp. ii–190. Mimeographed.

———: *The Story of the Blackfeet.* Pamphlet 6, Indian Life and Customs, U. S. Indian Service, Lawrence, Kan., 1944, pp. 1–66. Illus.

———: Letter to C. P. Russell, October 7, 1946. Detailed description of four pipe tomahawks, U. S. National Museum. MS and large photograph.

———: Personal letter to C. P. Russell, September 18, 19. 2 typed pps. Notes on trade axes and pipe tomahawks, early Far West.

———: Letter to C. P. Russell, October 1, 1946. Detailed description of 17 pipe tomahawks in U. S. National Museum. MS and measured sketches.

———: "The Indian Trade of the Upper Missouri before Lewis and Clark." *Missouri Historical Society Bulletin,* X (July 1954), pp. 429–46.

———: "Iroquois Indians in the Far West." *Montana, The Magazine of Western History,* XIII:2 (1963), pp. 2–10. 9 pls. Paper presented at

American Indian Ethnohistoric Conference, Albany, New York, October 1962.

Fairbanks, Charles H.: Typed memo, November 10, 1947, commenting on 25 trade objects recovered at Ocmulgee Fields, Ocmulgee National Monument. 3 photos, 8 x 10½.

Farrow, Edward S. (West Point instructor): *Mountain Scouting, A Hand-book for Officers and Soldiers on the Frontier*. New York: priv. publ.; 1881, pp. 1–284.

Ferris, Warren Angus: "Life in the Rocky Mountains," installment 14. *Western Literary Messenger*, II:40 (April 12, 1843), p. 318. (The entire journal by Ferris is in book form, ed. Paul C. Phillips [Denver: Old West Publishing Co.; 1940].)

Fish, Carl Russell: "The Relation of Archaeology to History." *Wisconsin Archeologist*, IX:4 (December 1910–February 1911), pp. 93–100. (The article is also in *Proceedings*, Wisconsin State Historical Society, Vol. LVIII [1910], pp. 146–52.)

Folmer, Bob: "The Battle of San Pasqual." *News and Views*, California Department of Parks and Recreation, October 6–9, 1965.

Forbes, Jack D.: "The Development of the Yuma Route before 1846." California Historical Society *Quarterly* (June 1964), pp. 99–118. Good for sources.

Ford, James A.: "Analysis of Indian Village Site Collections from Louisiana and Mississippi." Louisiana Geological Survey, *Anthropological Study No. 2* (November 1936).

Forsyth Papers, 1812–33, Vol. II, Draper Collection, Item 2 (MS). Wisconsin Historical Society, Madison.

Foster, Stephen C.: "A Sketch of Some of the Earliest Kentucky Pioneers of Los Angeles." *Publications of the Historical Society of Southern California* (1887), Los Angeles.

Franchere, Gabriel: *Narrative of a Voyage to the Northwest Coast of America in the Years 1811, 1812, 1813, and 1814*. New York: J. C. Redfield; 1854.

Franklin, [Sir] John: *Narrative of a Journey to the Shores of the Polar Sea, 1819–1822*. 2 vols. London, 1824.

Friederici, G.: "The Business of Scalping," in *When Peoples Meet*. New York and Philadelphia, 1949.

Ganong, William F., trans. and ed.: *The Description and Natural History of the Coasts of North America by Nicholas Denys*. Toronto: Champlain Society; 1908.

Garrard, Lewis H.: *Wah-to-Yah and the Taos Trail*. Norman, Okla.: Univ. of Oklahoma Press; 1955, pp. xvi–298. Map.

Garry, Nicholas: *Diary of Nicholas Garry . . . 1822–1835*. Proceedings, Royal Society of Canada, 2nd Series (1900), Vol. VII, Sect. II, pp. 3–204.

Garth, Thomas R.: "The Archeological Excavation of Waiilatpu Mission." *Oregon Historical Quarterly* (June 1948), pp. 117–36.

————: "A Report on the Second Season's Excavations at Waiilatpu."

Pacific Northwest Quarterly, XL:4 (October 1949), pp. 295–315.

Garth, Thomas R.: "Archeological Excavations at Fort Walla Walla." *Pacific Northwest Quarterly*, XLIII:1 (January 1952), pp. 27–50.

———: "*The Mansion House, Grist Mill, and Blacksmith Shop at the Whitman Mission. A Final Report*. Vancouver, Wash.: National Park Service; 1952.

Gebhard, Elizabeth L.: *The Life and Ventures of the Original John Jacob Astor*. Hudson, N.Y., 1915, pp. xix–321. Illus.

Gerard, William R.: "The Term Tomahawk." *American Anthropologist*, No. 2 (1908), pp. 277–80.

Gessler, E. A.: *Waffensammlung, Schweizerisches Landesmuseum*. Zurich, 1928, pp. 1–148. 48 pls.

Gibson, W. Hamilton: *Camp Life and the Tricks of Trapping*. New York: Harper & Bros.; 1881, pp. 1–300.

Girouard, Désiré: *Lake St. Louis, Old and New* (trans. fr. the French). Montreal: Poirier, Bassette & Co.; 1893, pp. viii–298.

Gluckman, Arcadi, and Satterlee, L. D.: *American Gun Makers*. Harrisburg, Pa.: Stackpole; 1953. 243 pp.

Gooding, S. James: "A Preliminary Study of the Trade Guns Sold by the Hudson's Bay Company," in Hamilton's *Indian Trade Guns* (1960), pp. 81–95.

Grabert, G. F.: Interim Report, Part I, Wells Hydroelectric Project, 1963, Old Fort Okanogan. Department of Anthropology, Univ. of Washington, Seattle. Typed MS, pp. 1–29. 10 pls., 4 maps.

Grant, W. L., ed.: *Voyages of Samuel de Champlain, 1604–1618*. New York, 1907.

Gregg, H. Raymond: "The Magnificent Rodent." *The Scientific Monthly*, LXVII:2 (August 1948), pp. 73–82.

Gregg, Josiah: *Commerce of the Prairies*. 2 vols. New York: H. G. Langley; 1844. Reprinted in Vols. XIX and XX, R. G. Thwaites, ed.: *Early Western Travels* (Cleveland, 1905).

Griffen, John W.: "End Products of Historic Sites Archeology." *Symposium, Role of Archeology in Historical Research*, Annual Meeting, American Anthropological Association. Washington, D.C., 1958. Mimeographed.

Grist: "On Making Charcoal." Park Practice *Grist*, X:4 (July–August 1966), p. 26.
  Grist is published bi-monthly in Washington, D.C., by the National Park Service, the National Conference on State Parks, and the National Recreation and Park Association.

Griswold, Bert J., ed.: *Fort Wayne, Gateway of the West, 1802–1813*. Indianapolis: Indiana Library and Historical Department; 1927, pp. xi–690.

Guinness, Ralph B.: "The Purpose of the Lewis and Clark Expedition." *Mississippi Valley Historical Review*, XX (June 1933).

435 · Bibliography

Hagglund, Lorenzo F.: *A Page from the Past. The Story of the Continental Gondola, "Philadelphia."* Whitehall, N.Y., 1936, pp. 1–24.

Hamilton, T. M., comp.: *Indian Trade Guns. The Missouri Archeologist* (December 1960), pp. vii–226.

———: "18th Century Gun Cache Uncovered." *Gun Digest* (1965), pp. 138–9. Illus.

Hanson, Charles E., Jr.: *The Northwest Gun.* Nebraska State Historical Society Publications in Anthropology, No. 2 (1955), pp. xii–85.

———: *The Plains Rifle.* Harrisburg, Pa.: Stackpole; 1960, pp. xi–171.

Harding, A. R.: *Deadfalls and Snares.* Columbus, Ohio, 1907. 232 pp.

———: *Steel Traps.* Columbus, Ohio, 1907. 333 pp.

Harding, Stanley: *The Amateur Trapper and Trap Maker.* New York: Dick & Fitzgerald; 1875. 134 pp.

Harrington, J. C.: "Historic Site Archeology in the United States," in J. B. Griffin, ed.: *Eastern United States Archeology* (Chicago, 1952), pp. 335–44.

———: "Archeology and Local History." *Bulletins,* American Association for State and Local History, II:6 (1953), reprinted from *Indiana Magazine of History,* XLIX:1, pp. 157–67.

———: "Archeology as an Auxiliary Science to American History." *American Anthropologist,* LVII:6 (1955), pp. 1121–30.

———: "The Artifact in History. Lessons from Archeology." Paper, Annual Meeting, Association for State and Local History, Columbus, Ohio, October 4–5, 1957. Typed MS, 9 pp.

———: *New Light on Washington's Fort Necessity.* Richmond, Va.: Eastern National Park and Monument Association; 1957, pp. 1–139.

———: "Search for the Citte of Ralegh." National Park Service Archeological Research Series, No. 6 (1962), Washington, D.C., pp. vii–63.

———: Personal letter to C. P. Russell, December 3, 1963, regarding historic site-archeology in southeastern United States. 3 pp.

———: *Archeology and the Historical Society.* Nashville: American Association for State and Local History, 1965, pp. 1–55. Illus.

Harrington, M. R.: "An Archaic Axe." *The Masterkey,* XXIII:6 (1949), p. 176.

———: "Archaic Axes Still Used in Mexico." *The Masterkey,* XXIV:3 (1950), p. 88.

Harris, Burton: *John Colter.* New York: Scribner's; 1952, pp. 1–177.

Hart, S. H., and Hulbert, A. B., eds.: *Zebulon Pike's Arkansas Journal.* Vol. I, Overland to the Pacific Series. Denver Public Library, 1932, pp. lxii–200.

Hart, Samuel S.: Personal letters to C. P. Russell, November 3 and November 20, 1964, regarding the manufacture of Blake and Lamb steel traps.

Hawkins Company: *Blake, Lamb & Co.'s Animal Traps Descriptive Price List.* [Jump Traps.] South Britain, Conn., 1925 (printed at Waterbury), pp. 1–14.

Hawks, Edward A.: "The Indian Buffalo Gun." *The Gun Report* (Akron, Ohio), I:5 (1940), pp. 1–2.

Held, Robert: "Kentucky Rifle Fact and Fiction." *Gun Digest* (1962), pp. 193–9.

Hendry, Anthony: *The Journal of Anthony Hendry, 1754–1755*. (L. J. Burpee, ed.) Ottawa. Royal Society of Canada. Transactions, Ser. 3, V. 1, Sec. 2, 307–364.

Henry, Alexander, and Thompson, David: *see* Elliott Coues, ed.: *New Light on the History of the Greater Northwest.*

Hicks, (Maj.) James E.: *French Firearms, 1702*, trans. from Pierre Surirey de Saint Remy. [Figures and proportions *des Armes de Guerre.*] Mount Vernon, N.Y., 1939.

———: *Notes on United States Ordnance*. 2 vols. Mount Vernon, N.Y., 1940.

Himsworth, J. B.: *The Story of Cutlery*. London: Ernest Benn; 1953, pp. 10–208. Illus.

Hockett, Homer Carey: *The Critical Method in Historical Research and Writing*. New York: The Macmillan Co.; 1955.

Hodge, Frederick Webb, ed.: *Handbook of American Indians North of Mexico*. 2 vols. Bureau of American Ethnology, Bulletin 30 (1907), Washington, D.C.

Hodgkinson, Ralph: "Tools of the Woodworker. Axes, Adzes, and Hatchets." *History News* (May 1965). American Association of State and Local History, Nashville, Technical Leaflet 28. 8 pp., 31 figs.

Holbrook, Stewart H.: *Dreamers of the American Dream*. New York: Doubleday; 1957, pp. ix–369.
Some reminiscences by Pierrepont Noyes on the making of Newhouse steel traps at the Oneida Community are on pp. 17–30.

Holmes, William H.: "The Tomahawk." *American Anthropologist*, No. 2 (1908), pp. 264–76.

Holmquist, June D., and Wheeler, Ardis H., eds.: *Diving Into The Past*. St. Paul: Minnesota Historical Society; 1964, pp. x–111.

Honig, Louis O.: *James Bridger*. Kansas City: Brown-White-Lowell Press; 1951.

Hopkins, Alfred F.: "Report on Indian Trade Objects Purchased by the U. S. Government through its several Superintendents of Indian Trade at Philadelphia, Penn., and George Town, D.C., from 1801–22, inclusive." Washington: National Park Service; 1942. Typed MS, 56 pp.

———: Personal letter to C. P. Russell, August 20, 1946.

———: Personal letter to C. P. Russell, August 20, 1946, regarding axes in early-day naval equipment.

Hornaday, William T.: *The Extermination of the American Bison*. Washington, D.C.: Report of the National Museum; 1887, pp. 369–548. 22 illus., 2 maps (bound as a separate vol.).

Howard, Robert West: "Cradle of Industry: U.S.A." *American Heritage*, II:4 (1951), pp. 26–31.

Hudson, J. Paul: "Historical Objects Unearthed at Wakefield." *The Iron Worker* (Spring 1951), pp. 8–10.

———: "The Story of Iron at Jamestown, Virginia." *The Iron Worker*, XX:3 (Summer 1956), pp. 1–14.

———: "Augustine Washington and the Iron Furnaces, 1725–1743." *The Iron Worker*, XXV:3 (1961), pp. 1–18.

Hunt, Wilson Price: The Wilson Price Hunt Papers, 1810 (MSS), Missouri Historical Society Library, St. Louis.

Hurlbut, Henry H.: *Chicago Antiquities*. Chicago: Eastman & Bartlett; 1881.

Hussey, John A.: *The Wolfskill Party in California*. Unpublished Masters thesis, University of California, May 1935. 210 typed pp.

———: *Preliminary Survey of the History and Physical Structure of Fort Vancouver*. National Park Service, Region Four, 1949, pp. xii–241. 29 pls. Mimeographed.

———: *The History of Fort Vancouver*. Tacoma: Washington State Historical Society; 1957, pp. xx–256. 54 pls.

Hutchings, J. M.: "Sketches from the Life of Peg-Leg Smith." *Hutchings California Magazine* (October 1860–March 1861).

Innis, Harold A.: *The Fur Trade in Canada*. New Haven: Yale University Press; 1930. 444 pp., illus. Later edns. 1956 and 1962.

Irving, Washington: *Astoria*. Philadelphia, 1836.

———: *The Adventures of Captain Bonneville, U.S.A.* New York, 1849, pp. xii–428. Map. Orig. edn. 1837.

Jackson, Donald, ed.: *Letters of the Lewis and Clark Expedition, 1783–1854*. Urbana: Univ. of Illinois Press; 1962, pp. xxi–728.

Jacobs, Wilbur R.: "Presents to Indians along the French Frontiers . . . 1748–1763." *Indiana Magazine of History*, Vol. XLIV (September 1948), pp. 245–56.

James, Thomas: *Three Years Among the Indians and Mexicans*, ed. Walter B. Douglas. St. Louis: Missouri Historical Society; 1916, pp. 1–316. Reprinted by the Rio Grande Press, Chicago, in 1965.

Jefferys, C. W.: *The Picture Gallery of Canadian History*. 3 vols. Toronto, 1945.

Jesuit Relations: see R. G. Thwaites, ed.

Johnson, Sir William: *The Papers of Sir William Johnson*, ed. James Sullivan and A. C. Flick. 3 vols. Albany: Division of Archeology and History; 1921–62.

Josephy, Alvin M.: *The Nez Percé Indians and the Opening of the Northwest*. New Haven: Yale University Press; 1965.

Kappler, Charles J., ed.: *Indian Affairs, Laws and Treaties, II*. Washington, D.C.: Government Printing Office; 1904.

Kauffman, Henry J.: *The Pennsylvania-Kentucky Rifle*. Harrisburg, Pa.: Stackpole; 1960, pp. 1–376.

Keener, William G.: *Bowie Knives from the Collection of Robert Abels*. Cleveland: Ohio Historical Society; 1962. 120 pp., 139 illus.

Kemper, Jackson: "American Charcoal Making in the Era of the Cold-blast Furnace." *The Regional Review*, V:1 (1940), pp. 1–14.

Kendrick, T. D.: *The Axe Age*. London, 1925, pp. xii–177. Illus.

Kephart, Horace: "The Hawken Rifle." *Saturday Evening Post* (February 21, 1920), p. 62.

Kidd, Kenneth E.: *The Excavation of Ste. Marie I*. Toronto: University of Toronto Press; 1949.

———: "Trade Goods Research Techniques." *American Antiquity*, XX (1954), pp. 1–8.

———: "Ethnohistorical Aspect of Archeology of the Canadian Frontier." *Symposium, Role of Archeology in Historical Research*, Annual Meeting, American Anthropological Association, Washington, D.C. 9 mimeographed pp.

Kivett, Marvin F.: "Excavations at Fort Atkinson, Nebraska. Preliminary Report." *Nebraska History* (March 1959).

Klemm, Gustav F.: *Das Alte Vorchristliche Europa*. Leipzig, 1850, pp. x–645. Illus.

———: *Allgemeine Kulturwissenshaft*. Leipzig, 1854–5, Vols. I and II.

Kreps, Elmer H.: *Science of Trapping*. St. Louis, 1909. 245 pp.

Kurz, Rudolph Friederich: *Journal of Rudolph Friederich Kurz; an Account of His Experiences . . . 1846–1852*, ed. J. N. B. Hewitt. Bureau of American Ethnology, Bulletin 115 (1937), Washington, D.C. 382 pp., 48 pls.

Lahontan, Baron de: *New Voyages to North-America*. 2 vols. in one. London: ptd. for H. Bonwicke, T. Goodwin, *et al.;* 1703.

La Rochefoucauld-Liancour, F. A. F., duc de: *Travels in Canada, 1795*. ed. W. R. Riddell. Toronto, 1917. 13th Rept., Bureau of Archives, Province of Ontario, 1916.

Lavender, David: *Westward Vision*. New York: McGraw-Hill; 1963.

———: *The Fist in the Wilderness*. New York: Doubleday; 1964.

———: *The Great West*. New York: American Heritage; 1965, pp. 1–416.

Lee, Ronald F., and Russell, Carl P., comps. and eds.: "Historic Objects; their place in research and interpretation." Minutes, interbranch conferences, February 29, March 8, March 14, and March 21, 1940. Washington, D.C.: National Park Service, Branch of Historic Sites and Branch of Research and Information. 56 pp. Mimeographed.

Lee, Ronald F.: "Recommendations for Office of Archeology and Historic Preservation" (14 pp.), and "Organization of Service Professional Staff," (7 pp.). Washington, D.C.: National Park Service; 1966. Multilithed interrelated reports.

Leitch, Adelaide: "Land of the Wendats." *The Beaver* (Winter 1963), pp. 14–19.

Leonard, Stephen R., ed.: "Reminiscences," accompanied by a compendium of orig. MSS and abstracts from MSS written by technicians engaged in the manufacture of Newhouse and other steel traps, Oneida Community, 1850's and 1860's (MSS).

In effect, this is a treatise on the transition from hand forging to machine work in the manufacture of steel traps. Identifiable among the pioneer blacksmiths who contributed to the writing: Sewell Newhouse, Leonard F. Dunn, Joel Higgins, Homer Barron, John Hutchins, William R. Inslee, George W. Hamilton, and John F. Sears. The MSS are in the possession of Mr. Leonard. Copy (partial) is owned by the Western Museum Laboratory, National Park Service.

Lesse, Andre: *Chasse.* Paris: J. B. Baillière et Fils; 1905. 532 pp.

Levinge, Capt. R. G. A.: *Echoes from the Backwoods; or Sketches of Transatlantic Life.* 2 vols. London: H. Colkurn; 1846.

Lewis, B. R.: *Small Arms and Ammunition in the U. S. Service, 1776–1865.* Washington, D.C.: Smithsonian Institution; 1960, pp. viii–338. Illus.

Lewis, Ralph: Detailed report on 13 French-type trade axes. MS and orig. measured sketches in Buffalo Museum. 15 pp.

————: Personal letter to C. P. Russell, October 22, 1937.

————: Detailed report on three trade axes and four historic broadaxes in the Holland Land Office Museum, MS, February 6, 1938. 6 typed pp. 7 drawings.

————: Critical analysis of proposed MS "The Iron Axe in America." Personal letter to C. P. Russell, September 4, 1946.

Lewis, William S., and Phillips, Paul C., eds.: *The Journal of John Work.* Cleveland: A. H. Clark; 1923, pp. 1–209. Illus.

Lorant, Stefan: *The New World: The First Pictures of America.* New York: Duell, Sloan & Pearce; 1946, pp. 1–292. 43 pictures of Florida, 1564.

Low, A. M.: *Musket to Machine Gun.* London: Hutchinson & Co.; 1942.

Lull, Francisco Ferrer, and Hefter, J.: "The Spanish Corps of Engineers in Florida, 1802." *Military Collector and Historian*, XVI:4 (Winter 1964), p. 112, Pl. 250.

Lundeberg, Philip K.: Personal letter to C. P. Russell, May 1, 1964. MS, 1 typed p.; 12 photos of four axes from the *Philadelphia*.

Macfie, John: "Short River Reveals Evidence of Long History." *Beaver* (Winter 1962), pp. 48–51.

Mackenzie, Alexander: *Voyages from Montreal Through the Continent of North America.* 2 vols. New York, 1904.

MacPherson, David: *Annals of Commerce.* 4 vols. Edinburgh, 1805.

Malcolmson, Wilson: "Trade Goods." *The Beaver* (December 1940), pp. 38–9.

Mascall, L.: *A Booke of Fishing with Hook and Line . . . Another of Sundrie Engines and Trappes to take Polecats, Buzards, Rats.* 1 vol. London: John Wolfe; 1590.

Mason. O. T.: "Traps of the Amerinds." *American Anthropologist*, Vol. II (1900), pp. 657–75.

Masson, L. R.: *Les Bourgeois de la Compagnie du Nord-Ouest.* 2 vols. Quebec, 1889.

Mattes, Merrill J.: "Jackson Hole, Cross Roads of the Western Fur Trade." *Pacific Northwest Quarterly* (April 1946), pp. 87–108.

———: "Behind the Legend of Colter's Hell." *Mississippi Valley Historical Review* (September 1949), pp. 251–82.

———: "Salvaging the Past in the Pacific Northwest." Paper presented at 10th Annual Meeting, American Association for State and Local History, Portland, Ore., August 28–31, 1950 (MS).

———: "Salvaging Missouri Valley History," in *Westerners Brand Book*. Chicago Westerners, 1952.

———: *Historic Sites Archeology on the Upper Missouri*. Bureau of American Ethnology, Bulletin 176 (1960), Washington, D.C., pp. 1–23.

Mattison, Ray H.: "The Upper Missouri Fur Trade." *Nebraska History*, XLII:1 (1961) (reprint), pp. 1–28.

———: "Fort Union: Its Role in the Upper Missouri Fur Trade." *North Dakota History*, XXIX:1 and 2 (1962) (reprint). 30 pp.

Maxwell, Moreau S.: *Excavations at Fort Michilimackinac, 1959 Season*. East Lansing: Michigan State University; 1961, pp. 1–130. 14 pls. and 19 figs.

McCracken, Harold: *How to Catch More Fur*. Lititz, Pa.: Animal Trap Co. of America; 1945, pp. 1–48.

McFarland, Lt. Col. Earl, comp.: *Catalogue of the Ordnance Museum, U. S. Military Academy*, West Point. U. S. Military Academy Printing Office, 1929, pp. 1–268.

McGuire, J. D.: "Pipes and Smoking Customs of the American Aborigines." *Report, U. S. National Museum*, Part 1 (1897), pp. 251–645.

McKenney, Thomas Lorraine, and Hall, James: *History of the Indian Tribes of North America*, ed. F. W. Hodge. 3 vols. Edinburgh: John Grant; 1933–4.

Mercer, Henry C.: "Ancient Carpenter's Tools, Part 1." *Old Time New England*, XV:4 (April 1925), pp. 164–97.

———: *Ancient Carpenter Tools*. Doylestown, Pa.: Bucks County Historical Society; 1929, pp. 1–328. 2nd edn. 1950, 339 pp.

Merk, Frederick, ed.: *Fur Trade and Empire*, Cambridge, Mass.: Harvard Univ. Press; 1931, pp. xxxvi–370.

Michigan Pioneer and Historical Society: *Historical Collections* (title of Vols. I–XI was *Pioneer Collections*). Vols. 1–40 (1827–1929). (Pub. suspended 1916–28.)

Miller, Alfred J.: "Rough Drafts for Notes to Indian Sketches." Washington, D.C.: National Park Service; n.d. MS, 66 typed pp.

Mora, Gen. Ignacio: *Elementos de Fortificación*. 2 vols. Mexico, 1830.

Mordecai, Maj. A., comp.: *The Ordnance Manual for the Use of Officers of the United States Army*. Confederate edn. Charleston, S.C., 1861, pp. xx–475. 19 pls. (Reprints a great deal of material from an *Ordnance Manual*, U.S., of 1841.)

Morgan, Dale L.: *Jedediah Smith and the Opening of the West*. Indianapolis and New York: Bobbs-Merrill; 1953, pp. 1–458.

Morgan, Dale L., ed.: *The West of William H. Ashley.* Denver: Old West Publishing Co.; 1964, pp. xlix–341. 15 illus., 3 maps.

Morgan, Richard G.: "An Engraved Tomahawk Pipe." *Museum Echoes* (February 1947), Columbus, Ohio, pp. 15–16.

Mumey, Nolie: *The Life of Jim Baker, 1818–1898.* Denver, 1931, pp. 1–234. Illus., map.

Museum of the Fur Trade Quarterly, publication of the Museum of the Fur Trade, Chadron, Neb. I:1 (1965) is the spring number.

Nadeau, Gabriel: "Indian Scalping Technique in Different Tribes." *Ciba Symposia* (January 1944), pp. 1676–81.

National Park Service: *Parks for America.* Washington, D.C.: Gov't Printing Office; 1964, pp. xiv–485. Illus., maps.

National Rifle Association Technical Staff: "Determining Muzzle Velocity." *American Rifleman* (May 1964), pp. 41–4.

New Hampshire Historical Society: *New Hampshire Historical Collections*, Vols. I–XV (1927–39). (Publication suspended 1916–27.)

Newhouse, S.: *The Trapper's Guide.* Wallingford, Conn.: Oneida Community; 1867, pp. 1–215. Orig. edn. 1865.

———: *The Trapper's Guide.* Community, N.Y.: Oneida Community Ltd.; 1887, pp. 1–224.

———: *Newhouse Trapper's Guide.* Oneida, N.Y., 1914. 171 pp. G. W. Noyes gives trap history in the Appendix.

Ney, Marshal: *Military Studies Written for Use of Officers*, trans. from the French. London: Bull and Churton; 1833, pp. 1–116.

Noël Hume, Ivor: *Excavations at Rosewell, Gloucester County, Virginia, 1957–1959.* United States National Museum, Bulletin 225. Washington, D.C.: Gov't Printing Office; 1962, pp. 154–228. 38 pls.

———: *An Archeological View of Colonial Life and History.* New York: Alfred A. Knopf; 1963. 316 pp.

Noyes, George Wallingford: *John Humprey Noyes; the Putney Community.* Oneida, N.Y., 1931. 393 pp.

Noyes, Pierrepont Burt: *My Father's House: An Oneida Boyhood.* New York and Toronto: Farrar and Rinehart; 1937. 312 pp.

Nusbaum, Deric: *Deric in Mesa Verde.* New York, 1929.

Nute, Grace Lee: *The Voyageur.* New York and London, 1931, pp. viii–289.

———, ed.: *Calendar of the American Fur Company Papers, 1831–49.* 2 vols. American Historical Association, Annual Report for the Year 1944. Washington, D.C.: Gov't. Printing Office; 1945.

———: "The American Fur Company's Fishing Enterprises on Lake Superior." *Mississippi Valley Historical Review*, XII (1945), pp. 483–503.

Nymeyer, Robert: Personal letter to C. P. Russell, January 1, 1949, regarding a skinning knife.

O'Callaghan, E. B.; Brodhead, J. R., et al., eds.: *Documents Relative to the Colonial History of the State of New York.* 15 vols. Albany: Weed, Parsons; 1853–87.

Oglesby, R. E.: *Manuel Lisa and the Opening of the Missouri Fur Trade.* Norman, Okla.: Univ. of Oklahoma Press; 1963.

Oliver, Edmund H., ed.: *The Canadian Northwest.* 2 vols. Ottawa, Publications of the Canadian Archives, No. 9 (1914).

Olson, Sigurd F.: "Relics from the Rapids." *National Geographic Magazine* (September 1963), pp. 412–35. Color photos, maps.

Ommundsen, H., and Robinson, E. H.: *Rifles and Ammunition.* New York: Funk and Wagnalls; 1915, and London: Cassell & Co. Ltd.; 1915.

Palmer, E. Lawrence: *Traps.* Cornell Rural School Leaflet Program, 1943–4 (September 1943). 37 pp.

Parker, Arthur C.: "History Is Written in Objects." Rochester Museum, *Museum Service* (1938).

Parker, Samuel: *Journal of an Exploring Tour Beyond the Rocky Mountains.* Ithaca, N.Y., 1838, pp. xii–371.

Parkman, Francis: *The Oregon Trail: Sketches of Prairie and Rocky Mountain Life.* New York: The Macmillan Co.; 1920, pp. 1–362.

Parsons, John E.: "Gun Makers for the American Fur Company." The New-York Historical Society *Quarterly* (April 1952), pp. 180–93.

———— and du Mont, John S.: *Firearms in the Custer Battle.* Harrisburg, Pa.: Stackpole; 1953, pp. 1–59.

Pattie, James Ohio: *see* R. G. Thwaites, ed.: *The Personal Narrative of James Ohio Pattie.*

Payette, B. C., comp.: *The Oregon Country under the Union Jack: [Alexander], Henry's Astoria Journal.* Montreal, 1961, pp. xiv–197.

Peet, Creighton: "History of Forest Tools: The Ax and the Adz." *American Forests* (March 1953), pp. 19 and 50.

Petersen, Eugene T.: *Gentlemen on the Frontier.* Mackinac Island, Mich., 1964, pp. 1–66. Illus.

Peterson, Harold L.: *Arms and Armor in Colonial America, 1526–1783.* Harrisburg, Pa.: Stackpole; 1956, pp. 1–350.

————: *American Knives.* New York: Charles Scribner's Sons; 1958, pp. 1–178. 186 illus.

————: *American Indian Tomahawks.* New York: Museum of the American Indian; 1965, pp. viii–142. 18 pls., 310 photos.

Petrides, George A.: "Snares and Deadfalls." *The Journal of Wildlife Management*, X:3 (1946), pp. 234–8. 4 pls.

Pettus, Terry: "Expedition to Russian America." *The Beaver* (Winter 1962), pp. 8–19.

Phillips, Paul Chrisler: *The Fur Trade.* 2 vols. Norman, Okla.: University of Oklahoma Press; 1961.

Pike, Zebulon Montgomery: *see* Elliott Coues, ed.: *The Expeditions of Zebulon Montgomery Pike.*

Pomeroy, Earl: *The Pacific Slope: A History.* New York: Alfred A. Knopf; 1965, pp. xiii–397.

Potter, Woodburne: *The War in Florida.* Baltimore, 1836.

Probst, Mary M.: Personal letter to C. P. Russell, November 10, 1965, regarding the history of the Mann Axe Factory, Mill Hall, Pa. MS, 5 typed pp.

Quaife, Milo M., ed.: *The Journals of Captain Meriwether Lewis and Sergeant John Ordway, 1803–1806.* Madison: Wisconsin Historical Society; 1916, pp. 1–444.

Quimby, George I.: "Dated Indian Burials in Michigan." *Papers*, Michigan Academy of Science, Arts, and Letters, Vol. XXIII (1937), pp. 63–72. 2 pls.

———: "European Trade Articles as Chronological Indicators . . ." *Papers*, Michigan Academy of Science, Arts, and Letters, Vol. XXIV, Pt. 4 (1938—pub. 1939), pp. 25–31. 2 pls.

———: "Indian Trade Objects in Michigan and Louisiana." *Papers*, Michigan Academy of Science, Arts, and Letters. Vol. XXVII (1941), pp. 543–51.

———: *Indian Culture and European Trade Goods.* Madison: Univ. of Wisconsin Press; 1966, pp. xiv—217.

Rich, E. E., ed.: *The Letters of John McLoughlin from Fort Vancouver to the Governor and Committee, Second Series, 1839–44.* Hudson's Bay Company Series, Vol. VI. Toronto: Champlain Society; 1943.

Roberts, Frank H. H., Jr.: "River Basin Surveys: The First Five Years . . ." *Annual Report of the Smithsonian Institution for 1951* (1952), pp. 351–83.

Roberts, Ned H.: *The Muzzle-loading Cap-Lock Rifle.* Manchester, N.H.: Clarke Press; 1944, pp. xvi–528. A 1952 edn. was pub. by Stackpole, Harrisburg, Pa.

Robinson, Harry B.: "Guide to the Custer Battlefield Museum." *Montana Magazine of History* (July 1952). Reprinted as a separate vol. by Naegete Printing Co., Helena. 48 pp., illus.

Rodee, Howard D.: Detailed report on the spiked axes and the trade ax in Rodee Collection, in a letter to C. P. Russell, February 22, 1960. MS, 1 p. typed, 7 sketches.

Rollins, Philip Ashton, ed.: *Discovery of the Oregon Trail.* New York: Charles Scribner's Sons. Pp. cxxxvii–391.

Ross, Alexander: *Adventures of the First Settlers on the Oregon or Columbia River*, ed. Milo M. Quaife. Chicago: Lakeside Press; 1923, pp. xxvii–388.

Ross, Marvin, ed.: *The West of Alfred Jacob Miller.* Norman, Okla.: Univ. of Oklahoma Press; 1951, pp. 1–400.

Rousseau, Jacques: "Mistassini Calendar." *The Beaver* (September 1949), p. 36.

Rue, Leonard L.: "Barriere Indians." *The Beaver* (Autumn 1961), pp. 31–51.

Russell, Carl P.: "The Use of Historic Objects as Sources of History." Presented at the History Museums Section, Annual Meeting, American Association of Museums, Hotel Statler, Detroit, May 21, 1940. MS, National Park Service Museums Library, Washington, D.C.

A paper advocating establishment of college courses for the training of historian-archeologists.

Russell, Carl P.: "Wilderness Rendezvous Period of the American Fur Trade." *Oregon Historical Quarterly* (March 1941), pp. 1–47.

———: "Trapper Trails to the Sisk-ke-Dee." Chicago Westerners *Brand Book* for 1944 (1946), pp. 57–79.

———: "History and Historic Objects." MS, National Park Service Museums Library, Washington, D.C. (1946). 20 pp.
A report on discussions engaged in by twenty scholars and technicians in conference at Colonial National Historical Park, Virginia, May 6 and 7, 1946, under the auspices of the National Park Service and the American Council of Learned Societies.

———: *Guns on the Early Frontiers.* Berkeley: Univ. of California Press; 1957, pp. xv–395.

———: "Preliminary Exhibit Plan for Lewis and Clark Memorial." National Park Service, Fort Clatsop, Ore., 1959. 144 typed pp., illus. Includes section, "Historic Objects of Lewis and Clark Provenance."

———: "Blue-eyed Men in Buckskin." Westerners Potomac Corral, *Corral Dust* (December 1960, March 1961, and May 1961).

———: "Some Handguns of the Mountain Man." Denver Westerners *Brand Book* (1962), pp. 149–59.

Russell, Isaac K., and Driggs, Howard R.: *Hidden Heroes.* [Numerous mountain men.] Yonkers, N.Y.: World Book Company; 1923, pp. xi–295.

Russell, Osborne: *Journal of a Trapper; or, Nine Years in the Rocky Mountains, 1834–1843.* Boise, Idaho: Syms Fork Co.; 1921, pp. 1–149. A 1955 edn. pub. by the Oregon Historical Soc. has been issued in paperback by the Univ. of Nebraska Press.

Ruxton, George Frederick: *Life in the Far West* (Hafen edn.). Norman, Okla.: Univ. of Oklahoma Press; 1951, pp. xviii–252. Appeared first in *Blackwood's Edinburgh Magazine* (June–November 1848).

Sage, Rufus B.: *Wild Scenes in . . . the Rocky Mountains . . . and the Grand Prairies.* Philadelphia, 1855, pp. 1–303.

Saint Remy, Pierre S. de: *Memoirs D' artillerie . . .* 2 vols. Amsterdam, 1702.
See also James E. Hicks: *French Firearms, 1702.*

Sandoz, Mari: *The Beaver Men: Spearheads of Empire.* New York: Hastings House; 1964, pp. xv–335.

Sarles, F. B., and Shedd, C. E., eds.: *Colonials and Patriots.* Washington, D.C.: Gov't Printing Office; 1964, pp. xvii–286.

Saum, Lewis O.: "Frenchmen, Englishmen and the Indian." *The American West*, I:4 (1964), pp. 4–11, 87–9.

Sawyer, Charles Winthrop: *Firearms in American History, 1600–1800.* Boston: pub. by author; 1910. 237 pp., illus.

———: *Our Rifles.* Boston: Cornhill; 1920. 409 pp., illus. 1941 and 1946 edns. pub. by Williams Book Store, Boston.

Schuchhardt, Carl: *Deutsche Vor- und Frühgeschichte in Bildern*. Munich and Berlin, 1936, pp. v–xi. 80 pls.

Schwerdt, C. F. G. R.: *Hunting, Hawking, Shooting*. 4 vols. London: Waterlow and Sons, Ltd.; 1928.

Scrivenor, Harry: *History of the Iron Trade*. London, 1854.

Sedergren, Oscar: Personal interview with C. P. Russell regarding practical use of double-bitted ax in logging (1958). (MS notes.)

Setzler, Frank M., and Jennings, Jesse D.: "Peachtree Mound and Village Site." Washington, D.C., Bureau of American Ethnology, Bulletin 131 (1941), pp. viii–99. Illus.

Severn, James E.: "The Hawken Rifle." *American Rifleman* (April 1951).

———: "Hawken Rifle." *American Rifleman* (December 1963).

Seymour, Flora Warren: *Indian Agents of the Old Frontier*. New York: D. Appleton-Century Co.; 1941.

Shankland, R. S.: Informal report on 13 brands of factory-made steel traps and miscellaneous hand-made traps in the Shankland Collection, Cleveland, Ohio. MS, November 2, 1964. 6 pp.

Shirk, George H., ed.: "Peace on the Plains." *The Chronicle of Oklahoma*, XXVIII:1 (1950), pp. 2–41.

Skarsten, M. O.: *George Drouillard, Hunter and Interpreter for Lewis and Clark*. Glendale, Cal.: Arthur H. Clark Co.; 1964, pp. 1–356. Maps.

Sloane, Eric: *A Museum of Early American Tools*. New York: Wilfred Funk, Inc.; 1964, pp. ix–108. Profusely illus.

Smith, Carlyle S.: "European Trade Material from the Kansas Monument Site." Plains Archeological Conference *News Letter*, III:2 (1950), pp. 2–9.

———: "Analysis of Firearms from . . . Fort Berthold I." *The Plains Anthropologist* (July 1955), pp. 3–12.

Smith, Cyril S., and Sisco, A.: "Iron and Steel in 1627." *Technology and Culture*, II:2 (1961), pp. 131–45.
Translation of the Mathurin Jousse chapters on hardening and tempering steel, 1627.

Smith, G. Hubert: "Interpretive Values of Archaeological Evidence." Symposium of the American Anthropological Association. Washington, D.C., 1958. 4 pp. Mimeographed.

Smith, Captain John: *A Map of Virginia with Description of the Country*. Oxford: Joseph Barnes, ptr.; 1612.

Smith, Reginald A., ed.: *Antiquities of the Bronze Age, British Museum*. Oxford, Eng., 1920, pp. xii–187.

———: *Early Iron Age Antiquities, British Museum*. Oxford, Eng., 1925, pp. xii–175.

Specht, F. U.: *Geschichte der Waffen*. 3 vols. Cassel and Leipzig, 1870–7, II, 674. 24 pls. (American axes here.)

Speck, Frank G.: "Ethnology of the Yuchi Indians." University of Pennsylvania *Anthropology Publications*, I:1 (1909).

Stevenson, Isobel: "Beginnings of American Military Medicine." *Ciba Symposia* (February, 1940), pp. 344–59.

Sullivan, James, ed.: *The Papers of Sir William Johnson.* Albany: Univ. of New York; 1921–33.

Sullivan, Maurice S., ed.: *The Travels of Jedediah Smith: Journal of the Great American Pathfinder.* Santa Ana, Cal., 1934.

———: *Jedediah Smith, Trader and Trail Breaker.* New York: Press of the Pioneers; 1936, pp. xiii–233.

Sunder, John E.: *Bill Sublette, Mountain Man.* Norman: Univ. of Oklahoma Press; 1959, pp. xv–279. Illus., maps.

———: *The Fur Trade on the Upper Missouri, 1840–65.* Norman: Univ. of Oklahoma Press; 1965. 295 pp., illus.

Swanton, John R.: *The Indians of the Southeastern United States.* Bureau of American Ethnology, Bulletin 137 (1946), pp. 1–943. 107 pls., 5 text figs.

Sweeney, Elizabeth: "Better Cutting with the Right Knife." *McCall's Magazine* (December 1947), pp. 88–9.

Swing, William: "Chain Saws Replace Ax and Hand Saw to Cut down Trees." Sunday *Oregonian* (Portland), March 21, 1965, p. RE 14. Illus.

Thomas, Earl A.: "Hopewell Iron Plantation." *Highway Magazine.* (Armco) (August 1949), pp. 172–5.

Thompson, David: *David Thompson's Narrative of his Explorations in Western America, 1784–1812,* ed. J. B. Tyrrell. Toronto: The Champlain Society Publications; 1916, Vol. XII.

Thorp, Raymond W.: *Bowie Knife.* Albuquerque: Univ. of New Mexico Press; 1948, pp. xv–167.

Thrasher, Halsey: *The Hunter and Trapper.* New York: Orange Judd & Co.; 1868, pp. 1–91. Illus.

Thwaites, Reuben Gold, ed.: *Jesuit Relations and Allied Documents—1610–1791.* 74 vols. Cleveland, 1896–1901.

———, ed.: *Original Journals of the Lewis and Clark Expedition, 1804–1806.* 8 vols. New York: Dodd, Mead & Co.: 1904–5.

———, ed.: *The Personal Narrative of James Ohio Pattie,* in *Early Western Travels,* Vol. XVIII. Cleveland, 1905.

Tose, Frank: *Trapping, Tanning, and Taxidermy.* Columbus, Ohio, 1928.

U. S. Congress: *Astoria Hearings.* 17th Cong., 2nd sess., H. Doc. 45. Washington, D.C.: Gales and Seton; 1823, pp. 1–80. (Invoice of Astor's properties, pp. 20–63.)

———: *Second Auditor's Report, Treasury Dept., to Lewis Cass, Secretary of War, March 5, 1832.* 22nd Cong., 1st sess., Sen. Doc. 101, Washington, D.C.: Gales and Seton; 1832, Vol. I, pp. 13–15.

———: *American State Papers.* Documents, legislative and executive, of the Congress of the United States. Washington, D.C.: Gales and Seton; 1832–61. [Contents date from 1789 to 1838.]

Class I. Foreign Relations, 6 vols.; II. Indian Affairs, 2 vols.; III. Finance, 5 vols.; IV. Commerce and Navigation, 2 vols.; V. Military Affairs, 7 vols.; VI. Naval Affairs, 4 vols.; VII. Post Office Department, 1 vol.; VIII. Public Lands, 8 vols.; IX. Claims, 1 vol.; X. Miscellaneous, 2 vols.

U. S. Congress: Report of Commissioners of Indian Affairs, 1837. 25th Cong., 2nd sess., Sen. Doc. 1. Washington, D.C.: Gales and Seton; 1837, pp. 525–8.

———: Report of Commissioner of Indian Affairs, 1838. 25th Cong., 3rd sess., Sen. Doc. 1. Washington: Gales and Seton; 1839, pp. 480–527.

———: Report, Board of Ordnance Officers, 1840. [Forging swords at Salingen.] 26th Cong., 2nd sess., Sen. Doc. 229, March 2, 1841. Washington, D.C.: Gales and Seton; 1841, pp. 84–91.

U. S. National Park Service: *Colonials and Patriots.* Washington, D.C.: Gov't Printing Office; 1964, pp. xvii–286.

U. S. Office of Indian Affairs: Letter Book, 1808. MS, National Archives, p. 198.

Van Laer, A. J. F., ed. and trans.: *Documents Relating to New Netherland, 1624–1626.* San Marino, Cal.: Huntington Library; 1924, pp. xxvi–276.

Vanstone, James W.: "Exploring the Copper River Country." *Pacific Northwest Quarterly* XLVI:4 (1955), pp. 115–23.

Vestal, Stanley: *Mountain Men.* Boston, Houghton Mifflin; 1937.

Victor, Frances Fuller: *The River of the West.* Hartford, Conn., 1870, pp. 1–602. Illus.

Warner, J. J.: "Reminiscences of Early California from 1831 to 1846." Historical Society of Southern California, *Annual Publications,* Vol. VII, (1907–8), pp. 176–93.

Watson, Douglas S.: *West Wind.* [Joseph R. Walker.] Los Angeles: priv. prtd. by Percy H. Booth; 1934, pp. 1–110.

Wellman, Paul I.: "Missouri as the Missionary of the American Idea." *Missouri Historical Review,* XLIX:3 (April 1955), pp. 217–29.

Wendorf, Fred: *A Guide for Salvage Archeology.* Santa Fe: Museum of New Mexico Press; 1962, pp. 1–128.
Contains 25-page essay by J. O. Brew on the cooperation of federal, state, and private interests in the recovery of archeological remains.

West, George A.: "The Aboriginal Pipes of Wisconsin." *The Wisconsin Archeologist* (April 1905).

———: "Tobacco Pipes and Smoking Customs of the American Indians." 2 vols. *Bulletin Public Museum, Milwaukee,* Vol. XVII (1934).

West, Helen B.: *Meriwether Lewis in Blackfeet Country.* Browning, Mont.: Blackfeet Agency; 1964. 28 pp.

Wilcox, Richard: "The Longknives of Collinsville." *Steelways* (January 1948), pp. 8–11.

Will, George F., and Hyde, George E.: *Corn Among the Indians of the Upper Missouri.* Lincoln, Neb.: Univ. of Nebraska Press; 1965. 323 pp.

Wilson, Clifford: "Founding Fort Yukon." *The Beaver* (June 1947), pp. 38–43.

Winsor, Justin, ed.: *Narrative and Critical History of America.* Cambridge, 1884. Vol. IV (1884), pp. 350–51.

Wisconsin Archeological Society: *Wisconsin Archeologist,* Madison, Vols. I–XXX (1901–49).

Wisconsin State Historical Society: *Collections* of the State Historical Society of Wisconsin, Madison, Vols. I–XXXI (1854–1931) (publication suspended, 1859–67).

Wittry, Warren L.: "The Bell Site; Early Historic Fox Village." *Wisconsin Archeologist*. XLIV:1 (March 1963), pp. 1–57.

Wodward, Arthur: "Notes on Axes, Tomahawks, Trade Values, and Blacksmithing." MS, n.d. 29 typed pp.; sketches.

———: "Those Green River Knives." Museum of the American Indian, *Indian Notes*, IV:4 (October 1927), pp. 403–18.

———: "Archeology—The Scrap Book of History." *The Regional Review*, National Park Service, Region One, I:1 (August 1938), pp. 8–10.

———: "The Metal Tomahawk." *The Bulletin of the Fort Ticonderoga Museum*, Vol. VII (January 1946), pp. 2–42.

———: "Up to Green River." Los Angeles Westerners *Brand Book* (1948), pp. 141–6.

———: "Green River Knives." *Western Folklore* (January 1950), pp. 56–9.

———: "The Knife on the Frontier." New York Westerners *Brand Book*, II: 1 (1955), pp. 10–14.

———: Pioneer historian-archeologists discussed in personal letter to C. P. Russell, March 26, 1963. MS, 4 typed pp.

Woolworth, Alan R., and Wood, Raymond W.: "The Archeology of a Small Trading Post [Kipp's Post] in the Garrison Reservoir, North Dakota." Washington, D.C., Bureau of American Ethnology, Bulletin 176 (1960).

Woosley, Walter J.: Affidavit regarding a Jim Bridger steel trap, 1934. MS, National Park Service, Fur-Trade Collections, Grand Teton National Park, Wyo.

Young, F. G., ed.: *The Correspondence and Journals of Captain Nathaniel J. Wyeth, 1831–1836*. Eugene, Ore.: Univ. Press; 1899, pp. xix–262. 2 maps.

Young, Stanley P.: "The Evolution of the Steel Wolf Trap in North America." *Western Sportsman* (February 1941), pp. 10–11, 30–1.

Zepp, E. C.: Detailed report on eight tomahawks, Ohio State Historical Society, 1938. MS and 8 measured sketches.

CARL P. RUSSELL, who was born in Fall River, Wisconsin, in 1894, graduated from Ripon College and received an M.A. and a Ph.D. from the University of Michigan. Until his untimely death in June 1967, Mr. Russell made a career of conservation work, joining the National Park Service in 1923 and serving successively in field and central office positions all of which more or less directly involved museum planning, operation, or administration. He worked on the early Park museums in the West and organized the original National Park Service Museum Division in Washington, D.C. As Regional Director of the Service's Eastern Region, Mr. Russell was a party to the initiation of the historian-archeologist program. From 1947 through 1952 he was superintendent of Yosemite National Park. He retired from the National Park Service in 1957. His published works include *One Hundred Years in Yosemite* and *Guns on the Early Frontier.*